Cover illustration.

A detail from "A View of [the] Passage of the Army under the Command of his Excellency Major General Amherst down the Rapids of [the] Saint Lawrence River for the Reduction of Canada in the Year 1760," executed by Thomas Davies (see Part Three for Biographical Note) sometime between 1762 and 1765.

The workmanlike monochrome wash, pen and ink and grey wash over traces of pencil on laid paper, measures 26.6 by 38.8 cm (10.5 x 16.06 inches). It was acquired by the Public Archives of Canada (today's Library and Archives Canada) in 1948 and bears the collector's mark of Sir Joshua Reynolds (who used it when painting the background to his famous dedicatory portrait of Jeffery Amherst in 1765).

In 1760 Davies was a 1st lieutenant in the Royal Artillery, part of Amherst's division in the three-pronged campaign against Montreal, where he commanded a row galley, taking part in the siege of Fort Lévis on Île Royale. On the way to Montreal, he would have first traversed the rapids at Long Sault, located just north of the modern community of Massena, New York, and then the much more dangerous rapids at the Cedars, closer to Montreal at the eastern end of Lac Saint-François.

Davies was obviously impressed by the rapids, executing this image which most likely depicts the Cedars. The composition, considered to be "a moving and extraordinary rendering of the difficulties faced by Amherst during his rugged journey," includes a number of what appear to be whaleboats transporting British troops, with Davies depicting one canoe carrying thirteen Indian allies (see detail below), part of the 200 warriors under the leadership of Sir William Johnson.

Most of the boats made it through the final rapids, although the army lost eighty-four men, predominantly soldiers of John Grant's 42nd Regiment of Foot and the American provincials, almost four times the number killed during the siege of Fort Lévis. The shocking loss in the rapids was due, according to John Grant, to the inexperience of the guides. (Image: Library and Archives Canada, Acc. No. 1948-13-1)

A Highland Light Infantryman, North American Theatre, 1760. It was determined early on in the war that the deeply wooded and rugged terrain of North America offered significant challenges for British troops. Add to the mix some wily and deadly enemies who did not play by Old World rules, and tactics and dress had to be modified quickly to cope with the "bush fight" or *la petite guerre*.

Shown here, a Black Watch private has discarded the regulation heavy frock coat in favour of his waistcoat with two leather pockets sewn onto the breast for flints and musket balls. Underneath a small cut-down kilt or *philabeg*, his legs are protected by a pair of Indian leggings or *mitasses*. Other nods to Indian equipment include his backpack mounted Indian style, a tumpline with carved powder horn on right hip and a tomahawk on left, a water canteen covered in Indian beadwork to cut down on glare, and his moccasins.

By 1760 the light infantrymen of Major General Jeffery Amherst's army were highly proficient veterans, adept at scouting, patrolling and leading the van of a large army through any wilderness. John Grant joined this elite corps of "chosen men" while on campaign in Martinique and subsequently encountered some close-quarter fighting in and around Havana during the 1762 siege. (Illustration from Reid and Chappell, *18th Century Highlanders*, Osprey Publishing)

A DANGEROUS SERVICE...

Memoirs of a Black Watch Officer in the French and Indian War – John Grant, 1741–1828

Edited by Earl John Chapman & Ian Macpherson McCulloch

Foreword by Stephen Brumwell

Published in collaboration with the Lake St. Louis Historical Society and the 78th Fraser Highlanders

ROBIN BRASS STUDIO
Montreal

Published 2017 by Robin Brass Studio Inc.
www.robinbrassstudio.com

Paperback: ISBN-13: 978-1-896941-74-5
Hardcover: ISBN-13: 978-1-896941-75-2

Printed and bound in Canada by Marquis Imprimeur Inc., Montmagny, Quebec

Library and Archives Canada Cataloguing in Publication

Grant, John, 1741–1828, author

A dangerous service… : memoirs of a Black Watch officer in the French and Indian War : John Grant, 1741–1828 / edited by Earl John Chapman & Ian Macpherson McCulloch; foreword by Stephen Brumwell.

Published in collaboration with the Lake St. Louis Historical Society and the 78th Fraser Highlanders.
Includes bibliographical references and index.
ISBN 978-1-896941-75-2 (hardcover). – ISBN 978-1-896941-74-5 (softcover)

1. Grant, John, 1741–1828. 2. Great Britain. Army. Regiment of Foot, 42nd. 3. United States – History – French and Indian War, 1754-1763 – Personal narratives. 4. Soldiers – Scotland – Biography. I. Chapman, Earl John, editor. II. McCulloch, Ian M., 1954-, editor. III. Lake St. Louis Historical Society, issuing body. IV. 78th Fraser Highlanders, issuing body. V. Title.

E199.G73 2017 973.2'6 C2017-902092-7

To Dr. John Johnson, the proud grandson and the first true editor of *A Dangerous Service*. He had the wit to recognize the historical value of his grandfather's eyewitness accounts and took it upon himself to diligently and patiently transcribe his memoirs. For his foresighted actions in preserving his grandfather's deeds and exploits for posterity, we are forever in his debt.

Baron Amherst of Montreal. On his return to England in 1765 from North America, Major General Jeffery Amherst dressed in ceremonial armour for this striking oil portrait by Sir Joshua Reynolds. Past the pensive commander's helmet (which rests on a prominent map of the Saint Lawrence and the Isles of Montreal), his "American Army" shoots the rapids on their way to capture Montreal in 1760. The detail for this part of the painting was inspired by a Thomas Davies watercolour found in Reynolds' possessions after his death, now in the collection of Library and Archives Canada, and found on the cover of this book. (Mead Art Museum AC 1967.85. Editors' photo)

CONTENTS

MAPS

FOREWORD

Stephen Brumwell

I first encountered Lieutenant John Grant of the Black Watch some twenty years ago, while researching my doctoral dissertation in the former Scottish Record Office in Edinburgh. It was late on a Friday afternoon, at the end of a hard week's work, and as I doggedly cranked my way through the fuzzy Register House microfilm I was rapidly running out of time and energy. With just an hour to go before the archive closed for the weekend, I was tempted to call it a day and adjourn to the Victorian splendour of the nearby Guildford Arms for a well-earned pint or two.

Yet I persevered, and finally reached the section of the reel beginning "Journal (part) of Lieutenant John Grant, 2nd Battalion 42nd Regiment, covering his service from 1758 to 1761." The document was filmed from the original held in Wellington, New Zealand, and I had to adjust the focus and squint to decipher the scrawled handwriting, only to discover that the "journal" itself mostly consisted of short, isolated phrases rather than properly-formed sentences.

As the editors of *A Dangerous Service* make clear in their scholarly introduction, the eccentric prose is explained by the fact that, while short sections are apparently based upon an earlier, written journal, the bulk of the material was taken down directly from Grant's mouth, dictated in the 1820s when he was an old man. As such, rather than giving the minute and sometimes mundane detail of a contemporaneous journal or diary, Grant's account of his early military services is far more impressionistic. It has the immediacy of oral history, in which the interviewee retains an extraordinarily vivid memory of key events despite intervening years.

As I worked through the microfilm, I had no doubt that, for all the decades that had passed between the events and their committal to paper, here was something fresh and original – a rare, authentic "voice" of a soldier from the mid-eighteenth century. It offered unique personal insights reflecting the reality of campaign life and combat, both often recalled with a certain self-deprecating humour.

Starting with his earliest, fragmented memories of a childhood disrupted by the Jacobite rebellion of the '45, Grant recounts his service as a subaltern in the 2nd Battalion of the 42nd Foot, the famous Royal Highland Regiment or "Black Watch," from his first taste of action at Guadeloupe in 1759, to the siege of Havana, on Cuba, in 1762. Between his stints of Caribbean service, Grant also fought on the North American mainland, participating in the conquest of Canada in 1760.

For my own purposes, Lieutenant John Grant of the Royal Highland Regiment proved a crucial witness. A main plank of my research argued that the "redcoats" sent across the Atlantic in increasing numbers from 1755 onwards slowly evolved, through hard and bloody experience, into a distinctive "American Army" that took pride in characteristics that set it apart from other British troops fighting on the more conventional battlefields of Europe. Campaigning on the mainland and in the West Indies, the officers and men of the "American Army" acquired unique experience in amphibious operations and irregular "backwoods" fighting. To a remarkable degree, John Grant's service reflected this story of adaptation and versatility.

Grant personified the "American Army," not least by conveying a strong sense of its corporate identity. By early 1762, when Grant participated in the conquest of Martinique, he was amused to observe that the officers of the 76th Foot, who had arrived fresh from the siege of Belle Isle on the French coast, were resplendent in full parade dress of "white Spatterdashes, Gorgets, & spontoons and sashes," and entrusted their provisions to their faithful servants. American veterans like Grant, "accustomed to backwoods expeditions," carried their own rations in haversacks, and "were ridiculed by the gay gentlemen for so doing." It's a typically vivid and telling vignette that leaves no doubt that, for all his years, John Grant's recollection was sharp. The same applies to his description of a subsequent firefight, in which a French sortie is rebuffed by "the brave fellows" of the 60th, or Royal American Regiment, bolstered by Grant and his Highlander comrades, who "instantly gave the Indian Halloo" – another legacy of their campaigning in the forests of Canada.

In their carefully-edited and fully-annotated edition of Grant's "Journal," Ian McCulloch and Earl Chapman present his *Dangerous Service* in context, finally making this credible eyewitness account of the Seven Years' War in the Americas readily available to the broad readership that it deserves.

ACKNOWLEDGMENTS

First of all, our sincere thanks to two descendants of John Grant who made our task all that much easier. Jo Ryan of Tauranga, New Zealand, first contacted Ian online several years ago while she was researching John Grant's ancestry. She provided him with her own transcript of the memoirs and family trees which she had privately published for family members. These and Ian's own transcript then formed the basis and impetus for this book. Her grandfather, Frederick Grant "Mick" Johnson, donated the original Grant Journal to the Alexander Turnbull Library in Wellington, New Zealand, in 1968.

Jo put us on to a distant Australian cousin from Melbourne, Marie Napier, a descendant of Isabella Robertson, John Grant's granddaughter, whose branch of the family immigrated to Australia in the 1880s. Marie generously provided many of the Grant and Johnson documents she had obtained from the Moray Council Archives and Local Heritage Centre in Elgin, Scotland, many years ago while researching her family tree. These were invaluable in piecing together the movements of John Grant's family during his long career.

Robin Brass, as always, bears special mention. Not only is he a staunch supporter of early Canadian military history; he has done a superb job in designing and publishing the book, with much-appreciated support from an anonymous donor and the encouragement of Lieutenant-Colonel Bruce D. Bolton, former commanding officer, The Black Watch (RHR) of Canada.

Additional material and assistance was provided by a number of generous individuals and institutions. Our special thanks to: Dr. Stephen Brumwell for graciously writing the superb intro to this book and sharing his thoughts on the character of John Grant; to friends Dr. John Houlding and Nick Westbrook, who both acted as readers for the final draft and provided us with information and advice that backstopped the narrative; to Jocelyn Chalmers at the Alexander Turnbull Library in New Zealand, and James Nock at the Elgin Local Heritage Centre in Moray, Scotland, who provided us with items gleaned from their respective collections; to R. Paul Goodman, who opened up his superb 18th-century British military library to our repeated calls for help; to Tim Todish, René Chartrand and marine artist Peter Rindisbacher for assisting with images; to Effie Rankin and Dr. John Gibson, Gaelic speakers from Judique, Cape Breton, who were consulted on several words and phrases in the MSS; to Todd Braisted of the On-Line Institute for Advanced Loyalist Studies who assisted with numerous Royal Garrison Battalion documents; and to Paul Pace, who provided us with biographies of Black Watch officers that served with Grant.

Finally, an old chestnut bears repetition. Despite the impressive array of talented and knowledgeable folks listed above, any errors or omissions in the book are entirely the editors' responsibility.

Abbreviations

The following abbreviations are used in the footnotes and picture credits.

Add. MSS	Additional Manuscripts
ASKB	Anne S. K. Brown Military Collection, Brown University Library, Providence, Rhode Island
BAL	British Army Lists
BL	British Library
BWCM	Black Watch Castle and Museum, Perth
CB	Commission Books, WO 25
CKS	Kent History and Library Centre (formerly Centre for Kentish Studies), Maidstone, UK
CO	Colonial Office Papers, TNA
DCB	*Dictionary of Canadian Biography,* Toronto
DNB	*Dictionary of National Biography,* UK
FARL	Frick Art Reference Library, New York, NY
HMS	His (or Her) Majesty's Ship
JCB	John Carter Brown Library, Brown University, Providence, Rhode Island
JGM	John Grant Memoirs, Alexander Turnbull Library, NLNZ
JGP	James Grant Papers (Microfilm), LOC
JSAHR	*Journal of the Society for Army Historical Research*
LAC	Library and Archives Canada, Ottawa
LOC	Library of Congress, Washington, DC
MCA	Moray Council Archives and Local Heritage Centre, Elgin, Moray, Scotland
MG	Manuscript Group
NLNZ	National Library of New Zealand
NPG	National Portrait Gallery, London
RG	Record Group
SB	Succession Books, TNA
SNPG	Scottish National Portrait Gallery, Edinburgh
TNA	The National Archives, UK (formerly PRO)
TPL	Toronto Public Library, Toronto
vol	volume
WLCL	William L. Clements Library, Ann Arbor, Michigan
WO	War Office Papers, TNA

Note on Typography and Usage

When a name in the text is set in small capitals (e.g., JEFFERY AMHERST), it indicates that there is an entry for that person in Part Three, Biographical Notes.

In new text we have followed modern practice of not using superscripts in such forms as 2nd, 78th and so on (as opposed to 2nd, 78th, etc.). However, we have kept these forms in material from Grant's memoirs.

In Part Two the text from John Grant's memoirs is distinguished from our introductory texts by a dotted rule on both sides.

The terms "Indian" and "Indians" appear in the text with reference to the indigenous peoples of North America. The use of these terms is in no way intended to convey anything derogatory, but simply to maintain consistency with the language used in quoted extracts appearing in this book.

EARL JOHN CHAPMAN
IAN MACPHERSON MCCULLOCH

INTRODUCTION

One of the most interesting and colourful accounts of a Highlander who soldiered in North America and the Caribbean during the Seven Years' War is found in an old manuscript now in the possession of the Alexander Turnbull Library in Wellington, New Zealand. Scrawled in a sometimes difficult-to-read script are the unfinished memoirs of Lieutenant John Grant, who served in His Majesty's 42nd (Royal Highland) Regiment of Foot (Black Watch) from 1758 to 1763. By war's end the young Highlander, who hailed from Glenurquhart, Scotland, was a veteran of Guadeloupe, 1759; the siege of Fort Lévis and surrender of Montreal, 1760; the siege and capitulation of Martinique and Grenada, 1762; and the siege of Havana, 1762.

John Grant was a minor player in the Highland gentry of 18th-century Scotland, a mere subaltern in the Royal Highland Regiment for the duration of the war. One might ask what the writings of a junior officer could add to the many illustrious histories already scribed on Britain's "Great War for Empire"? The answer is simple. He is a genuine Highland voice covering an important period in the evolution of Highland units in the Georgian king's army. As a friend of ours once said of another Highlander, James Thompson,[1] Grant speaks to us "in close-ups, not in panoramas." No wonder Colonel David Stewart (later, Stewart of Garth) pumped the elderly veteran for information for his famous 1822 best-seller, *Sketches of the Character, Manners, and Present State of the Highlanders of Scotland....*

Presented here for the first time, John Grant's dictated memoirs are a fresh and authentic window onto the human dynamics at play in the early mid-18th century Highland regiments raised for service in North America. By the spring of 1758 the three Highland regiments serving overseas totalled four battalions of 4,200 kilted men out of a total of 24,000 British regulars, nearly one fifth of the army. Twenty-five of these men were John Grant's first command.

1. **James Thompson** (1733-1830). Born in Tain, Scotland, Thompson served as a grenadier sergeant in the 78th Foot (Fraser's Highlanders). A veteran of the siege of Louisbourg in 1758 and three sieges of Quebec – by the British in 1759, the French in 1760 and American rebels in 1775-76 – Thompson lived out his postwar life in Quebec City. For more information, see *A Bard of Wolfe's Army: James Thompson, Gentleman Volunteer, 1733-1830*, E. J. Chapman and I. M. McCulloch, eds. (Robin Brass Studio, Montreal, 2010).

Secondly, John Grant's eyewitness accounts and anecdotes of military life on campaign and in garrison (what British historian John Keegan has termed "the personal angle of vision") are invaluable to historians of the period. Grant not only talks about the physical conditions of the fighting and the strange environments encountered, but provides valuable insights into the Highland soldier's behaviour and the emotions generated before and after combat, his will and ability to fight, and most of all, his proud resilience and perseverance in adversity. The Highlanders' exploits in the Americas during Britain's "Great War for Empire" were a critical factor in changing the overall image of Highlanders in the latter half of the 18th century from Jacobite rebels to Imperial heroes in British society, and here in John Grant we have a first-hand chronicler whose career straddled that remarkable transformation.

The John Grant Collection, archived as "MSS, Grant, John b. 1741: Journal" (reference designation, qMS-0871), is held at the Alexander Turnbull Library in Wellington, New Zealand, part of the National Library of New Zealand. It was donated to the library by Frederick W. Grant Johnson of Otorohanga, New Zealand, in 1968. The collection includes a coverless, bound group of manuscript pages, likely once forming part of a ledger book or letter book, covering the events in the life of John Grant from his birth in Scotland in 1741 up to his experiences during the British siege of Havana in 1762. Old age claimed Grant before he could tell his complete story.

While the Alexander Turnbull Library describes the manuscript as a journal, technically it is misnamed as such, as John Grant, the hero of our tale, never recorded anything in it. A more correct and accurate archival description would be "MSS, Grant, John b. 1741: Memoirs (as recorded by his grandson)." The collection also contains a few newspaper clippings, some typescript pages (one of which provides an overview of the collection while the others contain a rough transcript of the first few pages of the manuscript "Journal") as well as some photocopies of material concerned with the history of the Johnson family.

The misnamed "Journal," by far the most important item in the collection, consists of seventy-seven bound manuscript pages although the binding has come apart between pages 64 and 65. Oddly, the manuscript begins at folio page 15 (folio pages 1-14 are missing) and ends at folio page 92, although it is quite apparent that the original narrative went beyond page 92. Pages 55 and 56 are also missing (chronologically, these latter pages logically detail the deployment of John Grant's battalion back to Fort Ontario to join the gathering army under Major General Jeffery Amherst for the expedition against Montreal). Page 57 resumes with the army besieging Fort Lévis in the middle of the Saint Lawrence River on 23 August 1760.

John Grant's memoirs, page 15. The front page of the ledger or letter book, the misnamed "Journal" held at the Alexander Turnbull Library in Wellington, New Zealand. Oddly, the coverless, bound group of manuscript pages begins at folio page 15 as folio pages 1-14 are missing. The "Journal" ends at folio page 92, although it is apparent that the original narrative went beyond page 92. (Editors' photo)

"And the Wilderness shall become the Fruitful Field…." A self-titled 1843 sepia and ink wash drawn by Dr. John Johnson of his house and garden situated just below Government House in Auckland, New Zealand. In a previous life, the physician and amateur artist had actually studied at the Royal Academy Woolwich where he had first learned to sketch and record topographical features as a budding young artillery officer. Fronting the house, one can see a rich bank of grapevines and, in the immediate left foreground, a sprawling pumpkin patch. (Alexander Turnbull Library, Wellington, NZ, E-216-f-051. Editors' photo)

Following a detailed handwriting analysis in which journals and letters written by Dr. John Johnson after he emigrated to New Zealand were compared to the handwriting found in John Grant's "Journal," the editors have concluded that Dr. John Johnson actually wrote the manuscript held at the Alexander Turnbull Library, and not John Grant. This hypothesis is also supported by the fact that John Grant's "Journal" is part of the larger "Dr. John Johnson Papers" also preserved by the National Library of New Zealand. Dr. John Johnson was John Grant's grandson, and we can state now with some certainty that the "Journal" is, in fact, a first draft of the dictated memoirs of a Seven Years' War veteran recorded by a proud grandson.

Born in Portsea, Hampshire, in 1794, John Johnson Jr. (later Dr. John Johnson) was the son of Captain Lieutenant John Johnson of the Royal Engineers and his wife, Penuel Grant, the only child of Captain John Grant and his wife, Isobel. After the premature death of his father in November 1795, John Jr. was brought up by his grandparents. He eventually joined the Royal Artillery as a commissioned officer, later becoming an accredited medical practitioner, and still later emigrating to New Zealand, where he became the colony's first colonial surgeon. (See Part Three for Biographical Notes on Captain Lieutenant John Johnson and his son, John Johnson Jr.)

The missing front and back covers of the "Journal" can be explained if the bound manuscript was physically taken apart (i.e., intentionally damaged), likely by Dr. Johnson. This scenario would explain why the manuscript begins with John Grant's birth *at folio page 15*, with the remainder, for the most part, intact. It suggests that Dr. Johnson retained the part of the ledger which was most important to him (his grandfather's memoirs) but disposed of the first seven leaves (i.e., pages 1-14), perhaps for privacy reasons.

Folio pages 55 and 56, and one or more pages after folio page 92, are definitely missing as well, probably lost over the passage of time while in possession of the Johnson family. The missing covers and pages could also be explained by the manuscript suffering damage, perhaps by fire, where the "inner portion" (folio pages 15 through 92) survived at the expense of the "exterior portion" (the cover, the first seven numbered folio pages, and the unknown number of pages after folio page 92); however the extant manuscript shows no visible burn marks, which supports the first and more likely theory as to the manuscript's present incomplete condition.

Sometime after the battle of Waterloo in 1815, Grant was contacted by Colonel David Stewart (later, David Stewart of Garth), who was researching his famous book *Sketches of the Character, Manners, and Present State of the Highlanders of Scotland….* Colonel Stewart was looking specifically for John Grant's memories and stories of service during the French and Indian War. First published in 1822 when John was eighty-one years of age, Colonel Stewart's book would include the most complete history of the 42nd Foot (Black Watch) in the Seven Years' War and the American Revolution to that date. Thus, John Grant's first appearance before a British public and the world at large is not this book of his memoirs. He was first a 19th-century footnote in volume one of Stewart's bestseller: viz. "Capt. [John] Peebles, wounded at Bushy Run, and residing in Irvine, and Major John Grant [*sic*],[2] late of the invalids, are the only officers alive in the year 1822, who served in the regiment [the 42nd Foot] during the Seven Years' War." The editors surmise that this contact with Stewart was the impetus for John to write his own memoirs. However, by the time he had made this decision, old age had set in, and he was unable to write legibly, thus com-

2. **Major John Grant**. John Grant was never a major in the army. His final rank as captain is consistently shown (British Army Lists) as 25 September 1778. However, it is possible that he joined the Forres Volunteers or Militia during the height of the Napoleonic War and obtained a brevet majority.

pelled to dictate his memoirs to his capable and willing grandson. Dr. Johnson would use a blank, bound book for his grandfather's narrative, possibly one of his Royal Artillery ledger books.

The transcription of the manuscript was somewhat problematic for us as it was quickly determined it was only a first rough draft, that is, not fully expanded from the many short telegraphic phrases and isolated paragraphs that dot the narrative, some sitting in the middle of another event without any context or logic. For example, John Grant remembers additional details of events that happened three pages after describing them, and in some instances his grandson would make small stars or asterisks to mark where he saw that some events were out of chronological order and to remind himself to make corrections in the next more polished draft. Johnson never had the time to revisit his project conducted during his grandfather's last years, so, during our editorial process, we have moved a number of sentences or paragraphs that were clearly out of chronological order and duly footnoted the process.

Based on a careful study of the manuscript, the editors also believe that there was already something to copy from (Grant's personal rough notes) when the ledger book or letter book was first started by Dr. Johnson. For example, folio pages 78 through 90 are very well written with few mistakes, as if they had been hand copied from an early draft rather than reflecting on-the-spot hesitant dictation taken from an elderly man with failing memory. The pages that do have corrections on them are also rather neat, reinforcing our belief this is a fair copy with only some minor changes or deletions. These, we believe, Dr. Johnson was forced to make when reading back this fair working copy to his grandfather. Additionally, when an anecdote or event was remembered during this final read-through, some were too long for immediate inclusion and hence the creation of the four so-called "loose sheets" to capture the additional information for insertion at a later date.

The four "loose sheets" – each with handwritten notes on both sides – are clearly part of John Grant's narrative but are not part of the manuscript's original binding. There can be no doubt that these loose sheets were created *after* Dr. Johnson had made his fair working copy of his grandfather's dictation, and that the good doctor had planned to insert this additional material (some of the sentences are labelled with the folio page number for insertion) into the narrative in a final, more polished draft. A few of these loose sheets are damaged, particularly around the edges, which has resulted in some missing or unreadable text.

One particular reference in the "Journal" strongly indicates that John Grant's memoirs were recorded sometime between 1822 and 1828. There is an even more telling note on folio page 86, where in parentheses halfway down the page it states: "Monday, 12th January [1824][3] – Last day of personal dictation," a sure indication that John Grant (at eighty-three years of age) was not actually writing his memoirs but dictating them to someone else. On this particular date, 12 January 1824 and four years before his eventual death, John Grant was unable to continue dictation – something, perhaps a stroke, had affected his oral capabilities. However, the ever-dutiful grandson soldiered on. The last day of dictation noted in the manuscript was *not* the last day of the memoirs as the narrative continues after this notation.

The dictated "memoirs" up until John Grant's inability to use his speech faculties (we know he could no longer write, hence dictation) was very much a collaborative work in progress. If our hypothesis is correct, that Dr. Johnson's transcript was a *fair working copy* of his grandfather's reminiscences with perhaps the assistance of some rough notes, then the page annotated with "last day of personal dictation" was a section they were revisiting or reviewing, despite other follow-on pages. These latter pages are a *fair working copy* of the Havana campaign, which John Grant *had not yet reviewed or made final amendments to*, but likely had already dictated at an earlier time for Colonel Stewart. We know that Grant certainly did not dictate chronologically and there is much evidence showing that he went back often and changed things, or referred to earlier events mentioned in the manuscript. The approximate date at which the extant memoirs fall silent (folio page 92) is during the siege of Havana on or about the end of June 1762.

There can be no doubt that Dr. John Johnson was the first true editor of his grandfather's memoirs, and the task of the present editors has been to act in the spirit of his original intentions: that is, to move text forward from the "loose sheets," and to move fragments that are out of context but *still within the bound manuscript* into the final narrative. Our guiding principle throughout the editorial process has been to provide the best chronological sequence *and* logical flow to John Grant's memoirs with robust footnotes to indicate when and where text has been modified or moved from its place in the original.

We have structured *A Dangerous Service* in three parts. In Part One, we provide a detailed biographical essay of the man, his family and the turbulent times in which he lived, culled from a multitude of sources, including: the "John Grant Journal" (Archival Reference Number qMS-0871) held at the Alexander Turnbull Library in New Zealand; the "Family and Military Papers of Captain John Grant and Captain John Johnson of Forres, 1777–1888 (Archival Reference Code DJQ) held at the Moray Council Archives and Local Heritage Cen-

3. **Calculation of day.** The year 1824 is the only year (over the period 1819-1828) in which 12 January falls on a Monday.

tre, Elgin, Moray, Scotland; Colonial and War Office Records at the National Archives, Kew, England; Library and Archives Canada, Ottawa; the British Library, London; W.L. Clements Library, Michigan; and newspapers and magazines of the day.

In Part Two the narrative follows the natural sequence of John Grant's memoirs, but in addition places them into chronologically structured chapters complete with introductory paragraphs added to provide all-important context. In Part Three we have provided biographical notes for many of the people who had a significant impact on his life and career, a career spanning some fifty years of service to the British Crown, in Scotland, North America and the Caribbean. They are presented alphabetically and all officer entries are accorded their rank at the time of their *first* appearance in John Grant's memoirs.

John Grant's memoirs are written in a simple straightforward style, but the language is, in parts, quaint and the spelling of proper names and places is sometimes inaccurate (possibly due to Dr. Johnson's transcription). Since everything in Grant's memoirs occurred before 1828, we have not hesitated to occasionally – and silently – modernize the punctuation to make the meaning clearer, but leaving the commonly used 18th-century abbreviations, such as "corner'd" ("cornered") and "order'd" ("ordered") intact as these are fairly obvious.

In preparing the footnotes, we have kept in mind the needs of the general reader rather than the scholar, though a basic knowledge of the Seven Years' War and the American War of Independence is assumed. For the sake of brevity, we generally do not footnote our footnotes, but we do cite references for those readers wishing further details and up-to-date scholarship on certain battles, campaigns or aspects of the British Army that appear in the book. We occasionally cite other people's first-hand accounts of the same incidents described by John Grant to provide additional context and in some cases to corroborate or expand upon his own memory of the event.

A rule of thumb in our footnoting in Parts One and Two was to briefly identify places, things, foreign words and unfamiliar 18th-century terms at the bottom of the page for immediate reference. This was the lesser of two evils, as requiring the reader to turn to endnotes, we believed, would disrupt the flow and the reader's enjoyment of the narrative. To save space, however, we placed biographical notes on people mentioned in the text in Part Three, a move that allowed us to include additional contextual detail of the time and, more importantly, connect that person back to the events depicted by John Grant.

The editors' principal aim in this project has been to make this rare manuscript of fascinating insights into 18th-century soldiering available to both the general public and scholars alike. Now readers can enjoy a Highland officer's unique perspective on the events and personalities that shaped the French and

Indian War, the war in the Caribbean and the American Revolutionary War. We hope that John Grant, a faithful servant of the King, a gallant Highland officer and the "last of his line," would approve of our humble efforts.

Earl John Chapman
Burlington, Ontario

Ian Macpherson McCulloch
Kingston, Ontario

St. Andrew's Day, 2016

PART ONE

The Loch Ness monster observation deck. Urquhart Castle, one of Scotland's largest medieval castles, has a long and bloody history, but by John Grant's birth in 1741 it had become a "romantick" landmark of the Great Glen. Built in the early 1200s, not far from Inverness, it stood strategically astride the rocky Strone Promontory overlooking Loch Ness, guarding the river entrance to Glenurquhart. With the highest incidence of reported sightings, it is a favorite lookout spot for Nessie, the Loch Ness monster. (Illustration from Pennant, *A Tour in Scotland MDCCLXIX*).

"THE LAST OF HIS LINE ..."

THEY RODE LAZILY DOWN AT DAWN,[1] down through the stunted oak and silver birch, trampling black swathes through the dew-heavy grasses which sparkled in the early July sun. The troopers of Kingston's Light Horse[2] had their sabres drawn and resting on their right shoulders as the loyal Argyll militia followed on foot in an extended line, carrying their muskets at the ready. The Argyll Highlanders' leather brogans, hose and kilts were already soaked through as they had spent a wet night without tents on the Loch Ness side of *Sron Dubh*, which loomed behind them now.[3]

The Scots had led initially, creeping stealthily over the steep ridge before first light, the English troopers following, leading their horses on foot. The soldiers had followed the course of the Divach Burn down to a large deserted farm and its attendant fields of the same name which overlooked most of Glen Coiltie.

---

1. **The Harrowing of Glenurquhart**. With the exception of Argyll militia officer Captain Campbell, the people, places and events in this introductory scenario are all real. The key elements of the conversation between John Grant Sr. and the British major, James Lockhart, have been reconstructed from John Grant's earliest memories as a child – "the coming of troopers" – and are directly based on his recollections of what his father told him when he was older. See Part Two for John Grant's memoirs.
2. **Kingston Light Horse**, was raised for the duration of the Rebellion by the Duke of Kingston in the City of Nottingham. Shortly after their despoiling of Glenurquhart in the first week of July 1746, they left Fort-Augustus on 27 July 1747 for home, where they were disbanded in September 1746. Their standards were placed in the town hall with the following inscription: "These Military Standards, lately belonging to the Light Horse commanded by the Most Noble and Most Puissant Prince, Evelyn, Duke of Kingston, raised among the first by the County of Nottingham out of Love to their Country and Loyalty to the Best of Kings, in the year 1745, are here dedicated to the perpetual Fame and immortal Memory of their invincible Bravery in the Skirmish of Clifton Moor, the Siege of the city of Carlisle, but especially at the memorable Battle fought at Culloden, in the Highlands of Scotland, on the 16th day of April, 1746, where, amongst others, they performed many and glorious Exploits in Routing and entirely Subduing the Perfidious Rebels, stirred up and supported by the French King, an implacable Enemy of the Protestant Religion and Publick Liberty. God save our ever August King! Long may the County of Nottingham Flourish!" Quoted in William Mackay, *Urquhart and Glenmoriston: Olden Times in a Highland Parish* (Inverness, 1914), 292n. Hereafter, *Olden Times*.
3. ***Sron Dubh*** (Scottish Gaelic: "The Black Promontory"). It is 1,436 feet (438 m) high at its peak and runs eastward to its lower shoulder, which ends abruptly at the ruins of Castle Urquhart and is known as *Sron a' Chaistell* or "The Promontory, or Point, of the Castle."

When the thick pine forest had given way to fields though, the cavalry had mounted their horses and had taken the lead from the Highlanders. They were now in Grant country.

The British major in charge scowled when it became apparent that there were no human inhabitants at Divach Farm.[4] Worse, there was no livestock worth mentioning except a few scrawny spotted hens pecking hopefully around one of the low white-washed outbuildings. His wished-for surprise of Glenurquhart[5] had not worked. Rebel spies were everywhere.

"Burn it," he ordered brusquely. "Burn it all. And search the woods for the cattle and any other livestock."

Two months earlier, Major James Lockhart[6] and his men had launched a vicious raid on Glenmoriston,[7] further to the west, one of only two areas in the entire regality of Grant that had chosen to support "the Young Pretender," Charles Edward Stuart (Bonnie Prince Charlie), despite the express wishes of their clan chief for all gentlemen and their tenants to stay at home. On their earlier raid, they had started at Aeneas Grant *Daldreggan's*[8] estate which had been untouched by the previous harrowing of the glens because he was a loyal Whig gentleman, perhaps the only one in the entire valley. The troops had rounded up all his cattle, as well as every herd belonging to his tenants. When *Daldreggan* had appeared brandishing a certificate of immunity signed by the Earl of Loudoun himself and clearly stating that he personally had had no part in the Rebellion, Lockhart declared, "If you were to show me a warrant from Heaven it would not stop me."

Lockhart then ordered *Daldreggan* and his wife stripped naked and hung from a tree where three dead Highlanders were already strung up. His second-

---

4. **Divach Farm**. Located on the northern slopes of *Sron Dubh* on the western side of Divach Burn and the Falls of Divach. Overlooks the mouth of Glen Coiltie and present-day modern Lewiston that covers most of the river pasture or strath where the original Balmacaan Farm was located.
5. **Glenurquhart**, or Glen Urquhart (Scottish Gaelic: *Gleann Urchadain*) is a river glen in the Scottish Highlands that runs from Loch Ness at Urquhart Bay in the east to Corrimony and beyond in the west. The Glen is dominated by the River Enrick. Glenurquhart used to be part of the lands of the Grants of Glenmoriston.
6. **Major James Lockhart, later Sir James Lockhart-Ross**. See Part Three for Biographical Note.
7. **Glenmoriston**, or Glen Moriston (Scottish Gaelic: *Gleann Moireasdan*) is a river glen in the Scottish Highlands that runs from Loch Ness, at the village of Invermoriston, westwards to Loch Cluanie, where it meets with Glen Shiel. The Glen is dominated by the River Moriston, which in Gaelic might mean "River of the Waterfalls."
8. **Aeneas Grant, *Daldreggan*** (1702-79), a wadset (mortgage) holder in the larger estate of Dundreggan, Glenmoriston. Aeneas was married to Hannah Grant, the daughter of Alexander Grant of Shewglie.

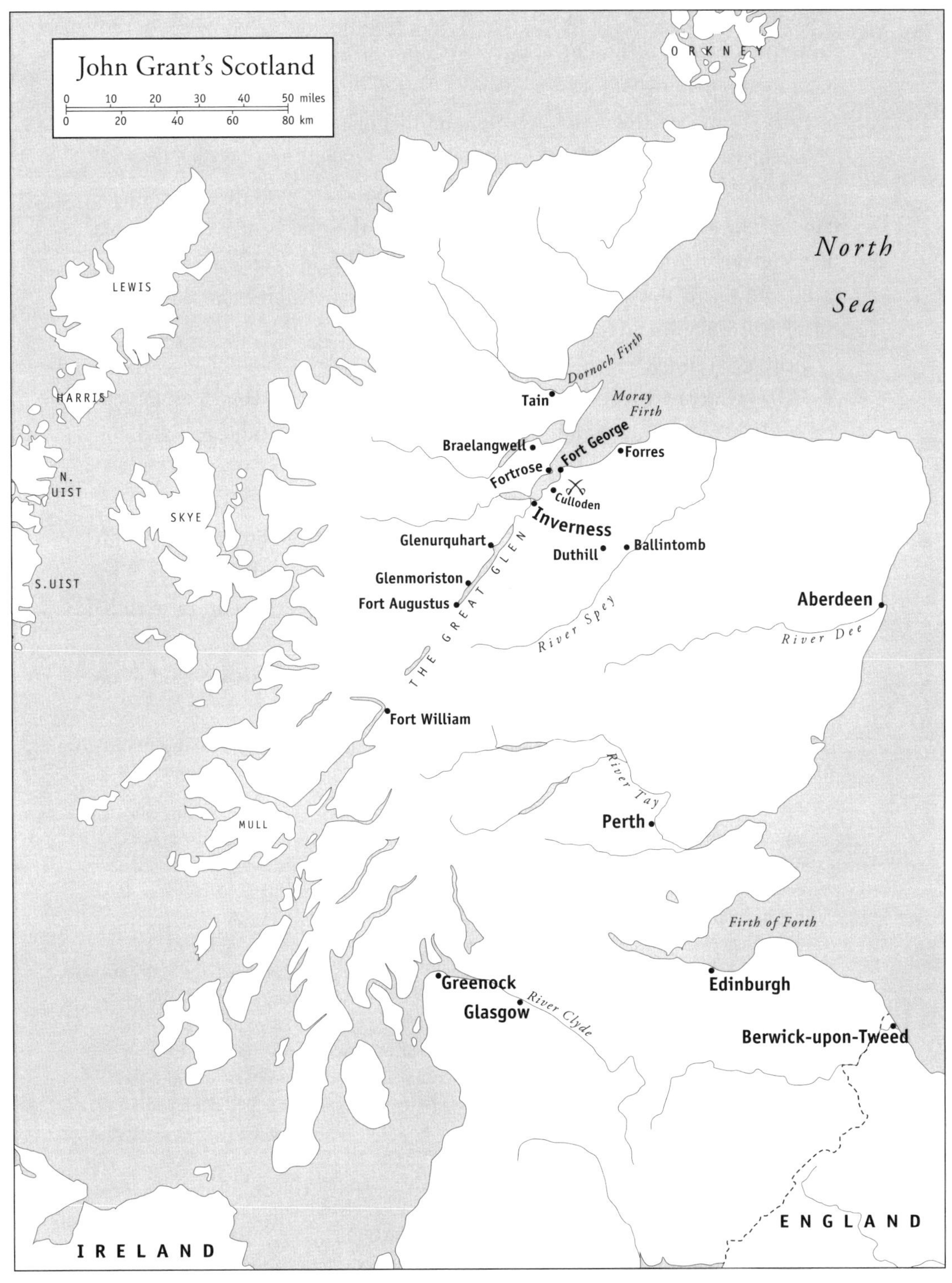

John Grant's Scotland. Born in Strathspey, raised in Glenurquhart, schooled at Inverness and Fortrose, and tutored in Tain and Aberdeen, John Grant's knowledge of his own country of birth before joining the British Army was limited to the eastern Highlands of Scotland. (Map: Robin Brass Studio)

in-command, Captain Alexander Grant[9] of Lord Loudoun's Highlanders[10] and certainly no choirboy himself when it came to reiving, stepped forward. With hand on the pommel of his broadsword, Captain Grant had then dared the sadistic major to carry on with his wanton murder of a loyal kinsman.

Lockhart had shrugged, released the terrified couple and let them run off into the woods naked. But his fury would be boundless with the other inhabitants of the glen. Woman were raped in front of their husbands, boys and old men shot down as they stood harmlessly in their cornfields, cattle driven off and farms laid waste. By the time Lockhart's men had marched the entire length of the glen, it was a smoking ruin.

And now they were here in Glenurquhart.

"Major Lockhart, sir," said his second-in-command, this time a more malleable Highland militia captain by the name of Campbell. "Rider approaching, sir."

Sure enough, a tall, hatless, dark-haired man, bestride a roan mare, was on the trail coming up from the rich pastures below. As the horseman and his mount drew nearer, the twenty-eight-year-old major of the 34th Foot could see the horse was blown and flecked with foam. The rider wore no uniform so he certainly was not a despatch rider.

"Another damn rebel with a piece of paper, no doubt," Lockhart said to no one in particular, his dark eyes hardening.

"Sir," said the well-dressed rider when he was ten yards away, slowing his ex-

---

9. **Captain Alexander Grant.** British army officer. Born c.1728 in Strathspey to parents who had sufficient means and influence to secure an ensigncy for their son in the 43rd Foot (Crawford's) on 24 June 1743. Historian John Prebble, among others, styles him as a younger son of the Laird of Knockando but the official genealogical and regimental records do not support this claim. Promoted to lieutenant on 18 August 1745 in the same regiment (though now styled Lord Sempill's) and served with Dugald Campbell of Auchrossan's lone Black Watch company at the battle of Culloden. Promoted to captain in the 64th Foot (Lord Loudoun's) and became notorious for his unforgiving harrowing of the Jacobite estates. With 200 men, he marched and plundered his way from Moy to the head of Loch Arkaig, burning and killing as he went. At Clunes Hill near Auchnacary he burnt the house of Cameron of Clunes, "stript his wife and others naked as they came into the world, and deprived them of all means of subsistence except five milk goats." He then deployed with his regiment to Flanders and was severely wounded at the defense of Bergen-op-Zoom, dying on 1 October 1747.

10. **Lord Loudoun's Highlanders**. A Highland regiment raised at Inverness and Perth in August 1745 for the duration of the War of Austrian Succession. Before its recruits could be trained and sent over to fight in Flanders, the Jacobite Uprising broke out. The regiment thus fought as part of the British forces under Sir John Cope at the battle of Prestonpans in 1745, where they were badly defeated and many taken prisoner. Designated the 64th Foot in 1747 after the uprising, the regiment served gallantly at the siege of Bergen-op-Zoom in the Netherlands, suffering heavy casualties. It returned to Scotland at the 1748 peace and was disbanded at Perth.

"Join no party." Sir James Grant of Grant (1679-1747), 6th Baronet, Grant of Grant and the 20th hereditary clan chieftain. During the Jacobite uprising he prudently removed himself to London in order to be seen dutifully attending Parliament as the member for Elgin Burghs. He left the day-to-day running of his regality back in Scotland to his eldest son, Ludovick, who was firmly instructed to "join no party" – in essence, to sit on the fence as long as possible. (Illustration from Fraser, *The Chiefs of Grant*)

hausted horse from a forced trot to a walk. Some militiamen had levelled their muskets at the man and a sergeant had stepped forward to try to seize his reins. "Sir. Are you in charge? I must ask you to cease and desist, sir."

"Damn your eyes, sir. Who the hell are you?" sneered Lockhart.

"John Grant, sir, Factor[11] to Sir James Grant,[12] owner of this farm and baron of most of the lands in Glenurquhart and Glenmoriston."

"Factor to a nest of vermin more like it," growled Lockhart. "Whose house is that down there by the river where you just came from?" he asked, pointing a buff-gloved finger at a large well established manse.

"Also the Laird of Grant's, sir. I live there with my family."

"And whose black cattle are those down there?"

"The Laird of Grant's also."

"Then that will be the next house I burn," said the major.

---

11. **Factor**. An 18th-century term for a deputy or representative, and in this case an estate manager. As factor, John Grant had delegated authority from the Laird of Grant to manage his properties in Glenurquhart and to supervise the tenantry and the collection of rents. During the Rebellion, his duties would also include acting as the Laird's intelligence officer and chief spokesman tasked to prevent the inhabitants joining the Rebellion. In other correspondence, he is referred to as "The Stewart of Urquhart." John replaced Major Walter Grant, the brother of the Laird, in 1742, who had replaced John Grant's father, John *Dhu* Grant of Dalrachney. See Part Three for Biographical Notes on John Grant and John *Dhu* Grant of Dalrachney.
12. **The Laird of Grant**. The Laird, during John Grant's tenure as factor, was Sir James Grant, who usually resided at Castle Grant in Strathspey near present-day Grantown-on-Spey. During the troubles, however, he had prudently removed himself to London to attend Parliament as the member for Elgin Burghs. Sir James left the day-to-day running of his regality to his eldest son, Ludovick Grant, who succeeded to the title in 1747 on his father's death. See Part Three for Biographical Note on Sir James Grant and his son.

Grant's face remained expressionless as he quickly produced an official-looking document from his frock coat. He proffered it to the British officer, but Lockhart looked away, shouting at one of his troopers at the corner of a burning cottage, "Kill those chickens, sergeant. I fancy something roasted for breakfast."

The second-in-command edged his horse closer and looked cursorily over the documents and handed them back to the factor.

"Sir, I must persist," said John Grant. "I ask you once more that you call off your men. This document is from the Duke of Cumberland[13] himself and grants my Laird's property immunity from insult and injury. Some of the Laird of Grant's own kin, including my nephew, Ensign Grant *Dalrachney* and my cousin Lieutenant Grant *Rothiemurchas*, serve our King in Lord Loudoun's regiment, sir. The Laird's own son, FRANCIS GRANT, is the major of the 42nd Foot in Flanders."

"Prattle, sir. Damned prattle. That house down there shall be the next house I burn."

"At your peril, sir," replied Grant matter-of-factly, then deciding he could do no more with the Lowlander with the cruel staring eyes, turned his horse to ride back down to Balmacaan Farm.[14] The second-in-command nodded at the sergeant to release the reins which the latter had secured at the first opportunity and also motioned for his Highlanders to lower their Brown Besses. As Grant rode off, the factor overheard the second-in-command behind him speaking in a muted but anxious voice to Lockhart: "Major. I saw the Duke's signature. Take care what you are about. This factor was in Fort Augustus[15] a few weeks ago."

---

13. **William Augustus** (1721-65). British army officer, member of the Royal Family. The third and youngest son of George II (reigned 1727-60), created Duke of Cumberland in 1726. Nicknamed "Butcher" Cumberland for his harsh suppression of the Jacobite rebellion of 1745. After being defeated at Hastenbeck in July 1757, he retreated to the fortified town on Stade on the North Sea coast. Hemmed in by the French, he agreed to the Convention of Klosterzeven which led to Hanover's withdrawal from the war and partial occupation by French forces. Ordered back to England, the Duke was treated badly by his father despite the fact that he had previously been given permission to negotiate such an agreement. "Here," the king remarked to his guests on the night that Cumberland reappeared at court, "is my son, who has ruined me and disgraced himself." In response, Cumberland resigned all his military and public offices and retired, switching his attentions to politics and horse racing. Obese and suffering from a past stroke, he died in London on 31 October 1765 and was buried in Westminster Abbey, Walpole writing: "He would have made a great King, but probably too great a king for so corrupt a kingdom."
14. **Balmacaan Farm**. A farm estate belonging to the Laird of Grant located at the mouth of Glen Coiltie adjacent to the mouth of Glenurquhart on the north side of Loch Ness.
15. **Fort Augustus**. Built at the southwest end of Loch Ness in the aftermath of the 1715 Jacobite rising by General George Wade, the fort took its name from William Augustus, the

John Grant rode slowly back down the hill with heavy heart, expecting any second to be called back, or worse, to feel the wet slap of a lead ball between his shoulder blades. He let the mare have her head and she picked her way delicately down the ancient trail alongside the turbulent Divach Burn, which had taken several hundred years to tumble and score its own path down the northern flanks of *Sron Dubh*. Smoke was now rising through the trees from the Clunemore holdings on the eastern side of the burn as well. It would seem that after a gut-wrenching year of arguing, cajoling, threatening and fighting to keep the Laird of Grant's obstinate Catholic tenantry in Glenurquhart from joining the Jacobite cause, the many were to be scourged for the sins of the few.[16]

After the night's heavy rains, the roar of the Divach falls nearby seemed particularly loud and the roar seemed to grow inside his head until it blotted everything else out. So, it was almost a surprise when his horse's hooves were stumbling and splashing across the ford amongst the cattle drinking their fill in the River Coiltie, the early morning sunlight still struggling to burn away the last patches of cool grey mist banked here and there on the low ground. He was still alive.

John Grant cantered the remainder of the way up to the white-washed stone manse and swung down from his saddle, passing the reins to his groom. He told him to give her extra oats for her efforts at getting across and up to Divach in such a hurry, then strode up to the front door of Balmacaan House, where his wife, Mary, was waiting. She had one of their young daughters on her right hip and held the hand of their five-year-old son, John Jr.

"Well?" she said.

"Well what?"

"Are they coming down here next?"

"I don't know," he said wearily, "but I will take my breakfast in my office. I have a letter to finish."

John Grant of Ballintomb went inside to his office, poured himself a couple of drams and collected his thoughts as he stared out the window. The morning's

---

Duke of Cumberland. Wade had planned to build a town around the new barracks and call it Wadesburgh, and a settlement indeed sprang up, but it eventually took the name of the prominent fortification. Completed in 1742, the fort was captured by the Jacobites in April 1745, just prior to the Battle of Culloden.

16. **Tally of Damages**. In a 23 January 1747 deposition, and witnessed by John Grant, Factor of Urquhart, at Kilmichael, twenty-eight "tacksmen" or gentlemen farmers of Glenurquhart sought redress as loyal subjects of the King to be reimbursed for livestock and effects carried off by Major Lockhart and his men, claiming that Lockhart's raid had netted some 740 pounds sterling of cattle, horses, sheep and goats. See "Accompt of Cattle, &c., Taken by the Duke of Kingston's Horse out of that part of Sir Ludovick Grant's Estate Called the Lordship of Urquhart." Annex H, *Olden Times*, 499-501.

"The Laird of Strathspey." Sir Ludovick Grant of Grant (1707-73), succeeded to the Grant estates on the death of his father on 16 January 1747, becoming the 7th Baronet, Grant of Grant and the 21st hereditary clan chieftain. In later years, John Grant would recall the elderly Laird singling him out by name at a fair at Castle Grant in 1757, the year before he went into the army. (Illustration from Fraser, *The Chiefs of Grant*)

events didn't change the decision he had made the previous evening. He was a tall man with a shock of black hair tied back with a black ribbon, and according to his son's memoirs years later, "a very handsome man, the best looking of his clan. Stout, well made, of 6 feet high, of a dark complexion and was an excellent companion when sober. It was said of him that he was one who a person would borrow a shilling to drink with."[17]

Grant turned from the window and sat down at a large oaken desk to write of what had happened that morning at Divach and Clunemore to Ludovick Grant,[18] the heir apparent to the Regality of Grant. Ludovick managed all estates on behalf of his father, Sir James Grant of Grant, the absentee Chief who now resided by design in London, far away from the troubles. His clan had given the government some help in suppressing the Jacobite Rising in 1715, but had held back during this particular rebellion, the Laird charging his eldest son "to stay at home and take care of his country, and join no party."[19]

Trying to enforce those instructions on the Catholic tenantry of Urquhart had been well nigh impossible due to the actions of three gentlemen of the glen – "The Three Alexanders" – Alexander Grant of Shewglie,[20] Alexander Grant of Corrimony[21] and Alexander Mackay of Auchmony. *Shewglie*

17. All quotes from John Grant are from Part Two.
18. **Sir Ludovick Grant of Grant**. See Part Three for Biographical Note.
19. **Join no party**. John Grant, Factor of Urquhart, to Ludovick Grant, 17 September 1745. *Olden Times*, 247.
20. **Shewglie, or Sheuglie**. A cadet branch of the Grant clan.
21. **Corrimony**. An ancient barony absorbed into the Regality of Grant in the 1500s and, by the 18th-century, a small hamlet or "farm toun" at the western end of Glenurquhart some 9 miles (14.5 km) from Loch Ness.

and his remaining son were now prisoners in England; *Corrimony*, wounded at Culloden, was still in hiding somewhere up the glen if rumours were true; and, Mackay was God knows where.

John Grant re-read what he had written the night before:[22]

> Am sory to tell you that I must remove my family from this country, as am not safe to have them here; ther's so many threats againest me by Shewglie's rebell Highland friends, that am sure my house will soon be brunt, and the few cattle left me by the rebells taken from me. Some days agoe, upon my way to Fort Augustus, Glenmoristone and Angus McDonald, Shewglie's sone-in-law, waylaid me in the hills of Glenmoristone, and Mr. McDonald then told me that all Shewglie's friends was fully convinced that he or his sone wou'd not be confinde was it not me; and as that was the case, after the armie left Fort Augustus, that I might depend upon my not being one night safe here, as he and all Shewglie's friends was positive to be revenged of me. So I hope you'll be so good to acomodate my wife in a posscession in Strathspey, or any other part of your esteate, as there [is] no master I'd chouse so soon; but if she's not imediatly acomodate, I must be excus'd to have her acomodate elsewhere, for I'le not keep her any longer here, as am afraid every night when wee goe to bed to be brunt to ashes or next day. James Grant in Killmore is equally threatn'd with me, and he beggs likways to be acomodate. Am determin'd, be the event as it will, not to leave this country, if I shou'd remove my family, at least till you come home. I understand that the Shewglies have landed at London, You'll please let me know how soon you expect there tryall. As I wrote you in my last, if ther's no other wittness call'd for then the prisoners that went from here and Glenmoristone, the Shewglies will be very safe, as these people would perjure themselves or they told any thing that wou'd hurt the Shewglies. I'le expect you'll be so good to lett me here from you in course, and I ever am, honourable Sir,
>
> Your faithfull and obedient servant,
> John Grant.

Resolved, he took up his quill with a steadier hand and quickly added his postscript, sealed the letter, then walked outside to see what the King's men were up to now.

All mist was now gone from the glen and the sky was a piercing bright blue, marred only by black plumes of smoke billowing from all the buildings at Divach and Clunemore. Three scarlet-clad horsemen were in the yard, one of whom was the dismounted Argyll captain dressed in breeches and riding boots talking to his wife, Mary. Two Balmacaan maid servants were handing up loaves of bread and wheels of cheese to the two mounted troopers, who were putting the food in sacks slung across their saddles.

---

22. **Grant's letter**. John Grant, Factor of Urquhart, to Ludovick Grant of Grant, 12 July 1746. William Fraser, *The Chiefs of Grant*, vol 2 (Edinburgh, 1883), 264. Hereafter, *Chiefs of Grant*.

Mary noticed him right away and called over to him brightly. "This is Captain Campbell, John. He knows your nephew John *Dalrachney* in Loudoun's." The young captain touched his hand to his bonnet.

"I know you too, sir. I saw you at Fort Augustus a month back when you were visiting after the Glenmoriston raid. Nasty brutish business." He then fell silent, at a loss for words.

"Indeed," said Grant. "Please pass my regards to Johnny next time you see him, Captain Campbell, and tell him to give my compliments to his father at Inverlaidnan the next time he's there. You can also tell him that I hope to return to Speyside shortly with my family. With tempers running high in the glens, it has become too dangerous to remain here."

Grant paused and looked to the southwest in the direction of Fort Augustus as if he could physically see it through the jumbled pall of black smoke that gently drifted up the glen, pushed by a freshening breeze off Urquhart Bay. He added sardonically, "The Duke and the protection afforded by his brave regiments will not remain in the Great Glen forever, Captain, nor do they offer much reassurance for British subjects loyal to the crown after this morning's sorry business."

"I will pass your regards with pleasure, sir," said the captain, ignoring the last remark, his face flushed. "Good day to you, my lady, and thank you once again for the food. My compliments to you, sir." The young officer swung up into his saddle, then leaned forward and saluted, touching the forward edge of his bonnet.

"We now ride to Corrimony up the main glen, sir, and hope to be there before eventide. Then onto Strathglass[23] the morrow to teach the Chisholms and Frasers a thing or two."

"Good luck with that," said Grant grimly. "They are hard men, Captain Campbell."

John Grant *Ballintomb* and his five-year-old son stood silently side by side, watching the three horsemen trot away eastwards along the small road that led to the stone bridge over the River Enrick some two miles distant.

"Remember this day, Johnny," said the father looking down at his son. "Mark it well." Then taking his son's hand he smiled and said, "Now, let's go inside and get our porritch."

* * *

23. **Strathglass.** Strathglass stretches from Glen Affric towards Beauly in the north-eastern Highlands of Scotland. Home to the Chisholm clan (Upper Strathglass) and the Fraser clan (Lower Strathglass).

The River Spey is 107 miles (172 km) long, making it the second longest river in Scotland. It rises at over 1,000 feet (300 m) at Loch Spey in the Corrieyairack Forest in the western Scottish Highlands, about 10 miles (16 km) south of Fort Augustus as the crow flies. The river then tumbles its way eastwards and down, down through Newtonmore and Kingussie, Clan Chattan and Macpherson lands, before reaching Aviemore.[24] There it gives its name to the lush river plain known as Strathspey, the traditional homelands of Clan Grant. Thence it flows the remaining 60 miles (97 km) north-east to the Moray Firth, reaching the sea 5 miles (8 km) west of Buckie.

As it is the fastest-flowing river in Scotland, the Spey is constantly prone to flash floods, a direct by-product of the heavy spate of rain or snow-melt fed into it by the numerous tributaries draining the large mountainous catchment area that flanks its easterly course. The origins of its name have been lost in time, though "hawthorn river" has been suggested (from a word linked to the Brythonic *yspyddad*) as well as a hypothesis that it is actually a derivation of the pre-Celtic word *squeas,* meaning vomit or gush.

It was at Ballintomb,[25] where the Dulnain River joins its cold waters with those of the Spey – the traditional gathering place for Clan Grant in times of celebration – that a son was born to John and Mary Grant of Ballintomb on 2 December 1741. They named him John, and unbeknownst to all he would be the last male representative of the old and trusted cadet branch of Clan Grant, the Grants of Dalrachney, who claimed their lineage from Sir Duncan Grant, first Grant of Freuchie (c.1400-1485).

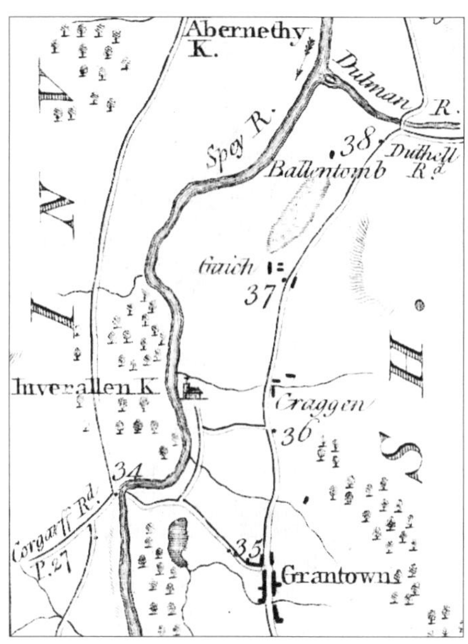

John Grant's birthplace. Ballintomb, where the Dulnain River joins its cold waters with those of the Spey, was the traditional gathering place for Clan Grant in times of celebration or war. Once a sizeable farming community, traces of an abandoned township still survive on a stretch of ground sloping southwards to the Spey. This 1776 detail of a touring map shows "The Road from Fochabers to Aviemore..." passing through Grantown (bottom of map) and thence westward to Ballintomb and Duthil (top of map). (Detail from Plate 59 of G. Taylor and A. Skinner's "Survey and maps of the roads of North Britain or Scotland," 1776, National Library of Scotland. Editors' photo)

24. **Aviemore**. A hamlet in the 18th century situated on the military road in the river plain on the western bank of the Spey River about 6 miles (10 km) due south of Carrbridge.
25. **Ballintomb**. A farm estate belonging to the Laird of Grant situated between the juncture of the Dulnain River and the Spey River, a mile (1.6 km) east of the village of Dulnain Bridge and 5 miles (8 km) west of present-day Grantown-on-Spey in Morayshire.

The Old Coffin Bridge of Carr. The oldest standing stone bridge in the Highlands, Carr bridge was erected by Brigadier General Sir Alexander Grant of Grant in 1717 to provide passage over the Dulnain for his clansmen, their horses and funeral processions to Duthil Churchyard, hence its local nickname "the coffin bridge." John would cross the River Dulnain every day via this bridge to go to his first school at the church. (Editors' Collection).

More accurately, that descent was through the illegitimate eldest son of John Grant, the second son of the chieftain, Sir Duncan. Named Duncan for his grandfather the chief, this Duncan was the first Grant of Gartinbeg and progenitor of several cadet branches, the most prominent being the Grants of Inverlaidnan, Dalvey and Dalrachney. Each branch was headed by a laird usually named for the principal estate he held, either by tack (lease) or by wadset (mortgage).[26]

"The Dalrachnie [*sic*] family were favorites of the Chiefs," Grant would write in later life, "My great grandfather [Alexander], John *Dhu*, my Grandfather, Father [John] and Uncle [Alexander][27] always acted as counsellors in matters of difficulty." His grandfather, John *Dhu*, had been factor of Glenurquhart earlier in the century. John's father, John *Ballintomb*, had followed in his father's footsteps, succeeding the Laird's brother, Major George Grant in 1742 as chamberlain, stewart, baron-baillie[28] and factor of Glenurquhart. His uncle

26. **Wadset**. A mortgage held by a wadsetter, someone who rented his land but had loaned money to the Laird, and in return, had been granted a wadset right to farm the land for a predetermined period, sometimes for generations.
27. **Alexander Grant of Dalrachney, later Inverlaidnan**, John Grant's uncle. See Part Three for Biographical Note.
28. **Baron Baillie or Bailey**. A magistrate appointed by a baron, in this case, Sir James Grant, to dispense justice and maintain the peace on his behalf in a designated jurisdiction, in this case the Regality of Grant.

"The Merry Ha." Castle Grant is the former ancestral seat of the Clan Grant chiefs of Strathspey in Moray, Scotland. It stands a mile (1.6 km) north of Grantown-on-Spey, the oldest part of the building dating from around the 15th century. The centre of all clan activity, "The Merry Ha" was the primary residence of the Chief of Grant where he not only gave grand parties on festive occasions, but meted out justice, resolved disputes and oversaw the running of his regality. (Private Collection)

Alexander Grant of Dalrachney, and later Inverlaidnan, was Ludovick's principal advisor during the Jacobite Uprising and the collector of *cess* (land tax) for the Regality of Grant.

John Grant would recall the elderly Laird of Grant, Sir Ludovick Grant, singling him out by name at a fair at Castle Grant[29] in 1757, the year before he went into the army. "Your family were always our *Lam á chrest* [*sic*], John," he said, supporting himself on the youngster's shoulder, the term literally meaning "hands closest to a belted shirt" – a feudal analogy reserved for family counsellors closest to the chief.[30]

---

29. **Castle Grant**. The former ancestral seat of the Clan Grant chiefs of Strathspey in Moray, Scotland. Castle Grant stands a mile (1.6 km) north of Grantown-on-Spey, the oldest part of the building dating from around the 15th century. The original building was a typical Z-shaped tower house but had a number of significant additions over the years, the largest expansion made in the 1750s by Sir Ludovick Grant. Two wings were added on the south side, which now encloses the courtyard and the Castle has remained roughly the same since that period. The centre of all clan activity, it was the primary residence of the Chief of Grant where he dealt with the various clan matters, meted out justice, resolved disputes, and gave grand parties on festive occasions. During the late 20th century, the castle became derelict and went through a series of owners. A major refurbishment project was completed in 2008 and the castle is now a private residence.
30. ***Lam á chrest*** (Scottish Gaelic: possibly *Leine chriosta* meaning "A belted shirt;" or *lamh ann an crios*, "hand in a belt"; or *làmh à crios* which can be translated as: "hands nearest the belt"). John Johnson Jr., the grandson who acted as scribe to his grandfather's dictation, was not a Gaelic speaker and wrote the word down phonetically so the phrasing is difficult

The Regality of Grant had been established in 1694 to form "ane great huge estait," its heart centred chiefly on Speyside between the two Craigellachies – one above Aviemore in the west and the other where the river entered the coastal plain of Moray in the east. It also included the district of Rothiemurchus on the northern slopes of the Cairngorm Mountains, and the far distant straths of Glenurquhart and Glenmoriston on the northwestern side of Loch Ness. The latter two glens were separated from the clan seat at Castle Grant in the Spey valley by only 40 miles (64 km) as the crow flies. Humans, however, had to go around a deep loch and traverse a high grey mountain range looming on its southern shores known as the Monadliath, the haunt of eagles and wild cats, as well as crossing the straths of the Nairn and Findhorn Rivers. Inverness, the acknowledged capital of the Highlands, by contrast, was only a half-day ride away. As a result of geography, the two distant glens were always managed by the most trusted of the Laird's relatives.

John's father, styled Grant of Ballintomb in later life, was the second son born to John *Dhu* Grant of Dalrachney, a powerful man in the clan. So much so, that people referred to him as "The Lord of Strathspey," but not to his face, nor to their chief, the Laird of Grant. It was said that his older brother, Alexander Grant of Inverlaidnan, had made enough money as a baron-baillie by 1740 to be able to lend the Laird of Grant 22,000 merks, as well as getting a very favourable wadset and a tack of Inverlaidnan for seventy-six years. John in his memoirs would note that his uncle "had nearly the whole of Dulnainside[31] [in wadsets] – these then considered as scarce redeemable and almost perpetual." Altogether, John's Uncle Alexander, and his grandfather, John *Dhu*, were said to have made £3,000 or £4,000 in the exercise of their authority. That power ended in 1748 after the '45 Rebellion however, when the Regality Courts, and the lucrative appointments of baron-baillie that went with them, were abolished.[32]

In his memoirs, John Grant confesses he was a sickly child and had three nurses before he was five months old. In 1742, his family moved from Strathspey to Balmacaan House at the eastern end of Glenurquhart as his father took

to decipher. But, given the context of his follow-on commentary, several Gaelic speakers are agreed that it literally means "hands closest to the belted shirt," the latter being the most intimate piece of wearing apparel without donning a belted plaid. The modern-day sense for this type of relationship would be "right-hand man." Norman MacLeod and Daniel Dewar, *Dictionary of the Gaelic Language* (Edinburgh, 1909), 201, 921; as well as help from Gaelic speakers; Effie Rankin and Dr. John Gibson of Judique, Cape Breton.

31. **Dulnainside.** The river plain found on either side of the River Dulnain, a tributary of the River Spey.

32. **Regality Courts.** "MSS Notes 1762 by Mr. Lorimer, Secretary to the Laird of Grant." Rev. W. Forsyth, *In the Shadow of the Cairngorm: Chronicles of the United Parishes of Abernethy and Kincardine* (Inverness, 1900), 260-1.

up his new post as factor to the Laird of Grant. It was there in 1746, that John's first memories were "the coming of troopers." John allegedly contracted smallpox that summer and "was treated in the usual way" with blankets "pinned up to the windows" and a large fire made in a sealed room. He was then fed a liquid diet of mulled wine, ostensibly to "keep it out of his heart." Such treatments smack of quackery by today's standards and his miraculous recovery from such a deadly disease at a young age might have been due to the possibility that he had actually contracted cowpox. A milder disease prevalent amongst Scottish dairy maids in the 18th century, cowpox was much less virulent and later used to inoculate humans against the more lethal variant.[33]

After John's recovery, his father, John *Ballintomb*, concerned for the safety of his family moved them north to the safety of Braelangwell[34] in Ross-shire, the estate of his wife's step-sister, Margaret Ross, and her husband, Charles Urquhart. Whether his father remained in Glenurquhart with his job or accompanied them is not recorded, but when John was of school age, he returned to live in his Uncle Alexander's house at Inverlaidnan[35] in Strathspey. He was sent to school in Duthil[36] near the old parish church to learn the basics of reading, writing and arithmetic.

At the age of ten, John was sent by his parents to board at the grammar school in Inverness with sixteen other sons of the Highland gentry and nobil-

---

33. **Smallpox**. The disease was usually deadly in the Highlands given its geographically remote settlements and relative isolation. D. Brunton, "Smallpox inoculation in eighteenth-century Scotland," *Cambridge Medical History*, vol 36, No.4 (October, 1992), 403-29.
34. **Braelangwell**. An estate of the Urquhart family situated in the heart of the Black Isle, Ross-shire, a peninsula, surrounded on three sides by water – the Cromarty Firth to the north, the Beauly Firth to the south, and the Moray Firth to the east. The last Urquhart to own the estate and property was David Urquhart born at Braelangwell in 1805, a famous diplomat and publicist who served for many years at the British Legation in Constantinople. In 1790, an elegant Georgian country mansion was built on the estate, of which only 76 acres (0.31 km^2) remain today, but it incorporates one of the last remaining areas of ancient woodland on the Black Isle.
35. **House of Inverlaidnan** was located approximately 2 miles (3.2 km) west of present-day Carrbridge, Inverness-shire, at the eastern apex where the Dulnain and Spey Rivers join. The Old Bridge of Carr was erected by Brigadier General Sir Alexander Grant of Grant in 1717 for estate purposes to provide passage for foot passengers, horses and stock for funerals to Duthil Churchyard, hence its other local name "the coffin bridge." Inverlaidnan House, now in ruins, was built to replace an older house that burned down in 1739. Its principal claim to fame is that Bonnie Prince Charlie stayed there one night in 1746 on his way to Inverness, and, according to John Grant, got a fairly frosty reception from his uncle, Alexander Grant.
36. **Duthil**. Parish in Strathspey one mile (1.6 km) east of present-day Carrbridge which straddles the Dulnain River just before it empties into the Spey. No trace of this school remains and may perhaps have been a church school run by the minister. At this time, the inhabitants of Duthil Parish lived at Dalnahaitnich, Foregin and Slochd on the southern side of the Dulnain.

Dunbar's Hospital. The structure where John Grant boarded with other sons of the Highland gentry and attended lessons in the town's grammar school. Originally an almshouse and hospital for the town, it was built on Church Street in 1668 by Provost Alexander Dunbar. The right side of the three-story building housed the school from 1727 until 1792 when it was closed on the opening of the newly constructed Inverness Royal Academy. (Editors' photo)

ity. The school was then housed in the right-hand section of the ground floor of Dunbar's Hospital, built in 1668, a long three-storey stone building situated on Church Street. Here John and his colleagues took their lessons from Dr. Alexander Ferguson,[37] the master, and Dr. John Boyd,[38] the first usher or assistant schoolmaster. Their curriculum would have included English and Gaelic grammar, Greek, Latin, mathematics, French and Presbyterian theology.

Inverness in 1751 was the principal town in the eastern Highlands with some 3,000 inhabitants and fewer than 500 houses, its small port the only economic gateway to the world for the region. The Highland gentry kept small townhouses there as winter residences, most of them marked on the outside with the owner's initials and those of his wife carved into the red sandstone. Despite be-

---

37. **Dr. Alexander Ferguson**, M.A., King's College, Aberdeen, 1738. A native of Insch and Master of the Inverness Grammar School in 1750. He had previously been a schoolmaster at Prestonpans. In 1755, Ferguson was dismissed and jailed when found guilty of immorality and making defamatory remarks against the parents of his students. "Masters and Doctors of Inverness Grammar School (from after the Reformation until closure in 1792)," Peter J. Anderson, *The Grammar School and Royal Academy of Inverness* (Inverness, 1907), 24. Hereafter, *Masters and Doctors*.
38. **Dr. John Boyd**. Dr. Boyd was at the grammar school from 1752 to 1754. He resigned without notice or explanation in 1754. *Masters and Doctors*, 24.

ing a royal burgh, Inverness had only four principal streets, three of which met at the market cross in the centre of town where merchants gathered every morning to conduct daily business. "There they stand in the middle of the dirty street and are frequently interrupted in their negotiations by horses and carts," wrote a British officer, "which often separate them one from the other in the midst of their bargains or other affairs."[39]

The Inverness merchants were vital to the bleak economy of the eastern Highlands, for they were the conduit for the principal exports of timber, salmon, beef, wool, malt and meal to the outside world. In return, they made Inverness into an emporium, bringing in for the Highland elite their "claret and books, their broadsword steel, Mechlin lace, Spanish silver, velvet, silk, shot, powder, spices and spies."[40]

When John's father dropped him off at the school in the fall of 1751, Inverness was still considered a Jacobite stronghold and thus the soldiers of His Majesty's 20th Regiment of Foot were very much in evidence. Their young twenty-four-year-old commanding officer, James Wolfe,[41] spent his first Scottish winter in Inverness at the same time as young John was boarding in Church Street. No doubt the two occasionally crossed paths in the small town. Wolfe attended the Presbyterian kirk every Sunday, as did all the Highland gentry, the Church regulating the entire town firmly by "Bible and by-law."[42] And while young John probably thought Inverness was a wondrous place, having never experienced anything other than the remote hamlets of the eastern Highlands, James Wolfe, by contrast, had been to Paris, Brussels and London, and thus his letters written home over the winter of 1751–52 are full of contempt for the town and its inhabitants.

"A little while serves to discover the villainous nature of the inhabitants," he wrote to his father on 3 October 1751, "and brutality of the people in its neighbourhood." And while it might have been natural for a Culloden veteran to harbour some ill feelings towards those he considered enemies of the Crown, Wolfe reserved his harshest comments for the Highland Hanoverians: "Those who pretend the greatest attachment to the Government, and who every day feed

---

39. **Affairs.** Edward Burt, *Burt's Letters from the North of Scotland,* vol I (Edinburgh, 1876), 52.
40. **Spices and spies.** John Prebble, *Culloden* (Harmondsworth, 1967), 143.
41. **Lieutenant Colonel James Wolfe (1727-59).** In January 1758 Wolfe was given local rank as "brigadier in America" and made one of Jeffery Amherst's three brigade commanders for the assault landing and siege of Louisbourg, 1758. He was killed outside the city of Quebec on the Plains of Abraham, 13 September 1758. For a more complete biography on Wolfe, see Part Three, *A Bard of Wolfe's Army: James Thompson, Gentleman Volunteer, 1733-1830*, E.J. Chapman and I.M. McCulloch, eds. (Robin Brass Studio, Montreal, 2010).
42. **Bible and by-law.** John Prebble, *Culloden* (Harmondsworth, 1967), 143

"Very unbecoming a soldier to complain of little evils." So wrote a newly-promoted and apologetic Lieutenant Colonel James Wolfe (1727-59) from Inverness in 1751 to his mother about his food, lodgings and fire in Inverness – all "bad." The twenty-four-year-old battalion commander of the 20th Foot was even less impressed with the hospitality of the alleged loyal inhabitants of Inverness, who, he claimed, displayed "greater rudeness and incivility than the open and professed Jacobites." Oil painting by Joseph Highmore, c. 1751. (LAC C-3916)

upon the public purse, seem to distinguish themselves for greater rudeness and incivility than the open and professed Jacobites."[43]

Winter was especially trying for the Kentish-born army officer. "The winds," he wrote "sometimes drive the snows with such violence that the roads are utterly impassable, and again, when it thaws, the rivers swell so prodigiously that there is no less danger and difficulty on that side." Confined to his room on account of the weather, he confessed to his mother in November 1751 that it was "unmanly and very unbecoming a soldier to complain of little evils such as bad food, bad lodging, and bad fire."[44]

According to John Grant, he and his fellow boarders were in a constant state of hunger and being "so scantily fed, it was a rule in our little band that when a few shillings were sent to any [of] us by friends it was put into a common purse and we purchased ale and hops, which we brought up to the room we had for our lessons." The niggardliness of the school's matron (also known as the mistress) to provide the growing boys with any nourishing food in any quantity caused them to retaliate with petty vandalism, destroying their eating utensils and burning all the peat as soon as it was provided.

In such a miserable environment, it is no wonder that the boys formed strong attachments to one another. On one occasion, John remembers the usher, John Boyd, attempting "to punish my chum Duff. He was a stout boy and made resistance. The brute drew his knife and in attempting to cut open his Clothes, cut him. I jumped up, was seconded by the others, and seized on his hands. He remembered this and punished me on the first occasion." This incident would

43. **Professed Jacobites.** James Wolfe to his Father, 3 October 1751, Inverness. Beckles Willson, *The Life and Times of James Wolfe* (London, 1909), 155.

44. **Confession.** James Wolfe to his Mother, 6 November 1751, Inverness. *Ibid*, 158.

be the cause for John's first beating, and later the pre-teen would be tortured by the same man after stumbling in on the usher and the mistress up in his room "in rather an equivocal situation."

In the days following the incident, Boyd was, at first, "very civil" records Grant and "many biscuits did I get from Miss Jessie Kirkland," but the laissez-faire truce did not last long. "One unlucky day he punished me severely [and] my prudence forsook me," confesses John. The youth rashly threatened to report the teacher and his paramour to the authorities and "from that moment I became his victim." As one of John's many ensuing punishments, Boyd would prick his head with a bodle pin under the pretence of killing head lice. John claimed that he "bore this torture as well as I could, but his treatment so frightened me that I could never say my lessons."

On Christmas Day 1752, in the middle of his second year at the school, disaster struck John's family. His father died suddenly from a botched medical treatment for severe tonsillitis. As a consequence, his mother and four sisters moved into Inverness the following spring to be closer to John at school and he no longer had to board. But the eleven-year-old's continual refusal to let the maidservant comb his hair made his mother suspicious, and on interrogation John told her of his daily torments at the school under the hands of Boyd.

The outraged mother examined her son's ravaged head and went directly to the town magistrate, where "the affair was taken up. The usher was cited. I appear'd and he received a severe reprimand." The torture ceased and the usher "took no more notice" of John. The following year brought closure with the scandal of Miss Kirkland, the mistress of the grammar school, becoming pregnant. This caused John to note, with some satisfaction, that his former "tormentor decamped, leaving the Lady in her shame." The school record would appear to corroborate this story, stating that Mr. Boyd resigned abruptly with no notice or reason in 1754.

John's deliverance was short-lived, for his mother died that same year. His memoirs state rather stoically that "she died of an apoplectic fit, or rather paralytic, brought on by the low nervous state she was left in, in consequence of grief from her husband's death. I heard of it casually in the street – rushed to the spot and saw them carrying her in, a corpse."

Surprisingly, that is the extent of Grant's commentary on what must have been a cataclysmic event in his young life. He offers no opinions or feelings on having become an orphan at the age of thirteen. Adding churn to the turmoil of the young teenager's world, the master of his school, Dr. Ferguson, was arrested shortly after his mother's death and charged with "gross immorality" (perhaps linked to the pregnancy of the mistress and Boyd's sudden departure) as well as defaming the parents of the students. Ferguson was found guilty and imprisoned and the town of Inverness was forced to find a new master.[45]

With both parent's dead, and the ongoing scandals at the school, his Uncle Alexander probably thought a change of scenery would be the best tonic for young John. He was duly sent to a boarding school in the small royal burgh of Fortrose,[46] some 6 miles (10 km) north of Inverness and on one side of a promontory known as Chanonry Point[47] which juts out from the Black Isle into the Moray Firth. The small ecclesiastical town, also known as the Chanonry, was home to the once famous Fortrose Cathedral, now in ruins, for Oliver Cromwell's Parliamentarian troops had plundered the its stone in the mid-17th century to build a fort at Inverness.

The small school John would attend owed its existence to the patronage of the Earls of Seaforth[48] and was administered by the town council. Over the years the school had been carried on in various buildings, usually private houses taken over for that purpose. In 1754 John's school was run out of the private residence of an Episcopalian clergyman whose name is lost in time. The annual rate for John's board was half of what his family had paid for him to attend the now discredited Inverness grammar school, a fact which probably appealed to his frugal uncle now footing the bills. By all accounts, the new school was acceptable, food was plentiful and John reported that he "passed his time pleasantly enough."

In 1756, as war clouds loomed over most of Europe, it was decided by his Uncle Alexander that John needed some final polish as a young gentleman before he sought his fame and fortune. His family decided that he would attend King's College in Aberdeen.[49] The War of the Austrian Succession, which had conclud-

---

45. **Headmaster**. James Miller, *Inverness* (Edinburgh, 2004), 163.

46. **Fortrose** (Gaelic: *A' Chananaich;* Scots: *Chainry*). Made a royal burgh in Ross-shire (Ross and Cromarty) in the Scottish Highlands in 1300 and comprises the towns of Chanonry and Rosemarkie. Located on the Moray Firth, about six miles (9.6 km) northeast of Inverness, the town is known for its ruined 13th-century cathedral, and was the seat of the bishopric of Ross.

47. **Chanonry**. A name deriving from the ancient enclosure comprising the residences of the Canons who had been associated with the Fortrose Cathedral built in 1485.

48. **Seaforth family**. The Earl of Seaforth was a title held by the family of Mackenzie from 1623 to 1716 (Scottish Peerage), and again from 1771 to 1781 (Irish Peerage). During John Grant's lifetime, Kenneth Mackenzie was the last Earl of Seaforth and Viscount Fortrose. Both peerages became extinct when he died in August 1781. During the American Revolution, Kenneth raised the 78th Regiment of Foot, later known as the 72nd Foot (Seaforth Highlanders).

49. **Aberdeen**. Situated on the North Sea coast between the Rivers Dee and Don, Aberdeen forms a natural port which has drawn people for around 8,000 years. Aberdeen's geography is reflected in its name, meaning either: "mouth of two rivers" (a corruption of *"aber da-aevin"*); or, a compromise between Aber-Don and Aber-Dee ("mouth of the Don/Dee"),

Showing off. The second division of the 42nd Foot undergoing a final review on Glasgow Green 23 April 1756 before shipping out to join the rest of the regiment already in North America. The following year, John joined a second battalion of the Black Watch raised on order of the King, who honoured them with Royal status in 1758, renaming them the Royal Highlanders. Grant stated his recruits had no time to learn drill or how to fire their muskets like the recruits depicted here and instead, were sent directly on military operations. (BWCM, Editors' photo)

ed when John was seven years old, had not really solved anything diplomatically in Europe. Empress Maria Theresa of Austria only signed the 1748 peace treaty of Aix-la-Chapelle to give herself enough time to rebuild her military forces and to forge new alliances. This she did with remarkable success during the so-called Diplomatic Revolution of 1756. The courts of Europe were surprised when Austria allied herself with her centuries-old enemies of France and Russia and ended her twenty-five-year alliance with Britain. Strongly dissatisfied with the limited help she had received from her supposed British allies, Empress Maria Theresa now saw France as the only continental ally powerful enough to help her retake Silesia and check Prussia's expansion.

Britain, feeling isolated, became Prussia's newfound ally, King George and his ministers concerned that his ancestral Hanoverian possessions in Germany were threatened by France. Britain thus brought the largest and most effective

---

combining the name of the city's two rivers. By the 18th century Aberdeen's industry was thriving: paper production; woolens, linen and cotton industries; quarried granite; flax-spinning, jute and comb-making factories; whisky distillation; and shipbuilding. After Glasgow industrialized, Aberdeen lost its position as Scotland's second city.

navy in the world into this new alliance, while Prussia, under the indomitable Frederick the Great, boasted the most formidable land force in Europe. The British hoped that the new alliances forged during the Diplomatic Revolution would serve to maintain the balance of power and keep the peace, but in fact they proved the catalyst for the eruption of hostilities in the summer of 1756.

The formal opening of hostilities in Europe would be preceded by fighting in North America, where the westward expansion of the British colonies along the eastern seaboard had butted up against French claims to the Ohio country and Mississippi valley. A major bone of contention was a line of forts the French built in the early 1750s to forestall the expansion of the British colonies westwards in what is now western Pennsylvania. Anglo-French rivalries in the teeming forests and rich river plains of the disputed Ohio River valley led to a fateful exchange of shots between Virginian provincials and British regulars led by a young officer named George Washington, and a force of French soldiers and their Indian allies. The result was a diplomatic incident that escalated into a crisis between Britain and France, both dispatching regular troops to North America in anticipation of hostilities.

Before the war was even officially declared in May 1756, Major General Edward Braddock advanced with 2,200 British regulars and American provincials against Fort Duquesne, a wooden French fort on the forks of the Ohio River and site of the present-day city of Pittsburgh in western Pennsylvania. One of three British expeditions against French frontier posts, Braddock's force was surprised 7 miles (11 km) short of its objective by a vastly inferior force of Indians and French colonial soldiers using Indian tactics of envelopment and concealment. Braddock was killed and his force dispersed.

The shocking news of Braddock's "Massacre" on the Monongahela River reached the Scottish Highlands in late 1755. It stoked an already busy rumour-mill that new Highland battalions (based on the model of the 42nd Foot) would soon be authorized and raised to go overseas to North America with Lord Loudoun, the newly-appointed commander-in-chief for North America, in 1756.

On the completion of his studies in Aberdeen, John Grant returned home to Strathspey to visit his relatives, and in his own words looked "quite a buck" wearing a new "pea green coat, a Waistcoat with flaps reaching half down the thigh, breeches, stockings and shoes and buckles, and a bag with the three-cornered hats then in fashion." His memoirs give a last glimpse of the old clan system and Highland society that had been in free-fall since the end of the '45 Uprising, a system that would ultimately disappear with the death of Sir Ludovick Grant in 1765.

"Strathspey was then a pleasant residence," he remembered, "filled with gen-

King's College, Aberdeen. A 19th-century depiction of the original college that John Grant attended before entering the army, the focal point here the 15th-century King's College Chapel with its distinctive crown spire. Originally founded in 1495, the college is now an integral part of the University of Aberdeen. (Private Collection).

tlemen cadets of the family or branches of the Lairds who had wadsets." His favourite time was Christmas when all

> ... met among each other ... and the dance and the Song with the Wine cup went round, punch and sometimes claret. It was rude but heady to be sure. We were somewhat polished by being admitted to the security of Castle Grant called the "Merry Ha'" – which was an epicure of open house or table. There was, to be sure, a good deal of conviviality – Sir Ludovic Grant being very convivial. The gentry intermarried among themselves so that they were almost one family.

The talk at Christmas 1756 would most certainly have centred on the rumours that new Highland regiments would soon be authorized and raised to go overseas to North America, the Duke of Argyll, or the "Governor" of Scotland as the Duke of Newcastle styled him, being the principal lobbyist for the creation of such new units. Argyll had astutely bided his time, believing that the foreign policy direction taken by the newly-appointed Secretary of State for the South, William Pitt, who had responsibility for the American colonies, would sooner support rather than hinder his proposals. By Christmas 1756, Pitt was calling for the vigorous acquisition and defence of colonies rather than making any further heavy military commitments to the European theatre of war.

On 4 January 1757, Viscount William Barrington, the Secretary at War, contacted Archibald Montgomery, brother of the 10th Earl of Eglington, and Si-

"The Old Squah." Major General James Abercromby *Glassaugh* (1706-81) was the unfortunate fifty-two-year-old commander of the British-American Army at Ticonderoga in 1758. His large army's defeat at the hands of a much smaller French force caused his aboriginal allies to term him "the Old Squah who should wear Petticoats." His own soldiers dubbed him "Mrs. Nabbycromby" after the debacle. (Oil on canvas by Allan Ramsay, Fort Ligonier, Editors' photo)

mon Fraser, son of the executed Lord Lovat, instructing each to "Raise a Highland Battalion of Foot, under your command, which is to Consist of Ten Companies of Four Serjeants [*sic*], Four Corporals, Two Drummers, and One Hundred Effective Private Men in each Company, besides Commission Officers." The commissions given to Montgomery and Fraser made them lieutenant colonels commandant of the 1st and 2nd Highland Battalions of Foot respectively, confirmed by Royal Warrant, "the 5th Day of January 1757 in the 30th Year of our Reign."[50] The Highland officers of these new battalions were to receive their initial commissions by raising men and not by purchase, and this created a flurry of willing candidates who aggressively lobbied their respective patrons.

"It was a frenzy," recalled James Boswell, the biographer of Samuel Johnson. Half-pay Highland officers and former Jacobites contended for a number of scarce vacancies, citing their military experience, but more importantly, their ability to raise men. The sixteen-year-old Boswell was swept up in the excitement and, though "timorous where firearms were concerned," was "set in a flame … to go among the Highlanders to America" in 1757. Wiser heads prevailed as "father prevented me," and Master Boswell remained at school.[51] John Grant, who was only a year older than Boswell, was also considering his options.

In early 1758 he went to stay with his maternal uncle, David Ross, later Lord Ankerville, a Lord of Session or supreme court judge in the Scottish legal sys-

50. **Commissions**. TNA, SP 44/189, fols. 342-46; *London Magazine* (January 1757), 41-2; Eric and Andros Linklater, *The Black Watch: The History of the Royal Highland Regiment* (London, 1977), 32. Both units were initially raised on a standard ten-company establishment. This was expanded to thirteen and ultimately fourteen companies. For a detailed discussion of the trends, problems and recruiting of the Highland battalions, see Andrew McKillop's useful, *"More Fruitful than the Soil": Army, Empire and the Scottish Highlands, 1715-1815* (East Linton, 1999). See also Stephen Brumwell, *Redcoats. The British Soldier and War in the Americas, 1755-1763* (Cambridge and New York, 2002), 264-89.

51. **Wiser heads.** *James Boswell: The Earlier Years, 1740-1769*, F. A. Pottle, ed. (New York, 1966), 31.

tem. After a short stint with a private tutor in Tain,[52] it was pronounced time for the seventeen-year-old John "to decide on a profession" and seek his fortune in the world. "Like most of my countrymen, I chose the army," wrote Grant, "and my friends obtained for me a Lieutenancy of the Highland Watch[53] under condition of raising 25 men." John's commission as a lieutenant in the 2nd Battalion of the 42nd (Royal Highland) Regiment of Foot was dated 22 July 1758.

It had not been his first offer however. A commission in the Honourable East India Company[54] in Calcutta had been first suggested, but his uncle rejected the proposal outright as in those days it was "considered rather an adventure." A vacant commission in the regular army opened up because LORD JOHN MURRAY, the colonel of the 42nd Regiment of Foot, was ordered to recruit seven new companies in the Highlands to add to the three "additional companies" already serving in North America.[55] Once joined they would form the new 2nd Battalion of the British army's senior Highland regiment. For the Highland gentry who had missed out on the first round of free commissions in 1757, seven new Black Watch companies meant seven new captains' commissions, fourteen new lieutenancies and seven new ensigncies.

King George II, however, had gone one step further. The monarch had graciously bestowed "Royal" status upon his "Old Highland Regiment," this before the disastrous news of the defeat of the British army under General James Abercromby at Ticonderoga[56] reached London on 20 August 1758. His special

---

52. **Tain** (Gaelic: *Baile Dhubhthaich*, Duthac's town). A town situated on the south side of Dornoch Firth, some 35 miles (56 km) north of Inverness. Granted its first royal charter in 1066, Tain is Scotland's oldest royal burgh.
53. **Highland Watch**. First formed as six independent companies in May 1725 to "watch" over the Highlands. With the addition of four newly-raised companies, the six companies were regimented as the 43rd Foot (Earl of Crawford's) in October 1739. In May 1749 the regiment was renumbered upwards to the 42nd Foot.
54. **The Honourable East India Company's Army**. An alternative to the British Army or European service if one did not have the funds necessary to purchase a commission. Ironically, many impoverished young Scots who went out to India and survived their military service, returned very rich men.
55. **Additional companies**. At the end of 1757, nine companies were raised in Scotland to reinforce the Highland battalions serving in North America: three to the 42nd Foot; three to the 77th Foot (Montgomery's Highlanders); and three to the 78th Foot (Fraser's Highlanders).
56. **Ticonderoga** (previously Fort Carillon). A large star-shaped fort built by the French between 1755 and 1758 at a narrows near the southern end of Lake Champlain. On 8 July 1758 4,000 French defenders were able to repel an attack by 16,000 British troops under the command of General James Abercromby near the fort. In 1759 the British returned and drove a token French garrison from the fort but not before the French, in withdrawing, blew up the magazines and eastern barracks. Renamed by the British as Fort Ticonderoga, it was repaired and improved between 1759 and 1760 but did not see any further action during the Seven Years' War.

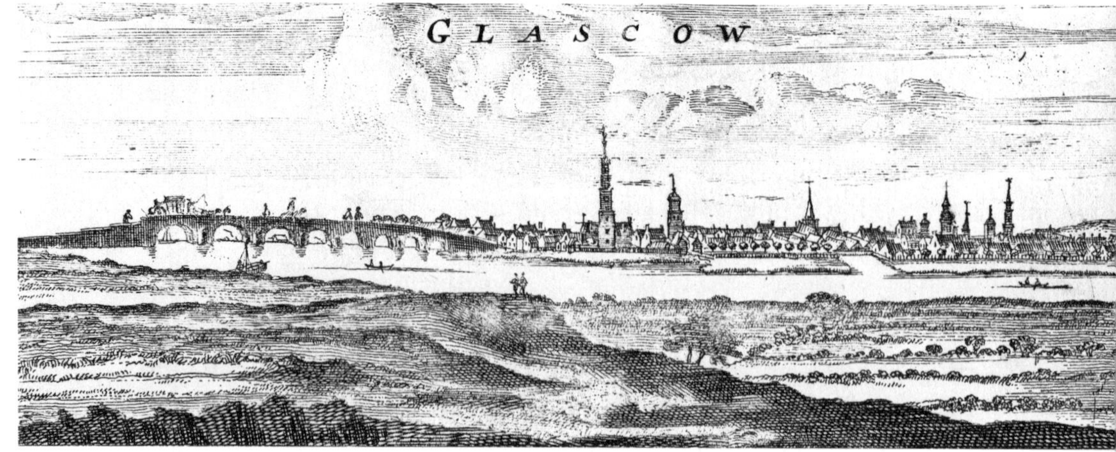

"Rising into commercial importance." Glasgow became the largest city in Scotland and third largest in the United Kingdom. Situated on the River Clyde in the country's West Central Lowlands, it grew from a small rural settlement to become Britain's largest seaport. It also became a major centre of the Scottish Enlightenment in the 18th century as well as a hub of transatlantic trade with North America and the West Indies. When John Grant passed through, he observed: "Glasgow was then just rising into commercial importance but was small in comparison to its present size." (Map detail from "The North Part of Great Britain called Scotland" by Herman Moll, published 1714. National Library of Scotland, Editors' photo)

warrant claimed that he was "desirous to distinguish Our Forty Second Regiment of Foot with some mark of Our Royal Favour" and directed that "from henceforth Our said regiment be called, and distinguished by the title and name of Our Forty-Second, or Royal Highland Regiment of Foot...."[57] With such an honour, the regiment was entitled to change its regimental colours, facings, collars, cuffs and drums to royal blue.

So successful were Black Watch officers in recruiting the 2nd Battalion that, within three months, seven companies, each 120 men strong, had been embodied at Perth[58] by October 1758. John's new unit marched down to Glasgow mid-October, where the new Highland companies were billeted and "well-received by the inhabitants." Grant remembered that his men, despite being issued arms, "were merely taught to march," while the officers attended balls and "had the honour of being made Burgesses" of Glasgow.[59]

---

57. **Royal warrant**. Eric and Andros Linklater, *The Black Watch: The History of the Royal Highland Regiment* (London, 1977), 32.
58. **Perth** (Pictish: meaning "copse" or "wood"). A city and former royal burgh in central Scotland situated on the Tay River. It had approximately 15,000 inhabitants in 1759 and its principal industry was linen weaving.
59. **Burgesses**. In this context, the Black Watch officers were granted honorary citizenships. Burgess originally meant a freeman of a borough (England) or burgh (Scotland). It later

The 2nd Battalion, 42nd Foot (Royal Highlanders), originally earmarked as a reinforcement for the army in North America in early 1757, had its orders changed at the last minute. At the end of November 1758 the officers and men learned at Glasgow that they would first be diverted to Major General PEREGRINE THOMAS HOPSON's[60] expedition to seize the French sugar islands of Martinique[61] and Guadeloupe[62] in the Caribbean, before carrying on to North America. The officers appointed to command the seven new Black Watch companies were; Francis MacLean; Alexander Sinclair; John Stewart of Stenton; WILLIAM MURRAY, son of Lintrose; Archibald Campbell; Alexander Reid; and Robert Arbuthnot. The latter officer would die before embarkation and be replaced by Captain DAVID HALDANE of Aberuthven, a kinsman of Colonel George Haldane, one of four brigadiers on the Hopson expedition and the governor-designate of Jamaica. He also happened to be John's first cousin on his mother's side and his new company commander.[63]

Due to a shortage of transports,[64] only 200 Highlanders could be sent forthwith to the Caribbean, the rest of the battalion to follow as soon as ships became available. John's company was one of the first two selected and they marched

---

came to mean an elected or unelected official of a municipality.

60. **Major General Peregrine Hopson**. See Part Three for Biographical Note. For an excellent account of Hopson's 1759 Campaign, see Marshall Smelser, *The Campaign for the Sugar Islands, 1759: A Study of Amphibious Warfare* (New York, 1955).

61. **Martinique**. Part of the archipelago of the Antilles, Martinique is located in the Caribbean Sea about 280 miles (450 km) northeast of the coast of South America and about 435 miles (700 km) southeast of the Dominican Republic. It is directly north of Saint Lucia, northwest of Barbados, and south of Dominica. In 1635 French settlers established the first European settlement at Fort Saint Pierre (now Saint Pierre). Except for the excellent and strongly fortified harbor at Fort Royal and a few quiet bays, the coast is uninviting with dangerous shores, coral reefs, shoals, rocky ledges, or cliffs 300 feet high. The land is scarred by deep ravines.

62. **Guadeloupe**. A group of islands situated among the Leeward Islands or the Lesser Antilles in the eastern Caribbean Sea, about 74 miles (120 km) north of Martinique.

63. **2nd Battalion officers**. Of these seven company commanders, all but one had had previous experience in the Dutch-Scots Brigade. Besides John Grant, other Lieutenants were: Alexander MacLean (Dutch-Scots); George Grant; George Sinclair; Gordon Clunes; Adam Stewart; John Robertson, son of Lude and brother of Captain James Robertson, 77th Foot; James Fraser; George Leslie; John Campbell; Alexander Stewart; John Murray; and Robert Robertson. Ensigns were: Patrick Sinclair; John Mackintosh; Neil Maclean; Thomas Fletcher; Alexander Donaldson; William Maclean; and William Brown. For complete biographical entries with details of each of the officers' careers see the 42nd Officers Register in Ian McCulloch, *Sons of the Mountains: The Highland Regiments in the French & Indian War, 1756-1767*, 2 vols (New York, 2006), II, 13-16. Hereafter, *SOTM*.

64. **Transports**. In most cases, transports were chartered merchant ships suitably modified to convey troops. The troop transports used at this time were about 80–350 tons and carried between 25 and 260 men. The men were allocated a "transport allowance" (a formula whereby the number of troops aboard was related to the tonnage of the ship) of between 1.5 and 2 tons per man, thus ensuring a cramped, smelly and very uncomfortable voyage.

to Greenock[65] in mid-November, where they embarked for the West Indies. As with the Highland regiments that had gone to North America the previous year, this advanced detachment of the battalion was subjected to the mandatory horrendous storm, spending two weeks buffeted by a tremendous gale in the Bay of Biscay.[66] They would not be the first Highlanders ever to visit the Caribbean, nor the first soldiers of the 42nd for that matter.

Convicted mutineers of the Black Watch in 1743 (with the exception of four Highlanders executed at the Tower as ringleaders) had had their death sentences commuted to exile and army service overseas. Thirty-eight men of the Black Watch had been sent to fill out the fever-ridden ranks of Lieutenant General Robert Dalzell's regiment, the 38th Foot, stationed in the West Indies. Other drafts of convicted mutineers were distributed to garrisons in Georgia, Gibraltar and Minorca. Ironically, it was the rumour that the Indies, considered by most in the British army as an automatic death sentence, was the destination of the Black Watch in 1743 rather than Flanders that had triggered the infamous mutiny in the first place. A few short years later after the '45 Uprising, convicted Highland rebels, some from Glenurquhart and Glenmoriston, also found themselves on transports to the Caribbean as indentured servants or to fill out Dalzell's diseased-thinned regiment in the British Leeward Islands.[67]

Martinique and Guadeloupe were just place names to the young Highlanders under Grant's command as they were tossed about on the Bay of Biscay. To William Pitt and the British government, however, the French islands in the Caribbean were just as valuable prizes as the British colony of Jamaica. Each of the islands produced over 20 thousand tons of sugar each year and their capture would serve several purposes. More than just economic and strategic feathers in Pitt's cap, possession would close down critical ports used as safe havens by French privateers. Ultimately, Pitt felt the Sugar Islands could be useful bargaining chips when diplomats met to discuss peace terms after the war, potential trades for the British island of Minorca, which had been captured in 1756. For John Grant and his fellow Highlanders of the 2nd Battalion, 42nd Foot, the islands would be their baptism of fire.

---

65. **Greenock** (Gaelic: *Grianaig*, meaning "sunny place"). A small port town on the south bank of the Clyde at the "Tail of the Bank" where the River Clyde expands into the Firth of Clyde and some 18.6 miles (30 km) due west of Glasgow.
66. **Bay of Biscay**. A gulf of the northeast Atlantic Ocean lying along the western coast of France from Brest, south to the Spanish border, and the northern coast of Spain west to Cape Ortegal. Infamous for its severe winter storms.
67. **Rebels**. For best account, see Chapter One, "Men Bred in the Rough Bounds," in John Prebble, *Mutiny: Highland Regiments in Revolt 1743-1804* (Harmondsworth, 1975), 13-87. The majority of the Grant tenantry transported went to the Barbados which was the 2nd Battalion's first port of call in January 1759.

The White Elephant. This 1759 watercolour view by Lieutenant Thomas Davies, Royal Artillery, looks northwards up Lake Champlain where the British are constructing the massive fortress at Crown Point, the largest British earthenwork fort ever constructed in North America. In 1761 John Grant and the two battalions of his regiment (some 1,500 men) spent two weeks on site helping build the still unfinished fort. With the Treaty of Paris in 1763, the military importance of Crown Point declined and construction ceased. Re-occupied briefly in the American War of Independence, it was abandoned in favour of Fort Ticonderoga by the Continental Army. (LAC C-13314)

John Grant's first war saw him fight over a large area of the Caribbean and North America in actions against the French, the Spanish, their native allies and slaves. It was nothing like the conventional warfare fought on the European continent. Campaigning in North America was essentially a massive problem of manoeuvre, communications and resupply. And while the principal task of generalship was simply moving a force of moderate size into contact with the enemy, the face of battle for John Grant and his Highlanders who had to penetrate hundreds of miles into trackless and unsettled country was a daunting one.

With such an environment, every aspiring commander needed a small highly-trained army of experts: auxiliaries such as light troops, rangers and friendly Indians for scouting and skirmishing; "Battoemen" to move the armies along the waterways which served as the only highways; and artillerymen and engineers to lay siege to the French forts once the army had closed with its ob-

Jumping off point. Detail from "A West View of Oswego and Fort Ontario with General Amherst Camp at Lake Ontario in the Year 1760" executed by Lieutenant Thomas Davies, Royal Artillery. The year before this sketch was made, the British started constructing a large pentagonal earthen fort on the heights overlooking the river mouth and dockyard. On their arrival from the Caribbean in 1759, John Grant and his Highland soldiers were immediately assigned one of the five bastions of the newly-named Fort Ontario to build. After wintering in Albany, John Grant and his regiment would return to Oswego the next spring as part of General Amherst's army on its way to conquer New France by way of the Saint Lawrence River. (LOC 2004661623)

jectives. Long lines of communication necessitated the building of well-garrisoned, defensible forts and depots along the way.

By 1764 John was a seasoned veteran, having soldiered from the torrid cane fields and swamps of Martinique and Guadeloupe to the thick Canadian forests lining each side of the mighty Saint Lawrence River draining the Great Lakes. He survived shooting the numerous rapids on the approach to Montreal, Canada, and experienced frigid winters with sub-zero temperatures in New France and amongst the Dutch inhabitants of the Mohawk valley. He worked on building forts at Oswego[68] and Crown Point[69] and was part of John Brad-

68. **Oswego**. Situated where the Oswego River enters Lake Ontario and the site of present-day Oswego, New York. A large stone blockhouse was first erected on the site in 1727 by New York fur traders. Oswego later saw three fortifications built: Ontario, Pepperell and George. In 1756 Oswego capitulated to the French and all three forts were destroyed. In 1759 the British built a larger new fort at Oswego on a pentagon plan with five bastions. In 1760 Oswego would be the jumping-off point for General Amherst's army on their way to conquer New France by way of the Saint Lawrence River.
69. **Crown Point**. The French erected a small, wooden stockade fort in 1730 where Lake Champlain narrows at present-day Chimney Point on Lake Champlain. In 1734 stone walls were added, including a four-storey masonry tower. Completed November 1737, it was named Fort Saint-Frédéric and used principally as a jumping-off point for Indian raiding parties into New England until the Seven Years' War. The fort became indefensible once

street's famous "Battoe Service" making the movement of large armies and their baggage through the wilderness possible.

What comes across clearly in Grant's unpublished memoirs of campaigning is a young man very interested in learning all facets of his profession, but at the same time making educated and astute observations on all that went on around him. That he dictated his memoirs to his grandson, JOHN JOHNSON JR., in his twilight years does not diminish the freshness and clarity of his recollections that emerge from the pages. For example, he fondly remembers his first winter in the New World and compares it to his return during the American War of Independence: "Society [was] somewhat rude, but women were pretty and had not that asperity produced by the Revolution, were uneducated but they danced...." His memory of his first combat, an amphibious landing on Valentine's Day, 1758, in our opinion, is one of the best first-hand accounts of such warfare in the 18th century.[70]

He was not averse to pulling his punches either. His stint of six weeks working with the Marines[71] on Guadeloupe in 1758 caused him to comment that they were undoubtedly "the worst troops in the service, looked down upon by both Services, without discipline & useless either on shore or at Sea." His opinion of the medical profession was not much better. When he fell ill with fever on Guadeloupe he was attended by "by two Men of War surgeons [who] bled us profusely [and] would have killed us but luckily their ships were order'd off and we were saved."

Experiences that hardened and strengthened his character as a Highland

---

the British captured Fort Ticonderoga to the south in 1759, and General Amherst, recognizing the strategic advantages of the Crown Point terrain, ordered the construction of new, extensive fortifications to secure his hold on the Champlain Valley. Once finished, "His Majesty's Fort of Crown Point" would be the largest British fortress ever built in Colonial America. With timber and earth ramparts 27 feet (8 meters) tall and a dry ditch up to 15 feet (5 meters) deep cut into the bedrock, it mounted 104 cannon and was designed to accommodate 4,000 troops. Outlying redoubts, wharves, storehouses and a village would spring up outside its walls. With the Treaty of Paris in 1763, the military importance of Crown Point declined and construction ceased. It was re-occupied briefly in the American War of Independence.

70. **Amphibious landings**. Perhaps the only other first-hand and gripping account of an amphibious landing during the Seven Years' War in North America that can compete with Grant's account is James Thompson's vivid description of the landing with Wolfe's division at Louisbourg, complete with a cannonball passing between his legs. See Anecdote 4, *A Bard of Wolfe's Army; James Thomson, Gentleman Volunteer 1733-1830*, E.J. Chapman and I.M. McCulloch, eds. (Montreal, 2010) 144-47.

71. **Marines**. On 5 April 1755, fifty companies, styled "His Majesty's Marine Forces," the infantry or land-fighting component of Britain's Royal Navy, were formed under the control of the Admiralty. Comprising about 5,000 men, the companies formed three divisions, stationed at Chatham, Portsmouth and Plymouth. The detachment on board the fleet approaching Guadeloupe in 1759 consisted of about 800 Marines.

officer ranged from quelling two mutinies and dealing with uncooperative Dutch settlers who refused to supply wood to the army during the winter, to a "fragging"[72] incident with soldiers of the 15th Foot at Staten Island[73] and preventing others from looting a liqueur factory on Martinique. It was on the latter island that Grant was selected, because of his size (he measured six foot six and was nicknamed "Long John"[74] by his brother officers), intellect and experience, to replace Lieutenant GEORGE LESLIE in the elite Light Infantry Corps. His company comprised fifty men of his own regiment and fifty soldiers from the 44th Foot.

The year Grant joined the army, 1757, had seen British commanders introduce an experimental, temporary corps that stemmed from the nature of North American terrain as well as the tactics of an elusive and savage foe. These warriors were called "light troops" or "light infantry" to distinguish them from their comrades serving as "heavy infantry" in the marching regiments. Similar to the widespread practice of 18th-century armies taking grenadier companies from their respective regiments to form special "shock troop" battalions, so the shorter, more agile men and marksmen of the other flank company of a regiment became part of an elite *ad hoc* corps specializing in scouting, patrolling, screening and skirmishing. By the end of the Seven Years' War in North America, these "chosen men" had become the most seasoned and useful veterans of Britain's "American Army."

It was at Havana that John Grant and his light infantrymen were given an independent command and sent out beyond the siege lines to blockade the city as well as to reconnoitre and scavenge off the land. His accounts of the siege are some of the most compelling recorded, but this exciting final chapter of his first war comes to an abrupt end as a number of pages have been lost over the

72. **Fragging.** The modern term "fragging" is used to describe the deliberate killing or attempted killing by a soldier of a fellow soldier, usually a superior officer or non-commissioned officer. US Army slang term deriving from World War Two and subsequent wars when a fragmentation grenade or "frag" was deliberately rolled into unpopular officer's tent or trench.

73. **Staten Island.** Roughly triangular in shape and almost 60 square miles (155 km²) in area, Staten Island has about 35 miles (56 km) of waterfront and sits in New York harbor. It was a staging area for the British army to assemble and train for operations southwards towards the Caribbean.

74. **Nickname.** "Long John" Grant was a possible Anglicization of the Gaelic diminutive that was commonly used in the Highland clans to distinguish the many folk of the same name in a clan from one another (e.g. Black John (*Ian Dhu*), Red John (*Ian Ruadh*), or Big John (*Ian Mhor*). The word "Long" in Gaelic however has several connotations (physically long or tall in body; long-winded; dull or stupid). But it is in one of John Peeble's diary entries that the riddle of John's nickname is finally revealed, for it refers to his enormous height, six foot six, an oddity in the day when the average height of most Highland soldiers was a mere five foot four, the minimum height requirement for the British army.

Powder horns. Personal pieces of kit, powder horns were decorated in scrimshaw by their owners or some of the more artistically-inclined men. Many were adorned with maps and the names of their owners. The darkest-coloured horn belonged to a Black Watch piper who was also a Freemason. John Grant and his light infantry men slung their horns off the left shoulder under the right armpit. Regular soldiers primed their muskets using powder from the same paper cartridge used to charge their musket, typically biting off one end and pouring a little into the priming pan before pouring the rest down the barrel. The powder horns contained "pistol powder" with its finer and more combustible grain, so priming one's musket was quicker and the musket was less likely to misfire, a big plus in life-or-death situations. (BWCM)

passage of time. John would die in 1828 at the age of eighty-seven, his memoirs left unfinished in mid-siege when he was just twenty-two years old. Thus, we are forced to glean the rest of this long-serving soldier's life and military service from a myriad of other primary and secondary sources.

John Grant's seniority as the fourth "eldest" lieutenant in the regiment by 1763 was sufficient to guarantee him a lieutenant's berth in the reduced "peace" establishment of the 42nd Foot. However, it would appear that he was unable to do so, perhaps because of an illness, or he was entertaining plans to resign his commission. In any event, he was not part of the 42nd contingent that force-marched westward with other siege of Havana survivors from Long Island in the fall of 1763 to put down Pontiac's Uprising. He does not appear in any of the surviving documents for that campaign, and it is known with some certainty that he did not participate in the subsequent Muskingum expedition to subdue the Shawnees the following year. Sometime over the 1763-64 winter, John decided to exchange onto half-pay with George Rigge of the 86th Foot, the latter taking John's place in the Royal Highlanders that spring. The regimental succession lists record this date as 2 April 1764 while the regiment was still quartered on Long Island.

John's motives are not that hard to divine. He had witnessed many of his colleagues killed or maimed on operations or succumbing to putrid tropical diseases or fevers on a duty he characterized as "a dangerous service." After six eventful years of soldiering in the Caribbean, Canada and the colonies, the seventeen-year-old lanky lad who had left Scotland a boy was ready to return home, a twenty-six-year-old man, ready to try his hand at more peaceful traditional pursuits. Another factor that probably tilted the scales for many young convalescing officers considering their future employment was the news of the substantial prize money they would receive from the staggering amounts of treasure, goods and shipping taken with the capture of Havana. In terms of today's purchasing power, John's subaltern share of £116 sterling was a small fortune, an impressive £15,600 (US$22,250) in today's currency.[75] This critical decision not to stay with his regiment, despite his hard-won seniority, and when many of his surviving comrades chose to soldier on, would not stand him in good stead when he tried to return to active duty with the regiment nine years later.

Whether John returned immediately home to Scotland in the summer of 1764 or stayed on in North America to scout out potential land grants in upstate New York is uncertain. He next appears in the public record back in Glenurquhart, Scotland, where he married Isobel Grant, the daughter of PATRICK GRANT of Lochletter, in 1771. The irony of this should not be overlooked, for his new father-in-law was the son of the afore-mentioned Alexander Grant, 4th of Shewglie, one of "The Three Alexanders" who had been the bane of John's father's existence during the Rebellion. Many of Shewglie's kinsmen and tenants, it should be remembered, had actually threatened the factor with physical harm and mischief, so much so that John Grant Sr., afraid for the safety of his family, had moved them to the Black Isle, north of Inverness.

The social *carte d'entrée* for Lieutenant John Grant back in Glenurquhart and Glenmoriston Highland society was probably the fact that he was a half-pay officer, late of the 42nd Regiment, now a brother officer of numerous other Grants from the area who had served the King faithfully and courageously

---

75. **Prize money.** C. B. Norman, *Battle Honours of the British Army* (London, 1911), 104-5.

overseas in the Americas. Foremost of these would have been his father-in-law's youngest brother and wife's uncle, CHARLES GRANT, the youngest son of Alexander Grant of Shewglie, and his second wife, Isabella Grant.

The same age as John, Charles Grant had gone to North America the year before the former's unit was raised. Charles went as a gentleman volunteer, serving in the ranks of the 77th Foot (Montgomery's Highlanders) until a free battlefield promotion came along. Captured by Indians during Major James Grant of Ballindoch's ill-fated raid on Fort Duquesne at the Ohio Forks, 14 September 1758, Charles and others were eventually exchanged for some French prisoners a year later. For his fortitude and service, Charles finally received his commission as an ensign in the Black Watch while his new regiment prepared for the conquest of Canada from Fort Oswego. From that moment on, John and Charles soldiered alongside each other at Montreal, Martinique and at the gruelling siege of Havana in 1762. Unlike John, Charles decided to remain in the regiment, taking a demotion to ensign but retaining his seniority as a lieutenant.

One of Isobel's cousins, as well as being the nephew of her Uncle Charles, was ALEXANDER GRANT, a son of Patrick Grant, 8th Laird of Glenmoriston. Alex, like Charles, had also soldiered in North America with Montgomery's Highlanders, but was lucky enough to secure one of the coveted ensigncies. Because of Alexander's previous experience as a junior officer in the Royal Navy, he ended his war in North America commanding warships on Lake Ontario and Lake Erie and went out on army half-pay in 1763. He never returned to Scotland, choosing to remain at Detroit after the war, where he married a French-Canadian wife, sired eleven daughters and built a comfortable estate at Grosse Pointe, Michigan, which he named "Castle Grant."

The seven intervening years between John Grant's decision to leave the army in 1764 and his decision to marry Isobel Grant in 1771, were tumultuous ones in the Highlands. Much had happened in the green straths of Glenurquhart and Glenmoriston since his departure in 1758. The New World he left in 1764 was now seen as the Promised Land by many of his countrymen. The clan system had been completely dismantled in the two decades since the '45, which meant that lands once considered common to the entire clan had become private property. New landlords managing the many forfeited estates, many of them rapacious Lowlanders, immediately raised the rents. This, coupled with the falling prices for black cattle (a mainstay of the Highland economy), several severe winters and crop failures coupled with the inevitable famines that followed, reduced much of the rural population of the Highlands to extreme poverty.

In 1769, a Welsh naturalist named Thomas Pennant, passing through the Great Glen, and with no particular axe to grind, noted astutely:

> The rage of raising the rents has reached this distant country. In England there may be reason for it (in a certain degree) where the value of lands is increased by accession of commerce, and by the rise of provisions; but here, contrary to all policy, the great men begin at the wrong end with squeezing the bag before they have helped the tenant to fill it by the introduction of manufactures. This already shows its unhappy effects, and begins to depopulate the country, for numbers of families have been obliged to give up the strong attachment the Scots in general have for their country, and to exchange it for the wilds of America.[76]

Notwithstanding all of the economic factors at play, John unwisely chose to become a gentleman farmer, renting "a considerable farm in the County of Urquhart, Inverness-shire."[77] In 1772 Isobel gave birth to their only child, a girl whom they named PENUEL, no doubt a nod to the sister of the Laird of Grant, Sir Ludovick, who was now the widow of Alexander Grant, 2nd of Ballindalloch, and mother to Colonel (later General) James Grant, 4th of Ballindalloch.

The following year, 1773, Samuel Johnson,[78] the famous diarist, journeying throughout the Highlands with his companion James Boswell, remarked on the palpable "epidemick [*sic*] of desire of wandering which spreads from valley to valley which spreads its contagion." He noted that wherever he went in the Highlands, people were contemplating emigration to America.[79] In September 1773 the *Edinburgh Advertiser* echoed his observations: "A spirit of emigration hath seized the people and the murmurs of discontent and painful distress are

---

76. **Thomas Pennant**. J. Cameron Lees, *A History of the County of Inverness (Mainland)* (Edinburgh, 1897), 219.
77. **Gentleman farmer**. Anonymous, 12 July 1774, *Aberdeen Journal*, No. 1387 (July 1774). See also "Extract of a Letter from Ft. William," 12 July 1774 in *The Weekly Magazine or Edinburgh Amusement*, vol XXV (July 1774), 190.
78. **Samuel Johnson** (1709-84). Often referred to simply as Dr. Johnson, Samuel Johnson was one of England's greatest literary figures: a poet, essayist, biographer, lexicographer and a critic of English literature. He was also a great wit and prose stylist, well known for his aphorisms. Between 1745 and 1755 Johnson wrote perhaps his best known work, *A Dictionary of the English Language*. During the decade he worked on his dictionary, Johnson, needing to augment his precarious income, also wrote a series of semi-weekly essays under the title *The Rambler*. These essays, often on moral and religious topics, tended to be graver than the title of the series would suggest. They ran until 1752. Initially they were not popular, but once collected as a volume they found a large audience. Johnson's final major work was his *Lives of the Poets* (1781), comprising short biographies of about fifty English poets, most of whom were alive in the 18th century. Amongst his other works are *The Idler* (1758-60), *Rasselas, Prince of Abissinia* (1759) and *The Patriot* (1774). A devout Anglican and committed Tory, Dr. Johnson has been described as "arguably the most distinguished man of letters in English history." He is also the subject of "the most famous single work of biographical art in the whole of literature" – James Boswell's *The Life of Samuel Johnson* (London, 1791).
79. **"Epidemick."** Samuel Johnson, *A Journey to the Western Isles of Scotland* (London, 1816), 119-20.

"A mere literary man is a dull man...." Samuel Johnson (1709-84), often referred to simply as Dr. Johnson, was one of England's greatest literary figures – a poet, essayist, biographer, lexicographer and critic of English literature. He was also a great wit and prose stylist, well known for his aphorisms. He was the subject of "the most famous single work of biographical art in the whole of literature" – James Boswell's *The Life of Samuel Johnson* (London, 1791). (Half-length portrait by Sir Joshua Reynolds. LOC 1994023114/PP)

everywhere echoed from the mouths of the poor, who groan beneath the weight of penury."[80]

In March 1773 several events occurred in rapid succession which uprooted families in Glenurquhart and Glenmoriston and set those neighbourhoods afloat. Sir Ludovick Grant, the elderly chief of Clan Grant who had always looked kindly upon John's family, died, and with him any last ties of loyalty or servitude that might have been traditionally passed on to the new chief by his clansmen. That summer, the "epidemick" struck home as several gentlemen tacksmen[81] spearheaded a group of some 300 Highlanders from Glenurquhart, Glenmoriston and Strathglass and emigrated to the fertile Mohawk River Valley[82] in New York colony to become tenants of Sir William Johnson.[83]

All over the Highlands a mass exodus was taking place. What had started as a modest flow of emigration following the Seven Years' War reached a frenzied

80. ***Edinburgh Advertiser*** (September 1773). Quoted in Lucille H. Campey, *After the Hector: The Scottish Pioneers of Nova Scotia and Cape Breton, 1773–1852* (Toronto, 2004), 2.
81. **Tacksmen**. The Macdonell gentlemen referred to above were Macdonell of Aberchalder, Leek, Collachie, and Scotus. J. P. MacLean, *An Historical Account of the Settlements of Scotch Highlanders in America* (Glasgow, 1900), 196-230. Also, Donald MacKay, *Scotland Farewell: The People of the Hector* (Toronto, 1980), 62-3; and Ian Graham, *Colonists from Scotland: Emigration to North America, 1707-1783* (Ithaca, NY, 1956), 35-41.
82. **Mohawk River**. The largest tributary of the Hudson River. Named for the Mohawk Nation of the Iroquois Confederacy, the river flows eastwards through the Mohawk Valley, passing Schenectady before entering the Hudson a few miles north of Albany.
83. **Sir William Johnson** (1715-44). British provincial army officer. Born in Ireland, Johnson went to America in 1738 as a land speculator and settled in the Mohawk Valley in upstate New York, quickly acquiring considerable influence with the Five Nations Indians. He became Superintendent of Indian Affairs in 1755. Granted the local rank of major general as commander in chief of the provincial corps in the expedition against Crown Point 1755, he was rewarded with a baronetcy for his victory. He was third in command to Brigadier John Prideaux on the successful expedition to take Fort Niagara in 1759. He died in 1774.

Frontier baronet. Sir William Johnson, 1st Baronet (c.1715-74), was appointed British Superintendent of Indian Affairs in 1756 for the northern colonies. Throughout his career as a British official among the Iroquois, the Irish-born Johnson combined his personal business with official diplomacy, acquiring tens of thousands of acres of native land and becoming very wealthy in the process. He commanded Iroquois and colonial militia forces during the French and Indian War (1754-63) and his role in the British victory at the battle of Lake George in 1755 earned him a baronetcy. His 1759 capture of Fort Niagara four years later brought him additional renown. (Illustration from Halsey, *The Old New York Frontier…*, Editors' photo)

floodtide in the year of Dr. Johnson's observations, the most for any year until the American Revolution stopped the flow in 1776. In the twelve years preceding 1776, it is estimated that some 23,000 Highlanders left for the colonies, which represented an astounding one-tenth of the total population of the Highlands, and this all before the introduction of the Great Cheviot sheep.[84]

The Highlanders of Glenurquhart and Glenmoriston were a small part of the swell that had begun early in the spring of 1773, the *Edinburgh Evening Courant* reporting on 3 April that 1,500 men, women and children had left Sutherland in the last two years alone seeking "the sustenance abroad which they allege they cannot find at home." In June the same newspaper reported that another 800 had sailed from Stornoway, across the Minch from Loch Broom, and in July another 800 from Greenock. In August it singled out the 425 Highlanders who sailed from Appin, Knoydart and Lochaber, once hotbeds of Jacobite sentiment. All told, some 4,000 Highlanders left their native land in 1773.[85]

John and Isobel Grant finally succumbed to emigration fever over the winter of 1773-74 and made the momentous decision to emulate their neighbours and kinsmen and cross over to America in search of a better standard of living. John was no longer able to keep up the payments on his lease and no longer had the financial support of his well-connected uncle, Alexander Grant of Inverlaidnan, who had died in 1765. John appears to have had enough money left however to hire the transport *Moore of Greenock* at his own expense for the conveyance of some twenty Glenurquhart and Glenmoriston families to America.

In July 1774 John Grant, his small family and followers went down the Great Glen to Fort William, where they took ship to Loch Doun, Mull. A letter writ-

---

84. **Emigration**. Donald MacKay, *Scotland Farewell: The People of the Hector* (Toronto, 1980), 62-8; *Edinburgh Evening Courant* (April, July, August, 1773).

85. **4,000 Highlanders**. *Edinburgh Evening Courant* (April, July, August, 1773).

View from Mount Defiance. An old photograph inscribed "Fort Ticonderoga and vicinity from Mount Defiance, c.1903" looks north across the ruins of Fort Ticonderoga just visible on the peninsula in the foreground. Behind can be seen a pontoon bridge similar to one that existed during the American War of Independence linking the fort to the American-built entrenchments at Fort Independence on the Vermont side of Lake Champlain (the pontoon bridge has been replaced today by a modern car ferry at the same spot). The 2,000 acres of land to which John Grant and his settler families were travelling in 1775-76 was just north of the Vermont side of the bridge. (LOC 1994002580/PP)

ten from Fort William reported their departure on 12 July 1774, their leader one John Grant "late of the 42nd regiment" who had tried farming in Urquhart for some years after retiring from the army until

> ... an extravagant rent [had] obliged [*sic*] him to abandon it, and retire to America, where he served for five years ...The Highlanders brought with him are chiefly from the country of Urquhart and wilds of Glenmoriston; and nothing but extreme poverty would oblidge [*sic*] these Highlanders to abandon their country. Such of these poor people as had not money to pay their freight, indent[ur]ed their families.[86]

John Grant and his settlers' ultimate destination is unknown and one is tempted to say they also went to the Mohawk River Valley where many of

86. **Farming in Urquhart.** *Ibid.*

Land baron. Phillip Wharton Skene (1725-1810), shown here in the uniform of the Royal Scots or 1st Foot, was the largest land baron on the lake after the Seven Years' War. In 1759, while still serving in the British Army, Skene had personally established a town named Skenesboro (present-day Whitehall) on the southernmost extension of Lake Champlain known as Wood's Creek. By 1765, and now on half-pay, Skene's various patents and tracts of land extended northwards from Fort Edward on the Hudson River in the south to Fort Ticonderoga in the north, totalling some 55,000 acres. (Private Collection)

their kinsfolk had gone the previous year. However, several factors strongly indicate that they may have all gone to Lake Champlain, the first and foremost clue being that all accounts of John Grant's arrest in 1775 by American rebels and subsequent recommendations for employment cite that his lands were "on Lake Champlain" or "near Lake Champlain." This geographic fact would thus appear to exclude the Mohawk River Valley as their final place of settlement. The question then is: what large tracts of land on Lake Champlain were available for settlement in the 1770-75 timeframe? Three possible locations come to mind.

The largest land baron on the lake after the Seven Years' War was Philip Wharton Skene, a fellow Scot and army officer who had served with Major General Jeffery Amherst's army. While still serving, Skene had established a town named Skenesboro (now present-day Whitehall) on the southernmost extension of Lake Champlain known as Wood's Creek in 1759. By 1765 Philip Skene's various patents and tracts of land extended northwards from Fort Edward[87] on the Hudson River[88] in the south to Fort Ticonderoga in the north, totalling some 55,000 acres. A broadside advertisement printed in New York[89] dat-

---

87. **Fort Edward** evolved from a trading post on the upper Hudson River into a substantial, albeit awkwardly sited, fort defended by almost thirty cannon. It was the main supply base for staging operations on the Lake George-Lake Champlain corridor. First called Fort Lyman, it was built in 1755 of timber and earth at the southern end of the "Great Carrying Place," a portage around the falls on the upper Hudson. It was renamed Fort Edward in 1756 by Sir William Johnson, the British Superintendent for Indian Affairs, in honour of Prince Edward, the grandson of George II. The fort was abandoned in 1766.
88. **Hudson River**. Named after the explorer Henry Hudson, the river originates in the Adirondack Mountains of Upstate New York, flowing north to south for about 315 miles (507 km) through the Hudson Valley, eventually draining into the Atlantic Ocean.
89. **New York**. Initially founded by the Dutch as New Amsterdam in 1620s. When the English conquered the area forty years later in 1664, they renamed it New York after the Duke of York. By the 1740s, the population had swelled to about 2,500 people making it the third largest city after Boston and Philadelphia.

"Will" Gilliland (1734-96). A New York merchant and land developer of Irish birth, Gilliland took advantage of French and Indian War veterans who had no intention of settling on their Lake Champlain land grants in 1764. He began buying up land until he had amassed upwards of 50,000 acres centred on the Boquet River on the western shores of Lake Champlain. His patent covered what is essentially Essex and Clinton counties today. (Private Collection)

ed 7 June 1765 promised prospective settlers "land on the most Reasonable Terms agreeable to their Circumstances and Character," "Three Years Rent free," soil "remarkably good for Grass, Flax, Hemp and Wheat and all Manner of Grains" and "Fish and Venison in Plenty."[90]

Second was William Gilliland's patent. A New York merchant and land developer of Irish birth, Gilliland took advantage of veterans who had no intention of settling their Lake Champlain land grants in 1764. He began buying them up until he had amassed upwards of 50,000 acres of land centred on the Boquet River on the western shores of the lake and extending north of Crown Point as far as Cumberland Head (the span of present-day Essex County). He too offered generous terms in order to lure tenants.

The third and perhaps the most likely destination was the vacant lot of 2,000 acres granted to Isobel's afore-mentioned cousin, Alexander Grant, from Glenmoriston in 1767 for his services to the Crown in the French and Indian War. According to Grant family documents, it was located "in Charlotte County, between Crown Point and Ticonderoga" but had remained vacant as Alexander had permanently settled near Detroit on Lake Erie to raise a family and supervise the fledgling Provincial Marine.[91]

A closer examination of New York colony patents for 1764 reveals that Alexander's land was actually just north of the Skenesboro grants and located in present-day Orwell, Vermont, on the eastern side of the lake and almost adjacent to Fort Ticonderoga. In all likelihood this is the piece of land where John Grant and several other families with him were headed when they arrived at New York in the fall of 1774. As they had nowhere to live on their arrival, they probably wintered over in New York city or vicinity, intending to move up onto their land in the spring of 1775 once the ice-bound Hudson River and deep snow up country had melted.

---

90. **Advertisement**. Plate X, Doris Morton, *Philip Skene of Skenesborough* (New York, 1959), 22-8, 31-5.
91. **Provincial Marine**. Peter John Anderson, *Major Alpin's Ancestors and Descendants* (Aberdeen, 1904, [privately printed]), 15.

In the New Year of 1775 John Grant's schemes began to unravel and his second war began. Troubles brewing between Patriots and Loyalists reached a head with clashes and much bloodshed at Lexington and Concord in April 1775. John was on his way to Lake Champlain at this time to prepare for the arrival of his settlers coming up from New York but he was arrested on his arrival mid-May 1775 and imprisoned at Crown Point, the largest fortress in North America at this time. The fort had fallen easily to rebel forces on 12 May 1775 while Fort Ticonderoga and the old French Lines, 10 miles (16 km) up the lake, had already fallen to a surprise attack the day before. One week later, Colonel Benedict Arnold and fifty New England militiamen boldly pushed north to raid Fort Saint John's on the Richelieu River in southern Quebec, seizing military supplies and cannon and capturing the largest sloop on Lake Champlain.

Sometime in early June 1775, John Grant was able to escape from his guards at Crown Point and quickly made his way northwards down Lake Champlain to Montreal. It was familiar territory for the former light infantry officer, as he had traversed it some twelve years earlier in his career, albeit in the opposite direction. His unit had travelled from Montreal down to New York in 1761 via the lake with a six-week stopover at Crown Point to assist in construction of the fortress.

John, upon arrival in Montreal, was offered the opportunity by Governor Sir Guy Carleton to join a provincial unit as many of his former Highland colleagues[92] who had remained in the New World had already done. John instead opted to return to England on the first available packet to find something better. Governor Carleton acceded to his wishes and wrote a letter of recommendation to Lord Dartmouth, the new Secretary of State for the American Department, from Montreal, dated 5 July 1775. The clerk to the Secretary of State penned on the outside of the docket: "Recommends Grant, a half-pay officer, who had settled on Lake Champlain and was driven off by the banditti, suggests his being employed in the raising of new levies."[93]

Here, then, is an insight into John's thought process. He was looking for authorization to raise a company, or perhaps even a regiment of Highlanders,

---

92. **Provincial commissions.** Former Highland officers joining provincial units such as the King's Royal Regiment of New York and the Royal Highland Emigrants (later taken onto the British Army establishment as the 84th Foot) included: Major John Small (42nd Foot); Major Robert Gray (42nd Foot); Captain Patrick Sinclair (42nd Foot); Captain Daniel Robertson (42nd Foot); Captain Ranald MacKinnon (77th Foot); Captain Malcolm Fraser (78th Foot); Captain John Nairne (78th Foot); and Captain Alexander Fraser (78th Foot). See *SOTM*, II, for career details on all Highland officers.

93. **New levies.** Governor Sir Guy Carleton to the Earl of Dartmouth, 5 July 1775, Montreal, Canada. William Legge, *The Manuscripts of the Earl of Dartmouth* (London, 1895), 571. Hereafter, *Dartmouth Manuscripts*.

back in his native Glenurquhart. This letter however was probably lost in the deluge of letters begging for posts or preferment that quickly inundated the new Secretary of State once it was clearly evident that all Thirteen Colonies were in open revolt. On his arrival in London in August 1775, John apparently made the rounds looking for friends, acquaintances and anyone of influence who could help him in securing an active commission or to support his scheme to raise new levies in his native Scotland.

Grant's experience as one of the rebellion's first victims gave him a certain cachet in London. Here was a live eyewitness to the troubles overseas, and it seems to have borne fruit in that it brought him to the attention of those who had the power to assist. On 24 August 1775 Major Gavin Cochrane, a half-pay officer of the Royal Americans (60th Foot),[94] as well as a relative of Lord Dundonald and a trusted and close confidante to the Earl of Dartmouth, wrote to the latter on Grant's behalf:

> My Lord,
>
> Dining yesterday at a friend's, there happened to be a half pay officer who had lately come from America; he had been a prisoner with the Rebels at Crown Point, had made his escape and got to Canada, from whence he came home. This officer's name is Lieutenant Grant of the 42nd Regiment and he will introduce himself to his Lordship if so desired.[95]

That the interview ever took place is highly unlikely. John Grant was still a half-pay lieutenant two years later in April 1777 when ordered by the Lords Commissioner to repair immediately to New York and await the commander-in-chief's pleasure with regard to employment on active service. What John actually did between August 1775 and April 1777 remains a bit of a mystery. It is known that he was unable to rejoin his old regiment the 42nd Foot (Royal Highlanders), which had been garrisoning posts in Ireland since its return from North America in 1767.

In the summer of 1775, while John languished in captivity at Crown Point, his old regiment was embarking at Donaghadee in Northern Ireland and crossing over to Scotland. It landed at Port Patrick, where many of its oldest soldiers dropped to their knees and kissed the soil, the regiment having been absent

94. **60th Regiment (Royal Americans)**. After Braddock's defeat in 1755, the British government raised an American regiment of four battalions of 1,000 men each, mainly recruited in the American colonies. Initially numbered the 62nd Foot, the Royal American Regiment became the 60th in 1757. The Royal Americans' 4th Battalion participated in this operation that concluded with the surrender of Montreal on 8 September 1760. For more information, see Alexander V. Campbell's excellent book, *The Royal American Regiment: An Atlantic Microcosm, 1755-1772* (Univ. of Oklahoma Press, 2010).

95. **Cochrane**. Major Gavin Cochrane to the Earl of Dartmouth, 24 August 1775, London, England. *Dartmouth Manuscripts*, 360.

The Parade Step. A modern representation of a Royal Garrison Battalion private soldier, c.1783, drawn by Derek Fitz James and entitled "The Parade Step." By using old veterans and invalid soldiers unfit for the fatigues of a long campaign to man key islands, forts and other static outposts of empire, General Henry Clinton freed up valuable (and scarce) combat troops to prosecute military operations on the mainland. (ASKB, Photo by R. Chartrand)

from its native country for thirty-two years. On reaching Glasgow it was authorized to add two additional companies and bring its war establishment up to 1,075 men. This was a crucial time for half-pay officers waiting to return to active service, for wartime triggered a bonanza of non-purchase commissions as new corps were raised or old ones needed to be augmented with experienced officers. Recruiting parties were quickly dispatched to the Highlands, and by the time John Grant returned to England, all the non-purchase vacancies in his old regiment had been quickly filled up.[96]

The regiment was deemed "fit for service" on 10 April 1776, and on 1 May 1776, along with the 71st Foot (Fraser's Highlanders), sailed from Greenock for North America. John spent all of 1776 and the first quarter of 1777 in Britain looking for employment. Finally, in April 1777, he was ordered to report to the headquarters of General William Howe, commander-in-chief in North America. That he did so is not in doubt. Three years later he would reference those same orders which had forced him to leave "England in such haste as made it materially inconvenient to his Private Affairs" in order that he might secure a long desired leave of absence to settle those affairs.[97]

By July 1777 John had returned to North America with a letter from the War Office recommending "Lieut. John Grant for promotion to a company, he having at the beginning of the dispute been driven from his home near Lake Champlain by the rebels and lost all his effects."[98] Not surprisingly, Grant's first preference for military employment on arrival in North America was to return

---

96. **Non-purchase commissions.** For an excellent explanation of how purchase and non-purchase vacancies were filled, see John Houlding, *Fit for Service: The Training of the British Army, 1715-1795* (Oxford, 1981), 100-111.

97. **Report to headquarters.** Memorial of Captain John Grant to Sir Henry Clinton, 5 February 1780, Fort Nassau, New Providence, Bahamas. *Henry Clinton Papers*, vol 84, item 21, WLCL. Hereafter, *Clinton Papers*.

98. **War Office.** John Robinson to General William Howe, July 1777, Headquarters, Philadelphia. *Report on American Manuscripts in the Royal Institution of Great Britain*, vol 29, No. 169.

to his old regiment. At this time, the Black Watch was stationed in Philadelphia as part of its garrison and most of its officers were waiting to see if Sir HENRY CLINTON would actually replace General Sir William Howe (General "Billy" as he was known to his men), and his brother, Admiral "Black Dick" Howe. Both had resigned over the winter of 1777-78 amidst charges at home that they were too conciliatory with the rebels and not prosecuting the war with sufficient vigour.

John was still looking for a "non-purchase" commission rather than purchasing one. There was a strict pecking order in the regiments with regards to purchasing commissions and achieving the next promotion or "step" up the ladder. When a regimental vacancy occurred through an officer's death, transfer or retirement on half-pay, the position was typically first offered to the officer next-in-line for promotion and seniority within the regiment (i.e. he had first refusal on purchasing the commission, and, if that officer was unable to pay, the next officer below him was then offered the vacancy and so on until all potential regimental candidates had been exhausted).

Usually it was only when a regiment could not fill the vacancy internally that it would look outwardly and consider officers of other regiments for the post. The two key players in peacetime for deciding all such personnel changes were Lord John Murray, the colonel of the regiment back in Scotland, and his lieutenant colonel commanding in North America, THOMAS STIRLING. However, in wartime they could be overridden by the commander-in-chief if there were operational reasons to the contrary, or another candidate was more suitable for the vacancy and it was considered "in the best interests of the service."

John's first inquiries were noted by a concerned Black Watch captain lieutenant in his diary. JOHN PEEBLES, a fifteen-year veteran who had stayed with the regiment since his commissioning as an ensign for gallantry after the Battle of Bushy Run, 1763, was a former colleague of John Grant, but junior to him when Grant went out on half-pay in 1764. The thirty-eight-year-old Peebles was now hoping for promotion to full captain himself and noted on Tuesday, 12 May 1778: "Spoke to Colonel Stirling in the Evening About a Report of Long John Grants attempting to get into the Regiment in [Alexander] Donaldson's vacancy & he seems to be warmly inclined to prevent it, & to carry the step in the Regiment."[99]

By the first week of June, the 42nd was packing up and preparing to leave Philadelphia for a route march across New Jersey to garrison New York. Having failed to get in on his first attempt, John Grant was still lobbying in New York

99. **Diary entry.** 12 May 1778. *John Peeble's American War: The Diary of a Scottish Grenadier, 1776-1782*, Ira Gruber, ed. (Stroud, 1998), 180. Hereafter, *Peeble's Diary.*

to return to his old regiment. When another captain's vacancy opened up in the regiment early that summer, Peebles' entry for Monday, 8 June anxiously read: "wrote a few lines last night to Colonel Stirling about long [*sic*] Grant trying to come into the Regiment in place of Captain [George] Mackenzie who is order'd home to take possession of his majority, hoping for his friendship & good offices & get succession in our favour." The colonel's reassurances were made in person the following day. With almost an audible sigh of relief, Peebles' recorded on 9 June 1788:

> ... [Colonel Stirling] told me he had seen ... General [Clinton] & spoke to him about Rutherford & me succeeding in the Regiment & he told him he would always pay a proper attention to [Stirling's] recommendation, but that these vacancys were not to be fill'd up yet – There are two or three applying to get into the 42nd on this occasion but Colonel Stirling thinks we need not be uneasy. [100]

Again "Long John" Grant would be unsuccessful in gaining entry to his old regiment, due mainly to the objections of Thomas Stirling, who was more inclined to reward loyalty and long service of officers within the regiment than those who had left it abruptly at the end of the Seven Years War. But John remained in touch with his old regimental comrades. The newly-promoted Captain John Peebles of the 42nd Foot noted on 25 October 1778 that he visited Mrs. "Long John" Grant on Long Island, her husband away in New York preparing his new command, a company of convalescing veterans of the newly-formed provincial unit, the Garrison Battalion. Peebles wrote as an afterthought to his visit: "I hope they are better match'd in temper than in size, he is 6 feet 6 inches & she [Isobel Grant] is as little as A[nna] H[amilton]," the latter woman being Peebles' fiancée, and later his wife.[101] John must have made travel arrangements at this time for his wife, Isobel and daughter, Penuel, to return to Britain. A memorial, written two years later from the Bahamas, requested a leave of absence

---

100. **Diary entry**. 8 June 1778. *Ibid*, 187. Peebles was finally promoted to captain two months later on 18 August 1778 in the place of the afore-mentioned Captain Alexander Donaldson, who was promoted to major of the 76th Foot (MacDonald's Highlanders). Rutherford, referred to in the same entry, was John Rutherford, Peeble's best friend and the next senior lieutenant below Peebles. When Rutherford moved up into the captain lieutenant's vacancy left by his friend Peebles on 18 August 1778, the latter thought that his friend had been treated unfairly in this transaction. Reflecting the clan-like nature of the regiment, Peebles recorded in his journal on 18 September 1778 that "one [Lieutenant James] Campbell from 57th put in on us [as Captain], with I think great injustice to Rutherford who has only got the Captain Lieutenancy ...," *Ibid*, 220. The implication was that the junior "outsider" should not have had priority over the senior lieutenant of the regiment in obtaining the promotion.

101. **"Long John."** *Ibid*, 228. See also footnote 74, "Nickname."

to go home to Britain to settle affairs which "together with Mrs. Grant's ill State of Health" rendered "his presence Indespencibly [*sic*] necessary in Britain."[102]

While John Grant had been lobbying to return to his old corps for almost a year, the idea had been coalescing to stand up a garrison battalion of older, unfit men and invalids to free up scarce combat units guarding key islands, forts and other static outposts of empire. When Sir Henry Clinton had taken over from Howe in the spring of 1778, his staff had pushed for the establishment of such a unit for several reasons. They claimed that the "Invalid'd Men of this Army" while "totally unfit for the fatigue of a Campaign [were] nevertheless, better calculated for the duty of a Garrison, or the defence of an Island or Fort than an equal number of Recruits sent from Europe." This would free up newly-arriving battalions to take the field rather than being shut up. Such a battalion of already-trained veterans would save the expense of sending them home or training new recruits. A proposal paper explaining the six-company structure also outlined the command and control arrangements, the most appealing being the suggestion that all officers should receive full pay for life after their active service:

> The Officers for this Corps should perhaps be Compos'd of such as are worne out, or disabled & of long Service, taken from the Regiments of the Line, & as such, be insur'd [*sic*] of a continuation of full or half pay for life, in case it should be hereafter found necessary to dissolve the Corps; especially as their chance of Promotion in this line of Service must be very small indeed.[103]

On 6 October 1778, *The Royal American Gazette of New York* announced that the Garrison Battalion had officially "stood-up" as a new provincial unit with "Captain William Sutherland, Aid [*sic*] de-Camp to the Commander in Chief, to be Major Commandant. Lieut. John Grant, upon half pay, and Lieut. Waldron Kelly, from the 10th regiment, to be Captains." John's commission was dated 25 September 1778, predating the announcement of the new battalion by nearly a month.[104]

The commissioning of the officers before the creation of the actual unit was a logical step in getting the administration and control elements in place before the subsequent intake of worn-out, infirm and recovering men from their

102. **Leave of absence.** "Memorial of Captain John Grant of the Garrison Battalion," 5 February 1780, Fort Nassau, New Providence. *Clinton Papers*, vol 84, item 21, WLCL.
103. **Garrison Battalion.** "A Sketch of an Establishment for a Garrison Battalion to be form'd from the Invalid'd Men of this Army," October [1777?], "Frederick Mackenzie Papers," WLCL.
104. ***The Royal American Gazette*** (New York), 6 October 1778. When the Garrison Battalion was taken on the regular British army establishment as the Royal Garrison Battalion three years later, all officers including John Grant had their commissions backdated to their original commissioning in order to preserve their seniority and time served.

respective regiments or their release from hospitals where they had been convalescing. John's company officers were experienced soldiers from the ranks: Lieutenant Alexander Chisholm, a Strathglass native, had been a gentleman volunteer and was recommended for a commission by his "Chief of that name"; and Alexander Rio was the late town adjutant of Philadelphia and a former sergeant major of the 44th Foot, with some forty-nine years of service under his belt.[105]

John, as the senior captain of the battalion, was given what amounted to an independent command in the Bahamas. His orders, signed and dated by Sir Henry Clinton, were quite explicit:

> Headquarters, New York
> November 12th 1778
>
> Sir,
>
> You will proceed with the Troops embarked under your Command to the Island of Providence where you are to be stationed for its Defence and Protection, as well as the Rest of His Majesty's Bahama Islands.
>
> Upon your Arrival you will wait on the Governor and inform him of the Orders you have received, who I am persuaded will afford you every Assistance in his Power, as well towards Quartering the Troops as any other Matters that may be necessary: and you will on your Part concur with him in every Measure that can tend to the Benefit of His Majesty's Service, paying due Attention at all Times to the Safety of the Fortresses of the Islands, which is the principal Object of your Station; and therefore my positive Orders to you that you do not undertake any Service which may occasion the smallest Risk to their Safety.[106]

With the hurricane season now at an end, John Grant and his two companies of invalid veterans boarded their transports for the Bahamas at the end of November 1778. Ironically, Grant had no idea that he was sailing straight into the stormiest period of his military career. In fact, the greatest enemy he would ever face in the Caribbean would not be American rebels or disease, but a former lieutenant he had served with at the siege of Havana fifteen years earlier.

* * *

Montfort Browne was a nasty piece of work. An Irishman by birth, he had served during the Seven Years War as a lieutenant in the 95th Foot (Burton's), and subsequently the 35th Foot, before going out on half-pay at the peace in 1763. A few years later, he had become a major landowner and developer of

105. **Grant's company officers**. "List of the Officers of the Garrison Battalion...." TNA, CO 5/184, fols. 88-9.

106. **Grant's orders**. Sir Henry Clinton to Captain John Grant, 12 November 1778, New York. TNA, PRO 30/55/1555.

"Better suited to the quarterdeck...." Commodore George Johnstone, Royal Navy, first governor of West Florida from 1763 until 1767, was a Scottish naval captain with a contentious disposition and a fiery temper which, according to one biographer, "was better suited to the quarterdeck than the council chamber." (Portrait miniature by John Bogle, c.1774. SNPG, Editors' photo)

British West Florida, sponsoring Irish and French Huguenot immigrants to the area. That a junior officer on half-pay was able to do so was only made possible due to a wealthy wife with some serious political connections with the current colonial secretary, the Earl of Hillsborough. In November 1764, to the surprise of many, Browne secured the lieutenant governorship of the new province of West Florida and arrived at Pensacola in January 1766 to take up his new post.

From the outset, his tenure as lieutenant governor of West Florida was rocky. Some of his alleged land claims were immediately contested and most of the lands where he had planned to settle his prospective Irish and Huguenot tenants were found to be uninhabitable. The relationship with his immediate superior, Governor George Johnstone,[107] can only be described as acrimonious. When Johnstone left West Florida under a cloud of his own making in January 1767, Browne assumed command of the province. Shortly afterwards, irregularities in Browne's bookkeeping, combined with numerous complaints lodged against him by the colonists, resulted in his being removed from power the following year and recalled to London. As Browne was preparing to leave the province he was also involved in a duel with a Pensacola trader, the latter being seriously wounded. If the man had died, Browne would have faced criminal charges, but fortunately for Browne he recovered.

Browne had then spent much of the next two years in England having his finances closely scrutinized by the Colonial Office. Convinced that it was merely some personal animosities holding him back and that he had done no wrong, the cocksure Browne continued to boldly lobby for establishing British settlements on the Mississippi. There was some speculation that the vast Mississippi portion of West Florida would soon become a province in its own right with

107. **George Johnstone** (1730-87). An officer of the Royal Navy who saw service during the War of the Austrian Succession, the Seven Years' War and the American War of Independence, rising to the rank of post captain and serving for a time as commodore of a squadron. In a multifaceted career, he was also a Member of Parliament, a director of the East India Company, a member of the Carlisle Peace Commission and the first governor of West Florida from 1763 until 1767.

Montfort Browne as its governor. When the plan fell through, despite the support of his patron, Lord Hillsborough, Browne continued to pressure his successor, the Earl of Dartmouth, for a Mississippi province. Probably in a move designed to shut him up, rather than a recognition of his merit, he was offered the governorship of the Bahamas in March 1774, which he accepted.

While governor of the Bahamas, Browne actively continued to promote his land interests on the Mississippi and made several trips there in 1774 and 1775. As a result, when the American Revolution broke out in 1775, the island was unprepared. Distracted by his development schemes, the erstwhile governor had only made cursory precautions to secure the principal port at New Providence, despite ample warning that the Americans coveted the garrison's numerous cannons and gunpowder stores. Browne was therefore caught off guard when American ships arrived off Nassau on the morning of 3 March 1776. Though he managed to get most of the island's gunpowder supply away to Florida on a schooner, he failed to hold the island. Taken prisoner back to Connecticut by the American rebels, Browne was released soon afterwards in exchange for the rebel commander William Alexander, the self-styled Lord Stirling, captured at the Battle of Brooklyn, 27 August 1776. Apparently Browne, while in captivity, had boasted in a letter to General William Howe that he could easily raise a brigade of 4,000 loyal Americans. Feeling the manpower crunch, the offer captured Howe's attention and he fast-tracked the prisoner exchange.[108]

On Browne's release, the immodest Irishman attempted to make good on his promise to raise a brigade and failed miserably. He was only able to raise one battalion of the Prince of Wales' American Regiment but was successful in obtaining the rank of brigadier general in the provincial forces. He briefly served with his battalion, then left them for virtually the remainder of the war. Still he did not return to his absent post in the Bahamas but spent some leisurely months in West Florida visiting his properties before finally returning to Nassau in July 1778 after an absence of two years.

In the five months preceding John Grant's arrival in December 1778, Browne faced repeated accusations of cowardice and incompetence from the inhabitants for his conduct during the 1776 Raid of the Island, and gross negligence in ensuring that the defences of the Bahamas were ready for another attack by the rebels. According to a list of complaints submitted to Lord Germain, who had replaced Browne's patron, Lord Dartmouth, as colonial secretary, Browne's reaction to censure had been to muzzle all criticism, removing most officers and officials of the colony from their posts and replacing them

---

108. **Browne's offer.** Governor Montfort Browne to General William Howe, 2 August 1776. *Dartmouth Papers*, Microfilm Edition, Reel 15, D (W) 1778/II/1695.

"Unfit to serve his Majesty." George Germain, 1st Viscount Sackville, styled Lord George Sackville from 1720 to 1770 and Lord George Germain from 1770 to 1782. Accused of cowardice at the battle of Minden, 1759, he was found guilty by court martial and given one of the strangest and harshest verdicts ever rendered against a British general officer. Not only did he become the first lieutenant general ever cashiered for life from the army, but he was deemed "unfit to serve his Majesty in any military capacity whatsoever" and the court martial's verdict was read out loud at the head of every regiment in the army. (Portrait miniature by Nathaniel Hone, 1760. NPG 4910, Editors' photo)

"with his own Creatures." Lieutenant Governor John Gambier also reported that Browne had arbitrarily "shut up the Courts of Law and Equity" and dictatorially "dissolved two Assemblys" and "lay'd aside his Council act[ing] entirely without them." Most serious of Gambier's charges was that Browne had "utterly neglected putting the Island in any Condition of Defence," one which, given John Grant's orders from Clinton, put them on a direct collision course with one another.[109]

John Grant and his two new companies of the Garrison Battalion disembarked at Nassau in December 1778 to find "no provisions of fuel or Candles for the detachment" as well as no "Barracks for Officers." Worse was the toxic climate of mutual enmity between the Governor and the inhabitants. As the assembly had been dissolved by the tyrannical governor before Grant's arrival, the new commanding officer was forced to apply directly for relief from the governor but was turned away. The first six months of Grant's command would become a sheer hell and, as he later claimed in a letter to Sir Henry Clinton, this "disagreeable Situation" had "occasioned me more than once to request that your Excellency would remove me from hence." Unfortunately for John, not a single one of his letters explaining the "disagreeable Situation" ever reached New York.[110]

By July 1779 conditions were so bad in the small colony that Grant was forced to put pen to paper. In an astonishing memorial to the lieutenant governor, John Gambier, he stated that he was now convinced, as many of the "Mem-

109. **Gambier's charges.** Lieutenant Governor John Gambier to Lord George Germain, 28 July 1779, Providence. TNA, PRO 30/55/2145.

110. **Missing letters.** Captain John Grant to Sir Henry Clinton, 5 February 1780, Fort Nassau, New Providence. *Clinton Papers*, vol 84, item 20, WLCL.

bers of his Majesty's Council" were, that Governor Browne was unfit to govern. In his summary, he concluded:

> From a total neglect of providing for the Defence of this Place, from the Company with which the Governor associates who are most of them known Rebels and disaffected to His Majesty's Government, From his turning out of their Employ, Gentlemen of approved Loyalty and Character and putting in their Rooms people disaffected & of infamous Characters, From his repeated Attempts to procure your Memorialist to be assassinated, your Memorialist has great Cause to suspect the Loyalty and Integrity of Governor Browne and great reason to fear very fatal Consequences to His Majesty's Government here and to the Lives & properties of his Majesty's Subjects should Governor Browne continue his illegal proceedings.[111]

It took great courage for John Grant to write such a letter, accusing a superior of trying to have him murdered, as well as implying he was guilty of treasonable activities. But he had the backing of the majority of the assembly, including the lieutenant governor, the latter sending a covering letter to Grant's memorial directly to Lord Germain listing "the just Causes of Complaint Captain Grant has against the Governor, the unhappy and distressed Situation of the Inhabitants and the Great Danger of the Peace and Safety of His Majesty's Government here from the flagrant ill Conduct of Governor Browne."[112]

On 5 August 1779 Lord George Germain, Secretary of State, laid several papers "relative to complaints of the misconduct of Montfort Browne, esquire, Governor of the Bahama Islands, in the administration of his government" before the Board of Trade and Plantations and asked them to prepare recommendations to His Majesty as to what should be done. Deliberations appear to have been swift and the following day the Board's recommendations for Browne's recall to London to answer charges were quickly drawn up and forwarded to the King the same day.

On 14 August 1779, the following week, Lord Germain returned and "acquainted the Board, that the King had been pleased to appoint JOHN MAXWELL, esquire, to be Governor of the Bahama Islands, in the room of Montfort Browne, Esquire, and that it was his Majesty's pleasure, that [the] Board should prepare and lay before his Majesty in Council, draughts of a Commission and instructions for the said Governor."[113]

---

111. **Grant's memorial**. "The Memorial of Captain John Grant," 12 July 1779, Fort Nassau, New Providence. TNA, PRO 30/55/2111.

112. **Covering letter**. Lieutenant Governor John Gambier to Lord George Germain, 28 July 1779, New Providence, Bahamas. TNA, PRO 30/55/2145

113. **Lord Germain**. Journal, September 1779. *Journals of the Board of Trade and Plantations*, vol 14: January 1776-May 1782 (1938), 271-274, fols. 171-5, 181.

The same week the Board had been deliberating in London, the commander-in-chief in North America had been desperately trying to recall John Grant to New York to answer the serious charges made against him by the lawful governor of the Bahamas. Some of Browne's letters had made it through to his superior. Sir Henry Clinton's letter to John's colleague and junior, Captain John Tyrell, who commanded the other company of the garrison in Providence, has survived and reads:

> New York, August 8th 1779
>
> Dear Sir,
>
> I have received your Letters, and answered most of them; but I find by some strange fatality none of mine to Governor BROWNE, Captain GRANT or yourself have been received.
>
> Captain GRANT's behaviour requiring Explanasion [*sic*, explanation], I have long since desired him to give up the Command to you & repair to this place; I take it for granted he will leave Providence immediately, it is therefore necessary that you should remain there 'till I can Send an Officer to relieve you.
>
> You will find by Lord RAWDON's Letter in what particular I think Captain GRANT has not conducted himself properly towards Governor BROWNE, and will regulate yourself accordingly.[114]

Clinton must have been supremely annoyed by the antics of the Garrison Battalion by this stage of its short existence. Earlier that summer, he had had to recall its thirty-eight-year-old commandant from Bermuda to New York – his own protégé and former aide de camp, Major William Sutherland. Several articles of complaint concerning that officer's conduct, as well as that of his men, had been filed by the governor of Bermuda.[115]

Ten days later after writing to Tyrell in the Bahamas, insult was added to injury. Paulus Hook, the last British fort on the New Jersey side of the Hudson River facing New York city, was attacked. The garrison, including a company of the Garrison Battalion, was under the temporary command of none other than Major Sutherland. The 19 August 1779 night assault was conducted by troops commanded by Henry "Light-horse Harry" Lee[116] of Virginia, which, accord-

114. **Clinton letter**. Sir Henry Clinton to Captain John Tyrell, 8 August 1779, New York, *Clinton Papers*, vol 65, item 34, WLCL.

115. **Governor of Bermuda**, George James Bruere, Esq.

116. **Henry Lee III** (1756-1818). Henry was an early American Patriot who served as the 9th governor of Virginia and as the Virginian representative to the United States Congress. During the American Revolutionary War, Henry served as a cavalry officer in the Continental Army. In 1778 he was promoted to major and given command of a mixed corps of cavalry and infantry known as Lee's Legion, with which he won a great reputation as a capable leader of light troops. It was during this time as commander of the Legion that he earned the

The father of Robert E. Lee. Henry Lee III (1756-1818) was an early American patriot and politician who served as the ninth governor of Virginia and as the Virginia representative to the United States Congress. During the American Revolution, Lee served as a cavalry officer in the Continental Army and earned the nickname "Light-Horse Harry." (Anonymous, American School, 1751-1800, c.1795. FARL)

ing to Clinton, "found the garrison so scandolously [*sic*] absorbed in confidence of their own security that they made themselves masters of a blockhouse and 2 redoubts with scarcely any difficulty" before withdrawing with 156 British prisoners.[117]

Clinton had no options but to have the major commandant of the Garrison Battalion arrested and charged with "general misconduct as commandant" of Paulus Hook on the morning of 19 August.[118] However, by 4 September 1779, Sutherland had been tried and honourably acquitted for his role in the entire affair. But there was no question of his returning to the command of the Garrison Battalion in Bermuda and thus Clinton appointed two new senior officers to command and regulate the disorderly unit. The six-company provincial battalion needed a seasoned lieutenant colonel commandant, and for this appointment he chose Brevet Lieutenant Colonel Robert Donkin on his staff, a recently promoted major in the 44th Foot.

Donkin was no stranger to the Caribbean, which may have been a key factor in his favour. As a young captain in the Seven Years' War he had participated in General Robert Monckton's[119] 1762 expedition to capture French Martinique,

sobriquet of "Light-Horse Harry" for his horsemanship. On 22 September 1779 the Continental Congress voted to present him with a gold medal – a reward given to no other officer below a general's rank – for the Legion's actions during the battle of Paulus Hook on 19 August of that year. Henry was the father of Civil War-era Confederate general Robert E. Lee.

117. **Clinton letter.** Sir Henry Clinton to Lord Germain, 21 August 1779, New York. Quoted in *Diary of the American Revolution*, Frank Moore, ed., vol 2 (New York, 1850), 213n.

118. **Misconduct.** *Ibid.*

119. **Major General Robert Monckton** (1726-82). British army officer. The most senior of James Wolfe's three brigadiers at Quebec, Monckton was a professional soldier who had served in North America since 1752. Promoted to major general in 1761, Monckton commanded the expedition to take Martinique and successfully captured it in February 1762. In addition, his forces took the islands of Grenada, Saint Lucia and Saint Vincent. In June 1763 he left America for good, later taking up the military governorship of Berwick-upon-Tweed in 1765.

in which John Grant had also served as a lieutenant. Donkin had subsequently served as the aide de camp and secretary for Brigadier General William Rufane, governor of Martinique, from the surrender of the island in January 1762 until July 1763.

For the now-vacant major's position, which rightly should have gone to John Grant, the most senior captain in the battalion, Clinton chose an outsider to fill the post, Captain William Anstruther, another half-pay Scottish veteran of the Seven Years' War. By strange coincidence, Anstruther had been a long-time captain in the 26th Foot (The Cameronians) and had blotted his copy-book while commanding at Crown Point in 1773 by allowing it to burn to the ground. Captured at Fort Saint John's[120] in Quebec shortly after John Grant's own capture, Anstruther had spent a year as a prisoner of war in Reading, Pennsylvania, where he remained until exchanged. In 1777 he retired from the army on half-pay and in 1779 was living at Bergen, New Jersey. Why Clinton decided to reinstate him as a major in the provincial Garrison Battalion effective 26 October 1779 is a mystery. Perhaps it was as a favour to Anstruther's older brother, Lieutenant Colonel John Anstruther, then commanding the 62nd Regiment of Foot.

John Grant would not find out about the new changes in command until the New Year, and then only second hand, when a damaged ship en route to South Carolina from New York put in for repairs. Because none of Sir Henry Clinton's letters requesting Grant to come to New York to explain his conduct *vis-a-vis* Governor Browne had ever made it through to the Bahamas, this was the first time Grant had an inkling that his character and conduct as a military commander had been called into question. Somewhat piqued and hurt that he had been passed over for command, he wrote on 5 February 1780:

> I have by some of the Gentlemen put in here in distress, been informed of the alterations in the Garrison Battalion, by the appointment of Lieut. Colonel Duncan [*sic*, Donkin] & Major Anstruther. I considered that from my long and hard service last war and my Sufferings in this; that although I was absent from Head Quarters, yet as Senior Captain I should not have missed any promotion in the Battalion, and your Excellency must be convinced that what I held by the King's Warrant, and at my own liberty, was preferable to a man with a family to any thing I could expect to get in a New Corps, and I can with truth declare that I have ever made it my study to risk & do every thing for the good of His Majestys Service.[121]

---

120. **Fort Saint John's.** The fort guarded the head of the Chambly portage and was built to defend Canada against Mohawk incursions. Today, the town of Saint-Jean-sur-Richelieu.
121. **Grant's letter.** Captain John Grant to Sir Henry Clinton, Fort Nassau, New Providence, 5 February 1780, New Providence. *Clinton Papers,* vol 84, item 20, WLCL.

Three months later, on 8 May 1780, everyone in the Bahamas would learn first-hand of Governor Browne's recall to London with the arrival of his replacement, the new interim governor, John Robert Maxwell, late of the 15th Foot. Maxwell was given a warm welcome by the inhabitants of Nassau, New Providence, and promptly took up residence in the governor's mansion. Grant's nemesis might have been gone, but he, as the senior military commander, was not off the hook in the whole disagreeable affair. Governor Browne would remain innocent until found guilty.

Lord Germain had written to General Clinton in November 1779 stating that "however culpable Mr. Browne may have been in the exercise of his Office as Governor," the character and actions of the military officer commanding, John Grant, was to be examined. Clinton was ordered to proceed with an official "inquiry into the behaviour of Captain Grant" to determine if his alleged insubordination had in fact been "highly disrespectful to the King's Representative and prejudicial to that Harmony between the Civil and Military Departments so essential to the Tranquillity [*sic*] of the Islands."[122] There could be no doubt in John Grant's mind now as to why he had been passed over. His good name had been called into question at the most inopportune time and his chances for promotion for the remainder of the war would be virtually nil.

No public record remains of any Inquiry taking place but John Grant appears to have gone to New York in the summer of 1780 and successfully answered all the allegations made against him to Clinton's satisfaction as he remained the senior officer in command of the Bahamas. By 2 September 1780 he was back on the public record with a memorial to Sir Henry Clinton requesting reimbursement for expenses incurred on his initial arrival in the Bahamas.

While in New York clearing his name, Grant no doubt made several inquiries about transferring to a regular establishment unit as a captain. He was still in a very precarious financial position: technically a half-pay lieutenant on the regular British establishment but holding a simultaneous commission in a provincial unit. When he was passed over for the major's position of the Garrison Battalion, despite being the senior captain in the unit, he probably saw the writing on the wall. As the unit would probably be disbanded at the end of the war, an anxious John Grant must have repeated his request of 5 February 1780 that the commander-in-chief "grant him leave of Absence to go to Britain, and for such time as your Excellency may judge it Expedient."[123]

122. **Inquiry**. Lord Germain to Sir Henry Clinton, 4 November 1779, Whitehall. TNA, PRO 30/55/2409.

123. **Leave of absence**. Memorial of Captain John Grant to Sir Henry Clinton, 5 February 1780, Fort Nassau, New Providence, Bahamas. *Clinton Papers*, vol 84, item 21, WLCL.

Perhaps feeling partially responsible for promoting William Anstruther over John Grant's head, Clinton acceded to the request, and from the public record one can see that Grant spent at least six months in Britain, for a letter to Lord Jeffery Amherst dated 18 March 1782 in London reveals that he had been on leave prior to October 1781. During his stay in Scotland and England, the now forty-one-year-old Grant was not idle. A surviving letter reveals that he still hoped to get authority to raise an independent company in Glenurquhart and Glenmoriston and was desperate enough at this stage of the war to willingly return to the regular establishment as a lieutenant. While waiting for a warship to take him back to his command in the Bahamas, he wrote a last-ditch letter on 18 March 1782 to the former general he had served under during the Seven Years War, Lord Amherst:

> The Particular attention always showen [*sic*] by your Lordship, to every Officer who had the honour of serving under your Lordships Command last War in America, emboldens me once more to address your Lordship, requesting that you would be pleased to appoint me to full pay as a Lieutenant, and afterwards to recommend me to his Majesty to have permission to raise an Independent Company in the Highlands of Scotland.
>
> I must beg leave to acquaint your Lordship, that the Garrison Battalion is upon a footing which puts me entirely out of the line of Promotion, and your Lordship will readily allow, that to an officer who wishes to be employed, being cooped up in a Garrison must be very disagreeable; And were I not certain of being able to Compleat my Company, in as Short a time, and with as good Men as any Officer that has been permitted to raise an Independent Company, I would not have presumed to have troubled your Lordship with a Second Application.[124]

The reply was quick, curt and final. Amherst in a one-liner said on the following day that he was glad to serve him "consistently with the Rules of Service" but that he was "sure His Majesty would not approve" of Grant's request to raise a company.[125] Nothing remained for Grant to do but return to duty.

The previous month, the bureaucratic wheels of the Admiralty and Navy Board had finally turned and issued orders that Captain John Grant of the Garrison Battalion serving in the islands of Bermuda should "be conveyed to New York on board some Vessels in the Service of the Government that sails thither with the next convoy …."[126] and it would now seem he sailed for New York

---

124. **Letter to Amherst**. Captain John Grant to Lord Amherst, 18 March 1782, London. TNA, WO 34/185, fol. 256.
125. **Amherst's response**. Lord Amherst to Captain John Grant, 19 March 1782, London. TNA, WO 34/238, fol. 280.
126. **Bureaucratic wheels**. Philip Stevens to John Fisher, Esq., 7 February 1782, Admiralty Office. TNA, PRO, State Papers, Class 42, vol 57, fol 116; TNA, CO 5/255, fol. 64.

shortly after receiving Amherst's reply, arriving in New York sometime in April to then take a reinforcement of some 180 convalescing men to Nassau later in the month. They had been in Nassau less than a week when a Spanish invasion fleet from Cuba loomed over the horizon.

While Grant had been on leave imploring his old commanding general for some meaningful employment in March 1782, the governor and captain general of Havana, JUAN MANUEL CAGIGAL Y MONSERRAT, had been planning a surprise descent on Grant's command. Ever since Spain had joined the war against Great Britain (though never formally allied with the Americans), Spanish shipping had been pillaged and harassed mercilessly by English privateers, operating mainly out of the Bahamas. Captain General Cagigal was joined in his quest to eliminate the constant menace of Bahamian privateers by Commodore ALEXANDER GILLON aboard the frigate *South Carolina* and several American brigs and sloops.

On 22 April, the joint Spanish and American armada sailed from Havana, arriving at New Providence on 5 May 1782. The American ships quickly blocked outlets on the north side of the island while the *South Carolina* took a position near the bar of the harbour within cannon range of Fort Nassau. Captain General Cagigal sent a flag of parley ashore to Governor John Maxwell on 6 May, stating that he wished to avoid senseless bloodshed as his large force outnumbered the British defenders six to one. He bluntly asked Maxwell on what terms he would be prepared to surrender the colony to Spain. Despite his reinforcement of 180 Royal Garrison men from New York under the recently returned John Grant, Maxwell decided he had no choice but to seek the most favourable terms possible. While the fleet waited, Commodore Gillon directed the transports to anchor before the town of Nassau so that General Cagigal might disembark his troops when he was ready.

At 9 A.M. the following day, 7 May, Maxwell sent his proposals on board the frigate *South Carolina,* which Cagigal immediately refused to accept, and sent them back with amendments. The revised proposal saw the military garrison permitted to march out of their two fortresses the following day with all the traditional honours of war: drums beating, flags flying and bayonets fixed towing a single field piece. While this honourable cessation of arms was probably no consolation to John Grant, who was now going into captivity for a second time, the generous terms included transportation of all garrison troops back to England by Spanish ships under a flag of truce. Five months later he and his men had been exchanged, the *London Chronicle* reporting: "The Remains of Col. Donkin's Regiment of Royal Bermudians, lately captured in the Bahama Islands by the Spaniards, consisting of 180 Privates, arrived on Friday last at

Landguard Fort. A 1788 view of the fort at the mouth of the River Orwell outside Felixstowe, Suffolk. Designed to guard the entrance to the port of Harwich, this was where John Grant and his men, captured in the Bahamas in 1782, were deposited by their captors under the terms of their prisoner exchange. A few of Grant's veterans strongly objected to serving past their terms of enlistment on arrival, forcing our hero to seize and hold them in Landguard's "black-hole" – the rest of the men returning to their quarters "with little murmuring." The old fort seen here no longer remains, replaced by more modern fortifications dating from the two most recent World Wars. (Editors' Collection)

Landguard Fort, under the Command of Capt. Grant, where they are ordered to do Garrison Duty."[127]

The Spanish allowed the Bahamian inhabitants eighteen months to remove themselves and their property from the Island, after which time they would become subjects of the King of Spain. However, these arrangements would be undermined by the French navy's decisive defeat at the battle of the Saintes (9-12 April 1782) a few weeks earlier, for it permitted the Royal Navy to quickly re-establish their dominance in the Caribbean. The Spanish only maintained control of the Bahamas for about a year, and when the Treaty of Paris was signed in 1783, the Bahamas, as well as Minorca and Montserrat, were duly returned to Great Britain in exchange for eastern and western Florida.

As the war wound down, one consolation for John Grant and his fellow officers was that the Garrison Battalion was taken onto the regular army establishment and given the prefix "Royal" which meant that he was now a full-pay captain and therefore entitled to half-pay as such with the peace. Colonel Robert Donkin, John's commanding officer, had nurtured a belief that his newly-named Royal Garrison Battalion might actually escape the army reductions of 1783. The previous year he had pointed out to higher authorities that if his "battalion was to be reduced, another must be raised for the defence of these important islands of Bermuda & Bahama."[128]

127. ***The London Chronicle***. Saturday, October 5, to Tuesday, October 8, 1782.

128. **Reduction**. Robert Donkin to William Know, Esq., 29 May 1781, Bristol. TNA, CO 5/184, fols. 86-7.

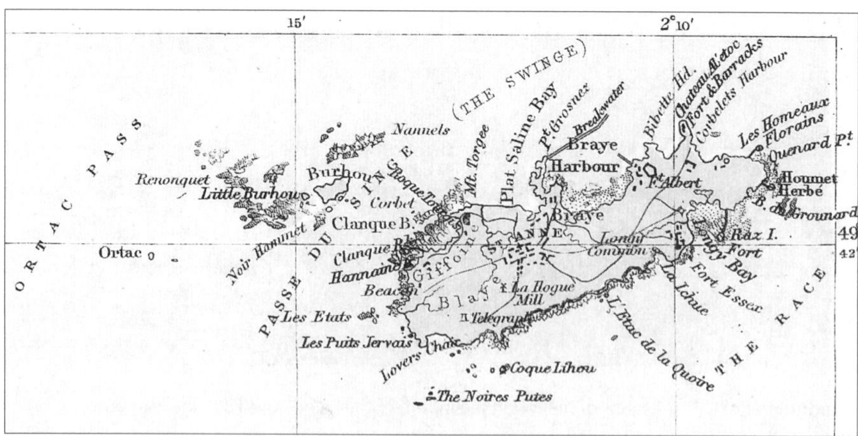

"Old Lady of the Sea." So a poet once called Alderney, the third-largest inhabited island of the Channel Islands and the closest to both France and the United Kingdom. The Channel Islands were the only British territory occupied by the Germans in the Second World War. (Map detail showing Alderney from "The Channel Islands" and published by Edward Standford in *Stanford's London Atlas of Universal Geography...*, 1901. Editors' photo)

In November 1783 Donkin wrote to Sir Guy Carleton from London that he hoped "the two companies here which were taken at Providence ... will be able to return to New York in the spring [1784]." Despite his colonel's lobbying efforts, John Grant and his fellow company officers at the Landguard Fort were placed on half pay, their fit rank and file absorbed into the existing garrison and the sick and infirm released or referred to the Royal Hospital at Chelsea.

John Grant would spend the next three years on half pay endeavouring to get back into the army full time, with a wife and young daughter to support. In September 1786 he succeeded in being reinstated as a captain with full pay commanding the North British Invalid Company in Berwick-on-Tweed. Five years later, on the eve of the Napoleonic War, he and his family would transfer south to Alderney, one of the Channel Islands off the coast of France, where he took up command of one of the Invalid Companies assigned to guard the island's meagre fortifications.[129]

John Grant's third war commenced on 1 February 1793. While stationed in the Channel Islands, his daughter Penuel, now twenty-one years of age, met and married a Royal Engineer officer, one Captain Lieutenant John Johnson. The forty-year-old bachelor, in a letter home to his sister Elizabeth, described

129. **Alderney** is the northernmost of the inhabited Channel Islands, part of the Bailiwick of Guernsey. Only 10 miles (16 km) off the coast of France, the tiny island (3 square miles, 8 km square) held some importance during the Napoleonic Wars as it could provide early warning of a French attack. However, it would have been a very isolated and remote posting for John and his family.

John Grant's only child as an "agreeable accomplished young lady of respectable family" and that her acceptance of his proposal was "highly flattering to himself and family."[130]

Just six months after the declaration of war against Napoleon, the Grant family, including their newly married (and pregnant) daughter, Penuel, moved to Gosport, the town opposite Portsmouth, where a fort guarded the entrance to the harbour. There, in July 1793, John took up command of another Invalid Company but he seems to have had immediate problems with the conditions his invalids had to contend with. The following year, his new engineer son-in-law confided to his wife from Flanders that her father would only come to grief with his propensity to never pass a fault. He remarked that it gave him "much concern to hear your father finds this situation at Portsmouth so disagreeable, I could wish he would attend to my opinion respecting the trouble he gives himself which serves no good purpose."[131]

The problems, and their resolution, are made more clear in two subsequent letters written in November 1794 by John Johnson in Flanders, wherein he describes his father-in-law's command as "a parcel of old vagabonds":

> I am not displeased to find your father intends leaving Portsmouth, it is by no means a pleasant place nor did I imagine Mrs. Grant would approve of the change of houses. I wish your father could get a station where, instead of attending to the continual wants of old soldiers who are a description of men never to be satisfied, he could find a small farm to divert his active mind....[132]

John Grant had thus received a transfer to a posting closer to home: one of the two Invalid Companies stationed at Kingston upon Hull in Yorkshire, his new commission dated 12 November 1794. His son-in-law, who had missed the birth of his first child, JOHN JOHNSON Jr., would finally return weakened and malnourished from service on the Continent in the spring of 1795. After a brief reunion with his family at Hull, he fell sick and died at Portsmouth, where he had been posted and was in the process of securing lodgings for his family. His brief stop at Hull, however, resulted in a second pregnancy for Penuel. His unfortunate widow, back with her parents in Yorkshire, would bear him an infant daughter the following year, May 1796. She would name her Isabella for the child's grandmother.

John Grant would serve there until age sixty, retiring on full pay in Decem-

---

130. **Penuel's character**. John Johnson to his sister, Mrs. Elizabeth Hope, 9 July 1793, Guernsey. MCA, DJQ J71/793/5.

131. **Portsmouth**. John Johnson to his wife, Penuel, 2 October 1793, Flanders. MCA, DJQ (no reference number).

132. **Vagabonds**. John Johnson to his wife, Penuel, undated, Flanders. MCA, DJQ J71/794/9; John Johnson to his wife, Penula, 16 November 1794, Flanders. MCA, DJQ J71/794/10.

ber 1802, the last commander of the Independent Company of Invalids assigned to Hull.[133] His Invalid Company was absorbed into the new Garrison Battalion structure[134] the following year, but by then John with his family, including his two grandchildren, had returned to Scotland for good, taking up residence first at Drynie on the Black Isle near his relatives, the Urquharts at Braelangwell, and by 1821, at Blervie near Forres.

It was sometime after the battle of Waterloo, 1815, that John was contacted by Colonel David Stewart (later David Stewart of Garth), who was writing his famous *Sketches of the Character, Manners, and Present State of the Highlanders of Scotland....* First published in 1822, Stewart's book was actually compiled, researched and written the decade before its publication and Stewart's inquiries for help from some of the veteran officers still living may have been the impetus for John Grant to record his memoirs. His grandson, serving with the Royal Artillery in the Mediterranean, would note in November 1816 that his grandfather had lost the sight of one of his eyes so it must have been a chore for John to write his own memoirs and another reason why they eventually had to be dictated to his grandson.[135] Stewart's book would include the most complete history of the 42nd Foot in the Seven Years' War and the American Revolution to date, benefitting from inputs from surviving veterans like John Grant, Thomas Stirling and John Peebles.[136]

One reference in Grant's memoirs strongly indicates that they were recorded sometime between 1822 and 1828. In attempting to describe the majesty of American forests in the latter half of his memoirs (see folio sheet 67 in Part Two) he would tell his grandson (John Johnson Jr.) taking dictation to add a telling postscript for his readers: "see The Last of the Mohicans," a novel first published

---

133. **Full pay.** The correct term is "retired full pay." The Retired Full Pay List dates from 1791, when twenty-five officers were established on the list (including thirteen captains).

134. **Garrison Battalions.** A Royal Garrison Battalion had been raised on 1 September 1795 to provide a home-based unit in order to release regular battalions from garrison duty for overseas service, taking all Invalid Companies in Britain under its umbrella for the duration of the war. This new Iteration of the Royal Garrison Battalion was disbanded on 24 December 1802 and replaced with seven new Garrison Battalions. These battalions were subsequently re-titled Royal Veteran Battalions on 30 June 1804, the main difference between the names being that the former were intended as a home for deserving old soldiers no longer fit for regular line duty, whereas the latter were intended for the left-over limited service men enrolled under the various forces acts of 1803 to 1806. However, this distinction blurred over time as both were used for depositing worn-out old soldiers for garrison duties.

135. **Blindness.** Lieutenant John Johnson, to his grandfather, John Grant, 9 November 1816, Corfu. MCA, DJQ J71/816/3.

136. ***Sketches.*** Colonel David Stewart, *Sketches of the Characters, Manners, and Present State of the Highlanders of Scotland: with details of the Military Service of the Highland Regiments*, 2 vols (London, 1822, reprint Edinburgh, 1977), vol 1, 588n. Hereafter, *Sketches.*

"The sweet smell of romantic anesthesia...." Major General David Stewart (1772–1829) was a Scottish soldier who secured his place in the history of the Highlands by becoming the first chronicler of the early Highland regiments and a staunch advocate of Highland dress. His two-volume book *Sketches of the Character, Manners, and Present State of the Highlanders of Scotland...*, first published in 1822, has underpinned every subsequent account of the Highlands to this day. Recent consensus on his *Sketches'* historical accuracy and objectivity however remains mixed. (Mezzotint engraving by S.W. Reynolds after a painting by James M. Scrymgeour, c.1825. ASKB)

by American author James Fenimore Cooper in 1826. There is an even more telling note in John Johnson's handwriting on folio sheet number 86 where, in parentheses halfway down the page, it states: "Monday, 12th January, Last day of personal dictation," a clear indication that John Grant in his eighties, was no longer able to speak, or remember.[137]

As stated earlier in the Introduction, the editors believe that John's grandson, John Johnson Jr., transcribed his elderly grandfather's oral memoirs while stationed nearby at Fort George.[138] A Royal Artillery officer, he married an Emily Anderson in September 1822, the first four of their eight children being born in Forres, Scotland. One letter from John's regimental agents dated 1821 indicates that John and Isobel lived at Blervie, a hamlet just south of the town of Forres. John Johnson Jr. was also the sole trustee and executor of his grandfather's last will and testament and his proxy signature appears on a codicil as his grandfather was too old and infirm to sign in the last months of his life.[139]

Despite the memoirs being abbreviated by poor health, and being recited in his twilight years, they do portray John Grant's first war with a crisp unadulterated freshness that only an actual eyewitness can provide. Grant's memories, carefully recorded by his grandson, are in our opinion one of the best first-hand accounts of the new kind of warfare encountered at the point of the bayonet in the New World during the French and Indian War. Undoubtedly, John Johnson cherished the manuscript enough to take it with him when he emigrated halfway around the world. There it was passed down through his New Zealand descendants, along with his other papers and paintings, to find a final resting place in the Alexander Turnbull Library in Wellington, New Zealand. And for that we are much indebted.

* * *

On 22 January 1828, the Iron Duke and victor of Waterloo, Sir Arthur Wellesley, set aside his field marshal's baton and his command of the British army to become Prime Minister of Great Britain. Two days later, one of the longest-serving officers of the British army quietly passed away at his home in Forres, Scotland. John Grant's death was reported after the fact in several British magazines, the longest entry being that found in the *Gentleman's Magazine*:

---

137. **Calculation of day.** The year 1824 is the only year (over the period 1819-1828) in which 12 January falls on a Monday.

138. **Fort George.** A large 18th-century fortress near Ardesier, to the north-east of Inverness. It was built to pacify the Scottish Highlanders in the aftermath of the Jacobite rising of 1745, replacing a smaller Fort George in Inverness constructed after the 1715 rising to control the area. The current fortress has never been attacked and has remained in continuous use as a garrison.

139. **Last will and testament.** London, 17 April 1828. TNA, PRO 11/1739. See also, MCA, DJQ/6.

"The last male representative of the ancient family of Dalrachney." So said the *Gentleman's Magazine* on the death of Captain John Grant "of the Royal Invalids" in March 1828. While there is no surviving record of his burial, his descendants believe he was interred in the graveyard of the original Forres Parish Kirk. The old kirk (known then and now as Saint Lawrence) and most of its surrounding graveyard were destroyed in 1904 to make way for a newer larger church. This image dates back to 1899 (about five years before its demolition) and it is possible that one of the tombstones in the foreground is John Grant's memorial. (Editors' Collection)

> SCOTLAND – Lately. At Forres, Capt. J. Grant, of the Royal Invalids. Capt. Grant was the last male representative of the ancient family of Dalrachney, in Strathspey, and one of the oldest officers in His Majesty's service. He entered the army in 1755, as Lieut. in the 42^{d} Highland reg.[140]

The eighty-seven-year-old Highland veteran, besides being "the last of his line," was the last living Black Watch officer to have soldiered in North America during the Seven Years' War. He literally was, in the words of David Stewart, one of "many Highland officers" to "have sunk in obscurity ... from want of money, or influence to procure early rank, or from a decay of constitution ... who under more favourable circumstances, might have risen to distinguished eminence in their profession."[141]

---

140. **Obituary**. John actually joined the 42nd Foot as a lieutenant in 1758 and *not* 1755 as the obituary states, perhaps a typo, or more probably garbled by his wife, Isobel, who was also getting on in years. *The Gentleman's Magazine*, vol XCVII (London, January-June 1828), 285. See also Blackwood's *Edinburgh Magazine*, vol XXII (Edinburgh, January-June 1828), 665.

141. ***Sketches***, vol I, 590.

Stewart might have also added that John Grant was part of a small elite corps of officers that styled themselves the "American Army" in the Seven Years' War to distinguish themselves from those troops serving in Germany. Proud of his family, his accomplishments and his regiment, John Grant pursued a shining young career while on "a dangerous service" as a Black Watch infantry officer in the French and Indian War. It marked and defined him for the rest of his life and is preserved for us here in his unfinished memoirs. So check your powder and flints and prepare for action.

PART TWO

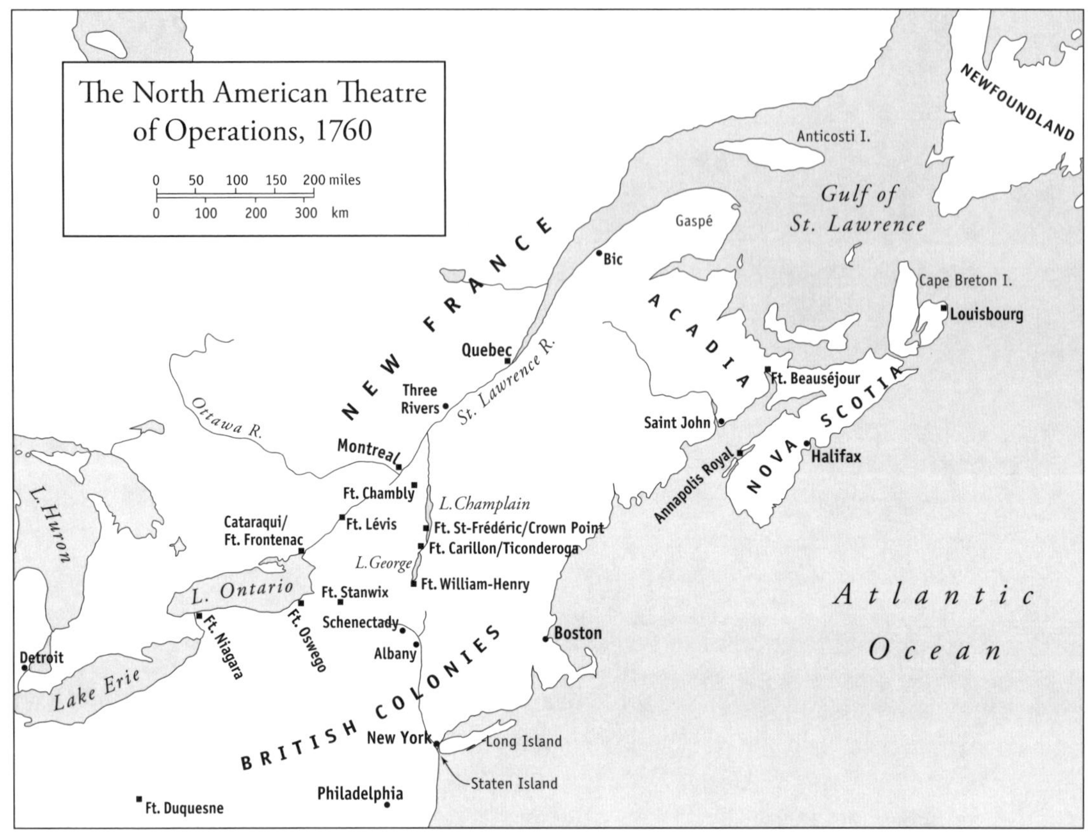

The cockpit of war. John Grant's campaigning in North America ranged up the New York–Albany–Lake Champlain corridor in 1759, up the Mohawk Valley to Oswego on Lake Ontario in 1760, then down the Saint Lawrence River from Cataraqui (present-day Kingston) to Montreal. In spring 1761 his battalion travelled from Montreal to Staten Island, by way of Crown Point. (Map: Robin Brass Studio)

"A DANGEROUS SERVICE ..." THE MEMOIRS OF JOHN GRANT

Chapter 1 | Scotland, 1741–58 – The Early Years

JOHN GRANT WAS BORN INTO TUMULTUOUS TIMES. During his lifetime, he would serve king and country abroad in three major wars before taking his final retirement in 1802 near Inverness, Scotland. His lifetime spanned the last Jacobite Uprising (and with it, the last battle fought on British soil), the Highland Clearances and the defeat of the tyrant Napoleon at Waterloo in 1815.

In the '45 rebellion's aftermath, the last vestiges of the feudal clan system were destroyed with a vicious harrowing of the glens. All Jacobite estates and lands became forfeit to the crown and the powers of so-called chieftains were curtailed. Highland dress was proscribed, and despite the Highland peoples' innate attachment and love for the land, tens of thousands, unable to afford the rents of new landlords, were forced to emigrate to the New World, including the hero of our tale.

John Grant would personally bear witness to all these events, but his first glimmering of a bigger, wider world than his pastoral Glenurquhart home was the arrival of the Duke of Cumberland's troopers on his doorstep one day in 1746. John Grant, the five-year-old son of a Highland laird, one day in the future would don the British red coat and become a long-time servant of the Crown. His only daughter, Penuel, would marry English soldiers, the first a captain lieutenant in the Royal Engineers, the second a lieutenant colonel in the Royal Artillery. His grandson, John Johnson Jr., who would transcribe these memoirs for his grandfather, would also serve in the Royal Artillery before retiring to become a doctor and emigrating to New Zealand.

Here then, in John Grant's own words, are the memoirs of a Black Watch officer of the French and Indian War.

* * *

15 [1] I was born at Ballintomb near Granton,[2] and not far from Muckrach[3] on December 2nd 1741. At a year, [I was] removed to Balmacaan where my father resided as factor, or chamberlain as sometimes called, and Baron Bailey to the Laird of Grant. **My Father was a very handsome man, the best looking of his clan. Stout, well made, of 6 feet high, of a dark complexion and was an excellent companion when sober. It was said of him that he was one who a person would borrow a shilling to drink with.**[4]

The first thing that I can recollect [is the] Coming of Troopers. [I] remember my Mother & Servants serving out bread, cheese & Butter. I remember their putting [the food] into their haversacks and the pawing of the Horses. Told it was to find out where treasure was hid [*sic*].

Major [James] Lockhart, brother to the famous Sir John Lockhart Ross[5] commanded the party & came to ravage and destroy the country. When burning Divach, which belonged to the Laird of Grant's property opposite, my father rode over. Major Lockhart addressed him & asked whose house that was, pointing to Balmacaan.

"It is the Laird of Grant's."

"Whose cattle are those?" For all the cattle of the county had been sent there for protection.

"The Laird of Grant's."

"It shall be the next house [that] I shall burn."

My Father produced the Duke's [Duke of Cumberland] protection to [the]

---

1. **Page 15**. John Grant's memoir begins on folio page 15 of the manuscript. Folio pages 1 to 14 are missing. The manuscript page numbers are indicated thus: 15. John Johnson Jr. numbered only the odd pages. The even numbers are the editors' interpolations.
2. **Grantown-on-Spey**. Did not exist at the time of John Grant's birth but was a thriving community when his grandson transcribed his memoirs from dictation in the 1820s. It was built by Sir James Grant of Grant in 1765 as a planned settlement on a low plateau at Freuchie beside the River Spey at the northern edge of the Cairngorm mountains, about 20 miles (32 km) south-east of Inverness.
3. **Muckrach**. A castellated Grant castle on the River Spey, c. 1598, built by the second son of John Grant of Freuchie, Laird of Grant. Situated 3 miles (5 km) to the east of Duthil, it stands on the brow of a hill looking west as far as Craigellachie and Aviemore, and eastwards over the Spey valley. At the time of John Grant's birth in 1741, it was in ruins. Now fully restored, it serves as an upmarket self-catering rental property for tourists.
4. **Description of father**. The last two sentences of this paragraph describing John Grant's father, originally appearing on folio page 18, were placed here to be more chronologically consistent with the narrative.
5. **Admiral Sir John Lockhart-Ross** (1721-90). Royal Navy officer. The younger brother of Major James Lockhart. He had a distinguished naval career, rising to vice admiral in September 1787, and was much beloved by his Ross tenantry on the Balnagowan estates for his improvements and devotion to agricultural reform.

Butcher or Sweet William? Prince William Augustus (1721-65), the Duke of Cumberland, was the third and youngest son of George II of Great Britain. He is best known in history for his heavy-handed and brutal role in putting down the Jacobite Rising in 1746, though at the time he was immensely popular with the British public for saving the realm. Cumberland would be nicknamed "The Butcher" by his English Tory opponents, "Sweet William" by his Whig Party supporters. (Mezzotint engraving by John Faber after a painting by David Morier, 1753. ASKB)

Laird of Grant's property. [He] would not look at it. Swore with oaths it would be [the] next place [that] he would burn.

"At your peril," said my father, who returned the protection into his pocket and rode off. As he was turning away he heard the next-in-command say, "Major. I saw the Duke's signature. Take care what you are about."

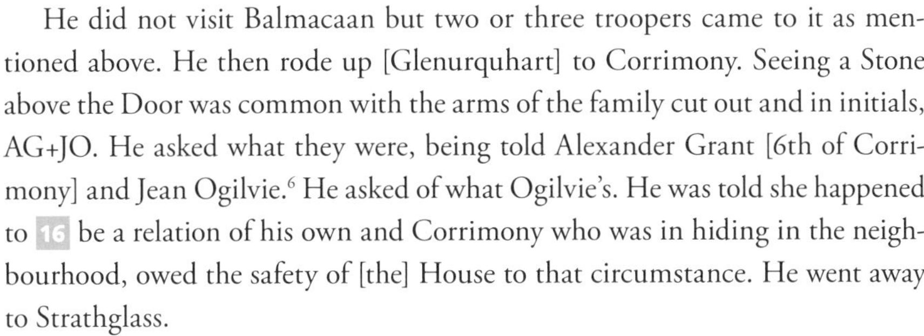

He did not visit Balmacaan but two or three troopers came to it as mentioned above. He then rode up [Glenurquhart] to Corrimony. Seeing a Stone above the Door was common with the arms of the family cut out and in initials, AG+JO. He asked what they were, being told Alexander Grant [6th of Corrimony] and Jean Ogilvie.[6] He asked of what Ogilvie's. He was told she happened to 16 be a relation of his own and Corrimony who was in hiding in the neighbourhood, owed the safety of [the] House to that circumstance. He went away to Strathglass.

At Glenmoriston, he went to Daldreggan,[7] took [him] out to be hanged.[8] He happened to be [the] only gentleman not concerned [with the] rebellion. Captain Grant[9] of Lord Loudoun's [Regiment], asked [the] gentleman who was stripped naked, "Who are you?"

"I am Grant of Daldreggan."

"Are you married to a daughter of Shewglie's?"

"Yes sir."

---

6. **Jean Ogilvie** (1724-97). The only child of Lieutenant John Ogilvie of Kempcairn and Anna Gordon in Keith. Married Alexander Grant, 6th Corrimony, in 1742 and had twelve children, several of whom died in infancy.
7. **Aeneas Grant, *Daldreggan*** (1702-79), married to Hannah Grant, the daughter of Alexander Grant of Shewglie.
8. **Burning of Dundreggan estate.** Chronologically this event took place two months earlier than the harrowing of Glenurquhart and Strathglass. For complete details of this incident, see Annex J, *Olden Times*, 501.
9. **Captain Alexander Grant**, 64th Foot. See footnote 9 in Part One.

"Major Lockhart," said he [Captain Grant], "He is he only loyal man in the Glen [and] has never moved from his house."

"By an oath I will hang him."

"Remember," said Captain [Grant], "I am now under your command, but if you do I will make you answer for it when we reach Fort Augustus."

Major Lockhart knew that Captain Grant was a favourite of the Dukes. The rope was taken off. Daldreggan ran naked as he was to Shewglie's 12 miles distant without stopping.[10]

From there [Balmacaan] I went to Braelangwell in Ross-shire to Mrs. Urquhart,[11] my aunt by the Mother. I had 3 nurses before I was five months old and was thin & poor[ly] fed on Formulayniac[12] [*sic*]. [I] remember my Mother used to give me sugar candy for eating, fresh butter from the churn without bread – rather hostile to the Bilious System of [the] modern medicals, [but] it did me no harm. **I had the Smallpox at 5 years and was treated in the usual way.[13] Blankets were pinned up to the windows, [a] large fire, Mulled wine to keep it out of my heart. Mother slept with me for 14 days to keep me warm.**

From there I went to Inverlaidnan, Dalrachnies[14] house, & went to school at Duthil. He kept an open house, the Highland road being then made by General Wade[15] and the Gentlemen passing that way spent a night with him and many

---

10. **Daldreggan**. John Grant neglects to mention that Grant *Daldreggan's* wife was also present and was stripped of her clothes, as well as her rings and jewelry.
11. **Mrs. Urquhart**. Margaret Ross, daughter of David Ross, 1st of Inverchasley and Tarlogie, by his first marriage to Isabella Munro. Her older sister, Anne Ross, married John Haldane, 2nd of Aberuthven, and her only brother, David, who succeeded to his father's estates. David became Lord Ankerville, a Lord of Session in Scotland's highest courts, and is referred to later in the memoirs by John Grant as stepping in to assist with his education. See Part Three for Biographical Note on Lord Ankerville. Technically, Margaret was John Grant's step-aunt, as Mary Ross, John Grant's mother, was the only child of David Ross (1st of Inverchasley) and his second wife.
12. **Formulayniac**. Likely a misspelling of "formulaic" (i.e., made according to a formula; a recipe), it was a barley and water mixture that was commonly given to sick infants in Scotland during this period.
13. **Editors' note**. The last two sentences of this paragraph concerning John's illness, originally appearing on folio page 23, were placed here to be more chronologically consistent with the narrative.
14. **"Dalrachnie."** John Grant's uncle, Alexander Grant of Dalrachney, later Inverlaidnan (1708-1765).
15. **General George Wade** (1673-1748). British army officer. Served in the Nine Years' War, War of the Spanish Succession, Jacobite rising of 1715 and War of the Quadruple Alliance. Best known for his construction of barracks, bridges and proper roads in Scotland during the 1720s and 1730s. He went on to be a military commander during the War of the Austrian Succession and Commander-in-Chief of the Forces during the Jacobite rising of 1745. John Grant implies in his memoirs that the road was still being constructed near Inverlaidnan when it fact it was one of the first to be completed in the 1720s.

"The most like to an English town of any at this end of the island." So an English surveyor road-building with General George Wade's troops in the Highlands described Inverness. By 1750, it was the principal town in the eastern Highlands with some 3,000 inhabitants, its small port the only economic gateway to the world for the region. Here, John Grant received his early education and a young James Wolfe spent his first Scottish winter as lieutenant colonel of the 20th Foot. (Illustration from Pennant, *A Tour in Scotland MDCCLXIX*, Editors' photo)

merry nights were spent there. The Inn at 17 Aviemore, now so comfortable, was then a poor hovel.

In 1751, I went to Inverness and was boarded at the School, [the] master's name then [Alexander] Ferguson. It was then a famous school. There were 16 Gentlemen's sons among others, Sir Roderick McKenzie of Scatwell,[16] [and] other McKenzies. The Bailey, afterwards Sir Ewen.[17] MacKays from Caithness and Colonel Duff of Muirtown,[18] &c. We paid a high board in those days, 16 £. They are now all gone.

---

16. **Sir Roderick Mackenzie of Scatwell**, 4th Baronet (1740-1811). First son and heir of Sir Lewis Mackenzie, 3rd Baronet. Succeeded to the Baronetcy, 13 September 1756; captain in the Foot Guards, 1762; rebuilt Rosehaugh House, 1796. He died 11 June 1811.
17. **The Baillie, or Sir Ewen Baillie,** later Sir Ewen Mackenzie (c.1740-1820). The Baillie (later the Mackenzie Baronetcy), of Berkeley Square in the County of London, was created in the Baronetage of the United Kingdom on 26 May 1819 for General Ewen Baillie, provisional commander-in-chief of The Bengal. Baillie had already been created a baronet of Portman Square in the County of London, on 11 December 1812. The 1812 creation became extinct on his death in 1820 while the 1819 creation was passed on to his nephew Alexander Mackenzie, the second baronet.
18. **Colonel Duff of Muirtown**. Alexander Duff, 2nd of Muirtown (1737-78), British army officer. Born 1737 (and thus four years older than John Grant), Alexander was son of solicitor

[We were] but poorly fed – morning meal [a] half mutchkin[19] of porridge, & milk and water in small wooden beakers, called luggies.[20] For dinner, a sort of broth of mutton & were exhorted that those who eat [the] most broth should get [the] most meat, which was then 3 halfpence per pound. Potatoes were then so rare that they were delicacies unknown to us. Gentlemen merely had a few in their gardens as now the vegetable marrow, and were presented on State occasions. Supper, porridge again. So scantily fed, it was a rule in our little band that when a few shillings were sent to any [of] us by friends it was put into a common purse and we purchased ale and hops, which we brought up to the room we had for our lessons, and discuss it over the fire. The niggardness of [the] Mistress made us destroy everything, burn as much peat and do all [the] mischief we could. [We] used to take the luggies, give them each a blow & the last finished it and threw it into the fire, so each had a share in [the] destruction.

Luggies. The Scots word for "ear" is "lug," so *luggies,* small wooden bowls often used for serving milk with porridge, were nicknamed for their small carved handles resembling ears (one "lug" or two). (Private Collection)

One day on going up to my room for some plaything I found the Usher and the Mistress there in rather an equivocal situation. I instantly left the room. Of course the Usher was very civil and many biscuits did I 18 get from Miss Jessie Kirkland. One unlucky day He punished me severely [and] my prudence forsook me – I let the cat out of the bag. From that moment I became his victim. He got an express tord[21] [*sic*] for me, well hardened. Among other punishments, he had a bodle pin with which he used to prick my head under pretence of there being insects there. I bore this torture as well as I could, but his treatment so frightened me that I could never say my lessons. My head was one sore.

At last in consequence of my father's death on December 25th 1752 who died

William Duff, 1st of Muirtown (1701-82), and grandson of the Provost of Inverness. Duff, like John Grant, also joined the army and served with Keith's Highlanders in Germany during the Seven Years' War. In the next war, Duff helped raise the 73rd Foot (Macleod's Highlanders) in 1777 but died in London the following year. Alistair & Henrietta Tayler, *The Book of the Duffs*, vol II (Edinburgh, 1914), 410.

19. **Mutchkin** (Gaelic: *mùisgein*). A Scottish unit of measurement of liquids that was in use from at least 1661 (possibly 15th century), until the late 19th century. A mutchkin is equivalent to 424 ml or four gills (Scots), equal to three imperial gills or three quarters of an imperial pint.
20. **Luggies**. Literally "ears" in Broad Scots, but refers to the handles on the small wooden bowls used for porridge (similar to Quaich cups).
21. **Tord** or **turd**. Excrement, from the Old English word *tord*. This term has been in use since the 10th century, considered ruder after the mid-13th century, becoming vulgar slang around the mid-18th century.

of a Quinsy[22] of the throat, at the age of 45 from ignorant treatment. My mother came into Inverness to live and I of course went to her. I did not mind my situation but would never allow the maid servant to comb my hair. This being reported to my mother, she asked me the reason. I told her. She went to [the] Magistrate [and] the affair was taken up. The Usher was cited. I appear'd [at the inquest] and he received a severe reprimand.

I remain'd at the school but he took no more notice of me. Time disclosed the issue of the circumstances I have alluded to and my tormentor decamped, leaving the Lady in her shame.

19 I shall never forget the feeling of revenge my young heart nourished against that man. The cause of my first beating was his attempting to punish my chum Duff. He was a stout boy and made resistance. The brute drew his knife and in attempting to cut open his Clothes, cut him. I jumped up, was seconded by the others, and seized on his hands. He remembered this and punished me on the first occasion.

My Mother died in 1754 leaving 4 daughters & myself. She died of an apoplectic fit, or rather paralytic, brought on by the low nervous state she was left in, in consequence of grief from her husband's death. I heard [of] it casually in the street – rushed to the spot and saw them carrying her in, a corpse.

My sisters were taken [in] by my friends and I was sent to Fortrose, or as it was then called, Chindy or the Chanonry, where there was a good school. The board was 6 £ in the Episcopal clergyman's house and our feeding was plentiful such as it was. I here learnt [*sic*] Quadrille[23] from my Mistress for pins, which I fear gave me a taste for play. I passed my time pleasantly enough.

One amusement was when the Synod[24] used to sit. There was riding their Horses to water. On one of these occasions [I] ran a race, [and] endeavouring to make a shortcut, ran against a wall. Knocked out a large stone – terrible wound on my leg. Streaming with blood I lost all command of [the] horse – my Master attempting to stop me. I fairly knocked him down and leapt over him & dashed into the stable. For 3 months [the] Doctor did no good and [an] old woman did what he could not 20 by applying Goldbaters skin,[25] or as it is called strippin [*sic*], the covering of Salt butter by simply applying it.

---

22. **Quinsy**. A severe swelling or inflammation of the throat, in this case probably severe tonsillitis.
23. **Quadrille**. A popular 18th-century card game played by four players in pairs and with a deck of 40 cards (the 8s, 9s and 10s being removed).
24. **Synod**. In the Presbyterian Church, a *synod* is a regional governing body (a *presbytery* is a local governing body).
25. **Goldbeater's skin**. A thin transparent membrane with great tensile strength usually taken from an ox or cow's stomach membrane and traditionally used in the 17th and 18th centuries as a base for the manufacture of gold leaf, hence its name. Here, John Grant is

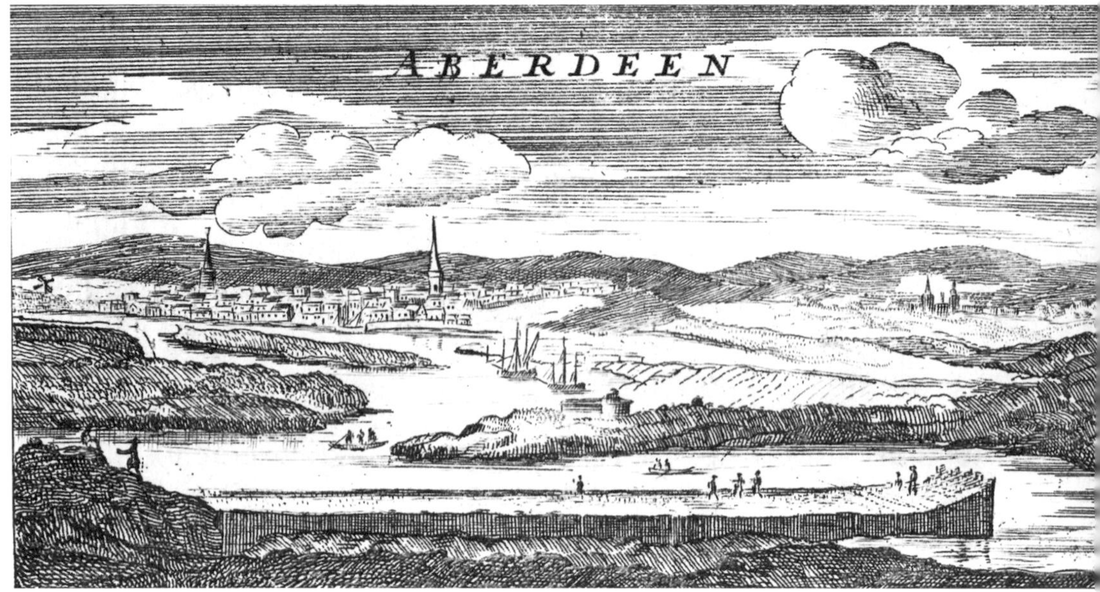

"The Granite City." Aberdeen, with its stately granite buildings, was the port city where John Grant would finish his formal studies before joining the army. Situated on the North Sea coast between the Rivers Dee and Don, Aberdeen was one of Scotland's first industrial centres. By the late 18th century, it was a major producer of ships, paper, woollens, linens, cottons, quarried granite, jute products and whiskey. (Illustration from "The North Part of Great Britain called Scotland" by Herman Moll, 1714. Editors' photo)

Gambling was then much in practice amongst all ages. With us it was carried on in a small way. A low fellow kept a public house and used to entice us to play Loo[26] for halfpence, which was laid out in his house on Whiskey and treacle. Some grievances on [the] part of the Master was the subject of conversation. He advised us to rebel.

A conspiracy was hatched. We laid in provisions, signed on the Usher or sub doctor as he was called. Got [the] key from [the] Janitor, locked the Doors [of our School]. The Master sent for the Magistrates. The town's officers appeared, we set them at defiance & remained in triumphant possession. Came to terms after 48 hours and escaped unpunished, some of the Lads being on in years.

I saw little change in Fortrose after an absence of 30 years, except that the old Castle at the east of the town was gone, round which I so often played. It was to the Seaforth family.

comparing it to the hardened skin of butter that was used as a breathable membrane to cover his open wound and prevent infection.

26. **Loo**. A card game.

"A Son of Aesculapius." So John Grant would style one of his fellow boarders while studying in Aberdeen. Walter Farquhar (1738-1819) would become a prominent Scottish physician whose clientele included many of the leading figures of the day, including the Prince of Wales (later George IV) and the Prime Minister, William Pitt. This is a pencil drawing by Henry Bone "after Sir Henry Raeburn," 1796. The drawing has been "squared in ink for transfer." (NPG D17262, Editors' photo)

In the year 1756 I returned to Strathspey[27] on my way to Aberdeen. There was no wheeled carriage in those days between Inverness & Aberdeen, there being only one two-wheeled chaise at the former place. A Horse & a man accompanied me to Aberdeen – the Horse carrying me and my baggage – the man on foot. There was no made road until I arrived at Keith[28] and that road was muddy.

Arrived at Aberdeen. I was boarded at the House of an old Lady at 10 £ a year, exclusive of washing. We were twelve in number, 11 of whom were either her nephews or grand nephews, and all medical students. One of them was the late Sir Walter Farquhar.[29] These young men found sufficient time notwithstanding 21 their pursuits to amuse themselves, and as there were a great number of young men of all counties, balls, suppers and Card parties were the order of the evenings.

Much is said about the demoralizing effect of manufactories [*sic*], but I must say that as much immorality existed at Aberdeen in those days, as can at present

27. **Strathspey**. The area around the upper part of the Spey River valley from its source down to its capital, Grantown-on-Spey.
28. **Keith** (Gaelic: *Baile Chèith*). A small market town located in the Isla valley in the Grampian Highlands of northwestern Scotland. It is divided into three sections: Old Keith, New Keith and Fife Keith. The town appears in written records as early as 1195 in the charter of William the Lion. The word comes from the Gaelic meaning "wind" or "pure air." The main part of the town is on higher ground above the river, laid out around 1750 by the Earl of Findlater.
29. **Sir Walter Farquhar** (1738-1819). A prominent Scottish physician whose clientele included many of the leading figures of the day, including the Prince of Wales (later George IV) and the Prime Minister, William Pitt. He left his medical studies and joined the 19th Foot as a surgeon. He retired from the army in 1769 and moved to London, opening an apothecary shop, eventually receiving his medical degree from King's College, Aberdeen. In 1796 he was awarded a baronetcy. With his reputation secured, Farquhar (pronounced "Farkwer") ran a very successful practice until his retirement in 1813 due to health problems. He died in London in March 1819.

Bodysnatching. A 19th-century illustration by Hablot Knight Browne depicting the the disreputable activities of so-called "resurrectionists" or "resurrection men" who secretly disinterred newly buried corpses at night, then sold them while still "fresh" to medical schools for dissection and anatomy lectures. Browne, who worked under the pseudonym "Phiz," was a well-known illustrator of Charles Dickens' works. (Illustration from Pelham, *The Chronicles of Crime; or, The New Newgate Calendar....*" Editors' photo)

when it is an essentially manufacturing place, and tho' luck, not old men, unwilling to allow improvement in the times. I must think the spread of information, tho' it may in some measure have deteriorated the simple manners of the country, has not had that effect upon towns.

Tho' well fed, the old Lady had one particular. She only allowed one biscuit to breakfast. My highland appetite could not tolerate it long – the third day I complained.

"What, have you not had your 'Stout'?"[30] So they called a [Stater?] allowance.

"Yes, but that, I complain of."

[So she] gave us plenty of bread and butter, but no Stout. The old Lady unwillingly acceded and I gained the good will of the Nephews. But she had her revenge. She engaged me to play Quadrille and won in a few nights my only guinea, in those days, no despicable sum.

I was often asked by these sons of Aesculapius[31] to accompany them in resurrection excursions[32] but I had always a horror. One feat of theirs I must record

30. **Stout**. A strong malted beer, also known as porter.
31. **Aesculapius**. The Greek god of medicine.
32. **Resurrection excursions**. The secret disinterment of corpses from graveyards by body snatchers (often called "resurrectionists" or "resurrection-men") in order to sell the corpses

The road that bankrupted a city. A print of Union Street, Aberdeen, as it looked in 1836. Not in existence when John Grant was at King's College, Union Street's construction started the year of John's retirement from the army, 1802. It was one of the most ambitious development projects ever undertaken in the city, eventually bankrupting it, but it left Aberdeen with its most emblematic thoroughfare. (Private Collection)

as it caused some sensation in the good town. A young man drowned himself for love, his body found at some distance was buried on the shore. They went at night, disinterred it, and laid it down at the door of the obdurate fair one.

22 Things went on pretty well 'till near the end of the first term. One morning having occasion to get up early, [my] curiosity [was] attracted by seeing something on [the] window seat cover'd up – found [in] it a dead infant. [I was] disgusted and left [the] house next day. I went to another House at the same board. I was well treated, lived on the fat of the land. Scotch breakfast & tea.

We lived in an upper flat. [I] used to practice my dancing steps [which] much annoyed an old woman below. She went to complain to the gentleman who had charge of me. He said that I must practice – that he could not help it. [The] old Lady, much irritated, said: "Hope he may dance in hell." Then [he said]: "You may hope to have him as a partner." But [she went] off in a terrible rage.

Our dancing school was in the Earl Marischal's House.[33] Aberdeen was then

---

for dissection or anatomy lectures in medical schools. In this case, the thrifty medical students of King's College appear to have been eliminating the middlemen.

33. **Earl Marischal's house.** The house of George Keith, 5th Earl Marischal of Scotland, who founded Marischal College in 1593, the second of Scotland's post-medieval civic universities after the University of Edinburgh. The university was founded with the expressed aim of training clergy for the post-Reformation Kirk. King's College and Marischal College were united to form the modern University of Aberdeen in 1860.

not above ¼ of its present size. The South bridge was not in existence nor Union Street[34] leading to it, nor any of the Houses beyond. The Ravine now below the bridge and filled with houses was then a green-sided hollow with gardens. The gallows gate and the old streets are now scarcely recognizable from their new extensions.[35]

Not one of the manufacturers was then in existence. Stockings knit by the hand were the sole occupation of the females. There was no whale fishing,[36] a large trade with Holland, and plenty of smuggled spirits. We used to go into [the] country with biscuits and get as much curds and cream as we could drink. We used to 23 dine at one or two. I cannot say much for the morality of the people. Marischal Street did not then exist, being called from the Earl Marischal's House alluded to as above.[37] Where the barracks are now, was the remains of an old Castle.

I left Aberdeen in 1757 & returned to Inverlaidnan.[38] Returned to Strathspey on Horseback, and only paid 3^{d} [three pence] in the different houses for dinner or breakfast. I returned quite a buck, my dress was a pea green coat, a Waistcoat with flaps reaching half down the thigh, breeches, stockings and shoes and buckles, and a bag with the three corner'd hats then in fashion.

Strathspey was then a pleasant residence. It was filled with gentlemen cadets of the family or branches of the Lairds who had wadsets. My uncle had nearly the whole of Dulnainside. These wadsets were then considered as scarce redeemable and almost perpetual. They met among each other particularly at Christmas and the dance and the Song with the Wine cup went round, punch

---

34. **Union Street.** One of the most ambitious of Aberdeen's development projects, work on Union Street started in 1801, eventually bankrupting the city but leaving it with its most emblematic thoroughfare. Made entirely out of granite, the street runs for about a mile (1.6 km) west-southwest and is lined by what is regarded as the world's most impressive granite buildings. This architectural heritage, the abundance of silver-grey granite edifices, has given the city its most well-known nickname: "the Granite City."
35. **Editors' note.** These memoirs, transcribed from dictation fifty years after the fact by the grandson of John Grant, John Johnson Jr., refer to changes that had taken place over the fifty years since John Grant had been at school.
36. **Whale fishing.** First introduced in Aberdeen in the mid-1750s when whales were hunted for blubber, which was boiled down to produce lamp oil. At first successful, it became less profitable when gas lighting was introduced. By the 1830s overfishing had greatly reduced the number of whales.
37. **Marischal Street** was built between 1766 and 1773 to improve the connection between the harbour and the main part of Aberdeen. In 1766 the town council purchased the unoccupied Earl Marischal's house and garden, which was then demolished to open up the way for the new street which was named in the Earl's honour.
38. **Editors' note.** This sentence concerning John Grant's departure from Aberdeen, originally appearing on folio page 22, was placed here to be more chronologically consistent with the narrative.

and sometimes claret. It was rude but heady to be sure. We were somewhat polished by being admitted to the security of castle Grant called the "Merry Ha'" – which was an epicure of open house or table. There 24 was, to be sure, a good deal of conviviality – Sir Ludovic Grant being very convivial. The Gentry intermarried among themselves so that they were almost one family.

There was plenty of red deer, roe, grouse, ptarmigan, black cock, &c. and no game laws. Only nets were not allowed. Sheep farms were not on to the extent so that game was not another reason. Every person left his sport to follow vermin or hawks – now but few sportsmen and don't follow. Plenty of salmon. Cervine [deer] not kept so close at Gordon Castle as now. There was no town at Fochabers,[39] a few houses clustered round the old Castle, most of the present being new. The Houses had only in general 4 rooms – only one room for eating and drawing room. When able the few rooms were filled, the rest used to sleep on shake downs, gentlemen in one, Ladies in another.

Whenever it was known a party was assembled, the piper, who also played the fiddle, made his appearance without invitation. [He] announced his arrival by a pipe tune, then partners were taken and dancing commenced at midday, so fond were they of dancing. They had every supply except groceries among themselves.

These were happy times. The Sons went into the army chiefly and returned with some little polish. Morals rather relaxed – a woman considered it no shame to bear a child to a gentleman. She got the [*sic*] 25 vestry married,[40] the Husband assured of the Father's protection.

The change in religion from the popish to Presbyterianism had done but little to change their practices. But in the one, absolution could be obtained, and, in the other, as the women themselves used to say, it was "foreordained" and they thus guilty and consciously submitted to what could not be altered. After a few months [I went] to my uncle, a Lord of Session,[41] who sent me to a private teacher at Tain.

---

39. **Fochabers** (Scottish Gaelic: *Fachabair* or *Fothabair*). A village in Moray, Scotland, 10 miles (16 km) east of the cathedral city of Elgin and on the east bank of the River Spey. Founded in 1776 during the Scottish Enlightenment by Alexander Gordon, 4th Duke of Gordon (1743-1827), Fochabers is a perfect example of a planned town with its straight, wide streets in mainly rectangular layouts, a central square and the houses built with their main elevations parallel to the street. Grantown, previously mentioned, is another example.
40. **Vestry married**. Fathers of illegitimate children were obliged by the parish to care for the child and often vestry minutes contained agreements for the care of bastard children.
41. **Lord of Session**. David Ross, Lord Ankerville. See Part Three for Biographical Note.

"Like lions breaking their chains…." So a British officer described the Highlanders of the Black Watch as they attacked through the *abattis* and fortifications near Fort Ticonderoga on Lake Champlain in July 1758. John Grant's regiment would suffer 65 per cent casualties in a single day's action, 649 men out of a total strength of about 1,000 all ranks, a loss unsurpassed by any regiment in 18th century North American history. Watercolour by C.C.P. Lawson and R.T. Cooper, executed c.1949. (Black Watch of Canada, Photo by P. Ferst)

Chapter 2 | Martinique and Guadeloupe, 1758–59 – Gone for a Soldier

While John Grant was recruiting his requisite amount of men to proudly take up his lieutenant's commission in the newly authorized 2nd Battalion of the Black Watch, the 1st Battalion, already serving in North America, was shot to pieces trying to storm the earthworks at Ticonderoga.[42] There were actually so many Black Watch officer and NCO casualties from this desperate battle at the head of Lake Champlain that the 42nd Regiment of Foot simply ceased to be an effective fighting formation.

"We had seven officers killed on the spot, and poor Major [Duncan] Campbell died since of his wounds," wrote a Grant officer. "Besides the killed, we had 19 officers wounded, 6 sergeants killed and 13 wounded, 4 drummers killed and 2 wounded, 186 rank and file killed and 263 wounded. Several have died since,

42. **Ticonderoga**. At that time, Fort Carillon.

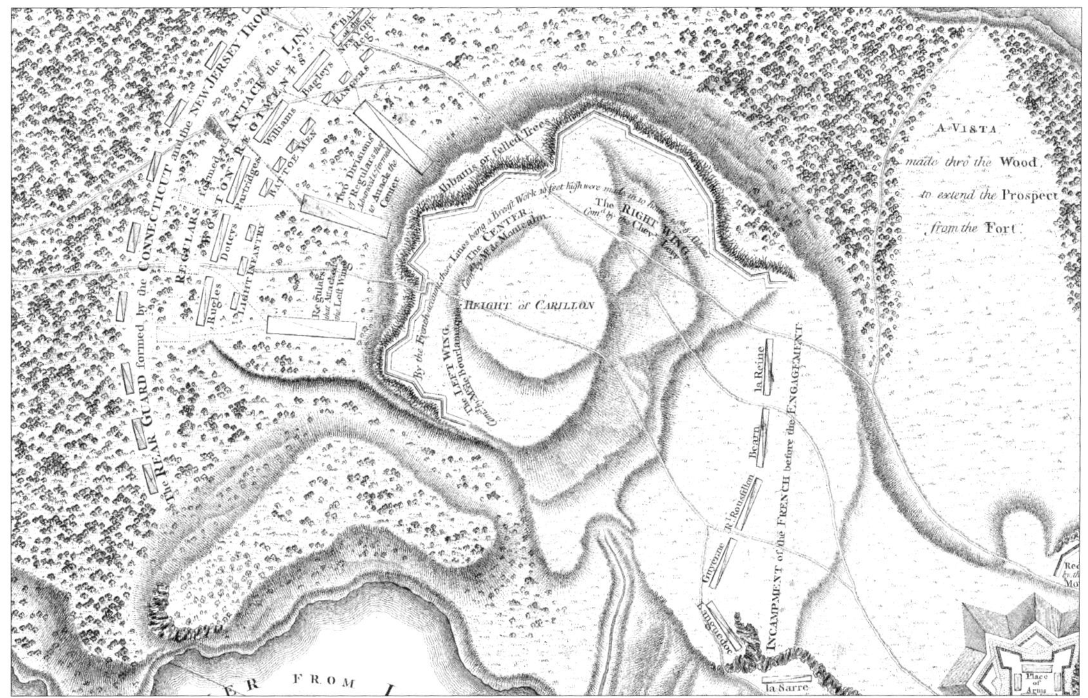

Desperate battle. At the battle of Ticonderoga (or Carillon, as the French victors called it) fought on 8 July 1758, only one British regiment – the Black Watch – penetrated the log and earthenwork defences of the French lines, built across the heights of Carillon like a giant inverted horseshoe. The penetration was made on the most northerly demi-lune at the top of the heavily entrenched position shown on map. (Detail showing the line of battle from "A Plan of the Town and Fort of Carillon at Ticonderoga..." published by Thomas Jefferys. LAC NMC 135020)

and are still dying of their wounds. How can we recruit, and when shall we have so fine a regiment again?"[43]

In fact, William Grant *Rothiemurchus'* plaintive question was already being addressed by the authorities back home. As the survivors of Ticonderoga sorted out their shattered companies and licked their wounds in America, their regimental colonel was completing the recruitment of the seven new Black Watch companies in the Highlands. These, when added to the three "Additional Companies" already serving in North America at Fort Edward, would form Lord John Murray's new 2nd Battalion.

Furthermore, King George II had gone one step further. On 22 July 1758 the monarch graciously bestowed "Royal" status upon his Old Highland Regiment, well before the disastrous news of the defeat at Ticonderoga reached

43. **Casualties**. Lieutenant William Grant, "Copy of a letter from North America," *The Scots Magazine*, vol 20, 698-99, quoted in Frederick B. Richards, *The Black Watch at Ticonderoga* (Glen Falls, 1920), 22-3.

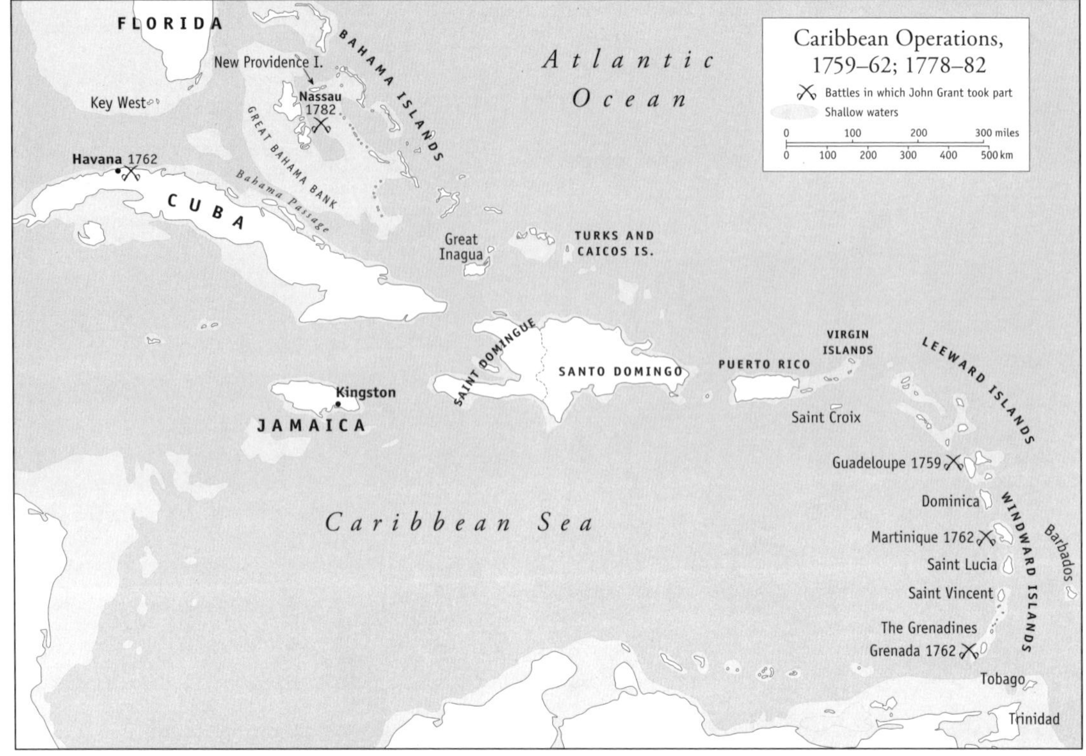

The southern cockpit of war. (Map: Robin Brass Studio)

London. His special warrant claimed that he was "desirous to distinguish Our said 42nd Regiment of Foot with some Mark of Royal Favour," and directed that "from henceforth our said Regiment be call'd and distinguished by the title and name of our 42nd or Royal Highland Regiment of Foot...."[44]

With such an honour, the regiment was authorized to change its regimental colours, facings, collars, cuffs and drums from buff to royal blue. While the 1st Battalion was no doubt pleased to receive this news, it was preoccupied in seeing to its wounded and in promoting junior officers, volunteers and NCOs to fill the vacant leadership posts that were crucial to getting the battalion back on its feet. The 1st/42nd Foot would move down to New York to reorganize, re-equip and rebuild over the winter, many of their wounded sent to the Jerseys to recuperate. Those unfit for further service were invalided home to Chelsea as soon as they could travel.

---

44. **Royal Highland Regiment.** TNA WO 26/23, p. 418. It was the King's "further will and Pleasure" that, with the further increase of seven companies (and the three Additional Companies already in North America), the regiment should be formed into two battalions to consist of ten companies each. It is not clear why the title "Royal" was given at this time. The Royal Archives, Windsor, hold archives only from the reign of George III in 1760 onwards.

Heart of oak, disease of kings. Commodore John Moore (1718-79) was appointed to his new post as commander in chief on the Leeward Islands Station in 1758 and after the successful capture of Guadeloupe, 1759, was promoted rear admiral for his efforts. Shown here later in his career as a baronet and Admiral of the Blue, he succumbed to a lifelong battle with gout in 1779. (Engraved by William Ridley from a painting in the possession of the Rev. James Stanier Clarke, domestic chaplain and librarian to the Prince of Wales (later George IV). Private Collection)

Originally the new 2nd Battalion of the Royal Highlanders was earmarked as a reinforcement for Jeffery Amherst's army in North America, but by the end of November 1758 the operational picture had changed. Their manpower was urgently needed to boost Major General Peregrine Thomas Hopson's expedition to seize the French sugar islands of Martinique and Guadeloupe. Owing to a shortage of transports, however, only 200 Highlanders could be dispatched immediately, so John Grant's company and another marched to Greenock and embarked for duty in the West Indies and their first baptism of fire.

By New Year's Day 1759, a substantial task force commanded by Major General Peregrine Hopson had assembled at Carlisle Bay in Barbados,[45] the rendezvous and assembly point for the expedition. The force comprised the 3rd, 4th, 61st, 63rd, 64th and 65th Regiments of Foot, a detachment of the 38th Foot from Antigua, a battalion of Marines and 500 artillerymen, for a total of some 6,800 men aboard 64 transports. There were eight ships of the line, a frigate, four bomb ketches and a hospital ship, making for an impressive fleet of eighty sail under the command of Commodore John Moore[46] of the Royal Navy.

---

45. **Carlisle Bay, Barbados**. A small natural harbour located in the southwest quarter of the island of Barbados, on which the island's capital, Bridgetown, is situated. The bay takes its name from Barbados' second Lord Proprietor, James Hay, 1st Earl of Carlisle. Barbados, settled by England in the 1620s, sits in the Atlantic Ocean, east of the other West Indies Islands and is the easternmost island in the Lesser Antilles.
46. **Commodore John Moore**. Royal Navy officer. Educated at the Whitchurch grammar school in Shropshire, he went to sea at the age of eleven, passing his lieutenant's examination on 6 April 1738. Enjoying the patronage of important relatives throughout his career, he was appointed to command the new frigate HMS *Diamond* (40 guns) on 24 December 1743. In 1747 he was appointed to HMS *Devonshire* (74 guns) then serving as the flagship of Rear Admiral Edward Hawke, seeing action at the Second Battle of Cape Finisterre. As a reward for his services, he was entrusted with taking dispatches back to Britain, Hawke writing, "I have sent this express by Captain Moore of the Devonshire.... It would be doing great injustice to merit not to say that he signalized himself greatly in the action." His next appointment was as commodore of the British Leeward Island's Squadron during the Martinique and Guadeloupe campaigns in 1759. Promoted to rear admiral in 1762, spending the rest of the war as commander in chief, The Downs. Appointed commander in chief,

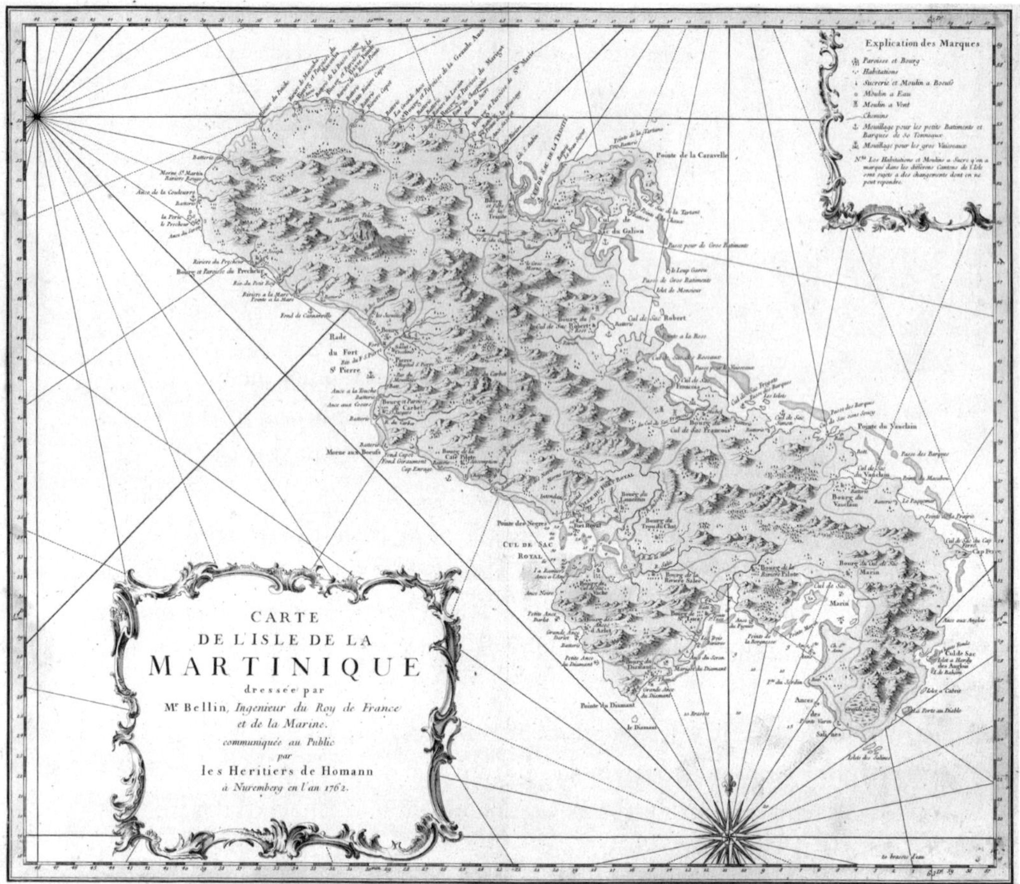

Martinique. "Carte de L'Isle de la Martinique dressée par Mr. [Jacques Nicolas] Bellin, Ingenieur du Roy de France et de la Marine. Communiquée au Public par les Heritiers de Homann à Nuremberg en l'an 1762." (JCB 30614)

The five companies of the 2nd/42nd that had left Scotland *after* John Grant's departure actually made it to Barbados first, arriving on 12 January, only to be ordered to remain on board, as the entire fleet would sail the next day. They were designated as an independent force or reserve. They also met their commanding officer for the duration of the expedition, one Captain Charles Anstruther of the 26th Foot, an officer on Hopson's staff and handpicked by William Pitt. The latter's particular instructions to General Hopson were: "Captain

Portsmouth in 1766, holding that post for three years. Created a baronet on 4 March 1766. A series of promotions followed, based upon his seniority within the service: vice admiral in 1770; a Knight Companion of the Order of the Bath that same year; and admiral in 1778. Suffered from gout since the 1760s, his health steadily declining. The attacks becoming violent by 1777, he died on 2 February 1779. The temporary rank "commodore" was typically used in referring to a senior officer (if not an admiral) in command of a detached squadron and ranked with an army brigadier.

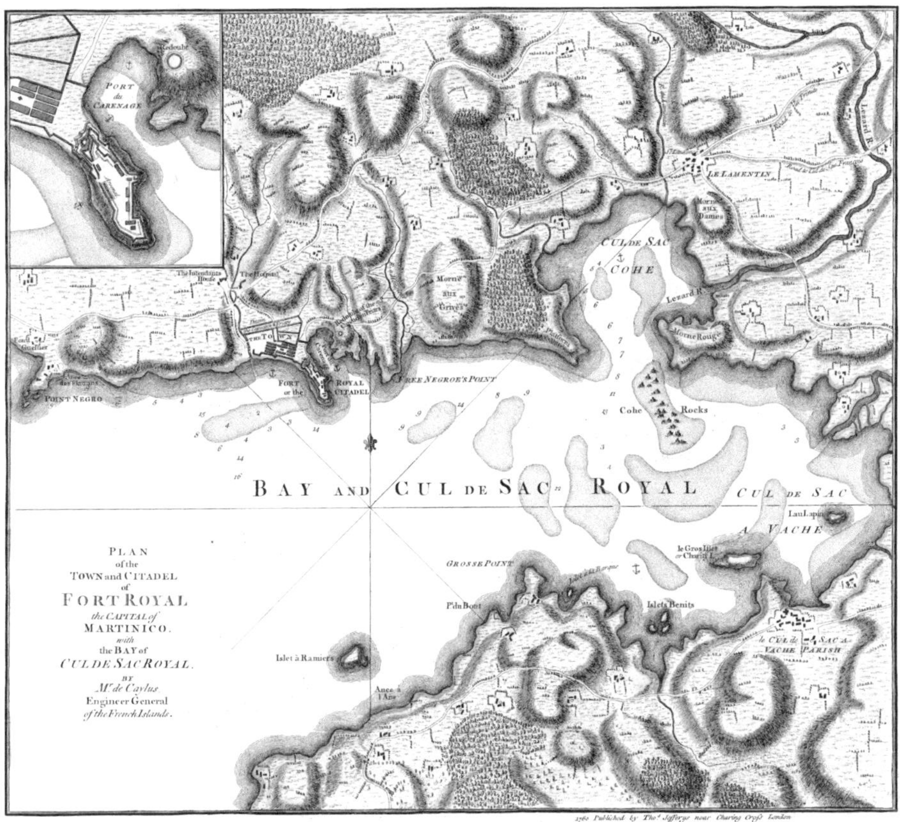

Fort Royal, Martinique. "Plan of the Town and Citadel of Fort Royal the capital of Martinico with the Bay of Cul de Sac Royal" drawn by Anne Claude Philippe Caylus, engineer general of the French Islands. Published by Thomas Jefferys, 1760. (JCB C-7544)

Anstruther, who is already with you, is to command these Seven Companies of Highlanders, with the rank of Major, and a Brevet for that purpose will be sent to Him by the first opportunity."[47]

On the morning of 13 January 1759 the whole force sailed from Carlisle Bay and two days later was greeted by the sight of the dusky-blue volcanic peaks of the island of Martinique poking up over the horizon. They soon bore down on Fort Royal Bay, a large harbour that could easily shelter the entire Royal Navy, even from hurricanes. The island's sharp volcanic crags and 300-foot (91 m) lava cliffs were unlike anything the Highlanders had ever seen and the sailors regaled the soldiers with tales of its rugged coast lined with dangerous coral reefs and shoals. Officers using spyglasses could see thorn and cactus forests on the

---

47. **Pitt's instructions**. William Pitt to Peregrine Hopson, 30 November 1758, Whitehall. *Correspondence of William Pitt ... with Colonial Governors and Military and Naval Commanders in America*, Gertrude S. Kimball, ed. (New York, 1906), vol 1, 412.

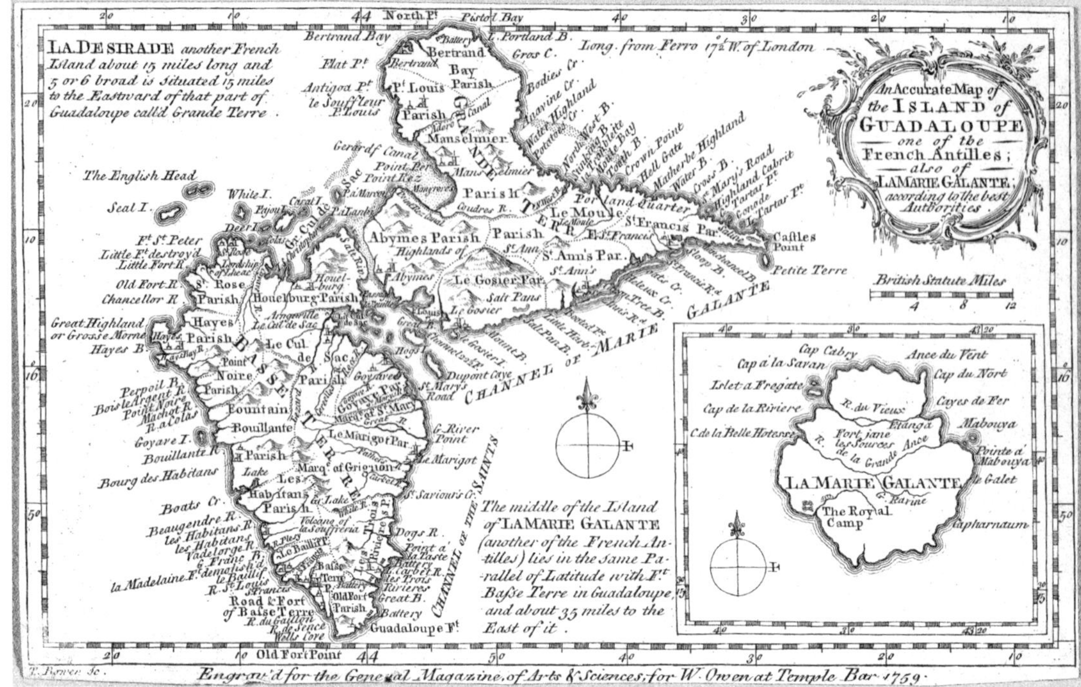

Guadeloupe. "An Accurate Map of the Island of Guadaloupe [*sic*] one of the French Antilles; also of La Marie Galante; according to the best Authorities" engraved by Thomas Bowen and published in 1759. (JCB 9012-3)

rocky ledges, small waterfalls cascading from black fissures in the rock, and river mouths that appeared choked with lush tropical vegetation, fronted by vast mangrove swamps or shielded by salt grass beaches.

The fleet hove to outside the bay for the night. Next day, British ships of the line sailed into Fort Royal Bay and speedily silenced Fort Negro, situated 2 miles (3.2 km) along the shore northwest of the citadel of Fort Royal.[48] A battery at Case des Navires was dealt with next and by midday of 16 January 1759 all British troopships were anchored in Case des Navires Bay.

Faced with the firepower of the British, some concerned citizens of Martinique had been considering sending deputies to the British commander to treat for surrender terms. They need not have worried. The guns of Fort Royal, particularly the westernmost battery, had to be silenced before any further progress could be made by Hopson's army. The British soon perceived that they would be unable to get heavy siege cannon up the slopes of Morne Tartenson and onto the top of the craggy ridge. They also saw difficulties in protecting the long sup-

48. **Fort Royal.** A Vauban-style fortress built in 1669 on the site of an earlier fort that protected a deep and well sheltered bay on the west side of the island. The fort's land approaches were defended by two fortified hills, Morne Tartenson and Morne Garnier.

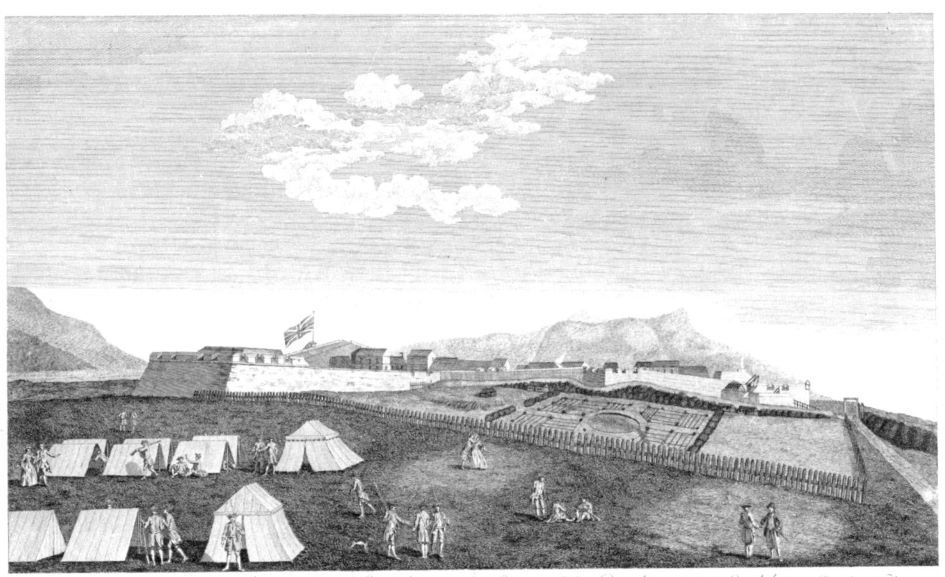

Fort Royal, Guadeloupe. "A North View of Fort Royal in the Island of Guadaloupe [*sic*], when in Possession of his Majesty's Forces in 1759" drawn "on the spot" by British engineer Lieutenant Archibald Campbell. Engraved by Charles Grignion and published by Thomas Jefferys in 1764. (JCB 32917)

ply lines necessary to support the artillery once they had fought their way up there.

"Never was such a country," a journal claimed. "The Highlands of Scotland for woods, mountains, and continued ravines are nothing to it." A discouraged and unnerved General Hopson ordered his troops ashore to fall back late on the afternoon of 17 January to re-embark with the rest of his force. The septuagenarian general was going to abandon the assault on Martinique.[49]

A joint council of war aboard decided to attempt the conquest of the islands of Guadeloupe, which were both richer and more lightly defended. The population there numbered about 2,000 Europeans and 30,000 Negro slaves. Guadeloupe was, in fact, an archipelago of six islands. The largest group consisted of two large islands resembling the wings of a butterfly separated in the middle by mangrove swamps and a brackish, saltwater river. The western half was called Basse Terre, French for "lower land," but it was a steep volcanic island.

49. **Wild terrain**. "Journal of an Officer," Peregrine Hopson to William Pitt, Basse Terre, Guadeloupe, 30 January 1759; William Pitt to Peregrine Hopson, 30 November 1758, Whitehall, *Correspondence of William Pitt ... with Colonial Governors and Military and Naval Commanders in America*, Gertrude S. Kimball, ed. (New York, 1906), vol II, 27-9.

The principal town of Basse Terre was situated on the island's southwest corner. The eastern half of Guadeloupe was called Grand Terre ("great" or "large land") and was composed of limestone instead of lava and dotted with flat, rich alluvial plains planted with tobacco, cotton and sugar. Isles des Santes, Marie Galante, Petite Terre and Désirade made up the rest of the archipelago.

On 23 January 1759 the British fleet of warships and troop transports, including the five re-embarked companies of the 2nd/42nd, appeared off Basse Terre, which was guarded by a small citadel, also named Fort Royal, built just south of Basse Terre on a small eminence. The ships of war stood in and opened fire on the citadel and other fortifications until nightfall. Around 10 p.m. the bomb vessels, which were lobbing large incendiary devices known as "carcasses" into the town, set alight one of the warehouses packed with rum, sugar and tar, which went up like a tinderbox. Flames soon engulfed most of the town and lit up the harbour and countryside for miles around. At 11 p.m. a powder magazine blew up, causing a spectacular fireworks display. At daybreak on 24 January the town was still burning fiercely and it was not until 1:30 p.m. that the British troops were ordered ashore.

The Highlanders of John Grant's regiment were the last contingent to land and marched into the smoking ruins of the town. They found "a miserable spectacle ... the earth ploughed by shells." By 5 p.m. all French defences had been abandoned. The town's garrison of regular troops had withdrawn 6 miles (10 km) inland, where they now armed plantation slaves and prepared to wage guerrilla warfare. The British entrenched camps on the hills of the town's perimeter to protect their new prize from the guerrilla forces now lurking about the countryside. Fortifications were repaired, guns unspiked and remounted, and new redoubts constructed. By the end of the week ashore, however, General Hopson's unseasoned troops began to sicken and die at an alarming rate.

Meanwhile, Brigadier General John Clavering had been detached with a small force to seize the island of Dominica[50] and, while en route, encountered the two errant companies of the 42nd, including John Grant's. The Highlander's little transport had first gone to Barbados, only to find that Hopson's force had sailed for Martinique without them. Clavering ordered them to heave to and for their company commanders to repair on board for orders. Having witnessed the aggressive utility of the hardy mountain men at the Fort Royal Bay landings at Martinique, Clavering was interested in adding the 200 men to his small force but soon discovered that the Highlanders had not yet received their muskets and were only armed with their broadswords and dirks. The brigadier

50. **Dominica.** An island in the Lesser Antilles region of the Caribbean Sea, south-southeast of Guadeloupe and northwest of Martinique. Its area is 290 square miles (750 square km) and its capital is Roseau, on the southwestern side of the island.

The Understudy. Major General John Barrington (1722-64) was appointed second in command with the local rank of major general to Major General Peregrine Thomas Hopson commanding an expedition against the French West Indies. Following Hopson's sudden death in February 1759 at Guadeloupe, command devolved on Barrington, who concluded the capture of the island successfully. (Oil on canvas by Sir Joshua Reynolds, c.1757. National Army Museum 1959-11-22-1. Editors' photo)

directed the Highlanders to continue onwards to Guadeloupe to be reunited with their comrades and carried on his way to Dominica.

Lieutenant John Grant and his company arrived too late to take part in the capture of Basse Terre in early February 1760 and they were kept aboard their transport due to the rampant sickness ashore. Assigned a few days later to a marine force dispatched to seize Fort Louis on the other side of the island, Grant and his men remained afloat yet another week while the Royal Navy sounded and charted the waters to find the best approaches to bombard the French fortifications. After the successful Valentine's Day assault on Fort Louis, John Grant and the two companies of Highlanders remained there with the Marine battalion for about six weeks during, which time John Grant came down with fever.

Back at Basse Terre, his countrymen were faring no better. Two weeks after Grant's company had gone ashore under fire at Fort Louis, General Hopson died on 27 February and command of the expedition passed to the Honourable Major General John Barrington,[51] an experienced, dynamic and much younger officer. Once the defences of Basse Terre were in good order, Barrington left the 63rd Foot to defend it while he shifted his focus of operations to Fort Louis on Grand Terre.

51. **Major General John Barrington** (1722-64). British army officer and colonial governor. Third son of John, 1st Viscount Barrington of Ardglass; younger brother of William, 2nd Viscount Barrington, the Secretary at War. John was commissioned into the 3rd Foot Guards in 1739 and transferred to the 2nd Foot Guards in 1746. In 1756 he was promoted colonel and appointed royal aide de camp to George II. On the formation of the 64th Foot in 1758, Barrington became its colonel and was appointed second-in-command with the local rank of major general to Major General Peregrine Hopson commanding an expedition against the French West Indies. Following Hopson's sudden death in February 1759 at Guadeloupe, command devolved on Barrington. In June 1759 he was made colonel to the 40th Foot, and in October of that same year colonel to the more senior 8th Foot. Died in Paris, 2 April 1764.

On 11 March 1759, after five days of wearily beating against the trade winds,[52] about half of Barrington's ships came to anchor before Fort Louis and the two Highland companies already there were overjoyed to see their comrades disembark and make camp alongside them. Barrington then learned that a French squadron had been sighted northward of Barbados and that Commodore Moore felt duty bound to fall back with his own squadron to Prince Rupert's Bay, Dominica, to cover the newly-captured Basse Terre as well as the British Leeward Islands.

Barrington agreed and, left alone with only his transports, decided to risk using them without warship protection to descend upon the various island settlements dotting the coastline of Grand Terre. While he could not starve the populace into submission, he reasoned he could certainly hurt the island's ruling elite in their pocket books by destroying their cash crops as well as burning their warehouses, curing sheds and sugar shacks. Most of the cultivated land in such mountainous terrain lay in the few river valleys that opened onto the sea. Here, the small settlements were clustered, connected by roads that followed the coastline. The French had raised an abundance of batteries guarding the key points of access but they could not man them all. By contrast, Barrington had the advantage of surprise and the ability to concentrate his forces quickly at a single point of attack anywhere along the coast and thus mounted a series of hit and run raids.

Once most of Grand Terre was burning, Barrington decided to shift his new brand of amphibious warfare to the western island. On 12 April Brigadier Clavering, with 1,300 men (including the 2nd/42nd) supported by six field guns, landed unopposed in a bay close to Arnouville. The French retired north to a strong position behind the river Licorne, vital ground to them because it covered Baie la Mahault, the principal port through which the island received its provisions from the Dutch island of Eustatia.[53]

These river defences were so naturally strong that they needed little defensive improvements to render them virtually impregnable. Access to the river mouth itself was barred by a mangrove swamp, across which there were two narrow approaches, both covered by redoubts, entrenched batteries, palisaded entrenchments and enfilading cannon. Undaunted, Clavering was determined to attack.

---

52. **Trade winds**. The prevailing pattern of easterly surface winds found in the tropics near the Earth's equator. In the Northern hemisphere, the trade winds blow predominantly from the northeast. The term derives from the early 14th-century late Middle English word "trade," meaning "path" or "track."

53. **Eustatia** or **Sint Eustatius**. Part of the Caribbean Netherlands, lying in the northern Leeward Islands portion of the West Indies, southeast of the Virgin Islands. The name of the island, "Sint Eustatius," is the Dutch name for Saint Eustace, a legendary Christian martyr, known in Spanish as *San Eustaquio* and in Portuguese *as Santo Eustácio.*

"We had seen from the ships in the morning large bodies of people moving about the Works, and we expected warm work," wrote John Grant before their landing, the first time all seven companies of the Royal Highlanders had fought together as a battalion.

An unidentified officer corroborates Grant's version that the Highlanders did not even bother firing their muskets but "drew their swords, and, supported by a part of the other regiment, rushed forward with their characteristic impetuosity, and followed the enemy into the redoubt, of which they took possession."[54] Pushing around to the rear of the entrenchments on the French right, the Highlanders forced the enemy to evacuate them also, and captured seventy prisoners. Casualties for the Royal Highlanders in this action were: Ensign William MacLean and thirteen men killed; Lieutenants George Sinclair and John Robertson wounded, as well as fifty-two rank and file.

The French then retreated southward, setting fire to the cane-fields as they went to delay any pursuit, and took post behind the river Lézarde, breaking down the bridge behind them. It was too late in the afternoon for Clavering to attempt an assault crossing that day, the only ford across the river being covered by the fire of an earthwork redoubt mounting four guns. The Royal Artillery, however, kept up their fire all night to distract the enemy. In the darkness, Clavering sent his light infantry in boats across the river below the position of the French, who no sooner saw their right flank turned in the dawn than they retired hastily, abandoning all their guns.

The French retreated southward to their next line of defence at Petit Bourg,[55] where they had prepared more entrenchments and armed redoubts, but an anchored British bomb vessel, HMS *Grenada,* was waiting for them, its targets already accurately ranged. When the French appeared, *Grenada* lobbed shells into the identified positions. The French were yet again forced to hastily abandon their positions, including their guns.

The next day, Grant and his company were ordered with a company of the 3rd Foot (the Buffs)[56] to garrison Petit Bourg as well as a neighbouring redoubt. The French defenders of the island by now had become thoroughly disheartened as position after fortified position was flanked and turned by the British. They sued for terms and a capitulation was granted on very liberal conditions. Guadeloupe, one of the wealthiest colonies of the Antilles, passed into the possession of the British Crown.

---

54. **Highland charge**. Anonymous, "Letter from Guadeloupe." *Sketches*, I, 319.
55. **Petit Bourg**. A small town on the east side of the island of Basse Terre near the mouth of the Lezarde River.
56. **"The Buffs."** Nickname given to the 3rd Regiment of Foot because of the buff facings and cuffs of their uniforms.

The timing of the capitulation was fortuitous, for with the ink of the signatures hardly dry, news came of a force of 600 French regular troops and 2,000 buccaneers coming from Martinique to support the Guadeloupians. Had they arrived a day or two earlier, this reinforcement would probably have steeled the inhabitants' resolve to carry on the struggle, but the latter had been given good terms and were unwilling to take up arms again. The French commander, on hearing of their capitulation and desire for peace, re-embarked his troops and sailed away back to Martinique.

Nothing remained for Barrington to do but to settle the administration of the captured islands and to leave sufficient garrisons to hold them. The 4th, 63rd and 65th Regiments of Foot were tapped for this task, while the 38th Foot detachment returned to its old quarters in the Leeward Islands. Barrington, with the remnants of the 3rd (Buffs), 61st and 64th Regiments, returned to England. So ended the 1759 campaign of Martinique and Guadeloupe.

Ironically, the two units suffering the highest combat casualties of the West Indian campaign were the two smallest: the detachment of the 38th Foot from the Leeward Islands; and the 2nd/42nd. One historian deemed "the levy of death on the Forty-Second" to be "the penalty of merit," as "these rugged hardy youngsters of a shiny new battalion were sent in wherever there was a particularly rough job to do." Lieutenant John Grant and his young Highlanders would probably have concurred.[57]

* * *

It was now necessary to decide on a profession and like most of my countrymen I chose the Army and my friends obtain'd for me a Lieutenancy of the Highland Watch under condition of raising 25 men. Before that I had an offer of a commission in the Companies service at Calcutta [The Honourable East India Company's Army], but my friends rejected the proposal as it was then considered rather an adventure. Didn't I have cause to regret it.

Recruiting was somewhat difficult. I first got a good piper and then 4 young men [who were] good dancers, [and] established myself at an ale House. My "sergeant kite"[58] made a flowerly [*sic*, flowery] harangue [speech], extolled the Regiment &c. [and] then commenced dancing, sometimes even on the plain stones. This collected a crowd & drink was not scarce. Mariners were more fa-

57. **Casualties.** Once 700 men strong, the 2nd Battalion had suffered 193 other ranks killed, died of fever or wounded on their first campaign. One quarter of the battalion officers were combat casualties (two killed, one dead of fever and five wounded) and all the others were recovering from various bouts of fever and dysentery, including the hero of our tale, John Grant.

58. **Sergeant Kite.** A character in the 1706 play "The Recruiting Officer" by Irish playwright George Farquhar.

A brother officer. Captain John Campbell *Melfort*, 42nd Foot, wears the same dress uniform (c.1763) that John Grant would have worn at the end of the Seven Years' War with royal blue facings edged with gold lace on the lapels and cuffs. The head-dress is a large blue woolen tam with a red band, and a black ostrich feather worn as a large hackle on the left side of the head. These black feathers would evolve into the iconic feather bonnets worn by some of Scotland's most famous regiments during the nineteenth century. (Oil on canvas by an anonymous artist. BWCM, Editors' photo)

Gorget. Worn by all Georgian army officers, the gorget was the last vestige of medieval neck armour, reduced to a small engraved crescent of gilded brass or silver bearing the King's royal cypher and the regimental number. It was worn suspended below the throat (*gorge* in French, hence gorget) with a ribbon of the regiment's facing colour. By the mid-18th century it had become a ceremonial symbol denoting an officer. In the North American and Caribbean campaigns, Black Watch officers and other veterans of the "American Army" quickly learned to remove all telltale signs such as sashes, gorgets and gold lace that identified them as officers to enemy sharpshooters. John Grant wrote: "We were equipped in jackets without lace made to resemble [the] soldiers', with a haversack with provisions on one side and a canteen of liquor on the other. Our few change of shirts &c. wrapped in our plaid which was wound round our chest." (Dmitry Zhukov-Gelfand)

miliar [*sic*, friendly], mixed among the people at Strathspey & Inverness, Insch[59] and Keith.

I soon completed my number and **26** set out for Perth in September [1758]. Recruiting in those days [was] not without danger. At a Market in Tomintoul,[60] [I] enlisted a man, [his] friends formed a party – wished to rescue him. [We] barricaded [the] door – [they] attempted to unthatch the House.

59. **Insch** (Gaelic: *An Innis or Innis Mo Bheathain* meaning island). A village in Aberdeenshire, Scotland, approximately 28 miles (45 km) northwest of the city of Aberdeen on the road to Inverness.
60. **Tomintoul** (Gaelic: *Tom an t-Sabhail*, meaning Hillock of the Barn). Tomintoul was a small village in John Grant's day on the military road leading south from Strathspey through the Cairngorm Mountains to Perth. Improved by Alexander Gordon, 4th Duke of Gordon (1743-1827) in 1775.

"Give me a cockade"[61] said the man, "and let us go out."

Went out [and the] mob surrounded [us]. [I was] obliged to draw a sword [and] would have been roughly handled but [the] other recruit parties came to [our] assistance. A Gentleman came up [and] said: "Young man (I was only 17), take my advice and don't remain here. The man's friends are all Romans and but a wild set." Took [his] advice [and] left [the] place. I got 3 Guineas for each recruit and the Bounty was a Guinea and a Crown.

We reached Perth by the Highland road. Lord John Murray was the Colonel. **Our dress was a red coat turned up with blue, laced button holes, blue waistcoats.[62] The belted plaid, which was passed round the body, [was] pleated behind [and] kept up with a belt – the remainder was pinned to the left shoulder. A Bonnet with a small black ostrich feather from the side for a cockade. Hose, shoes and buckles [and] a purse. Broadsword [and] Dirk attached to [the] belt that held [the] kilt. One pistol [held] by a small belt on the left breast, [the] other attached to sword belt.**

Perth was then a large town and gay. They were accused of being Zealous Jacobites – certainly they did not like us. Nine of us lived together and coming home one night, the butchers set their dogs upon us. We were armed and [the] dogs suffer'd a good deal. We had other rows chiefly arising from drinking, much then in fashion, when Claret could be got for one shilling a bottle. Port was not used except as a medicine. Plenty of Balls. Our men had arms, were merely taught to march.[63]

I recollect a story of English ignorance and pride amongst us happening
27 when I was there. An Englishman arrived there – asked [the] Landlord of Municipal Inn what he had for dinner.

Landlord – "What would you like?"

"Oh, give me all you have" with a sneer.

Landlord was a very good cook, famous for confections and had a good Larder. [He] placed a most sumptuous dinner on [the] table. [The] traveller stared.

Landlord – "You order'd everything."

Bill presented next day, 20 £. [The Englishman] refused to pay. [He was]

61. **Cockade.** A rosette or knot of ribbon worn on the hat as a badge. The use of cockades as marks of military distinction became very general about the beginning of the 18th century, particularly in France and Britain, where "to mount the cockade" was synonymous with becoming a soldier.

62. **Highland dress.** The sentences concerning dress, originally appearing on folio page 27, were placed here to be more chronologically consistent with the narrative. For a complete description of all aspects of a Black Watch officer's uniform and his equipment of the period, see Part Two "Dress, Weapons, Equipment & Specialties," *SOTM*, II, 113-49.

63. **Editors' note.** By "arms" John Grant meant swords, dirks and pistols, for as he reveals later on in his memoirs, muskets were not issued to the men until they were in theatre.

brought before [the] Magistrates [and] forced to pay. I'll mark the Englishman know[s] that Johnstown can turn out a good dinner.

After a short time at Perth we marched & formed the 2nd Battalion of [the] 42nd [Highland] Regiment. Arrived at Glasgow, remained a month there, well received by the Inhabitants. Glasgow was then just rising into commercial importance but was small in comparison to its present size. However, cold punch from the produce of their wee beet fields 28 against the water.[64] We had all the honour of being made Burgesses.

Marched to Greenock and embarked the 19th November 1758 on board transports which had been sent round from England. Being this [my] first essay,[65] I was dreadfully seasick. The Hills of Argyllshire[66] were in view, cover'd with snow. I would have given the world to have been on the top, they would not have caught me.

After 7 or 8 days [I] got well. [The sea] was dreadfully rough in [the] Irish Channel. Soldiers very sick. Seamen ignorant. We managed to part convoy on the Bay of Biscay in a gale of wind of 14 days when we could not light a fire. At last [we] got into the trade winds, but before that [we] had four days of terrible rolling. On the passage, by mismanagement, we exhausted our sea stock about half the passage and were obliged to live on our rations – poor food in approaching the tropics.[67]

In 10 weeks our Port was Barbados but our reckoning was out 5 weeks before we reached it. Not knowing our situation, the evening before we reach'd Carlisle Bay, we saw a light in a different direction from what we were going. Anxious to hail any vessel that might let us know where we were, we put about and made all sail after it. Went on for several hours but [we] did not come nearer to it. At last, daylight broke and we found ourselves almost among the vessels in Carlisle Bay.

It was a curious circumstance – no vessel had arrived that morning. Had we

---

64. **Wee beet fields**. The Scots and Irish made moonshine from potatoes and sugar beets, the Irish calling it *poteen* (or *poitín*). Meaning "little pot," the spirit's name refers to the tiny, home-made stills in which it is normally produced. Here John Grant is referring to cold punch made with "poteen" (the produce of the wee beet fields) as opposed to a rum punch that was usually heated.

65. **Essay**. Derives from the French verb *essayer*, which means "to try." John Grant uses this word in a number of other locations in his narrative.

66. **Argyllshire**. A maritime county in the west of Scotland bounded on the north by Inverness-shire, on the east by the counties of Inverness, Perth and Dumbarton, and on the south and west by the Firth of Clyde and the Atlantic Ocean. It is about 115 miles (185 km) in extreme length and about 55 miles (89 km) in average breadth, comprising an area of about 3,800 square miles (9,842 square km).

67. **Editors' note**. This sentence concerning rations during the voyage, originally appearing on folio page 30, was placed here to be more chronologically consistent with the narrative.

Rendezvous. "A Prospect of Bridge Town in Barbados, 1695, by Samuel Copen" shows a thriving harbour, underlining the importance and extent of the prosperous sugar industry in Barbados, already well established before the outbreak of the Seven Years' War. Sugar cane was introduced by Dutch Jewish merchants in the mid-17th century and it quickly replaced Barbados's staple crops of tobacco and cotton. Irrigation of cane fields thus became top priority, and by 1700 Barbados had built so many windmills to this end that the island had the second highest density of windmills per square mile in the world, second only to the Netherlands. (LOC 3c24469u)

held our first course we should have made the coast of South America before any other. 29 We had been reported as lost, and found all our Comrades were at Guadeloupe. Whether [the light was] supernatural or not, the Sailors thought it so – but it saved us.

Much struck on landing at Bridgetown, with the number of emaciated looking whites and the wretched looking negroes, gave no favourable impression to newcomers.[68] But our landing from ships made us view it with a more favourable eye. Made ourselves acquainted with the oranges, pineapples and shaddocks and considered the beauty of the tall coconut trees and spreading tamarinds. Carlisle Bay affords fine anchorage.

Bridgetown, the capital, is on the shores of the Bay. The Island is low but rich in the extreme. It was a most pleasant place, here formed of small properties. At that time there was a most general intercourse. The third day after our arrival,

---

68. **Editors' note**. This paragraph, originally appearing in one of the four loose quarto sheets, was placed here in the narrative. These loose sheets contain several anecdotes, some marked by John Grant's grandson, John Johnson Jr., with a folio page number to remind himself where to insert them in his next, more polished draft of his grandfather's memoirs.

walking with a friend, a well-dressed gentlemanly man came from a neat house. [He] stopped us [and] said, "You are encroaching on my property and are my prisoners."

We stared & said [we] thought it had been the Highroad.

"No, you must be my prisoners until such an hour – in plain English you must take a share of my family dinner." We did so. Found a fine family [and] spent a pleasant day. It was hot but not unpleasant. From 4 'till 8 in p.m. was very warm – then came [the] sea breeze [known as] the Doctor[69] [*sic*] and was quite cool. [We] received great hospitality.

After a week we sailed to join the Army at Guadeloupe. But on our way we fell in with 2 line-of-battle ships[70] and 2 Gunships with a detachment of Marines on board under Brigadier General Clavering destined to make a decent on Dominica. He made us join him.

But from some reason or other, he changed his mind. He [first] called our

---

69. **The Doctor.** The name used in many countries for the cooling sea breeze that relieves the stifling (and unhealthy) heat of the day, thus the name, "The Doctor" (conversely, a land breeze is sometimes called "The Undertaker"). Sea breezes are the result of differential heating of the land and the sea. Given the sometimes telegraphic shorthand that John Johnson Jr. utilizes throughout the unfinished manuscript, the editors believe that this is a note he left for himself (underlined) in order to remember to include a more detailed description of this phenomenon in a more polished future draft.

70. **Line-of-battle ship**. A contraction of "ship-of-the-line-of-battle," a warship armed powerfully enough to fight in the *line of battle*, usually having cannons ranged along two or more decks. From the 17th through to the mid-18th century, the *line of battle* was a naval tactic in which two columns of opposing warships would manoeuvre to bring the greatest weight of broadside firepower to bear. By 1755 the Royal Navy no longer considered 50-gun ships powerful enough to serve as ships of the line. HMS *Victory*, in dry dock in Portsmouth Harbour, is the only surviving example of a ship of the line.

two Captains on board, and said: "Gentleman, I could not bear a Scotch talk lately for I got so many wounds from the Highlanders at Prestonpans[71] that I could not bear them. But now I have changed my mind and [I] would 30 command them sooner than other people, so I order you to join me." We had two Captains, 4 Lieutenants, 2 ensigns and 200 men. Brigadier Clavering however changed his mind [and] left us.[72]

[We were] order'd to attack Grand Terre and Fort Louis.[73] We entered the Bay and remained there for a week after sounding[74] and finding water enough. Captain Lynn[75] of the *Roebuck*[76] went in to attack a Battery of 48 pounders[77] *a fleur d'eau*.[78] He got within 150 yards of it and in less than 40 minutes not a stone was standing. The two line-of-battle ships battered the fort which was 200 yards from the shore. [They] soon silenced and dismantled it, we were only mere spectators.

As soon as that was done, we and the Marines were order'd into flat bottomed boats[79] to land and take possession. We set off. There were some French,

---

71. **Prestonpans**. A small town east of Edinburgh founded in the 11th century and where the first significant battle in the Jacobite Rising of 1745 took place on 21 September 1745. The Jacobite army, led by Charles Edward Stuart, defeated George II's army, led by Sir John Cope. The inexperienced government troops were outflanked then routed by a determined Highland charge.
72. **Editors' note**. John Grant fails to mention here that the two Black Watch companies in question were not in possession of any firearms, nor trained in their use.
73. **Fort Louis**. A small Vauban-style masonry French fort built to protect the small bay known as Le Petit Cul-de-sac Marin situated between the south coast of Grand Terre and the east coast of Basse Terre near the mouth of the Salt River.
74. **Sounding**. The act of measuring the depth of an area of water by throwing a line with a leaden weight.
75. **Captain Thomas Lynn** (1715-81). Royal Navy officer. Commissioned a lieutenant in 1747, then promoted to commander and made post captain in 1756. He commanded the frigate HMS *Roebuck* (44 guns) from 1757 to 1760. Given command of a larger ship of the line, HMS *Chatham*, he was court martialled and reduced in seniority in 1763 for misconduct in the East Indies. Reinstated in 1766, Lynn's last sea command was HMS *Garland* (20 guns). He died in 1781.
76. **HMS *Roebuck***. A fifth-rate warship with a complement of 44 guns. Built in 1743, it saw service in the Mediterranean Sea and spent the last three years of its commission in the Caribbean under the command of Captain Thomas Lynn. Paid off in September 1759.
77. **48-pounder cannon**. About 1700 the French tried to mount extra-large 48-pounder cannon to the decks of warships. However, they proved too heavy and were relegated to the coastal forts.
78. ***À fleur d'eau***. A French naval gunnery expression meaning that the British gunners were skipping or ricocheting their round shot off the surface or the "flower" of the water."
79. **Flat bottomed boats**. The boats were of a novel construction, built at Portsmouth specifically for the West Indies expedition, "to be employed in landing troops on the enemy's coast ... they carry 63 men each, are rowed with 12 oars, and draw not above two feet [of] water." *Gentleman's Magazine*, 28 (1758), 243.

Landing craft. A scale model of a flat-bottomed landing craft, first used in the Americas by British troops conducting amphibious operations off the coasts of Martinique and Guadeloupe in early 1759. Later in the year, General Wolfe's infantry used them for their night descent of the Saint Lawrence River to surprise the French on the Heights of Abraham at Quebec. (National Army Museum 1961-07-180-1. Editors' photo)

about 400, who had returned into the ruined Battery as soon as the Ships, for fear of striking us, had ceased firing.

A marine who was sitting just before me was shot.[80] **He sprang up, fell back nearly knocking me down. I gave him a push [and] desir'd him to take care but a stream of blood soon undeceived me. He had been shot through the heart. I began to think matters were serious, but an accident occurr'd which even in our circumstances caused a laugh.**

The piper had been playing 'till the firing became heavy & many lay wounded. He gave up and put the pipes down without quite expressing the wind beneath his coat. A ball struck him between the pipes & flesh, he clapped his arms to his side & said, "Oh!" The same movement of course squeezed the remaining air out with a responsive groan.

They opened a fire upon us and Colonel Rycaut[81] order'd us back along-

80. **Editors' note.** The next two paragraphs, originally appearing on folio page 35, were placed here to be more chronologically consistent with the narrative.
81. **Lieutenant Colonel Edward Rycaut** (c.1715-63). British marine officer. Originally commissioned as a 2nd lieutenant in the 1st Marines on 25 November 1739, he was promoted to 1st lieutenant in 1741 and captain lieutenant that same year. He obtained his captaincy on 12 June 1742, going on half-pay when his regiment disbanded in 1748. He returned to active service as one of fifty company commanders of the Marines raised in 1755, his captain's commission dated 11 February 1755 (8th Company, Plymouth Division). He eventually reached the rank of brevet lieutenant colonel in the Marines on 19 October 1758. He

"Looked down upon by both Services." A modern reconstruction of Britain's sea soldiers c.1750, the Marines, before their Royal designation in 1802. John Grant called them "the worst troops in the service, looked down upon by both Services, without discipline & useless either on shore or at Sea." (Drawing by Victor Huen. Illustration from Field, *Britain's Sea Soldiers: a History of the Royal Marines*.... Editors' photo)

side [the transports]. The Commodore, Captain Harman,[82] no sooner alongside, than [*sic*] he called out: "Don't give the d[amne]d cowardly fellows a rope."

---

commanded the Marine detachment that formed part of Commodore Moore's expedition to take Guadeloupe in 1759. In 1761 he held the office of governor of Roattan Island, Honduras. He died at Piccadilly, London, on 8 July 1763.

82. **Captain William Harman** (c.1715-66). Royal Navy officer. Enlisted in the Royal Navy as a lieutenant in 1741, promoted to captain in 1746 (commanding HMS *Richmond*, 24 guns). Served at Louisbourg in 1758 (commanding HMS *Berwick*, 64 guns) and the West Indies in 1759.

Captain [WILLIAM] MURRAY[83] immediately got up in 31 the Boat and said, "Captain Harman, we are under command and were forced to obey, but rest assured you shall answer to me for the expression you have used."

"My dear Captain Murray, I beg a Thousand pardons. It was not you I meant, but our own fellows, the Marines."

Captain Murray was however so indignant that he order'd his boat to pull off – the others, ashamed, followed. Next we were landed and drove the French before us as the others had landed.

(I must mention a story of Highland fidelity when we were ordered to land. My faithful servant, who had enlisted merely to act as my servant, called me aside and said, "We are going to land John (such was the familiarity of servants in those days) and I trust you will behave yourself like a man and not disgrace your family – don't take amiss what I say. I do it as you are so young.")

When we were going on [the assault] the second time under a very heavy fire, having lost several killed and wounded, He stood up, although the rest sat, in order to show me an example. A ball happened to pass through his hat, he instantly presented [his musket] and fired. Captain Murray called out to cease firing, however, all in the boat followed his example. It had the good effect, for afterwards all the balls which before had fallen like hail, in a good measure ceased and the rest went over our heads.

32 Getting out of the Boat, I stumbled over a stone and fell forward into the water. My servant, thinking me mortally wounded, seized me and was dragging me on shore, in so doing he scraped my shins against the Grapnel.[84]

We all rushed in pell-mell and the French ran like hares up the hill which rose almost from the water at the back of the battery, which being covered with brushwood, was difficult to ascend. When we arrived at the top, we found a 4-gun battery with the guns loaded. The French were about 100 yards off and ran so fast that it was useless to attempt overtaking them.

We were satisfied with our success and halted. Seeing the Guns loaded, I thought they might be fired, and with the assistance of the men, I got one turned. I could not find a match. I turned to Major [JOHN] CAMPBELL of Glenlyon of the marines and said, "If you will point them I will fire." I pulled out the

---

Detached on 6 February by Commodore John Moore at Guadeloupe with six warships to take Fort Louis (still commanding HMS *Berwick*). He died in 1766.

83. **Captain William Murray**. The senior Black Watch officer present. See Part Three for Biographical Note.

84. **Grapnel**. A small anchor with three or more flukes used for grappling or dragging, or for anchoring a small boat. Grapnels were flung ashore on first contact so that John Grant's boat and others would not be sucked backwards in the surf's strong undertow.

pistol and snapped it on the priming.[85] The shot went bounding and ploughing up the soil 'till it reach'd the retreating French, whose motions it much accelerated.

The others joined us immediately after, tho' we certainly had *the honour of the thing* [Editors' emphasis] in our boat. The *Roebuck*, which was the nearest ship, manned its yards and gave us three cheers, which we answered. It was my happiest moment as it had been my first *fait d'armes*[86] and had been successful.

33 Before however this, I had been under fire. It was my morning business [prior to the day of assault] to go out in a boat for my amusement with four oars and 3 or 4 men, armed. We perceived small logs floating, these we found were buoys marking fishing lines. [We] hauled them up [and] got a dish of fish. This we practiced for 2 or 3 days 'till at length we were suddenly startled one morning by a shower of musket balls from the shore. We returned the fire but pulled out of the way as quickly as possible.

We bivouacked [after the assault] on the hill all night. We lighted a fire from the fascines,[87] got a bullock – from which we cut slices and that was all our supper. I was quite wet from my fall [during the assault] and tho' in a tropical climate I suffered much from the cold, and my shirt thin having neglected to put on my plaid.[88] And we had no communication with the ships 'till next morning. We lost no men after we landed.

I forgot to mention that the men had only their arms deliver'd to them the day on which the landing was to take place, nor had I ever commanded men under arms (such was the state of the Army in those days). But at Aberdeen, I had attended the drills of the Regiment quartered there and had seen their manner of loading. I had charge of a platoon of 25 men and I showed them the way to load, describing the manner of putting down the cartridge. When I came to examine [their weapons] I found that 15 were going to put the Ball in foremost.[89]

---

85. **Snapped it on the priming**. Here John Grant produced the required spark by striking his pistol to the powder in the priming pan.
86. ***Fait d'armes***. First combat, or literally "use of weapons."
87. **Fascines**. Sticks bound together in large bundles, used as reinforcement in the construction of earthworks, dikes and ramparts.
88. **Plaid**. This indicates that John Grant and his Highlanders were wearing kilts or *philabegs* (in Gaelic, *feileadh beag*, meaning "little wrap"), and not their full belted plaids (or *feileadh mór*, meaning "big wrap"). This was common practice on campaign, especially in a tropical climate. The usual rule of thumb in the Highland regiments was to convert full belted plaids into kilts after one year of wear, the wearing of the bulkier belted plaid being usually reserved for dress parades or reviews only.
89. **Loading**. The cartridge was a pre-measured amount of black powder and a round ball wrapped up in a cylindrical tube of paper about the size of a finger. The soldier would tear open one end of the paper cartridge (usually with his teeth), pour some of the powder into the priming pan and then pour the remainder down the barrel. The round ball was then

34 Yet these men pressed on with the courage of old and tried soldiers.

About dusk we were alarmed by a shot from one of our sentinels. I [was] immediately followed by some of the men nearest to the spot and was met by Colonel Rycaut, who appeared much disconcerted. Said a mistake had occurred and that he had been fired at. The fact was, the Colonel, much nettled by the spirited conduct of the Highlanders under Captain Murray, his boat with 60 men having almost unassisted drove the enemy before him, was determined from knowing the Highlanders to be young soldiers, to get them into a scrape.

He accordingly in company with two others remained down near the Battery 'till night fall. He then came up the hill by rather an unfrequented route very silently. The Highlander however was on the alert and challenged. No answer a second and a third time, he then fired. The ball passed between the Gallant Colonel's legs who immediately fell flat on his face, crying out: "Friend – Friend – Friend." There was a good deal of joking at the Colonel's expense.

When we first went on [the assault] the Band of the *Roebuck* played "Britons Strike Home," but ceased as they saw us return [the first time]. However, when they saw us in possession of the hill they sang their cheering & manning the yards to "God Save the King." It was not a pleasant feeling sitting in a boat, but the very impetus and motion of the boat had a good effect. The falling of the dead, the moans of the wounded, all in so small a 35 space is far from pleasant. Of all species of warfare, that of landing is the most unpleasant. You present a mark [target] for your enemy and you are not in your element.

Next morning, we got tents from the ships and encamped below the hill near the shore, maintaining a post upon the Hill, which terminated in a ravine on our left. And on the right, at some little distance, were some salt lakes filled by the sea, and the ground was hilly around us. In front of the hill was a long plain stretching into the country covered with houses, sugar canes & all other West Indian produce. We remained in this station for about six weeks, under very unpleasant circumstances. We were too weak to advance into the country, and we had no provisions but from the ships. Beef and musty bacon, which had been in store since the former war, and Biscuits full of maggots so 36 that after endeavouring to clear them of vermin, we used to wet them and toast them.

Water we had none but what came from the ships, so putrid that we could not drink it without holding our noses. I and some other officers got into a large deserted house and made ourselves more comfortable. Our situation was very irksome. We could not move 500 yards without being fired at with long wall

inserted into the barrel muzzle, followed by the empty paper cartridge wadded up, and then both pushed firmly down to the base of the barrel by a metal or wooden ramrod.

pieces,[90] which they had mounted particularly on the opposite side of the ravine, which was accessible to either party.

Of course we had a number sick, but I held out pretty well. We had continual alarms from firing, [text missing] wounding our Centinels [*sic*]. Once when I was on guard, I heard a shot in the direction of one of my double sentries. I ran to the spot and coming in contact with some person, I found it was the other Centry [*sic*] coming in to tell [of the] wound[ing] of his companion. [I] order'd him back and desired him to fire in [the] direction where I thought I saw an object. He did so – brought in [the] wounded man next morning. A black fellow was lying dead 60 yards from the post on the hill.

They used to fire at our Mess House from the neighbouring high ground, and often when at dinner, a cannon ball used to pass – they could only see [the] top of it. A week passed thus, when I was order'd in the morning with a party to protect some Men of War boats[91] sent to fish in the salt lake. We took post in front of a bridge which cross'd the stream leading into the sea, the only point at which [the] enemy could come to fire upon the 37 Boats as [the] lake then opened wide out. The enemy hover'd about the hills, and I brought one of the wall pieces we found in the batteries with me. With a boyish ardour, I remained out in the sun all day, firing shots.

I paid for my temerity. When the fishing was over the Boats were passing through the Bridge without offering us a share. I stopped them and insisted upon a division. [The] Officer resisted. I remained firm, swore [they] should not pass, & having [the] means of preventing them, he was forced to do so. Made a division. Carried off, it made a fresh meal for the party and our Mess but alas, exposure to [the] sun had fever'd me. I could not eat a morsel when they were presented, got rapidly worse and as they had no Surgeons on shore, our Regimental surgeon[92] being sick on board, there I was sent, also, on board our own transport. I was attended for four days, Surgeon & I, by two Men of War surgeons [who] bled us profusely [and] would have killed us but luckily their ships were order'd off and we were saved.

Remained 3 weeks almost living on toast and water. Got better at last, but miserable enough. About the 9th day we found ourselves so well that we proposed going on shore. Not finding myself strong however, when our Clothes

---

90. **Wall pieces**. Large muskets, usually fixed on a bracket, and used for sniping at long range during sieges.

91. **Men of war boats**. Here John Grant is referring to ships' boats, the utility boats carried by all larger warships to act as tenders amongst other roles (landing craft, picket boats, lifeboats, rescue boats, etc.). During the age of sail, ship's boats had different names (admiral's barge, captain's gig, cutter, launch, longboat, pinnace, etc.) depending on hull form, rig, size and role.

92. **Surgeon Robert Drummond**. See Part Three for Biographical Note.

were already in [the] boat, I said I would go tomorrow. Tomorrow we relapsed and lay for 10 days afterwards without assistance 38 of any kind, except that before mentioned, and the care of my faithful servant. Nature bore us out. In this interval, what must have been the suffering I know not, but the miserable looks of many of the men spoke volumes, so different from their *mien*[93] on landing.

The fever of the West Indies is very rapid in their course, two or three days often prove fatal.[94] Fever and ague occur in marshy situations. Dysentery and bowel complaints from bad food & water. About Christmas is the best time for arriving, and the best preventative [is] unnecessary exposure to the Sun or night air. New rum is very deadly in its effects. The climate requires generous liquor in moderation & water unmixed with wine or spirits is unwholesome. Meat & fish are very dear, except turtle. Pineapples, [illegible], mangoes, shaddocks, granadillas, guavas, melons, and the alligator pear [avocados] are the fruits. Plantains, yams, okras, sweet potatoes, beans, peas and cauliflowers are the vegetables. Mangoes which made into flour, called cassava, and then made into crisp cakes like Scotch bannocks, are much used among the French. The weeds are beautiful flowers. The Palm, orange and box, cocoa, tamarind, Bamboo are all natives of the West Indies. The palmetto or cocoa nut with their bushy tops are most conspicuous. Flamingos, ramies, apes, parakeets and monkeys are abundant. Creole women are very pretty but their intercourse with the slaves gives them a drawling, [d]ry pronunciation.

On one occasion we revenged ourselves of the French who annoyed us. A Guard of French used to mount on the opposite side of the ravine, which lay only about 500 yards off – of course [we] could see them distinctly. From this post we were annoyed. One day a Sergeant of Artillery asked permission to have a shot at them from one of the 48 pounders which had not been disabled in the attack by the *Roebuck*. He was allowed. He layed it. The shot struck and carried off so many of the front rank, the guard ran off and did not reappear again. The Sergeant was made a Lieutenant & afterwards rose to rank.

I did not land again 'till the Expedition which had been at Grand Terre, and had failed in making their way by land to Petit Bourg which was nearly opposite the Bay in Grand Terre where we were, [joined us]. Grand Terre is only separated from the rest of the Island by a narrow Strait.

It was 6 weeks after our first landing. The expedition was commanded by General Barrington after General [Peregrine Thomas] Hopson's death and con-

93. ***Mien***. Air, bearing or demeanour, as showing character or feeling.

94. **Editors' note.** This paragraph, originally appearing in one of the four loose quarto sheets, was placed here in the narrative.

Grant's sketch. The rough sketch on page 39 of the manuscript journal shows the terrain around Petit Bourg, Guadeloupe, as John Grant remembered it. The editors, however, have been unable to match the features of this sketch to contemporary maps. (Editors' photo)

sisted of the 3rd, 4th, 38th & 42nd Regiments.[95] We now joined our Battalion and bid adieu to our comrades the Marines who were then, the worst troops in the service, looked down upon by both Services, without discipline & useless either on shore or at Sea.

39 The third day after our combination [with the other five companies of the Black Watch] we were order'd to land and, at day break, the whole were embarked in boats. The ground was low but rather sloping upwards and the works were at about 500 yards from the shore. The whole country was cover'd with sugar canes and Sugar Houses. To our surprise we were suffered to land without opposition, in all about 1600 men, and formed on the shore.[96]

– – – – – – – – – – – –[97]

I knew nothing, but from Hear-say, of the operations of our small body but that the same system of annoyance was kept up and it was found necessary to erect a work in the hill as a point d'appui.[98]

– – – – – – – – – – – –

95. **Regiments.** 3rd (Howard's), commanded by Lieutenant Colonel Cyrus Trapaud, ranking locally as a brigadier general; 4th (Duroure's), Lieutenant Colonel Byam Crump; 38th (Ross's), Major Robert Melville; 42nd (Murray's), Brevet Major Charles Anstruther.
96. **Editors' note.** This was the unopposed 12 April 1759 amphibious landing near Arnouville, just north of Petit Bourg, by a force of 1,300 men led by the aforementioned Brigadier Clavering.
97. **Dashed line.** Here and there John Johnson Jr. inserted dashed lines into the rough draft of his grandfather's memoirs, apparently to separate paragraphs. These dashed lines also appear in the so-called loose pages, apparently to keep sections together for re-insertion later when producing a more polished final draft.
98. ***Point d'appui.*** Supply point or base. This stand-alone sentence appears to be a note referring to an earlier anecdote about the enemy annoying them nightly on folio page 38. John Grant records the event as "hearsay" because he was still recuperating on board his company's transport anchored offshore.

On one occasion at Grand Terre, I had wandered a little in advance of the Works into a place looking for some limes in the hedges when a man suddenly rushed out and fired his piece at me. I instantly drew one of my pistols and returned his fire, but without effect. I immediately retired and went no more lime hunting.[99]

The Works we were about to attack was a continued line of Intrenchments [*sic*] extending from the shore of the little bay at [the] bottom of which was Petit Bourg, to which there was only a very intricate passage, reaching a sort of point and resting on a hill there.

40 We had seen from the ships in the morning large bodies of people moving about the Works, and we expected warm work. No sooner [had we] landed than we formed line, our Regiment in the centre, and advanced slowly towards the Work. Not a shot was fired until a masked battery[100] open'd upon us with grape[101] and knocked down almost a whole platoon of the 4th Regiment opposed to it, and a heavy fire of musketry opened.

We did not fire a shot, but giving a cheer, instantly ran on, jumped into the ditch and when we scrambled to the top, the whole body of French were retreating, or rather running, into the Sugar cane grounds in the rear of the battery from which they opened a fire upon us. The word was given to set fire to the Canes and the sea breeze blowing, in an instant there was a blaze. This soon dislodged the French and a good many were killed in getting off. Our Regiment lost but few men. The Major[102] was wounded.

[Bottom third of page blank, apart from a faint list in pencil, faded from water damage, and appearing in a different handwriting.]

41 In a few minutes the whole opposing force disappeared and as the country was thickly covered with Sugar Houses, we were order'd to halt and to proceed to destroy them. This was done most systematically, reconnoitring each before we did so. Before nightfall 25 were reduced to ashes & the whole beau-

99. **Editors' note.** Again, another stand-alone anecdote referring to when John Grant was still healthy ashore, before coming down with sunstroke.

100. **Masked battery.** A battery hidden from view by camouflage and then "unmasked" to surprise an enemy.

101. **Grapeshot.** A type of artillery round that is not one solid element, but a mass of small metal balls or slugs packed tightly into a canvas bag. When assembled, the balls resembled a cluster of grapes, hence the name. On firing, the balls spread out from the muzzle in a conical formation, causing a wide swath of destruction.

102. **The wounded major.** A reference to Brevet Major Charles Anstruther, a captain of the 26th Foot (Cameronians) on Hopson's staff, placed in command of the 42nd companies. He died a few days later on 19 May 1759 of his wounds and a severe fever.

tiful face of the country was a smoking ruin. We halted for the night in some Houses after throwing out pickets,[103] quite exhausted with our exertions. Our attack had been so sudden and complete that we found plenty of provisions to regale ourselves with.

Next day I was ordered with the Company I commanded & another of the Buffs to Petit Bourg to garrison that place and a redoubt in its neighbourhood. We marched amidst fine clumps of Bananas & Cabbage trees to that place. It was small but the houses were luxuriously furnished and as most of the owners were fled, we had it all to ourselves.

It was amazing to see the careless recklessness of the Soldiers, stinted as they had been for such a time – they revelled in abundance. I recollect entering a quarter and seeing a large loaf of a kind of brown sugar which, tho' unrefined, was made in that form-in-[a]-pot and pounded when used, placed in the middle of the Table. A hole was made in it and a wax 42 candle, for all the silver candelabra and valuable plate was carried off, was stuck into it. The party were drinking punch and whenever sweetening was wanted a piece was chipped off for the purpose.

After remaining about 3 weeks there we were order[ed] to join at headquarters by marching by land. I forgot to mention that 3 days after the attack of Petit Bourg the whole Island surrendered.[104] We set out and marched through a piece [of] rich country cover'd with plantations and swarming with slaves, whose lot, tho' pretty well as to clothing and food, were yet treated very cruelly, unlimited power being in the hands of the Masters.

We halted for several days at a negro village. We had one side of it and 1500 negroes on the other, all with their families. We then passed through some wooded rocky passes, in attempting which the [previous] Expedition before they joined us, was endeavouring to force their way into the middle of the Island. At Basse Terre, which is seated on the sea shore, having the fort on the left on a rising ground, the Town had been almost destroyed and presented a miserable spectacle and the inside of the fort was fairly ploughed with shells.

---

103. **Picket or picquet.** A soldier or detachment of soldiers placed on a line forward of a position to warn against an enemy advance. Interestingly, John Grant's memoirs uses both "picket" and "picquet." In a military sense, "picket" is an American term, while "picquet" is British.

104. **Surrender.** The island of Basse Terre capitulated on 19 April 1759.

Chapter 3 | New York Colony, 1759–60 – "The Scene was Terrifick"

On 2 July 1759, the seven diminished companies of the 2nd/42nd left Guadeloupe in convoy under the watchful care of the frigate HMS *Rye*. With Acting Major Francis Maclean in command, they arrived at New York on 15 July 1759 after a passage of fourteen days. Only pausing to drop off their wounded, they continued up the Hudson in smaller shipping and alighted at Albany[105] with orders to join Amherst's army, poised and ready to capture Ticonderoga further north at Lake George.[106]

On 3 August 1759 the tanned but emaciated men of the 2nd/42nd started their march northwards from Albany, following the towpaths along the banks of the beautiful Hudson and pulling their bateaux[107] filled with their baggage and provisions. Lieutenant John Grant and his men were in good spirits, happy that they would soon be joining their kinsmen on their victorious march into the heartland of New France. They already knew of Amherst's bloodless victory at Ticonderoga, as their landing at Albany had coincided with the arrival of Lieutenant Colonel Roger Townshend's[108] body sent down from Amherst's siege lines outside Fort Ticonderoga.

---

105. **Albany**. A bustling port and trading centre established by the Dutch as Fort Orange in 1624 at the head of navigation on the Hudson River. Renamed by the British in honour of the Duke of Albany, the future James II of England and James VII of Scotland. Its population by 1750 was about 1,500 people.
106. **Lake George**. A long, narrow lake located at the southeast base of the Adirondack Mountains in the northeastern portion of New York State. The lake extends about 32 miles (52 km) on a north-south axis, is quite deep and varies from 1 to 3 miles (1.7 to 5 km) in width, presenting a significant barrier to east-west travel. The lake is situated along the historical natural (Amerindian) path between the Hudson River valley and the Saint Lawrence River, on the direct land route between Albany and Montreal. Lake George drains into Lake Champlain to its north through a short stream, the La Chute River, with many falls and rapids, dropping about 230 feet (70 m) in its 3.5-mile (6 km) course. Ultimately the waters flowing via the 106-mile-long (171 km) Richelieu River empty into the Saint Lawrence River downstream from and northeast of Montreal.
107. **Bateaux**. The bateau was one of the most widely used types of watercraft for carrying men and supplies. Bateaux came in various sizes but were all double-ended with flat bottoms and a shallow draft. They had the ability to carry great weight in proportion to their size.
108. **Lieutenant Colonel Roger Townshend** (1731-59). British army officer. Fourth son of Charles, 3rd Viscount Townshend of Raynham Hall in Norfolk, and younger brother to Brigadier General George Townshend. Commissioned as an ensign in the 1st Foot Guards, 26 February 1747/48, and captain in the 3rd Foot ("Buffs"), 18 June 1751. Promoted to brevet lieutenant colonel (in America), 1 February 1758. Served as deputy adjutant general in the expedition against Louisbourg in 1758 and during the 1759 Quebec campaign. He was killed by a cannonball on 25 July 1759 as he was reconnoitring the French lines at Ticonderoga and his remains were buried at Albany, New York.

Workhorse of the wilderness. The *bateau* or *batteau* was a standard flat-bottomed boat made of pine about 24 feet (7 m) long used for transporting goods and cargo on the rivers and lakes of North America. John Grant and his Highlanders became experienced "battoemen" working on the "Battoe Service" between Fort Ontario and Fort Stanwix in the fall of 1759. (Fort Stanwix National Monument, National Park Service. Photo by R. Chartrand)

"Before we reach'd our proposed destination," recorded Lieutenant John Grant, "we were chagrined by receiving an order to march to Oswego ... with Major Graham who took the command." Major Gordon Graham of Drainie had been dispatched "with all Expedition" by Amherst on 1 August 1759

> to command the Second Battalion of the Royal Highlanders and to march them to Oswego, that in case, from the unfortunate death of Brigadier Prideaux, the Reduction of Niagara should not have taken place, Brigadier Gage may return to the attack with the utmost vigor & dispatch, and if Niagara is taken Brigadier Gage then to go to la Galette and take Post there & proceed to Montrealle [*sic*] that the Enemy may be pressed and attacked in every Corner, which cant [*sic*] fail of Success.[109]

It was from Graham that they learned that Crown Point further up Lake Champlain had also fallen and that they were now to be part of a strategic stroke that could potentially end the war.

Amherst believed that Brigadier Thomas Gage[110] could push down to Mon-

109. **Major Gordon Graham**. Entry, 1 August 1759, *The Journal of Jeffery Amherst: Recording the Military Career of General Amherst in America from 1758 to 1763*, J. Clarence Webster, ed. (Chicago & Toronto, 1931), 149. Hereafter, *Amherst's Journal*. With Major Graham's promotion to major, and commandant, of the 2nd/42nd Foot, his vacant majority was taken by the next senior captain, Major John Reid. See Part Three for Biographical Note on Gordon Graham.
110. **Brigadier Thomas Gage** (1719-87). British army officer. Gage served in Flanders (1747-48) as aide de camp to Lord Albemarle and in 1751 became lieutenant colonel of the 44th Regiment, one of two regiments sent to America under General Braddock in late 1754. Gage led the advanced detachment on Braddock's march towards Fort Duquesne in 1755 and was wounded in the rout of that expedition. In 1757 he proposed raising a regiment of light infantry that received royal approval in December, designated the 80th Foot in 1758 and known as Gage's Light Infantry, the first of its kind in North America. Appointed brigadier general and third in command under Abercromby in the 1758 expedition against Fort Ticonderoga. After the capture of Fort Niagara in 1759, he replaced Sir William Johnson as commander in that region. For his laxness and poor performance in proceeding against Oswegatchie (La Galette) on the Saint Lawrence River above Montreal as ordered, he was assigned the rear guard of the army under Amherst that moved against Montreal in 1760. Left at Montreal as governor for three years, he rose to the rank of major general.

PTSD victim? A survivor of Braddock's massacre in 1755, Brigadier General Thomas Gage (1719-87) was conspicuously absent during the battle of Ticonderoga in 1758. This coupled with his inexplicable inaction in launching a force towards Montreal as ordered by Amherst in 1759 gave rise to charges of the good general being not "over valiant." Some now believe he was suffering from post-traumatic stress disorder (PTSD). (Oil on canvas by John Singleton Copley, c.1768. Yale Center for British Art, Paul Mellon Collection B1977.14.45. Editors' photo)

treal now that Niagara had fallen to British arms. He reasoned that Gage's left flank and rear were now secure and that the only French forces remaining in Canada that could possibly oppose him were fixed by James Wolfe at Quebec, and at the northern end of Lake Champlain by himself. His subordinate could thus walk in through the back door and take one of the richest and most important cities of Canada, but only if he moved quickly. Gage, who had been sent some weeks earlier to the siege of Niagara to replace Brigadier John Prideaux,[111] was not the best choice however, to execute such a bold and daring plan.

Major Graham soon had his column of Caribbean veterans turned around and they retraced their steps to within 16 miles of Albany. At Half Moon[112] they paused to draw three days rations before ascending the Mohawk River to Schenectady.[113] After a week of marching, Graham's Highlanders reached Fort Stanwix,[114] most of them, according to John Grant, convinced "nothing could

---

Placed in command of all British troops in North America when Amherst returned home in November 1763. During the American Revolutionary War, one of his first tasks was to close the port of Boston as punishment for the infamous "Tea Party," which incensed the merchant classes and led to an illegal Provincial Congress being set up.

111. **John Prideaux** (1718-59). British army officer. Lieutenant Colonel of the 55th Foot appointed brigadier by Amherst 5 May 1759 to command the expedition to capture the French fort at Niagara. Prideaux was accidentally killed by one of his own mortars during the siege.

112. **Half Moon**. A small town on the west side of the Hudson River just north of Albany, first settled about 1680. Named for the crescent shape of the land between the Hudson and Mohawk rivers.

113. **Schenectady**. Derived from a Mohawk word meaning "beyond the pines," the town was founded on the south side of the Mohawk River, near the confluence of the Mohawk and Hudson rivers, by Dutch colonists, many from the Albany area, in the 17th century. Prohibited from participating in the fur trade, residents of the new village developed farms on strip plots along the river.

114. **Fort Stanwix**. A square earthwork fort with wooden palisades and bastions built in early 1758 to protect the Oneida Carrying Place and the lines of communication between Lake Ontario and Albany. The nearest inhabited house was located 60 miles (97 km) away. Named for Brigadier John Stanwix, it had walls about 300 feet long (91 m) and 14 feet high

be more wild or grand than the scenery. There was no habitation within 40 miles of it."

By the end of August, the 2nd/42nd were rowing down Wood Creek,[115] swollen from the rains, and out onto Lake Oneida.[116] They crossed the lake to its western outlet that connected it to the Onondaga (Oswego) River, which in turn took them down to Lake Ontario. The 2nd Battalion arrived at Oswego the following day and were assigned to their tent lines near the rapidly rising walls of Fort Ontario.[117]

In addition to the 2nd/42nd Foot, there were other detachments of regulars in camp, the 46th and 4th Battalion of the 60th Foot (Royal Americans), each assigned a bastion and a curtain wall of the new fort to complete before the winter set in. In addition, to assist them with the task, each had a regiment of provincial soldiers who, in John Grant's candid opinion, were all "bad workers."

Grant and the rest of the 2nd/42nd would labour at their "unpleasant work" until ordered at the end of October to down tools and march back to winter quarters in Albany. Though unhappy with their contribution to the campaign so far, they could take solace in the knowledge that their fellow Highlanders in

---

(4 m) with pointed bastions at each corner to protect the flanks, with the whole completely surrounded by a dry ditch. Fort Stanwix remained garrisoned until the end of Pontiac's Rebellion (1763-66) but was then abandoned. Rebuilt in the spring of 1776 and renamed Fort Schuyler while members of the Continental Congress were drafting the Declaration of Independence. A modern reconstruction of the fort was built in the 1970s on the original foundations in downtown Rome, New York.

115. **Wood Creek** flows into the eastern end of Oneida Lake and provides the connection between that body of water and the Oneida Carry, or portage, at present-day Rome, New York. Early in the war, two small forts protected the portage, Fort Williams on the Mohawk River, and Fort Bull, 4 miles (6 km) to the west at Wood Creek. Eventually, the much stronger Fort Stanwix was built in the middle to protect the portage.

116. **Lake Oneida**. Named for the principal tribe in the region, Oneida is the largest lake found entirely within the colony (later state) of New York (80 square miles or 207 square km). Located 11 miles (18 km) west of present-day Rome (Fort Stanwix), it now serves as one of the links in the Erie Canal–Mohawk River system. It empties into the Oneida River, which subsequently flows into the Oswego River, which, in turn, flows into Lake Ontario. While not officially included as one of the Finger Lakes, it is sometimes referred to as their "Thumb." Twenty-one miles (33 km) in length and about 5 miles (9 km) wide, it is shallow (average depth 22 feet or 7 m) and freezes solidly in winter. Its name in the Iroquois language was *Tsioqui*, meaning White Water, no doubt a reference to the dangerous summer squalls that could turn the lake into a seething mass of white water and an instant watery grave for incautious boatmen.

117. **Fort Ontario**. First built in 1755 at Oswego as a wooden stockade to accommodate 300 men. Destroyed by the French a year later in August 1756, the fort remained deserted for the next two years until the British expedition to capture Fort Niagara in 1759 mounted operations from the site. Captain Thomas Sowers of the Royal Engineers, utilizing the latest European military technology in earth and timber construction, designed and oversaw the building of the five-bastioned, pentagonal fort that was started in 1759 and completed the following year.

the 1st Battalion had been engaged in fort building as well, stationed at Crown Point for most of the autumn. They also heard of Amherst's brief expedition north on the icy slate-grey waters of Lake Champlain in early October. Stalled by storms, the operation was quickly cancelled on the receipt of the news that Quebec had fallen to British arms and that the remnants of Montcalm's army had fallen back on Montreal.

By the time Major Graham and his Highlanders arrived back at Albany at the end of November 1759, winter came "so suddenly," according to Grant, that "some of the Regiments who were marching down to canton in some villages on the river, had their hair and bodies frozen to the ground in their tents." Grant, billeted with a Dutch family near Albany for the winter, did duty as an officer supervising wood collection and enforcing quotas from the Dutch settlers. His second winter in the New World would be a stark contrast to his campaign the year before, when he was cruising the sun-drenched but fever-ridden isles of the Caribbean.

* * *

We re-embarked on board a Transport, armed [with] a Letter of Marque,[118] of 24 guns, and sailed for New York. We landed after a passage of 14 days at New York. We sailed up the beautiful Hudson with Long Island on one side and Staten Island on the other. New York was then a fine City.

43 The cheapness and abundance was astonishing. We had an excellent dinner at a Tavern for 14^{d} [pence]. After two days we embarked in small sloops for Albany. The sail up the Hudson is very beautiful. Every six hours we anchored for six to wait for [the] tide and landed at the farmers' Houses, who were chiefly Dutchmen, where we revelled in good cheer and fruits or took our guns, unchecked by game laws.

– – – – – – – – – – –

I forgot to mention that General Barrington sailed with part of the Regiments for England at the same time as us [June 1759].

– – – – – – – – – – –

At Albany, which was a fine fort village inhabited by Dutchmen. While the 3 days we were there, the body of Colonel Townshend, brother of Lord

118. **Letter of marque**. A government licence authorizing a person (known as a privateer) to attack and capture enemy vessels, bringing them before Admiralty courts for condemnation or sale. Cruising for prizes with a letter of marque was considered an honourable calling as opposed to uncontrolled, unlicensed piracy.

New York, c.1766. "Plan of the City of New York in North America Surveyed in the Years 1766 and 1767" drawn by Lieutenant Bernard Ratzer, a Swiss officer with engineering experience serving in the 60th Foot (Royal Americans). (BL Maps K.Top.121.36b. Editors' photo)

New York, New York. Above: "A Plan of the City of New York Reduced from an Actual Survey by F. Maerschalck, 1763." No. 1 in *A Set of Plans and Forts in America, Reduced from Actual Surveys 1765*, published by Mary Ann Rocque. Below: "Landing of English Troops at New York, 1776." Hand-coloured engraving by Franz Xaver Habermann, published 1777. (Top: TPL 11900690, Editors' photo. Bottom: JCB UP1776f-2a)

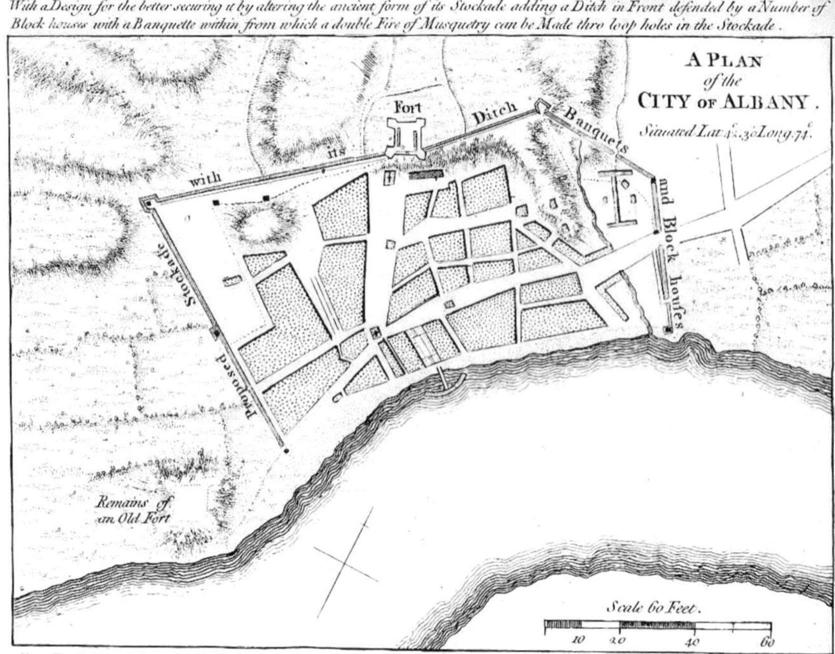

"A Plan of the City of Albany." No. 2 in *A Set of Plans and Forts in America, Reduced from Actual Surveys 1765*, published by Mary Ann Rocque. (TPL 11900690. Editors' photo)

Townshend,[119] came down for interment. This gallant officer was much regretted by the Army. He fell at Ticonderoga.

He had been outside the lines reconnoitring with his Spy Glass, some cannon shots had been fired at the party and they retired. He forgot his Spy glass case and some officer wanted to pick it up. Said no, [he] would go himself. A shot carried off his arm by the Shoulder & [he] died immediately. At [his] funeral [I] got a Scarf & Hat band. It is so large of cambrick[120] [*sic*] as to make several shirts for me.

---

119. **Brigadier General George Townshend**, 4th Viscount and 1st Marquess Townshend (1724-1807). British army officer. Older brother of Lieutenant Colonel Roger Townshend. Fought as a junior staff officer at Dettingen in 1743, also fighting at Culloden in 1746 and at Laffeldt in 1747. He was the government's choice to command a brigade in the Quebec expedition, serving under Major General James Wolfe and later criticized for trying to steal the dead general's glory. Promoted to major general in 1761, he served with the Allied army in Germany and saw fierce fighting at Vellinghausen. Master General of the Board of Ordnance from 1772 to 1782, he was promoted to full general in 1782 and created a marquess in 1787. Promoted to field marshal in 1796, he died in Norfolk in 1807.
120. **Cambric**. A thin, plain white cotton or linen fabric of fine close weave.

Sturgeons[121] called "Albany Beef" [are] numerous in the Hudson. In the small canoe belonging to the officers, [we] used to be rather startled by large fellows of 100 pounds springing out of the water close to us. Sometimes a shole[122] [*sic*] used to play some prank, large ones but coarse eating.

44 Leaving Albany, we marched along the banks of [the] Hudson past detached farms via a log road, boats carried our baggage. Were sadly tormented by mosquitoes. Encamped at night if not able to get a farm house. Plenty of fruit amidst these peaceful abodes.

At Saratoga[123] cultivation ceased, but few clearings. Marched amidst splendid forests before we reach'd our proposed destination, Fort Edward, from whence we were to join the army besieging Ticonderoga. We were chagrined by receiving an order to march to Oswego. Order came with Major [Gordon] Graham who took the command.

We retraced our steps 'till within 16 miles of Albany at Half Moon, a small village where [the] Mohawk river runs into the Hudson. We ascended the Mohawk River to Schenectady and next day we had to set out for Fort Stanwix. We marched 8 days in cultivated country, that is, what was cleared, 'tho not answering our description of cultivation, and then for several days in the Wilderness 'till we reached our destination.

Highlanders have a great antipathy to Pork and it was the provision issued to the Regiments for their march. At Half Moon, 3 days' provisions were served out, but as the Soldiers had plenty of money and could get bread, butter, cheese, &c. to purchase at the Towns, they threw the "odorous flesh" away. Before they entered the wilderness the provisions were 45 again thrown away, tho' they were warned not to do so, but ignorant of the country, they thought that they could still find other food. To their consternation however, the halt was made at night in an uncultivated spot *[124] where nothing could be got. They were ashamed to murmur, but next day when the halt was made for breakfast, they

---

121. **Sturgeon**. The largest and longest-lived of any of the freshwater fishes, sturgeon live only in the Northern Hemisphere. Of the twenty-six species found worldwide, three occur in New York State's waters: Atlantic sturgeon, lake sturgeon and shortnose sturgeon. In the western United States during the 1700s, sturgeon as large as 1,500 pounds (680 kg) and over 100 years old were common. Populations decreased drastically with industrialization and as man became aware of the value of sturgeon for its meat and eggs (caviar).

122. **Shole (shoal)**. Fish are said to be shoaling when they swim somewhat independently, but in such a way that they stay connected, forming a social group. When they swim in the same direction in a coordinated manner, they are said to be schooling.

123. **Saratoga**. A small town on the west side of the Hudson River about 30 miles (48 km) north of Albany. First settled at the end of the 17th century as Fort Saratoga, it quickly became contested land between British and French colonial forces.

124. **Asterisk**. The asterisk marks an original footnote to the manuscript that appears at the bottom of the page.

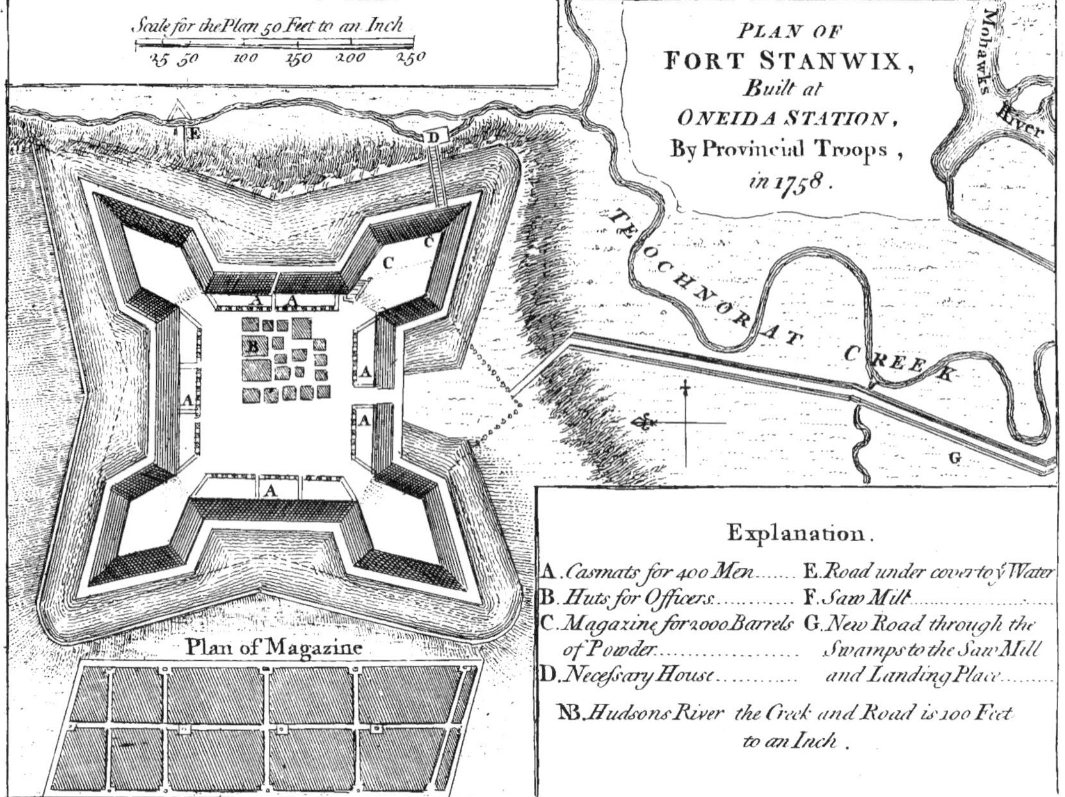

The Fort at Oneida Station, 1758. The first garrison of the newly-built Fort Stanwix comprised four companies of Fraser's Highlanders (one of the two junior Highland battalions raised on the model of the Black Watch for service in North America) and a company of Rogers' Rangers. "Plan of Fort Stanwix Built at Oneida Station by Provincial Troops in 1758," No. 12 in *A Set of Plans and Forts in America, Reduced from Actual Surveys 1765*, published by Mary Ann Rocque. (TPL 11900690. Editors' photo)

could no longer hold out and sent a deputation to the Major, telling him [the] circumstances. He said he was sorry for it but he could issue nothing. There was a general gloom, but luckily it was remember'd a day's provisions had not been issued some previous period. It was found correct and the day's provision was fixed, to suffice them for two, but not a morsel of pork but was cherished with as much care as it had been before rejected with disgust.

After 6 or 7 days we arrived at Fort Stanwix situated on the Mohawk River. Nothing could be more wild or grand than the scenery. There was no habitation within 40 miles of it. It was an earthen fort with 4 Bastions with log Houses within for 500 men.

* Forgot to mention that after we entered the Wilderness we came to an open space called the Big Indian field, a large open meadow running down to the River, which carried our provisions and equipages; [the river was] quite clear

of wood, perhaps by Beavers. We also came after a day's march to another [open space] called the Little Indian field. The rest was wilderness.[125]

46 We also passed an Indian Mohawk Village[126] where [I] had my first view of Indians, those fine warriors. Officers had no horses but marched.

We only remained at Fort Stanwix 'till they unloaded our other boats and carried them across [the portage] to Wood Creek about a mile off. We embarked in five large Boats, 20 men and twenty barrels. We were obliged to use poles as in the Mohawk River but we had not the current to contend with, but still being heavier laden by 20 instead of 5 men, our progress was slow in the sluggish stream, and through unskillfulness went often on the logs which lay in masses in the bed of the creek, which is about 15 miles long.

– – – – – – – – – – – –

Forgot before – that before we reached one of these Indian fields, a most terrible storm overtook us, rain, wind, thunder and lightning. The scene was terrifick [*sic*], the boldest trembled. Trees falling in every direction, deluge of rain, and as we were afraid of an attack from the Indians, we took off our bonnets to protect our pieces[127] and thus bare headed we bore the pelting of the pitiless storm, the water running out of our shoes. Some of our men were hurt and the Adjutant [Lieutenant Alexander Donaldson] was nearly killed by the falling of a tree. [This] happened in [the] middle of August, insects annoying. Storm cleared the air, made it cool.

47 At the mouth of Wood Creek [we] entered Lake Oneida and rowed down its course. It is narrow 2 miles and long 30. A few hours brought us to the north end of the lake and we landed at a block House[128] where a Major of Militia was posted. But we could get nothing to eat and were forced to put up with our Beef & Pork. Next morning, we embarked and enter'd the Oneida River[129] and

---

125. **Indian fields.** The Little Indian field was on the Mohawk River, approximately 14 miles (23 km) west of Fort Herkimer near German Flats. The Big or Great Indian field was 17 miles (27 km) further west along the Mohawk and comprised some 40 acres (0.2 square km) cleared by the Indians where the Oriskany Creek joins the Mohawk, some 11 miles (18 km) before Fort Stanwix.

126. **Mohawk village.** This most likely was the Mohawk settlement outside Fort Hunter where the Scoharie River joins the Mohawk River from the south. The land along the Mohawk River was the tribal territory of the Mohawk Nation, who were styled "The Guardians of the Eastern Door" within the powerful Iroquois confederacy.

127. **Editors' note.** Viz. They placed their hats over their flintlock firing mechanisms to keep the powder in their priming pans dry.

128. **Blockhouse.** This was the first fortification built on the site of what would later become Fort Brewerton, incorporating three more blockhouses enclosed within star-shaped earthen ramparts and ditch similar to Fort Stanwix.

129. **Oneida River.** In 1759 this river was actually known locally as the Onondaga River, as all maps of the period attest, then was later renamed the Oswego River.

rowed all day along Banks where solitude reigned and large pines and magnificent forest trees.

At night landed, where we had a serenade of the Bullfrogs and wolves. I never shall forget going down to the river's edge and imitating the yelp of a dog when all around rose such a yell as if Pandemonium had broke [*sic*] loose. We were almost afraid of them but as wood was not scarce, [we] had rousing fires. We were also obliged to keep a picket [*sic*] of an officer and 50 men against the Indians.

Next day at the junction of the 3 rivers with the Oneida[130] there are dangerous roughs or rapids, and as it was our first essay, we had some little alarm at their appearance, boiling and foaming. In the lea day [late afternoon], [we] reached Oswego Falls.[131] Here we landed and next morning reached Oswego, twelve miles. There had been a blockhouse on the eastern side [of the mouth of the Oswego River] but a Fort was constructing on the West side on a rising ground.

48 There were 4 Regiments of Regulars and 4 of Provincials: 42nd, 44th, 46th [and a] Battalion of [the] 60th. Each Regiment of [the] Regulars and of Provincials had a Bastion and a curtain [wall] to finish, unpleasant work. The Yankies [*sic*] [were] bad workers [and I] near got into a scrape. One fellow challeng'd and kept my men and others from work. [I] chided him, [but] still [he] continued. [I] threw a chip [*sic*] of wood at him, knocked him senseless. A shabby looking fellow came up with a belt & sword, took him for a Sergeant. He said, "You serpent, you. I vow you shall not kill my men." "Get about your business," he continued. I ordered two [42nd] men to carry him to [the] guard house.

When going, "I vow" said he, "I am a Captain."

[I] released him. Afraid of a scrape, [I] went immediately to Brigadier Gage [and] mentioned [the] circumstance. He said, "It was lucky you had not confined him, otherwise you would have been broken to keep the provinces in good

---

130. **Junction of the 3 rivers.** The Three Rivers Junction is where the Oneida and Seneca rivers in upstate New York meet to form the Oswego (Onondaga) River.

131. **Oswego Falls.** Rapids on the Oswego River near present-day Fulton, New York, and about 5 miles (8 km) below where the Oneida River (from the south and formerly known as Seneca River) empties into the Oswego River. It was the halfway point between Fort Brewerton on Oneida Lake and Oswego on Lake Ontario. It was also a significant obstacle to river traffic in that all bateaux had to be unloaded and moved around the falls. A post for 100 men was built above the falls in the summer of 1759 to protect convoys bound for Oswego. Mary Ann Roque's "Sketch of the Stockade Fort, at Oswego Falls" shows an eight-pointed star fort with a central blockhouse. It also shows the portage route around the site which General Amherst viewed in 1760 commenting that the post was "a bad one" and that bateaux were moved over log rollers for some 60 yards (55 m) without being unloaded. *Amherst's Journal*, 217.

Fur post turned fort. In 1727 a large stone blockhouse was built by enterprising New York fur traders on a hill overlooking the mouth of the Oswego River where it emptied into Lake Ontario. This strategic entrée onto the Great Lakes and the vast interior of the continent later saw three additional fortifications built, but all were destroyed by the French in 1756. Only Fort Ontario was rebuilt, commencing in summer 1759. This illustration, "The South View of Oswego on Lake Ontario," was engraved by T. Mynde and published by Thomas Wilcox in 1757. (JCB 06369)

humour." Next day an order was given out that King's officers should command the working parties.

We were encamped. I made a trench for my tent, found that I had encroached upon the burying ground of the Yankies [*sic*], numbers of whom had died last year in building a small fort. Some died whilst I was there. They used to say [of the regulars] "Look at those Vipers, they drink, they eat, they swear, they follow women and they live. We neither eat nor drink, and pray, and we die."

We were always upon the alert, as we expected to be attacked by the French and Indians. Badly off for provisions, all salt, sometimes [we] got salmon.

49 About 10 days afterwards I was ordered to form part of 250 destined to carry provisions between Fort Stanwix and Oswego. Hard work, often obliged to sleep in swamps. It took us between two or three days to reach Fort Stanwix and the same to load and return. It was very monotonous work but the Captain, Johnstone,[132] who commanded soon tiring of the work, shamed Abraham

132. **Captain Alexander Johnstone** (1729-82). British marine and army officer. Commissioned a 2nd lieutenant in the 4th Marines, 8 June 1742, but transferred to the army in 1747 with a commission as a lieutenant in the 62nd Foot. Placed on half-pay the following year, but returned to active duty with the 47th Foot on 2 July 1750. By April 1759 he was a captain serving in the 46th Foot, one of the four regiments at Oswego. Promoted to major of the 70th

and remained at Fort Stanwix. An old drunken Swiss, a Lieutenant in the Royal Americans, also fell sick, and I being older a week than the others, the younger in age got the command. This pleased me and made me, in the importance of my office, think lightly of the disagreeables.

Once at Wood Creek whilst loading there was some instance of insubordination and grumbling on the part of the men. Some were tryed [*sic*] and, the most guilty were to be punished. The Captain and two Subalterns arrived to attend [the court martial],[133] and I and two others were permitted to dine with the commandant at Fort Stanwix, a Major Browning.[134]

My Servant came after dinner to inform me that the Men had mutinied. The two Subalterns, who had no great love or affection for the Captain said, "Let him quell it himself." I jumped up and seizing my fusee,[135] an arm we all carried, ran down about a mile. When I arrived I found that the man they had been in the act of punishing was cut down and that the Captain was engaged with a tall soldier, who armed with a long clasp knife, was menacing him, whilst he armed with a small dagger was endeavouring to seize him.

50 There was no time to be lost. I instantly cocked my fusee [and] told him to drop the knife or he was a dead man. The rest of the soldiers were at *order arms*, looking on. He dropped the knife.

I then asked what was the matter. He said all the troops had mutinied. I said I was sure the 42nd had not, and turning to them addressed them in Gaelic to that effect. [Hearing] their native language had its effect. Order'd them to shoulder arms – they obliged. I called 4 men out, "Take prisoner that man." It was done.

Foot on 26 April 1763 and lieutenant colonel the following year, spent the next ten years in the West Indies. He retired in that rank in 1775 and is presumed to have died in 1783 when his name disappears from the Army Lists.

133. **Regimental courts martial**. For most soldiers, crime and punishment was administered by regimental courts martial (RCM) yet there are no extant records and few surviving accounts of their procedures. By 1718, however, rules and procedures governing RCM were formalized, with commanding officers allowed to inflict various corporal punishments for such crimes as neglect of duty, insolence or disorderly conduct in quarters. All such trials had to be conducted by a court of five commissioned officers with conviction decided by a plurality of votes. By contrast, general courts martial (GCM) were reserved for capital offenses (e.g., murder, rape, robbery, mutiny, desertion). *Articles of War, 1718*. TNA WO 72/2.

134. **Major William Browning** (c.1740-67). British army officer. Joined the army as troop quartermaster of the 5th Dragoons, then commissioned lieutenant in the 57th Foot (later the 46th Foot), 26 January 1741. By the fall of 1759 was major of the 46th commanding at Fort Stanwix on the Oswego–Albany lines of communication. The same year he claimed to be the "oldest" major in Amherst's army. Made lieutenant colonel of the 46th, 9 July 1761. He retired in April 1767, selling his colonelcy to Major Francis Legge.

135. **Fusee**. A lighter-weight musket or carbine used by officers instead of a slender pike known as a spontoon.

The Captain seemed at a loss what to do. [He] took liberty to try [the] man instantly and [to] punish. The arrival of two other Lieutenants who had taken their time to [the] scene of [the] action, made the number [required to form the court martial]. It was done and sentence executed. I then begged as a favour, that all might be forgotten and made up. It was granted. Thus by a little firmness and a little lenience I gained the good opinion and obedience of [the] detachment.

The Provincials wore no uniform.[136] At the Blockhouse at [the] mouth of Wood Creek was a provincial Captain. I had received civilities from him, got provisions, used to take my bearskin and sleep in his room. When leaving [I] asked what I could do for him. [He] said, "I guess [when] you pass through such a village, well then, I am the Blacksmith there and when you or your Brother Officers pass through there, you will repay me by getting your horses shod at my forge. I promised.

51 We carried on this [task] for 56 days until the beginning of November [1759]. It was becoming very cold and we were often obliged to lay in wet places, yet we had very little sick being constantly in the open air, working hard either in loading, rowing or polling the Bateaux as each boat carried 30 barrels and were flat bottomed. The men had always their set provisions, regular and plenty of liquor in moderation. I however got into a habit of drinking about ½ pint of spirits every morning in the swampy districts, and had great difficulty in getting rid of it when at Albany. But afraid of bad habits, [I] made a strong resolution.

We occasionally got a duck and sometimes some fish to vary our salt provisions. We only got 14 pence a day as [an] extra allowance.[137]

In the beginning of November therefore we prepared to enter winter quarters and we embarked our whole regiment in boats containing 10 men and 10 sick of [the] different Regiments & Provincials. We went on Smoothly 'till we entered Lake Oneida [when] a violent storm arose. We had in my boat extended a plaid as a sail and were getting on. I saw a sudden squall, jumped up and with

136. **No uniform**. The provincial battoemen with whom Grant worked were brigaded into ten independent companies of forty men each and did not wear uniforms. The provincial marching regiments however did wear an assortment of regulation uniforms depending on the largesse of their respective colonies. For example, Marylanders wore blue, Massachussetts men brown, Connecticut soldiers scarlet, and Roger's Rangers (on the provincial establishment) green

137. **Extra allowance.** Typically paid to officers for difficult or extraordinary assignments. In this case, John Grant was receiving 14 pence per day as boat convoy commander carrying supplies between Fort Stanwix and Oswego.

Schenectady, c.1763. Established in 1661 by the Dutch, Schenectady boasted a small, stockaded fort built adjacent to the Mohawk River, numerous town lots with houses and outbuildings, a rebuilt church, and farms and pastures. The Black Watch spent their first winter in North America billeted in homes throughout the community. "A Plan of Schenectady," No. 8 in *A Set of Plans and Forts in America, Reduced from Actual Surveys, 1765*, published by Mary Ann Rocque. (TPL 11900690. Editors' photo)

my dirk cut the plaid from top to bottom. In a moment it flew into shreds. It blew then a perfect hurricane – "*Sauve qui peu*"[138] was the cry.

We were at its mercy; the only danger was from permitting the flat bottomed boat to broach to. The blood started from the Helmsman's fingers as he endeavoured to steer her straight. As we neared the shore we looked for the best point for 52 running on shore, which we did in a bay. No other boat was near us and I began to fear they were lost, nor could we see a vestige of them in the stormy water. Got [the] poor sick (much to [be] pitied) out. Dried our tents with them but it poured torrents and we were all wet to the skin.

Next morning, we found our boat 20 yards from the water, such had been the elevation of the water in the storm. Had rollers on board, got [the] boat down [to the water and] sailed for Wood Creek. When there, all the other boats got safe in and we proceeded to Fort Stanwix. From there we embarked in boats and where we had been so many days marching up, we descended the rapid current in a day to Schenectady. From that village we marched across to Albany.

138. **Translation:** "Save yourselves, if able!"

Winter convoy. John Grant and his men worked well into the month of November on the arduous "Battoe Service" between Forts Ontario and Stanwix during the 1759 campaign. Grant remembered it was "very cold and we were often obliged to lay in wet places, yet we had very little sick being constantly in the open air, working hard either in loading, rowing or polling the Bateaux as each boat carried 30 barrels and were flat bottomed." (Pencil sketch by Peter Rindlisbacher)

At Albany we spent our time pleasantly enough. When the winter set in which it did about the end of November so suddenly that some of some [*sic*] Regiments who were marching down to canton in some villages on the river, had their hair & bodies frozen to the ground in their tents. And on arriving in Albany and embark[ing] in small sloops to go down the river, they were enabled to walk on shore next morning on the Ice. Then our amusements began – slaying [*sic*: sleighing], dancing, shooting, skating, and dancing [*sic*]. Society [was] somewhat rude, but women were pretty and had not that asperity produced by the Revolution, were uneducated but they danced. After a Ball the country parties, well muffled in their furs, dashed off in their sledges.

All the houses were built of wood with their gables to the street, peaked in the Dutch style, most 53 of the people being Dutch. Without a pavement, very cheap and plentiful. Spent a merry christmas [*sic*] but these [activities] had an end. I was order'd on a command to press wood, that is, making the people carry in wood at a certain price in the country 12 miles from Albany on the Mohawk.

I had a district. It was not a pleasant occupation, constant squabbles with the Dutchmen who were the settlers. I established myself at the best looking farm house in the district, but [the] owner was a surly Dutch boor and I left it next day and pitched on another. Most fortunately he was a plain, blunt, honest fellow. A large log house and plenty of good cheer, and abundance of Cakes of every denomination at Tea. During the day I went about to see that the wood was sent in, and at night over a blazing fire and an occasional newspaper with which I used to enlighten Mijnheer Claus.[139]

When it came to the turn of my first Host [the surly Dutch boor] to send in his quota, I was told that he would not send it. I went, he refused – I persisted. I said I would send him a prisoner to Albany. He took out his gun and threatened to shoot me. I sprang in, seized the gun, discharged it and broke the stock and made him send in a double quota, in spite of his doggedness. I was kept 6 weeks. I used often to go to their Frolics, as they were called, with the sons of the family.

54 [I] used to scamper off in a sledge, 10 or 12 miles. Lots of food – fat misses, uncouth sort of dancing, old folks smoked, cider the chief drink.

When going away [I] asked what I had to pay. Not a farthing, "I wish you could always live with us." During the whole winter he used to send me in jams, &c. and sent in 4 loads of wood. Told him he need not send in wood, his quota [met]. Said he would, if he did not, others would complain and get me into trouble – a really smart, hospitable man. We flirted with the Ladies &c. during the winter which broke up in April [1760], and the turbid Hudson rolled majestically along being a mile across, strange after its immoveable face for so many months of ice.

Messes were not then enforced by an order. The Captains messed together, more expensive than we could afford, and they occupying the only room large enough in the only good Inn, we were left to shift for ourselves. I boarded at a Dutch House and had good cheer, dinner and cider for 1 shilling per diem. We had our parties at our quarters every evening, gambling & Drinking as we got stout and Madeira.

In the beginning of May [1760], we returned to Schenectady and encamped on a hill near the town for a week 'till [the] boats were ready. We then embarked 20 in a boat and retraced our route to Fort Stanwix.

---

139. **Mijnheer Claus.** John Grant must have learned some Dutch from his landlord and family. "Mijnheer Claus" in English means "Mister Claus." Claus (pronounced *klows*) is a common Dutch family name.

Chapter 4 | The Montreal Campaign, 1760 – "It was a Glorious Sight"

When Jeffery Amherst's army set off from Oswego on 10 August 1760 to capture Montreal and complete the British conquest of New France, his command consisted of 5,586 British regulars, including John Grant's 42nd Highlanders, 4,479 provincials and 706 allied Indians,[140] the latter under the command of Sir William Johnson. It was the largest of the three forces converging on Montreal that summer, which together totalled some 17,000 men in theatre. Brigadier William Haviland's[141] British-American force moving northwards in the centre on the Lake Champlain approach comprised about 3,300 British regulars and provincials, while Brigadier James Murray's[142] small contingent of regulars coming upriver from Quebec initially totalled 2,500 men but swelled to almost 4,000 with the arrival of the Louisbourg reinforcements.

---

140. **Amherst's army.** "Embarkation Return of His Majesty's Forces under the Command of Major General Amherst from the Camp at Fort Ontario, 9 August 1760," LAC MG 11, CO 5, vol 59, part 1, f.123, microfilm B-2173.

141. **Brigadier William Haviland** (1727-1784). British army officer. William Haviland arrived in North America as lieutenant colonel of the 27th Foot and led the right wing of Abercromby's army at the unsuccessful battle of Ticonderoga in July 1758. In 1760 appointed brigadier general commanding the centre army assigned the Lake Champlain approach to Montreal. By February 1762 he was senior brigadier general serving under Major General Robert Monckton at the reduction of Martinique. Appointed major general, 10 July 1762, he served at the siege of Havana and returned to England after the war, dying in 1784.

142. **Brigadier General James Murray** (1721-94). British army officer and colonial administrator. Born at his family's seat of Ballencrieff in Lothian, Scotland, the fifth son and fourteenth child of Alexander Murray, Lord Elibank, and his wife, Elizabeth Stirling. A short man with bright staring eyes, a hawk-like nose and a fiery disposition, James did not suffer fools gladly. Two of his four brothers were avowed Jacobites and his military career was an uphill struggle to prove his loyalty and worth to the British Crown. Enrolled as a cadet in Colyear's 3rd Scot's Regiment of the Dutch army in 1736, later claiming he had "served in all ranks except that as drummer." Obtained a commission in Wynard's 4th Marine Regiment in 1740 and participated in the British-American expedition against Cartagena in Central America, later transferring to the 15th Foot as a captain. Purchased a majority in the 15th Foot in 1749 and a year later the lieutenant colonelcy. At the outbreak of the Seven Years' War, he met James Wolfe for the first time on the Rochefort expedition in September 1757, serving under Wolfe at Louisbourg the following year. Served as the most junior of James Wolfe's brigadiers during the 1759 siege, but was actually the oldest at thirty-nine years of age. He was left in command of a bomb-shattered Quebec for the winter of 1759-60 and is perhaps best known for his six tempestuous years as Quebec's first peacetime British governor, making his greatest impact as one of the first champions of French-Canadian rights. Commanded one of the three armies that converged on Montreal in 1760 and forced its capitulation. After facing his last siege as the governor of Minorca in 1782, he retired to his Sussex estate, where he spent his twelve remaining years. Promoted to full general in February 1783. He died 18 June 1794 at Beauport House, near Battle, Sussex.

The Swiss colonel. Frederick Haldimand (1718-91) was one of several Swiss army veterans brought into the British Army to fight in North America during the Seven Years' War, initially commanding a battalion of Royal Americans with the rank of lieutenant colonel and ending the war as a brigadier general. From 1778 to 1786 he served as governor of the province of Quebec and by the end of the American Revolution was the general responsible for establishing the Loyalist refugees from the Thirteen Colonies in what is now Ontario and reconciling the Six Nations to their resettlement with them in Canada. (Oil on canvas by John Singleton Copley. FARL)

On 7 August the vanguard commanded by Colonel Frederick Haldimand[143] departed ahead of the main army. It comprised two companies of Roger's Rangers, the light infantry, the grenadiers of the army and the 1st/42nd Foot. Two days out, Haldimand reported back that they had reached the commencement of the large river, which was full of large and small uncharted islands.[144] The remainder of the army sailed on 10 August 1760 and made about 30 miles (48 km) that day before putting ashore. Meanwhile, the vanguard was now in striking distance of Oswegatchie,[145] about 40 miles (64 km) down the Saint Lawrence from Lake Ontario.

---

143. **Colonel Frederick Haldimand** (1718-91). British army officer and colonial administrator. Christened François-Louis-Frédéric Haldimand in Yverdon, Switzerland, the second of four children of François-Louis Haldimand and his wife Marie-Madeleine de Treytorrens. Entered the Prussian Army in 1740 and the Swiss Guards "in the Dutch Service" in 1748, promoted to "captain commandant" in the latter in 1750. Part of a group of foreign officers recruited to serve in the Royal American Regiment, a new-raising unit recruiting the German and Swiss inhabitants of Pennsylvania, commissioned lieutenant colonel of the regiment's 2nd Battalion on 4 January 1756. Throughout his career, he would encounter the animosity of some British-born officers, who resented the presence of foreigners in their ranks. Promoted to brevet colonel (in America) on 17 January 1758 and that same year transferred to the 4th Battalion, seeing service at Ticonderoga, 1758, Oswego, 1759, and Montreal, 1760. His language skills made him invaluable to his commanders and in 1760 he was chosen by Jeffery Amherst to negotiate the terms of surrender of New France. Became military governor of nearby Trois-Rivières at the end of the conflict. Promoted to brigadier (in America) on 12 December 1765. Following a political reshuffling in Canada, he left to manage military affairs in Florida from 1767 to 1773. At the outbreak of the American Revolutionary War, British authorities considered foreigners too untrustworthy to hold command positions, and as a result he left North America in 1775, returning to Yverdon, where he purchased an estate. Promoted to lieutenant general (in the Army) on 29 August 1777. Replaced Sir Guy Carleton as governor of the province of Quebec in 1778, serving until 1786. Appointed to the Order of the Bath in 1785. He died at the age of seventy-three in his birthplace, Yverdon, Switzerland, on 5 June 1791.
144. **The Thousand Islands.** An archipelago of 1,864 islands that straddles the Canada–US border in the Saint Lawrence River as it emerges from the northeast corner of Lake Ontario. They stretch for about 50 miles (80 km) downstream from Kingston to Brockville, Ontario.
145. **Fort La Présentation** (now Ogdensburg, New York). The first fort built at the confluence of the Saint Lawrence and Oswegatchie rivers consisted of a small house and barn, with three soldiers for its garrison. A wooden stockade was built in 1749 and expanded in 1750. The

Surviving journals show that the officers had extreme difficulty navigating amongst the countless small islands choking this stretch of the river. Three days later, Amherst's army had closed up behind the vanguard and the following day, 16 August 1760, the whole army embarked on the river at 10 a.m. with Gage's Light Infantry,[146] the grenadiers of the army and five row-galleys,[147] each mounting four 12-pounders and a howitzer, leading. As they neared Oswegatchie in the dusk, word came back from downriver that an armed French brig[148] was anchored off its point. General Amherst immediately ordered his army to the shores of the river while the vanguard proceeded downriver to seize the point and take post there; and if the vessel tried to intervene, they were to capture her. They arrived after dark, however, and the French did not detect their presence.

The next morning at first light, the British row-galleys under the command of Colonel George Williamson,[149] the chief gunner, audaciously attacked the French schooner, which mounted seven 12-pounder guns, two 8-pounders and an 18-pounder and had a crew of 100 men. "The vessel seeing our boats row towards her, she did not chuse [*sic*] to hazard being boarded & struck," said

---

new fort consisted of four large timber towers erected on masonry foundations connected by wooden palisades, "a remarkably attractive arrangement that was meant to impress the Indians but certainly could not withstand anything like a siege by an Anglo-American army equipped with artillery." Sometimes known by its Indian name of Oswegatchie, Fort La Présentation was also known as La Galette because of the proximity of an old and usually abandoned trading post of that name. A sawmill and three Indian villages would eventually spring up outside its walls. The fort was abandoned and dismantled in August 1759.

146. **Gage's Light Infantry**. The 80th Regiment of Light Armed Foot, raised in North America on 5 May 1758, the first light infantry regiment in the British Army. While intended to be a more disciplined corps than the Rangers, the men of Gage's Light Infantry were often the cast-offs of other regiments or prisoners released from jail. Men of the 80th were frequently mentioned in court martial proceedings and desertion advertisements, giving rise to Grant's derisive comments later about "jailbirds of America." Gage's was disbanded in late 1763.

147. **Row-galleys**. A hybrid type of vessel derived from similar ships that operated in the Mediterranean. Commanded by Royal Artillery officers and rowed by provincial troops, they could be readily rowed, or sailed in nearly any wind, as each galley was fitted with oars and a keel and rigged with lateen sails.

148. **French brig**. The *L'Outaouaise,* built by the French at Point au Baril in 1759 after the destruction of most of their Lake Ontario fleet at Fort Frontenac two years previously. The French brig was renamed the *Williamson* by General Amherst in honour of his artillery commander, Colonel George Williamson.

149. **Colonel George Williamson** (c.1704-81). Royal Artillery officer. Williamson entered the Royal Artillery as a cadet on 1 February 1722, rising to colonel commandant on 20 November 1759. He had commanded the Royal Artillery at the siege of Louisbourg in 1758 and commanded Wolfe's artillery at Quebec in 1759 (where he claimed "General Montcalm was killed by my grapeshot from a light 6 pounder"). The fifty-six-year-old senior artillery officer "with extensive command experience in North America" was characterized as "energetic and aggressive." Promoted to major general in 1762 and to lieutenant general in 1772, he died at Woolwich on 11 November 1781.

"Don't disgrace me." Colonel George Williamson (c.1704-81) commanded Major General James Wolfe's artillery at Quebec in 1759 (where he claimed "General Montcalm was kill'd by my grape shott from a light sixpounder"). Characterized as "energetic and aggressive," the fifty-six-year-old senior artillery officer had extensive command experience in North America. John Grant remembers him taking aside his son, John Williamson, a Royal Artillery lieutenant commanding one of the five row galleys, and saying, "God bless you my Boy, but do your duty, and don't disgrace me." (Illustration from *An Historical Journal of the Campaigns in North America … by Captain John Knox*. Editors' photo)

Lieutenant Colonel William Amherst with evident satisfaction. Casualties were light: one artillery sergeant killed and a New York provincial wounded. General Amherst named the captured schooner *Williamson* and the entire army moved down to Oswegatchie and took post. The main French defensive position was then sighted, "an island fortified a little below this place," wrote William Amherst. His older brother immediately ordered a reconnaissance to find out what actually lay in his path.[150]

After the fall of Fort Niagara in 1759, engineer *capitaine* Jean-Nicolas Desandrouins[151] was ordered to build a fort on a tiny island[152] in the St. Lawrence near present-day Ogdensburg, New York, and it was named for the man

---

150. **Capture of schooner.** Entry, 17 August 1760. William Amherst, *Journal of William Amherst in America, 1758-1760*, John Clarence Webster, ed. (Shediac, NB, 1927), 64.

151. ***Capitaine* Jean-Nicolas Desandrouins** (1729-92). French army officer. Born at Verdun, France, Desandrouins was commissioned lieutenant in the Régiment de Beauce in 1746. Five years later, following active service in the War of the Austrian Succession, he entered the military engineering school at Mézières and graduated with distinction, joining the engineer corps in 1752. Sent to Canada in 1756, he played a key role in the siege and capture of Oswego. He also made important contributions to Montcalm's victories of 1757 and 1758. In 1759, as Bourlamaque's senior engineer, he constructed new defensive positions in the Richelieu River–Lake Champlain sector against Brigadier Haviland's cautiously advancing force. From mid-August until March 1760 he was responsible for the construction and command of Fort Lévis, then went as engineer and aide de camp to Lévis in his attempt to retake Quebec from the British. Later that year, after the surrender of the colony, Desandrouins returned to France and continued a distinguished career in the engineer corps for another thirty-one years before being forced to retire by the Revolution. He died in 1792.

152. **Isle Royale**. A small, low-lying, rocky island that was situated in the middle of the Saint Lawrence River near present-day Ogdensburg, New York. Any remains of the British fort, William Augustus, built to replace the battered French fortification, have disappeared underwater with the completion of the Saint Lawrence Seaway in 1959. Today only a small portion of the former island, now known as Chimney Island, is visible above water.

who ordered it built: Major General François-Gaston de Lévis.[153] Its only purpose was to guard and defend the western "back-door" approach to Montreal from the Great Lakes. When Desandrouins left the site in the fall, only the ramparts were finished and much work remained to be done.

Capitaine Pierre Pouchot[154] of the Béarn Regiment, who had extensive experience of sieges and engineering himself, was left in command and put his tiny garrison to work to complete the fort over the winter. The barracks, storehouses and officers' quarters, all of log and plank construction, were finished first to shelter the men and vital stores. Then gun embrasures were sited to best advan-

---

153. **Major General François-Gaston de Lévis** (1719-87). French army officer. Born near Limoux, France, son of Jean de Lévis, Baron d'Ajac, and Jeanne-Marie de Maguelonne. He entered the army in his teens, merely another "impoverished Gascon cadet" but one with excellent family connections. Commissioned 2nd lieutenant in the Régiment de la Marine on 25 March 1735, rising to lieutenant that same year and captain by 1737. Served with distinction in the War of the Polish Succession and the War of the Austrian Succession, rising to brevet colonel and serving as assistant chief of staff. Known as a "brave and competent officer noted for his sang-froid," he served as second-in-command to Major General Louis-Joseph de Montcalm in the defence of New France during the Seven Years' War. Following Montcalm's death at the battle of the Plains of Abraham, he was appointed commander of French forces in North America. After the surrender of New France, he was returned to France on parole but released for service in Europe by William Pitt. Retired from active military service when the war ended in 1763. Appointed governor of Artois in 1765. Promoted to Marshal of France in 1783, raised to the inheritable title Duc de Lévis in 1784. He died in 1787 in Arras, France.

154. ***Capitaine* Pierre Pouchot** (1712-69). French army officer. Born at Grenoble, France, the son of a merchant, Pouchot joined the regular French army as a volunteer engineer in 1733 and the following year obtained a commission as a *lieutenant en second* in the Régiment de Béarn, with service in Italy, Flanders and Germany. He won distinction during the War of the Austrian Succession as an engineer, receiving the cross of the Order of Saint-Louis, and in 1745 a brevet promotion to *capitaine*. In 1755 his regiment was selected for service in Canada and on arrival he was sent to Cataraqui in July, and later detached as commandant of Fort Niagara, tasked to complete the fortifications. In 1758 he and his company fought at Fort Carillon (later Fort Ticonderoga), where they and other French regulars defeated Major General James Abercromby's British and provincial army. In 1759 he was back in command of Fort Niagara, where he was a helpless spectator on 24 July 1759 at the battle at La Belle-Famille. He was compelled to surrender the fort the following day. After being exchanged in 1760, the capable Pouchot was tasked to complete and command Fort Lévis on Isle Royale near Ogdensburg, New York. His mission was to delay the British army's descent down the Saint Lawrence River for as long as possible. After the fall of Montreal in 1760, Pouchot returned to France and retired to Grenoble to write his memoirs. Coming out of retirement, and while employed as a military engineer in Corsica, he was killed on 8 May 1769. For a more complete French account of the siege of Fort Lévis, see Pierre Pouchot's own *Mémoires sur la dernière guerre de l'Amérique septentrionale entre la France et l'Angleterre, suivis d'observations, dont plusieurs sont relatives au théatre actuel de la guerre, et de nouveaux détails sur les mœurs et les usages des sauvages, avec des cartes topographiques*, Brian Dunnigan, ed., 3 vols (Yverdon, 1781, reprint Niagara, 1994).

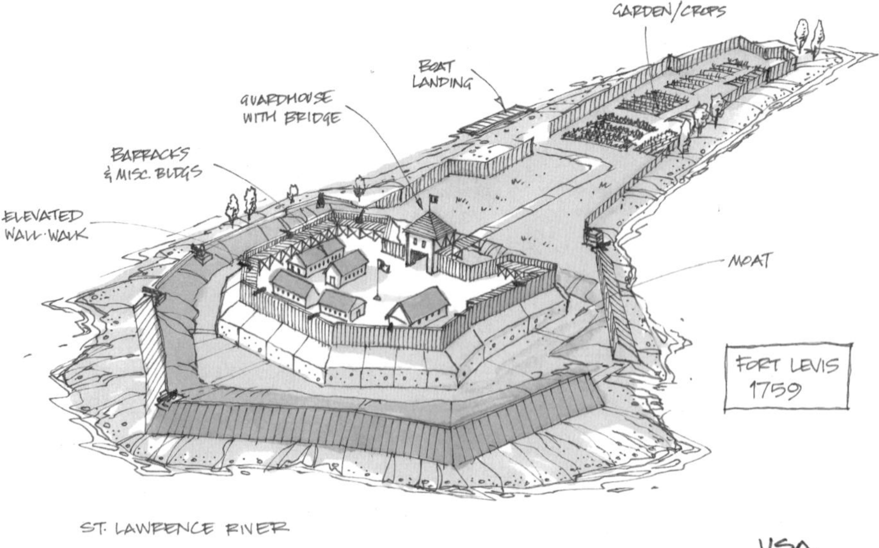

"An awful spectacle." A modern-day recreation of Fort Lévis as it appeared in 1759 to the besieging British. John Grant visited the island after its surrender, noting "the small fort presented an awful spectacle within, scarce a y[ar]d that was not marked by shot or shells. Their log houses, which contained the miserable wounded, were riddled." (Ink sketch by Andrew King)

The victor of Sillery, 1760. François-Gaston, Chevalier de Lévis (1719-87), was the second in command of French forces in North America until 1759, when he replaced General Montcalm, the overall commander, who was killed at Quebec. Best known for his April 1760 siege of Quebec and his defeat of the British army under General Murray at the battle of Sillery (second battle of the Plains of Abraham), he died the Duc de Lévis and a Marshal of France in 1787, just months before the outbreak of the French Revolution. A frenzied mob would desecrate his grave and execute his wife and two daughters. (Artist unknown. Chateau Ramezay. Photo by R. Chartrand)

tage and cut into the thick earthen walls, while a gun platform made of oak timbers was constructed around the ramparts (see fort plan).

Now Jeffery Amherst put this tiny fort under siege. The always careful and methodical Amherst first surrounded the small island with gun batteries lining the adjacent shores and islands. Once this was done, he ordered the first salvoes fired on the morning of 23 August 1760 and the guns did not cease their bombardment until two days later. He then ordered Sir William Johnson to send his Indians downriver to reconnoitre "at least two days march" and give any advance warning "in case Mons de Lévis should attempt to come up."[155]

155. **Indians**. Entry, 21 August 1760. *Amherst's Journal*, 236.

An unhappy issue. *Onondaga,* a three-masted merchant vessel constructed at Oswego, armed with sixteen 6-pounders, was the last of Major General Jeffery Amherst's three large vessels to be crippled in the short but furious 1760 amphibious assault on Fort Lévis in the middle of the Saint Lawrence River. The *Onondaga*'s grounding was not considered controversial but rather who aboard actually ordered the British colours struck to the French – the ship's captain or the commodore? Colonel Williamson, the artillery commander, commented that "if he & crew could not stand it on bd they ought not to strike under our Noses [*sic*] so near our batteries but come over to us leaving everything standing, waiting for a happier issue." (Pencil sketch by Peter Rindlisbacher)

William Amherst recorded the battle plan in his journal: orders were issued to the grenadiers of the army to storm the fort on the same day as the batteries opened fire. The plan was to mount an amphibious assault using the captured *Williamson* and the two British snows, *Mohawk* and *Onondaga,* which were "to fall down close to the Fort as they can, to man their tops and keep the enemy from their guns, the grenadiers to row in with fascines & scaling ladders, in their shirts, taking only their broadswords and tomahawks."[156]

However, the moment the three ships got close and anchored, they were targeted by the French gunners, who had held their fire until that moment. The *Mohawk* was first to cut her cable and she fell below the island when she was stove in below the waterline. An "unlucky shot cutting the Cable of the *Williamson*, Lt. Sinclair was obliged to follow the *Mohawk*," wrote General Amherst. The third ship, *Onondaga*, went aground on the fort's island and was

156. **Plan of attack**. Entry, 23 August 1760. William Amherst, *Journal of William Amherst in America, 1758-1760*, John Clarence Webster, ed. (Shediac, NB, 1927), 65. *Mohawk* and *Onondaga:* two three-masted merchant vessels known as snows and constructed at Oswego. Both carried sixteen 6-pounders and a crew of ninety seamen.

"Frightful in appearance but not dangerous." Major General Jeffery Amherst recorded that "the current of the River was very strong" at the Long Sault and that while "I took water several times in the whale boat" the rapids were "frightful in appearance but not dangerous." Unfortunately, the following day, "a Bateau of the 1st Batt[alion] of the R[oyal] Highlanders in coming down the Long Seau [*sic*] this morning & keeping too near the shore was staved & a Corporal & three men drowned." (Detail from a watercolour by Lieutenant Thomas Davies, Royal Artillery. LAC 1948-13-1)

pounded by the French artillery until she filled with water and struck her colours.[157]

During the afternoon of 25 August 1760 the French defenders finally ran out of ammunition, and their commandant, Pouchot, beat a parley. An officer carried a letter asking for terms and Amherst sent back his terms of capitulation: the French must surrender the fort immediately and all would be treated as prisoners of war.

"I ordered Lt. Col. [Eyre] Massey with three Companys [*sic*] of Grenadiers to take Possession of the Fort," wrote Amherst. "I did not permit an Indian to go in." Understandably, this annoyed many of Sir William Johnson's Indians and a large number of them left.[158]

Pouchot's surviving garrison numbered 291 all ranks, with casualties of 12 men killed and 35 wounded. By comparison, British casualties were 21 killed

157. **Failure of attack.** Entry, 23 August 1760. *Amherst's Journal*, 237. Lieutenant Sinclair was Patrick Sinclair of the 42nd Foot. See Part Three for Biographical Note on Patrick Sinclair.
158. **Surrender**. Entry, 25 August 1760. *Amherst's Journal*, 239.

and 23 wounded. The tiny fort, which had been reduced to earth and splintered logs, yielded up thirty-five pieces of artillery of various calibres, some of them British guns taken at Oswego in 1757. Jeffery Amherst had the fort rebuilt and garrisoned so the French could not reclaim it. It was renamed Fort William Augustus in honour of the Duke of Cumberland.

Unbeknownst to Amherst and the Highlanders under his command, heavier casualties lay in wait for them downstream, but not at the hands of the French or Indians. The killers would be a series of dangerous rapids on the final approaches to Montreal with names like "cotau [*sic*] du lac, battures des Cedres, Buisson, trou et le Cascade, of which the two last are the most dreadful that can be imagined," wrote an artillery officer.[159]

On 1 September 1760 Amherst's army first negotiated the Long Sault, an extensive set of rapids just north of modern-day Massena, New York, and west of Cornwall, Ontario. Private Robert Kirkwood, serving with Montgomery's Highlanders, wrote that they ran "with great rapidity and are extremely dangerous: but we had the good fortune to have a guide who knew the falls perfectly." The guides were seventeen *Canadien* crewmen, originally captured from the French sloop, and two Oswegatchie Indians, now distributed amongst the

---

159. **Rapids.** The artillery officer was likely Captain Lieutenant Thomas Skinner of the Royal Artillery, a friend and correspondent of John Knox, *An Historical Journal of the Campaigns in North America for the Years 1757, 1758, 1759 and 1760*, A.G. Doughty, ed., 3 vols (Toronto, 1914), II, 557.

flotilla. Kirkwood remembered one guide sitting upright "in a whale boat, in company with the General [Amherst], proceeded in our front, the rest of the battoes followed in a direct line. Six men was the compliment to a boat, and they occupied her as follows; one man at the helm, while four rowed, and another sat in the bow, in order to break waves, that arose by the great current of the stream."[160]

Amherst recorded that "the current of the River was very strong" at the Long Sault and that while "I took water several times in the whale boat" the rapids were "frightful in appearance but not dangerous." Unfortunately, the following day, "a Bateau of the 1st Batt[alion] of the R[oyal] Highlanders in coming down the Long Seau [*sic*] this morning & keeping too near the shore was staved & a Corporal & three men drowned." At the next set of dangerous rapids, greater caution was taken, for here Amherst found "the greatest Part of the Rapids I had to pass could only be passed with one boat abreast." He put most of his men ashore to march from the Cedars to the end of the Cascades, but confessed that "the Rapids cost us dear, notwithstanding every Corps had a Pilot."[161]

Private Kirkwood reckoned the high loss of life "was occasioned, by their not being careful to keep their boats in the right channel, which can only be distinguished by the smoothness of the surface, and it is always fatal to any who deviate from this rule." A light infantry man adept with canoes, whaleboats and bateaux, Kirkwood noted that they ran "15 miles in 15 minutes, and if you offer to turn out of this current, which you would imagine would precipitate you in ruin, nothing but being dash'd to pieces, and unavoidably lost will be the consequence."[162]

Amherst recorded in his journal: "We lost 84 men, 20 bateaus of Reg[imen]ts, 17 of Artillery, 17 whaleboats, one Row Galley, a quantity of Artillery Stores & some Guns that I hope may be recovered." Of this total, the light infantry who were leading the way lost twenty-five men drowned, while John Grant's battalion, the 2nd/42nd Foot, and the provincials seem to have suffered the remaining casualties. Amherst regrouped his army below the rapids on 5 September 1760.[163]

---

160. **Private Robert Kirkwood**. Robert Kirk[wood], *Through So Many Dangers: The Memoirs and Adventures of Robert Kirk, Late of the Royal Highland Regiment*, Ian McCulloch and Tim Todish, eds. (Limerick, 1775, reprint New York, 2004), 70. Hereafter, *TSMD*. First printed in 1775, this is a rare personal narrative of the Seven Years' War seen through the eyes of a private soldier who served in two of the three Highland regiments in North America, the 77th and the 42nd.

161. **Amherst's description**. Entry, 1 & 2 September 1760. *Amherst's Journal*, 242-4.

162. **Running the rapids.** *TSMD*, 73.

163. **Casualties**. Entry. 4 September 1760. *Amherst's Journal*, 244.

At daybreak on 6 September, Amherst's army was re-embarked in its boats and was moving toward the capital of Canada. "I rowed in four Columns," he recorded. "We had a fine day & I rowed down to La Chine[164] on the Isle of Montreal ... here I landed without any other opposition than some Volunteers and a sort of Cavalry who run into Montreal after a very few shots." The capitulation of Montreal two days later, 8 September 1760, effectively completed Britain's conquest of New France in the Seven Years' War. The war itself would continue until 1763, at which point the French colony formally became a British possession. Amherst proudly wrote, "I believe never three Armys [*sic*], setting out from different & very distant Parts from each other joined in the Centre, as was intended, better than we did, and it could not fail of having the effect of which I have just now seen the consequence."[165]

On 9 September, the day after the Governor of New France signed the terms of capitulation, two companies of British grenadiers and three companies of light infantry were accorded the exclusive honour of entering the city, led by a symbolic 12-pounder cannon and "many Drums & Fifes [and] a Band of Musick [*sic*]." All other troops remained outside the city, prohibited from entering, Amherst "having no intention of releasing hundreds of bored, curious, mischievous, and exclusively Protestant soldiers loose in the city to wreak God only knew what havoc."[166]

Ten days later, after dispatching all the provincial regiments home, Amherst let the regiments allocated to Brigadier Thomas Gage for the garrison of Montreal draw lots for their quarters, with one exception. "I put the 1st Royal Highland Battalion in the town," he recorded, but they did not march in until 20 September 1760.[167]

Two days later, the Highlanders were joined by their 2nd Battalion, which was then parcelled out to some outlying parishes on the island. John Grant and his company would spend their first Canadian winter snugly billeted in

---

164. **La Chine**. The parish of "La Chine" was located on the Island of Montreal. In the early 1760s the parish consisted of seventy-two families with ninety-eight men "able to bear arms." The name "La Chine" was formally adopted when the parish of Saints-Anges-de-la-Chine was created in 1689, with the form "Lachine" first appearing with the opening of a post office in 1829. "La Chine" stems from the French *la Chine* (China), first used in 1667, supposedly in mockery of Robert Cavalier de La Salle, who explored the interior of North America, trying to find a passage to Asia. When he returned unsuccessful, he and his men were derisively named *les Chinois* (the Chinese). Today Lachine is a borough (*arrondissement*) within the city of Montreal on the Island of Montreal in southwestern Quebec.
165. **Boast**. Entry. 8 September 1760. *Amherst's Journal*, 247.
166. **Amherst's precautions**. Douglas R. Cubbison, *All Canada in the Hands of the British: General Jeffery Amherst and the 1760 Campaign to Conquer New France* (Univ. of Oklahoma Press, 2014), 205.
167. **Entries**. 18, 19, 20 and 22 September 1760. *Amherst's Journal*, 253-4.

Montreal, c.1762. "An East View of Montreal, in Canada," drawn "on the Spot" by Thomas Patten. Engraved by Pierre-Charles Canot and published by Thomas Jefferys in 1762. (JCB 6369)

the homes of French-Canadian farmers on the west side of the island, a winter chillier and more challenging than his sojourn in the Mohawk Valley the year before.

* * *

[Pages 55 and 56 are missing. The missing pages must detail the 2nd Battalion's deployment back to Fort Ontario to join the gathering army under Jeffery Amherst for the expedition against Montreal, Canada. Grant's memoirs resume with the army besieging Fort Lévis in the middle of the Saint Lawrence River on 23 August 1760.]

57 I was order'd on Picquet where we had to construct abattis[168] for defence against the Indians who were hovering about. No sooner [was] that duty done than I was order'd on duty to the trenches, so that I was really three days with scarce sleep.

I was so tired at last that when the work was finished shortly before daybreak (on the fourth day of our arrival) I leant against the parapet[169] of the battery and fell fast asleep. My party missing me, [they] went off before dawn to avoid the

168. ***Abattis***. Chopped-down trees laid lengthwise, their branches sharpened then intertwined to form an impenetrable barrier designed to slow down and fix attackers in front of trenches or defensive positions similar to the later use of barbed wire in modern times.

169. **Parapet**. A breastwork or protective wall over which defenders, standing on a fire step (banquette), fired their weapons.

fire of the Fort [Fort Lévis] on the Island [Isle Royale] which was heavy, and reported me killed or missing. When I awoke 2 hours after dawn, the Batteries had opened and had been firing, that so sound was my sleep as not to disturb me. On [my] return to [the] Regiment, [the] Ensigns looked disappointed, taking me for a Step.[170]

When the French Brig was taken, it was enquired if there was an officer who had been at Sea. An Ensign in our Regiment by [the] name [of] [PATRICK] SINCLAIR had been for some years at sea. He was appointed to the command and she was manned in the same manner. She was warped[171] down in the evening opposite to the Fort and at night opened on it to distract its fire from the batteries and trenches [being dug by us]. She suffered a good deal and lost many killed and wounded. Before dawn she was warped back again out of fire to repay [*sic*, repair] damages.

58 Next morning Commodore Rawling[172] [*sic*] with his 16-gun Brig arrived & another vessel, and all three[173] were order'd to take a station in order to distract the attention of the besieged. As the works having suffered a good deal, it was proposed to storm, by dashing at the Island by boats. By some error a wrong station was taken about 12 o'clock by the Commodore and after a few rounds his [anchor] cable was shot away and the strong stream carried him down to within 300 yards of the fort where he grounded. He immediately struck. A boat was dispatched to take possession from the fort.

Old Colonel Williamson, who commanded the Artillery, was in the Battery at the time and laying a gun, cut the boat right in two. There was a loud cheer from our army. They [the French] all perished, afraid to send another boat, but continued firing at it. A boat with a Lieutenant and 30 men was sent on board [by the British] and kept possession in spite of the fire.

In the meantime, Captain Pouchot who commanded, seeing the determined

---

170. **Step.** A step in promotion, as a death vacancy would have allowed one ensign to move up the ladder of promotion, improving the other's position in line and seniority.

171. **Warping or kedging.** A method of moving a sailing vessel, typically against the wind or out from a dead calm, by hauling on a line attached to a kedge anchor, a sea anchor or a fixed object, such as a bollard. In smaller boats, the anchor may be thrown in the intended direction of progress and hauled in after it settles, thus pulling the boat in that direction. In larger ships, a ship's boat is used to carry the anchor ahead where it is then dropped.

172. **"Commodore Rawling."** John Grant's recollection of the commodore's name commanding the naval contingent is incorrect. The commodore was actually Captain Joshua Loring, RN, and he and the other ship arrived on 19 August 1760. There *was* a Joshua Rowley serving in the Royal Navy at the same time as Loring, but John may have only remembered the first name Joshua in his old age, then looked it up incorrectly in the naval lists.

173. **Three vessels.** The snows *Onondaga* and *Mohawk* and the newly-christened *Williamson* (formerly, the French brig *L'Outaouaise*).

preparations that [we] were making, beat the *chamade*[174] about 3 o'clock. Curious circumstance of [the] drummer. When shot [was] falling near him, he laid down on his belly and, when [the shot] exploded, jumping up and beating. The White flag was 59 then hauled and firing ceased. Informed one of the officers and parties, after preliminaries were settled, to take possession [of the Fort]. The small fort presented an awful spectacle within, scarce a y[ar]d that was not marked by shot or shells. Their log houses, which contained the miserable wounded, were riddled. They had made [a] sort of pits for them, cover'd with logs and earth. These, miserable as slums, were their only refuge. The garrison consisted of 280 men, two Hundred of whom were either killed or wounded.[175] He [Captain Pouchot] made a brave defence, considering the odds against him.

- - - - - - - - - - - -

I was the first who thought of making an abbatis [*sic*] against the Indians when on picquet.

- - - - - - - - - - - -

Old Colonel Williamson took his young son,[176] a boy, by the hand when getting into the Boats to storm the Brig. [He] said, "God bless you my Boy, but do your duty, and don't disgrace me." I was standing near the old man at the time, as those officers not on duty were permitted to go down to the place of embarkation as spectators.

- - - - - - - - - - - -

Shores around Isle Royale low, as well as the Island itself. A village of Saint Francois Indians opposite.[177]

---

174. **Chamade**. Drum beating indicating a wish to parley. Usually accompanied by a white flag by the French and a red flag by the British.
175. **Casualties**. John Grant's recollection of some 200 French killed or wounded is somewhat exaggerated. The entire garrison of Fort Lévis numbered 291 all ranks. The French lost a total of 12 men killed and 35 wounded. British casualties, by comparison, were 21 killed and 23 wounded.
176. **1st Lieutenant John Williamson** (c.1738-94). Royal Artillery officer. The son of Colonel George Williamson, he was commanding one of the five row-galleys accompanying Amherst's army as fire support. John entered the Royal Artillery as a matross in December 1752, rising to 1st lieutenant on 19 April 1758. Served as adjutant to the 1st Battalion, Royal Regiment of Artillery, between November 1760 and October 1770. Rose to the rank of colonel on 25 September 1793. Died at Shooters' Hill, Greenwich, London, on 19 October 1794.
177. **Saint François Indians**. Not to be confused with the infamous Saint François-de-Sales Indians who came from a mission settlement established for the western Abneki at the confluence of the Saint Lawrence and Saint-François rivers at the edge of Lac Saint-Pierre further downriver. Also known as Odanak, this village served as the principal launching point for all Indian raids south into New England for the previous hundred years until it was destroyed in October 1759 by Rogers' Rangers. By contrast, the Indians of the mission settlement at Oswegatchie were predominantly Christian Iroquois converts who had

— — — — — — — — — — — —

One Thousand of our warriors returned home because they were prevented from scalping the French taken in the fort.[178]

— — — — — — — — — — — —

60 The Guns we used were carried in the boats attached to the Artillery and were 2 Brass eighteen pounders and some field pieces and some small mortars and Howitzers. General [Jeffery] Amherst commanded. No Brigades were formed.

We remain'd three days to prepare and we set out at daybreak, leaving the [Navy?] & ships in charge. We got about 40 miles the first day, in the best manner we could without meeting any rough water or rifts as they were called. The next day the same, the country still uninhabited. [The] next day an order was issued that in order to avoid confusion, the Boats should go two and two abreast, and each Regiment [to] keep together. It was said that we had no rapids to fear. In this order we set out and had proceeded some hours along this majestic river in full security.

On a sudden I saw the boats ahead of me suddenly disappear, and felt the suction of the water. [I] immediately divined the cause. I jumped up [and] called out "a rapid" and to keep to the right, & to pass the word. [I] instantly turn'd the head of the boat, clapped two [hands] to the oars and pulled hard. Caught however by the suction on the edge of the rapid, the boat was whirled about and filled with water. The casks floated & one struck me a blow in the side that almost stunned me. We however got down safe & saw several boats upset, and poor fellows swimming and struggling in the eddies below the falls and calling piteously for help. I ordered some men 61 to bail out the boat with the camp kettles, whilst I pulled into the bottom of [the] fall and succeeded in saving 13 of my Regiment.[179] The other boats, from having timely notice, got down safe & two or three came in time to save a few more. But 50 or 60 found a watery grave – Bonnets, casks, baggage, all floating about in the eddy.

The cause of this disaster was the mention made that there were no rapids,

---

moved north from the Five Nations with their Jesuit missionaries. The appellation "Saint François" is therefore a geographical reference, as the section of river near Fort Lévis was also known as Lac Saint François.

178. **Returned home**. This is an exaggeration since there were only 706 Indians with Amherst's command. According to Sir William Johnston, 506 Indians had departed in disgust along with twenty whaleboats. Those who remained were principally members of the Iroquois Confederation who stayed because of personal loyalty to Sir William.

179. **Saving 13**. Captain William Sterling of the 42nd wrote that one of his regimental boats "spilled with three drowned and thirteen saved." NAS, GD 24-1-458-2.

so that the people were not on their guard. The Guide[180] who led the Army had passed clear and a number of boats followed him but, as there happened to be occasionally a distance between the boats, they gradually obliqued [*sic*] to the left imperceptibly and thus got within the suction of the fall, which fell about 12 feet. The rest of the Army past [*sic*] safe and we arrived at our camping ground. **We were only allowed as officers, soldiers' tents.**[181]

Next morning as usual we set out and proceeded 'till midday when we approached the formidable rapid of the Long Suie[182] [*sic*]. We all approached the shore and landed leaving some men to direct the boats down the rapids. Most of the regular boats[183] got safe but a number of the Provincials perished through unskillfulness, with the loss also of the Bateaux and most of the provisions.

It was rather a dangerous service and [an] officer of ours, an excellent swimmer, volunteered by [the] name [of] HERRING.[184] The prodigal of his own life, he was not with his baggage for I remember to have seen his servant, a little man sweaty under the weight of his portmanteau[185] which he had not taken with him. The reason for the loss of the Yankies [*sic*] was that they were New England men and when they were in danger they sung psalms and prayed instead of [taking] caution, whilst our fellows swore and worked. Some of the [Regular] Regiments, however, lost a few.

As yet the country on either side of the magnificent river was quite in a state of nature and only frequented by the Indians and the Voyageurs in the fur trade. The shores sometimes rocky, sometimes low, were all cover'd with the most 62 superb forests.

Next day we proceeded in the same manner to the Isle Perrot.[186] Here we

---

180. **Guides**. The guides were seventeen *Canadien* seaman captured with the French brig *L'Outaouaise* and two Oswegatchie Indians who were distributed amongst the flotilla.
181. **Editors' note**. This sentence, originally appearing in one of the four loose quarto sheets, was placed here in the narrative.
182. **Long Sault**. John Grant implies in his memoirs that the army ran a dangerous rapid *before* running the rapids at Long Sault. His memory is a little hazy, putting the two most dangerous rapids (Long Sault and Cedars) out of chronological order. The rapids at Long Sault were located just north of the modern community of Massena, New York, while the more dangerous rapids at the Cedars were closer to Montreal at the eastern end of Lac Saint-François.
183. **Regular boats**. In other words, boats containing British regulars.
184. **Lieutenant Elbert Herring**. See Part Three for Biographical Note. This paragraph, originally appearing in one of the four loose quarto sheets, was placed here in the narrative.
185. **Portmanteau**. A large trunk or suitcase, typically made of stiff leather and opening into two equal parts.
186. **Isle Perrot**. About 7 miles (11 km) in length and nearly 3 miles (5 km) in breadth, the Island was granted by Intendant Jean Talon to Sieur François-Marie Perrot, a captain in the Régiment d'Auvergne and governor of Montreal, on 29 October 1672. By the mid-18th century the island was an important supplier of wheat to the Montreal market. A

landed and took prisoner the only family on the island. We remained there 48 hours to re-organise and arrange the troops for the landing at La Chine.

At daybreak therefore the whole Army were embarked with 2 days' provisions in their haversacks but without their baggage. Marshalled in divisions, Colours displayed, drums beating, pipes playing, the River was like glass, the morning beautiful, it was a glorious sight. We landed in a few hours at La Chine.

The 42nd Regiment was immediately order'd to advance. We pushed along at double quick along a narrow path bounded by brushwood, only 4 abreast. We were afraid of a surprise. It was 9 miles and in less than two hours we had debouched from it and formed on the plain in front of Montreal. Our situation was not pleasant as we expected an attack every moment and were not sure of a support. However, we could always retreat in the wood.

We remained under arms 'till Sunset, when the rest of the Army arrived. We had no tents and spent but a miserable night, our bodies heated by our rapid march and the hot day, & the chilly night dew and the damp swampy ground threw some of us into fever. [The] next day we stood to our arms, but the Capitulation of the Canadas was signed. Our tents arrived and I retired to mine 63 in a high fever. As a complaint, curious. Whilst I lay a-bed, I was well but could not eat, but whenever I attempted to get up, I fainted. I took no medicine. I was confined for about a fortnight when we were order'd into winter quarters or cantonments.[187]

Montreal was then a place of some consequence. But the inhabitants from the long blockade and non-intercourse with Europe, were badly off for groceries, wine and spirits, but above all, salt.

It was in September [1760] I was quartered 20 miles from Montreal in the Parish of Saint Genevieve[188] with my Company – the others of the 2nd Battalion were quartered around. The 1st Battalion was quartered in town [Montreal], the other Regiments were scatter'd about in different parts of the Settlements.

We were billeted on the best houses, we were on a river half a mile broad

---

stone windmill built c.1707 is still standing despite the island being a growing suburb of Montreal. R. Paul Goodman, *The General Slept Here: The Amherst British Army Encampment, Ile Perrot, 4 & 5 September 1760* (Privately Published, Île Perrot, 2014), 5.

187. **Cantonments**. An army's temporary resting place, where the men are placed in people's homes in adjacent towns and villages, as opposed to being placed under canvas in camps.

188. **Sainte-Geneviève**. Located on the northwest shore of the Island of Montreal overlooking the Rivière des Prairies and across from Isle Bizard located to the north. The village was established by French habitants in 1701 after the signing of the Great Peace of Montreal with the Iroquois. In 1739 the Roman Catholic Archdiocese of Quebec approved the establishment of a parish dedicated to Saint Geneviève and the first church was erected in 1751 under the supervision of Antoine Faucon, father of Saint-Sulpice.

opposite the Isle Jesus.[189] I was with a Lieutenant of Militia and his family. The houses consisted only of two rooms and a cooking place and were of logs. One of the rooms I had. A stove was between the two rooms warming both, and also a fireplace. Our amusements when off duty, which was only visiting twice a week the different quarters of the soldiers, was shooting, visiting, [and] going into Montreal.

The Winter set in the beginning of November. By the sides of the river being frozen for about 30 or 40 yards on either side, it was cold yet fine & clear in the middle of the day (Saint Genevieve was on the west side of the Island). Before the frost set in I had been sent to Montreal for provisions, pork, flour, &c. I was laughed at for purchasing 4 or 5 barrels of salt, but remembered that salt was very scarce at Saint Genevieve. When I returned we began to lay in our winter fresh stock of 64 provisions which are killed at the beginning of the Winter and remain frozen during it, cutting off a piece when wanted. My salt now came into play, and my speculation sufficed to lay in Beef, Mutton, [and] Poultry enough for our mess for several months. Our men were well off, two were quarter'd in every house, and the Canadians who prefer pork and scarcely eat at that time any other meat, exchanged poultry & beef &c. for the men's rations.

I paid 5^{d} [pence] for a pound of Sugar and 2 pounds [Stirling] for a gallon of rum, wine and other luxuries in proportion.[190] The severe frost does not generally set in 'till after the Snow has fallen so that the ice in the centre of bodies of water is unset by it. Thus the Lac de deux Montagnes,[191] 16 miles long, where Gage's Light Infantry, formed of all the Jail birds of America, and the 44th [Regiment] all quartered, was frozen over for 3 days and we passed along it in sledges.

Curious circumstance. One night, I was surprised to see my Servant up and dressing and taking care of the fires after I awoke from my first sleep, and to observe my fusee and cartridge box lying near my bed. I asked him what he was doing. He said he was cleaning his arms. I fell asleep and early next morning I woke and found him up. It struck me as strange but I thought nothing more 'till going on my rounds next day. There was a general complaint that all the men had fright-

189. **Isle Jésus**. French for Jesus Island. The island is separated from the mainland to the north by the Rivière des Mille Îles, and from the Island of Montreal to the south by the Rivière des Prairies.

190. **Editors' note**. The next two paragraphs, originally appearing in one of the four loose quarto sheets, were placed here in the narrative.

191. **Lac des Deux Montagnes** (English: Lake of Two Mountains). Originally named Lac des Médicis in 1612 by Samuel de Champlain, the French colonists named it as Lac des Deux Montagnes around 1684. The lake is part of the river delta widening of the Ottawa River in Quebec at its confluence with the Saint Lawrence River. The lake has four outflows: Rivière des Mille Îles and Rivière des Prairies, bordering Isle Jésus, and two branches of the Ottawa River, flowing into the Saint Lawrence via Lake Saint-Louis, on either side of Isle Perrot.

ened Him by sitting up all night, armed. Upon questioning the men, I found out that they imagined that there was a plot to rouse all the French that night & murder them [while sleeping] and this had been kept a secret amongst the men. Could never learn origin of [the] reports.

On the 9th of November we celebrated the King's birthday, tho' dead, not knowing it.[192] Up to our knees in snow which had that night commenced, and snowed for about a fortnight, 'till it was 7 feet upon a level, there being no drift. Then every sleigh was in motion. To keep the track open, branches of trees being put in the evening to mark the track for the next morning.

After that we had a bright and clear sky for the whole winter. About the latter end of November in one night the river was frozen over. My Captain and I lived on the opposite of a bay, a mile round, ¼ [mile] across. I crossed it after 2 night's frost. The cold now becoming more intense, I had my ears frost bitten from running across that distance without the precaution of a Cap with flaps. To make myself warm I got a French tent and nailed it up to the roof which was not sealed nor boarded. Within that, a Soldier's tent, and within that, my bed & curtains. Still it was so cold that 'tho there was a fire and stove and great heat before I went to bed, yet in the morning icicles were on the spot of the sheets where I breathed.

Our men 65 exchanged their kilts at [the] beginning of winter for leggings of green cloth like the backwoodsmen,[193] but suffered much from cold, having only their plaids, but still we had not a sick man during the winter. As there were no spirits to be got until next spring would permit the river Saint Lawrence to be open, we had brought up spirits and wine but at a great expense.

The Priest was a pleasant man. We went about in sledges, sometimes in snowshoes. We used sometimes to dine with the Priest, lived well & plenty of Liquors and Burgundy & Champagne. We were badly off for vegetables, there being none but onions, garlic and cabbage, and but little of them. One of their dishes every day [was a] piece of pork, boiled down in a mass of Cabbage, and then slices of bread put in.

---

192. **Death of King George II**. Unaware that King George II had died on 25 October 1760, John Grant writes that they celebrated the king's birthday on 9 November, although his birthday was on 10 November. As he was writing in later life, perhaps he got the date wrong and the celebration actually took place on the correct date.

193. **Leggings of green cloth**. Standard operating practice during winter months as can be seen by an earlier 6 November 1759 orderly book entry at Crown Point: "The Non-Commissioned Officers & men will be allowed until further orders to do duty in there [*sic*] Kilt over their leggans [*sic*]." Sometimes known as "Indian spatterdashes," leggings were also used by non-Highland troops to protect their legs from walking hazards "that may happen by briars, stumps of trees, or underwood, etc. in marching through a close, woody country." For a complete description of all aspects of a Black Watch soldier's dress, weapons and equipment of the period, see Part Two "Dress, Weapons, Equipment & Specialties" in *SOTM*, vol 2, 113-49.

Spruce beer[194] was the common drink. Fond of dancing but priests forbade the young women from joining the parties where the officers were, but still they shirked the Priests. Of course a good deal of our time was spent in the house, and having but few books, the time sometimes hung heavy. So we welcomed the first appearance of winter's [end] in March.

In April the Pigeons came in most uncommon flocks, myriads.[195] The first flight we had seen occurred thus, when in the commanding Officer's house, a sudden darkness came on with a rushing noise, we ran out to see what was the matter. A flock extending to a distance all around, the Highland Sentinel was laying [*sic*] flat on his belly in a paroxysm of fear.

They lighted in a field near us of several acres, as thick as they could lie. We took our guns and shot a number, the whole country were [*sic*] out, like a skirmish.

66 We caught a great many by means of traps and confined them in a barn and fed them. We thus prolonged our pigeon pies and Soup for some time beyond the fortnight of their appearance.

The snow melts from below and a number of odd accidents occur from breaking through the crust and being suddenly up to the neck. By [the] latter end of April snow had disappeared and the vigorous vegetation of Canada appeared in full vigour.

Chapter 5 | Crown Point and Staten Island, 1761 – "Determined to brave all fears of assassination"

In September 1760, when the Royal Highlanders marched into Montreal, they found every house, mansion and warehouse intact, as there had been no siege with its attendant bombardment. So, unlike their 78th brethren further to the northeast who had spent a terrible winter in Quebec in 1759-60, the Royal Highlanders were blessed with snug, comfortable billets for the winter of 1760-61.

After an uneventful winter and spring, a grand review was ordered for 4 June 1761, the new King's Birthday, a sure indicator to all troops quartered on

194. **Spruce beer**, a natural source of vitamin C, was utilized extensively by the British army in North America as a preventative for scurvy. A Canadian recipe from 1757 states: "It is made of the tops and branches of the spruces-tree, boiled for three hours, then strained into casks, with a certain quantity of molasses; and, as soon as cold, it is fit for use...."

195. **Myriads**. John Grant had likely witnessed a passenger pigeon migration. Once the most common species in North America, the passenger pigeon has been extinct since 1890. Constantly migrating in search of food, shelter or nesting grounds, the dense pigeon flocks were typically described by awe-struck spectators as blackening the entire sky for miles.

"The coils of a gigantic serpent...." An artist's attempt to give "a correct representation" of the dense flocks of passenger pigeons that used to inhabit North America, "the weight of the immense flocks frequently breaking and twisting the limbs of the forest trees as if a hurricane had passed through the woods. Sallying out from their resting-place, they move through the air in compact form, wheeling and twisting in graceful and undulating lines, which resemble the coils of a gigantic serpent. They fly with inconceivable velocity, every one striving to be ahead, and produce a noise similar to that made by a gale at sea passing through the rigging of a close-reefed vessel. As the torrent rolls along, the gunners keep up a continued fire upon the flying birds, and but little skill is required to soon obtain a game-bag well filled." "Shooting wild pigeons in north Louisiana" executed by Smith Bennett, 1875. (Illustration from the Louisiana Digital Library hwj000438. Editors' photo)

the island of Montreal that they would be going on active duty very soon. On the day of the parade, they finally received their marching orders – their destination Crown Point:

> The "General" to beat at 4 o'clock and the "Troop" at 6, after which the regiment will embark in their Battoes at the rate of 9 men in each Battoe, and will have as many artillery boats as they can. After the baggage is thus loaded, one man per company beside the guard which is ordered, will take charge of their own Battoes. If it should happen to rain, the men are to be in little kilt with their plaids cloaked. They are to reserve their old coats for work, which they are to put on at the first halting place, the boats are always to row two in a breast where the river will admit and are to keep as close to one another as possible."[196]

196. **Orders**. Entry, 4 June 1761. James Stewart of Urrard's *Orderly Books, 1757-1761* (Black Watch Museum, Perth), 42.

The Royal Highland battalions crossed over the Saint Lawrence River to La Prairie on the south shore the following day, 5 June, where they marched overland to Sainte-Thérèse on the Richelieu River. Boats sent down from Saint-Jean picked up their provisions and regimental baggage and brought them back to Saint-Jean to meet the men, who continued on by road. At Saint-Jean, both supplies and men were loaded into larger bateaux and shipping for the voyage to Crown Point, some 90 miles (145 km) south up Lake Champlain.

Twenty-five men were assigned to each bateau and four days' rations issued. Escort vessels included a row-galley, a captured French schooner and the sloop *Boscawen*,[197] all of which were loaded with the heavy gear such as regimental tents and equipage. The companies drew lots to determine in what type of vessel they would travel. The lucky ones secured passage in the sailing ships, which meant they were excused from the onerous task of rowing up the lake.

The 1st/42nd went up the lake first on 11 June 1761, with Colonel Francis Grant leading in the schooner, followed by the laden bateaux in line, four abreast. As they had done for the 1759 campaign, the Highlanders took shifts at the oars. They rowed day and night and three days later arrived at Crown Point, the largest fort in North America, huge parts of it still unfinished. The camp colour-men conducted the Highlanders to their designated tent lines, but first they had to clear their allocated ground of tree stumps, "brush and rubbedge." Their empty boats were towed back north by the sailing vessels, so that John Grant and the 2nd/42nd could repeat the process.[198]

Four weeks later, they received orders to proceed to Staten Island, a staging area for the British army to assemble and train for operations southwards towards the Caribbean. Both battalions marched south together to Lake George, then sailed up the lake to Fort George, which had replaced Fort William Henry. From there, both battalions travelled overland to Fort Edward and thence staged down to Albany and the Hudson to Staten Island.

The 1st Battalion arrived there on 25 July 1761 and their colonel, Francis Grant, was immediately made commandant of the Staten Island camp at Watson's Ferry by Major General Amherst. The 2nd Battalion came over on 28 July. Colonel Grant, a younger brother of the Laird of Grant, Sir Ludovick, was quick to issue stringent orders for the discipline and good order of the camp. No officers or soldiers were "to stir off the Island without Colonel Grant's Especial Leave in writing"; guards were detailed for all the ferries, boats and water-

197. ***Boscawen***. A sloop built at Ticonderoga under the direction of Captain Joshua Loring, RN, September 1759. She was armed with fourteen 4-pounder guns and carried a crew of fifty sailors and forty marines.

198. **Camp**. Colonel R. F. H. Wallace, "The Black Watch in 1761: From Montreal to New York," *The Red Hackle*, (July 1935), 18-9.

"An amazing useless mass of earth." "A South View of Crown Point, 1760" executed by Lieutenant Thomas Davies, Royal Artillery. Built after any real threat of French invasion from the north had ended, Crown Point was used largely for staging rather than as a position in its own right. On 21 April 1773, a chimney fire broke out in the soldiers' barracks. It quickly spread, burning for days. In May 1774 an engineer sent to investigate the extent of damage reported back that "the conflagration of the late fort has rendered it an amazing useless mass of earth only." John Grant was briefly interred at the "useless mass" a year later by American rebels so *some* outbuildings survived. (LOC 2004661622)

ing places to prevent desertion; and no soldier was to rob gardens or orchards or pull down fences for firewood. "In order to preserve health," read the Orders, "the Regiments to be out at exercise twice a day; the Rolls to be called at least three times a day" and so on. Francis Grant was taking no chances.[199]

Focused on the campaign at hand, the Caribbean veterans of the 2nd Battalion knew what they were in for and shared their hard-won knowledge with their countrymen. Both battalions of the 42nd underwent complete overhauls of their camp equipment in preparation for the upcoming campaign. On 30 July all tents and bells of arms were struck, washed in the brook beside the regimental lines, then hung up to dry. Every company was issued fourteen new tents, while the grenadier and light infantry companies each received fifteen. The two Black Watch battalions remained encamped on Staten Island until the end of October 1761, waiting for the hurricane season to pass and their orders to embark for a yet undisclosed Caribbean destination.[200]

---

199. **Orders**. Colonel R.F.H. Wallace, "The Black Watch in 1761: From Montreal to New York," *The Red Hackle*, (July 1935), 19.
200. **Refitting**. Entry, 30 July 1761. James Stewart of Urrard's *Orderly Books, 1757-1761* (Black Watch Museum, Perth), 45.

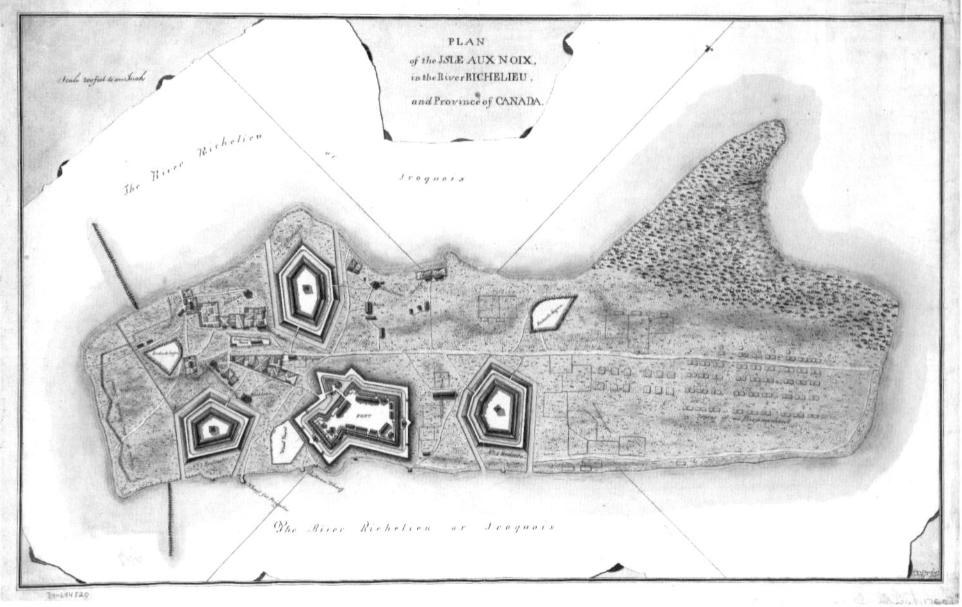

"The Island of Nuts." Named for its once-profuse walnut trees, Isle-aux-Noix, at the northern end of Lake Champlain where the Richelieu River (originally named the Iroquois River) commences, was considered by the French to be an important first line of defence against the Iroquois nations to the south and, later, British and American encroachments. "Plan of the Isle aux Noix, in the River Richelieu, and Province of Canada," a pen and ink drawing executed by Thomas Walker, c.1760. (LOC 74694520)

* * *

In May[201] we embarked at Montreal and bateau'd as far as Chambly,[202] a day's and a half march. Landed there and marched 4 miles on account of the rapids to Saint John's, a few houses and little cultivation. At Saint John's the river is half a mile broad. At 16 miles above, in the centre of the river, is the Isle aux Noix.[203]

---

201. **Embarkation date.** John Grant's memory is faulty. The two battalions embarked 5 June 1761, not May.
202. **Fort Chambly.** A stone fort located at the foot of the Chambly rapids on the Richelieu River, roughly 19 miles (31 km) southeast of Montreal. Built by the French in 1711, the last of three forts to be built on the same site, to protect New France from Iroquois attacks. With the construction of two other forts further south – Fort Saint-Frédéric (1731) and Fort Saint-Jean (1748) – Fort Chambly lost most of its defensive *raison d'etre* and was used as a warehouse. It was re-fortified and reoccupied during the Seven Years' War but failed to stop the British from approaching Montreal and Quebec.
203. **Isle-aux-Noix.** The fortifications on Isle-aux-Noix in the Richelieu River near Lake Champlain were the only significant French defences between Montreal and the British army at Crown Point. The island's position in the middle of the Richelieu River made it possible to control all river traffic. The island itself is about 0.8 miles (1.4 km) long by roughly 437 yards (400 m) in width. Before the start of the fortification work in 1759, the island was nearly all covered by walnut trees, hence its name; a year later, few trees were left. Today, the island is the site of Fort Lennox, built by the British between 1819 and 1829 and named

Looking north. A view of Major General Jeffery Amherst's encampment at the southern end of Lake George during the 1759 campaign against the French forts of Carillon (Ticonderoga) and Saint-Frédèric (Crown Point) on Lake Champlain to the north. In the foreground of this oil painting by Lieutenant Thomas Davies, Royal Artillery, are two figures. One is a member of Rogers' Rangers and the other is a Stockbridge Indian. Both battalions of the Black Watch, assigned to participate in the British expedition to capture Martinique in 1762, staged southwards on their way to Staten Island through this encampment where Fort George was still under construction. (Fort Ticonderoga Museum. Editors' photo)

We were two days reaching Lake Champlain at Crown Point, the river got broader towards Lake Champlain. We encamped at Crown Point where they were building a Fort. There is a splendid view of the Lake from the hill on which it was building. There was no cultivation around or in view. We worked for six weeks at the Fort, very unpleasant on account of the heat. We were forced to be out at 5 o'clock, poor living.

We marched then to Ticonderoga, 12 miles off through the wilderness, our baggage coming round in boats. Ticonderoga was taken the year before, whilst we were at Fort Stanwix, and the fort was ruined & burnt by accident in consequence of the soldiers being permitted to cook at the foot of the rampart, which being faced with logs, the whole took fire.

after Charles Lennox, 4th Duke of Richmond, governor general of North America from 1818 to 1819.

At Ticonderoga I visited the site of our unfortunate disaster of 1758.[204] The Fort was on a low point running into the lake between two Bays. In front of this the French had erected, on some rising ground in front, a breastwork across from water to water. It was made of Logs and earth and in front a strong abbatis [*sic*] of trees pointed [sharpened] for about 20 yards. The left [side] of the work was unfinished and the French had only 4 Regiments[205] when they heard of the force coming against them. They objected to remain in so defenceless a state from the opening at the left. Montcalm[206] had boats prepared and told them that if a single cannon shot was fired he would let them embark.

The English under Sir Jeffery Amherst,[207] [*sic*] 15,000 strong, arrived. A reconnaissance was made and two officers reported the breastwork not to be unfinished, but that it was so weak as to be easily surmounted without the use of cannon. Accordingly, none were brought up.[208]

The attack was made on the right by the Grenadiers of the Army. Entangled in the abbatis [*sic*] they were exposed to a murderous fire without being able to effectively return it or close with their enemies.

A cask of Cartridges exploded in our line and the report so terrified the French

---

204. **Editors' note**. The next four paragraphs, originally appearing in one of the four loose quarto sheets, were placed here in the narrative.

205. **French regiments**. When the battle commenced (12:00 p.m.), Montcalm actually had seven regular infantry battalions (*troupes de la terre*) on the firing line, all 2nd battalions of their respective regiments: Guyenne; La Reine; Languedoc; Royal-Roussillon; La Sarre; Berry; and, Bearn. The 3rd Battalion, Berry, was in support. Montcalm also had about 450 colonial regulars (*troupes de la marine*) and 200 *Canadien* militia.

206. **Lieutenant General Louis-Joseph, Marquis de Montcalm** (1712-1759). French army officer. A professional soldier with considerable campaign experience in Europe, Montcalm assumed command of all regular French troops in New France in 1756. His defensive victory at Carillon in 1758 was short-lived as he faced James Wolfe the following year on the Plains of Abraham, where he was out-generalled and died of his wounds the day after the battle, 14 September 1759.

207. **Major General Jeffery Amherst**. Grant is mistaken. The commanding general of the unfortunate disaster of 1758 was Major General James Abercromby, not Major General Jeffery Amherst, who commanded forces that actually took Ticonderoga the following year. Amherst took the fort just as John Grant was first setting foot in New York colony with the 2nd/42nd, fresh from the Caribbean.

208. **Use of artillery**. John Grant is repeating the "traditional" claim that General Abercromby did not intend for his artillery to come forward. This is incorrect. Abercromby had put a plan in motion for a battery of four 6-pounders to be positioned on the south bank of the La Chute River at the base of Rattlesnake Mountain (now Mount Defiance), from where it could easily enfilade the left flank of the enemy line. Since one French battalion broke during the battle merely from flanking musket fire due to the incomplete breastworks, one might argue that the effect of four field guns raking their positions would have been most influential. As it turned out, the boats carrying the artillery battery went too far downriver, were fired on from the fort and repulsed.

"War is the tomb of the Montcalms." An old saying in the family of Louis-Joseph, marquis de Montcalm (1712-59). The victor of Carillon (1758) would die of wounds on the Plains of Abraham outside Quebec in 1759. Buried in a crater beneath the choir floor of the Ursuline Convent, his skull and a leg bone were accidentally dug up during renovations in 1830. Inexplicably, they were put on permanent display in the convent museum for a paying public instead of being reinterred. In a long-overdue ceremony on September 2001 at the cemetery of the Hôpital général de Québec, Montcalm's remains were finally reunited with the other parts of his body from the museum and placed in a specially built mausoleum. Today Montcalm lies peacefully in Canada's first war cemetery alongside hundreds of Canadian, French and British soldiers who died with him on that fateful day almost 260 years ago. (Portrait by Antoine-François Sergent-Marceau. Published in Paris, 1790. LOC 2001696990)

that two Regiments proceeded to embark.[209] Our Grenadiers retired, other Regiments were ordere'd up in detail [and] suffer'd the same fate. The 42nd Regiment lost 400 men killed & wounded, in all 3,000 men were lost.[210] Had the whole line been formed and advanced, the weak point would have been discovered and the place taken without difficulty.

67 We reached Lake George, which is but a few Miles from Ticonderoga and embarked at a few nameless huts on the north end. It is a beautiful lake (see Last of [the] Mohicans),[211] fine wooded hills on either hand and very clear. We rowed across to the south end in a day, 36 miles in length, and landed at the ruins of Fort William Henry, destroyed in 1757 by Montcalm when the troops & women marching off under the protection of the Capitulation, the women & the Baggage were in the rear and the Indians murdered many of them & plun-

---

209. **French retreat**. Here John Grant alludes to the entire French right wing, composed of several companies of the French colonial marines down in the low ground (without the benefit of the extensive log entrenchments higher up on the rising ground). They did run for the boats at one point in the battle, but returned to their duty when their own cannons in the fort fired upon them.

210. **Casualties**. Out of a total of nearly 2,000 British casualties, almost a third were from the 1st Battalion, 42nd Regiment: 316 Highlanders died, including eight officers; 333 were wounded, including seventeen officers, making a total of 649 casualties out of a total strength of about 1,000 men (this represents a casualty rate of 65 per cent for a single day's action). It is not clear how many died of their wounds (between July and October seventy men were taken off the payroll).

211. ***Last of the Mohicans***. This one reference to the famous best-selling 19th-century novel by James Fenimore Cooper, first published 1826, places the date of the writing of this manuscript (at least this portion of it) in the last two years of John Grant's life, 1827-28, when he was eighty-six years of age.

dered the baggage to the eternal shame of the French who stood spectators. The troops forming themselves into a square prevented much massacre, guarding the remnants of the children & women. The massacre was said to have been instigated by Luc le Corne,[212] Superintendent of Indians, who, tho' appearing to prevent the massacre, said in an undertone: "*Tuez! Tuez!*" [Kill! Kill!]

After the taking of Montreal, Sir William Johnson, the English Superintendent was dining at the Marquis de Vaudreuil's[213] table. The question was put by Luc Le Corne, how Sir William managed to prevent the Indians from massacring and scalping. "Tell him," said the old man (who did not understand French), "that if he had wished to prevent it as much as I did, he could easily have prevented it."

From there we marched 14 miles through the wilderness, by a most excellent broad road made for the conveyance of provisions to the troops at [Fort] William Henry. Fort Edward is on a high plateau above the river Hudson which is but 300 yards wide there, enclosed by high banks, finely wooded. We encamped there that night. Our baggage was sent down by water and we marched next day to Stillwater[214] 68 14 miles further on, so named from the stillness of the water,

---

212. **Luc de la Corne** (1711-1784). French colonial officer and Indian interpreter. An officer in the Compagnies Franches de la Marine and awarded the Cross of Saint Louis in 1759. Served as an experienced Indian interpreter for Louis-Joseph de Montcalm at Fort William Henry in 1757 and was held partially responsible for the attack on British troops. In 1761, on returning to France, his ship, *Auguste,* ran into terrible weather off the coast of Cape Breton, Nova Scotia, and sank. With a few other survivors, he managed to get back to Quebec City during the dead of winter – a trek of some 1,700 miles (2,736 km). He would fight for the British during the War of American Independence. The massacre at Fort William Henry was used as the principal reason for denying the surrendering French regular regiments at Montreal the full honours of war, an action which precipitated them to resentfully burn their colours rather than handing them over to the British as trophies of war.

213. **Pierre de Rigaud, Marquis de Vaudreuil** (1698-1778). French colonial officer; governor of New France. Born in Quebec, Vaudreuil was commissioned ensign in Les Compagnies Franche de la Marine while a boy, attaining the rank of lieutenant by age thirteen and captain by fifteen. In 1733 he was appointed governor of Trois-Rivières, and in 1742 of French Louisiana, serving there between 1743 and 1753, proving himself a skilled officer and capable administrator. He lived in France for two years before returning to Canada as the first native-born governor of New France in 1755. After the surrender of New France in 1760, Vaudreuil sailed back to France and was imprisoned for a short time in the Bastille prior to trial for his complicity in the corruption that had helped to ruin Canada. He was exonerated in 1763, and the king invested him with the Grand Cross of the Order of Saint-Louis and granted him an additional pension of 6,000 livres as compensation for all that he had endured while implicated in the *affaire du Canada.* For the next fourteen years he resided in quiet retirement at his Paris home where he died on 4 August 1778.

214. **Stillwater.** A small town on the east side of the Hudson River about 20 miles (32 km) north of Albany, between Half Moon and Saratoga. First settled about 1730. According to John Grant, it was named "from the stillness of the water, a beautiful stream" although this is not mentioned in any of the modern official histories of the town.

The ultimate partisan. The French-Canadian answer to the bold American-born ranger captain Robert Rogers and his audacious raids was Luc de la Corne (1711-84), also known as Saint Luc. An officer of the colonial marines, Saint Luc served as an interpreter for Louis-Joseph de Montcalm at the Massacre of Fort William Henry and was held partially responsible for the French Indians' attack on British troops, a rumour perpetuated in these memoirs by John Grant. Saint Luc served as General John Burgoyne's interpreter for the British Indians that accompanied the army during the Saratoga campaign of the American Revolution. Intimately involved in the fur trade throughout his career, Saint Luc died in 1784, one of the wealthiest men in Canada. (Artist unknown. McCord Museum M22334. Editors' photo)

a beautiful stream. We reached it through a fine Vale, as yet little cultivated by the hand of man. Around Stillwater there was some cultivation, and a few houses. From there we marched along the banks of the river on a made road to Saratoga, which was as yet a bloodless field.[215] The whole of our route was through a Vale in which the river ran.

[At] Half Moon we crossed the Mohawk after halting for the night and [the] next day [we] arrived at Albany. At Albany we remained 3 days, which left me time to visit my old landlord, the Dutchman, who would scarce part with me. We embarked in sloops and sailed in 3 days by tiding[216] to Staten Island opposite New York where we encamped with 11 other Regiments forming the expedition intended for taking Martinique.

We arrived in June[217], the latter end, at Staten Island and remain'd there 'till November, drilling, etc. We occasionally went to New York a few miles off. About a week after I was there I fell sick of a kind of ague.[218] After remaining 3 or 4 weeks in a precarious state, I was ordered into the country for [a] change of air about 3 miles from the Camp.

I lived at a Dutchman's house, had the use of a horse and soon gained strength. In the beginning of September my Landlord complained to me that Soldiers used to come and steal his vegetables and fruit. I promised to protect [him] and detected 3 of the 15th Regiment in the act. I rode with them into

---

215. **Saratoga**. A reference to the two battles of Saratoga fought on 19 September 1777 and 7 October 1777, the latter resulting in the surrender of Burgoyne's entire army and giving a decisive strategic victory to the Americans in their fight for independence.
216. **Tiding**. To float or drift with the tide.
217. **Arrival at Staten Island**. Again, John Grant's memory is faulty. The Royal Highlanders arrived at Staten Island 25 July 1761. They left with their expeditionary fleet 15 November 1761.
218. **Ague**. Any fever marked by fits of shivering.

Camp and reported the circumstance. They were tried and then upon their trial they explained the reasons that made them do so, being that money which 69 was allowed the other Regiments for the purchase of vegetables to put their bodies in order, against the ensuing campaign when they would be obliged to live on salt provisions (which indeed by some bad arrangement they were forced even to do now on beef and pork brought at an immense expense from Ireland when plenty of fresh might have been procured in America) was withheld for them. This was not thought a valid excuse and they were sentenced to punishment which was executed, for in those days Courts Martial was [*sic*] not forwarded to the General Commanding.

A few nights afterwards I heard a shouting whilst in bed and several shots fired near the house. I took no notice, but next morning before daylight, my Landlord came to tell me the house had been fired into and showed me the ball marks. I instantly mounted, rode into Camp, called on Major Loftus,[219] explained my suspicions and requested a search to be made amongst the men's arms for dirty ones.[220] He refused.

I went to the Brigadier commanding the Brigade. He reported the subject to the General. An order came to search the arms but sufficient time had elapsed to have them cleaned. The Major got a rap on the knuckles on the whole circumstance being explained and was ordered to pay up the men's arrears and vegetable money. By this means the Soldiers got their money to spend which, if they had died in the West Indies on expedition, would have fallen into Officers Commanding hands, for Soldiers [allowances] were then only settled with once a year, which was a great hardship and the pay was not distributed 70 regularly as at present. **It was so cold in the tent when I returned into Camp that I was determined to brave all fears of assassination and return to my former quarters.**[221] **So glad were the people to have me back that they refused to take anything for board.**

219. **Major Arthur Loftus** (c.1720-81). British army officer. Then major and second-in-command of the 15th Foot, General Amherst's own regiment. His father, Lieutenant Colonel Simon Loftus, and his younger brother Dudley had also served in the 15th Foot, but they had died at the siege of Cartagena in 1741. Arthur retired on half-pay as the major of the 2nd Foot to take up a seat in the Irish Parliament. He died in 1781.
220. **Dirty ones.** In other words, muskets recently fired.
221. **Editors' note.** These two sentences, originally appearing in one of the four loose quarto sheets, were placed here in the narrative.

Chapter 6 | The Martinique Campaign, 1761–62 – "Turn Out, Highlanders"

The Second Battalion, Royal Highlanders, with John Grant in tow, arrived in Bridgetown, Barbados, with ten other regiments from Staten Island on Christmas Day of 1761. Totalling some 13,000 men, the force was mostly drawn from Amherst's "American Army," but some hailed from the West Indies garrisons, some from Britain, and some had recently arrived from the successful expedition against Belleisle in the Bay of Biscay, France. Their mission was to capture Martinique, the sugar island the British had failed to capture in 1759. Major General Robert Monckton, one of Wolfe's former brigade commanders, was in command.

General Monckton knew that campaigning in the tropics necessitated drastic adaptations to dress. These were mandated in a General Order issued to all twenty-three battalions of his command on New Year's Day when they were finally assembled at Bridgetown: "The Commanding Officers of the Corps will order the linings to be ript [*sic*] out of the men's coats, the lapels taken off, and the skirts cut shorter. The General recommends to them, providing their men with something that is thin, to make sleeves for their waistcoats, as the troops may be ordered to land in them."[222]

The naval part of the expedition was commanded by Rear Admiral George Brydges Rodney[223] and consisted of eighteen sail of the line, as well as frigates, bomb-vessels and fire-ships. They sailed from Barbados on 3 January 1762 and anchored in Sainte-Anne's Bay, Martinique, on 8 January 1762. The bulk of the army went ashore immediately. This was familiar territory to many of the men

---

222. **General Orders.** 1 January 1762, Bridgetown, Barbados. "Hamilton Notebook," *National Army Museum,* MSS 6707-11, 211-12.

223. **Rear Admiral Sir George Brydges Rodney,** 1st Baron Rodney (1718-92). Royal Navy officer. He came from a distinguished but poor background, going to sea at the age of fourteen. Rising swiftly through the ranks, he became a post-captain by 1742 and a rear admiral by 1759. With prize money won during the 1740s, he purchased a large country estate and a seat in the House of Commons. During the Seven Years' War, Rodney was involved in a number of amphibious operations including the raids on Rochefort and Le Havre, and ultimately his stalwart support of the army ashore in the capture of Martinique in 1762. Promoted to vice admiral following the Treaty of Paris, 1763, he returned home to find his finances in disarray. Forced to flee abroad to escape his creditors, he found himself in a French jail at the outbreak of war with France in 1778 but was able to secure his release. Returning to Britain, Rodney was given a new command with the rank of admiral. Severely criticised for his taking of Sint Eustatius in 1781 and, on the verge of recall, he won a decisive victory at the battle of the Saintes off the coast of Dominica, 9-12 April 1782, ending the French threat to Jamaica. On his return to Britain, Rodney was created a peer and awarded an annual pension of £2,000. He lived in retirement until his death in 1792.

Monckton. An early portrait of a rather young and corpulent Ensign Robert Monckton of the 3rd Foot Guards, painted ten years before his posting to Nova Scotia as lieutenant colonel of the 47th Foot. There, he served as lieutenant governor of Annapolis Royal in Nova Scotia, commanded the successful 1755 expedition against Fort Beauséjour, and had the dubious honour of overseeing the subsequent expulsion of the Acadians. He was James Wolfe's hand-picked second-in-command for Quebec in 1759 where he was severely wounded in the lung and evacuated to New York. He was chosen by Pitt to lead the army component of the 1761-62 expedition against Martinique. (Painting by John Michael Williams, 1742. FARL)

still serving in the 2nd/42nd Foot for it was here, in early 1759, they had experienced their baptism of fire in the expedition commanded by Major General Peregrine Thomas Hopson.

Lieutenant John Grant, however, had not been part of the campaigning on this "fine picturesque island" as his company and one other of the 2nd/42nd had been delayed by storms and were diverted instead to the attack on Guadeloupe. This time he and his men landed at les Anses-d'Arlet along with the rest of their battalion, commanded by Major Gordon Graham. They were brigaded with the other Highland battalions: their own 1st/42nd (commanded by Major John Reid) and the 77th (Montgomery's Highlanders) fresh from Dominica. To this seasoned "American Army" brigade of veterans was added the newly-arrived 76th Regiment of Foot, commanded by Lieutenant Colonel David Erskine, all under the command of Brigadier Francis Grant.

They landed light with no tents or baggage, encamping "amidst a low hilly country cover'd with brushwood," which they used to construct shelters as best they could. Les Anses-d'Arlet was to be a temporary camp, for on 16 January 1762 General Monckton re-embarked his troops and made a landing near Case des Navires, under Morne Tartenson and Morne Garnier, two high ridges commanding the town of Fort Royal. As it was vital ground, the French had heavily fortified both and occupied them in force.

Monckton, undaunted, was resolved to attack Morne Tartenson first and ordered a body of troops and 800 marines to advance along the beaches towards the town on the morning of 24 January 1762. Their mission was to attack and destroy two redoubts near the shore, and to support this movement he sent some flat-bottomed boats mounted with guns in their prows to provide some close fire support. Aided by this diversion, and with the fire of new British bat-

Moonlight admiral. George Brydges Rodney, 1st Baron Rodney (1718-92), was best known for his actions in the American War of Independence, particularly his victory over the French at the battle of the Saintes in 1782. An experienced fighting admiral, Rodney was also responsible for defeating a Spanish fleet during the 1780 battle of Cape Saint Vincent (also known as the "Moonlight Battle" because it took place at night) and effecting the resupply of the British garrison besieged at Gibraltar. It is often claimed that Rodney pioneered the tactic of "breaking the line," a move later favoured by Nelson. (Painting after Sir Joshua Reynolds. NPG 1398. Editors' photo)

teries raised on the opposite ridges by some tenacious sailors from the fleet, the army's light infantry was to try to get around the enemy's left flank while the main attack went in on the central ridge of Morne Tartenson. "We attacked and drove the enemy from all the redoubts, with only 200 of ours killed and wounded," wrote Captain Henry Pringle, an Ulster Scot serving in the light infantry. "This brought us within reach of the Town & Fort."[224]

In this assault the Royal Highlanders lost Captain William Cockburn and Lieutenant David Barclay of the light infantry company killed, as well as one sergeant and twelve rank and file. Major John Reid commanding the 1st/42nd and ten other Black Watch officers were wounded, as well as three sergeants, one drummer and seventy-two rank and file.

After the quick capture of the hill-top, one last ridge remained looming over them. "A high hill called Morne Grenier [*sic*, Morne Garnier] and the Capuchin redoubt," wrote Pringle, "that commanded everything near it, well-fortified & furnished with Cannon & Mortars, & the great support of the Fort, as it looked into it."[225] It was the last piece of vital ground Monckton needed in order to take the capital of Martinique, and while he made the necessary preparations for what would be his final assault, the enemy struck without warning.

Late on the afternoon of 27 January 1762, John Grant's battalion were pitching their tents, which had come ashore, and the regimental women[226] were wash-

224. **Assault.** Henry Pringle to Robert Pringle, 5 February 1762, Fort Royal in Martinique. Henry Pringle fonds, LAC MG 18-L8, microfilm reel H-1954. Hereafter, *Pringle's Letterbook.*

225. **Morne Garnier.** *Ibid.*

226. **Regimental women.** It was customary for a specified number of women to accompany the regiments on campaign, the majority of whom appear to have been wives of enlisted men. Expected to perform a myriad of chores ranging from cooking and sewing, to nursing and laundering, in exchange for their government rations, those that lost a husband in battle

View of Fort Royal, Martinique. "View of Fort Royal in Martinico [*sic*] from the Esplanade 1762." Ink on paper. Artist's initials marked on drawing at bottom right – "W.B." (JCB 66-109-9)

ing clothes in a stream. Suddenly, three French shells burst over the Highlanders' tent lines and "we saw our Adjutant who had been at headquarters, rushing down the hill," remembered Grant, calling out: "Turn out Highlanders...."

The men, some still stripped to the waist, dropped what they were doing, grabbed for their stacked muskets, powder horns and cartouche belts and ran up the hill, forming as they advanced. By the time they reached the brow of the hill and stopped, they were in extended order and formed there in two ranks until the slowest caught up and fell in behind to form the third rank. Over on the next hill they "saw a large body of French immediately opposite to us, driving in the 60th who were slowly retiring before them to our right down the hill," remembered Grant. "We instantly gave the Indian 'Halloo,' part of our Backwoods acquirements and the brave fellows of the 60th instantly stood as if riveted to the spot and advanced with us."[227]

---

or to disease would quickly remarry within their companies to maintain their ration status for themselves and their children.

227. **Indian "Halloo."** Grant, who first encountered the Indian "halloo," "howl" or "whoop" while fighting in the "backwoods" of North America, is clearly stating that the veterans of the "American Army," despite regulations to the contrary, had appropriated one of the most effective psychological weapons used against them by their Indian adversaries. Lord Albemarle, one of the commanders during the following campaign against Havana, remarked to his friend Jeffery Amherst that the troops he had provided for the expedition had conquered Martinique "in the American way, running, or with the Indian whoop."

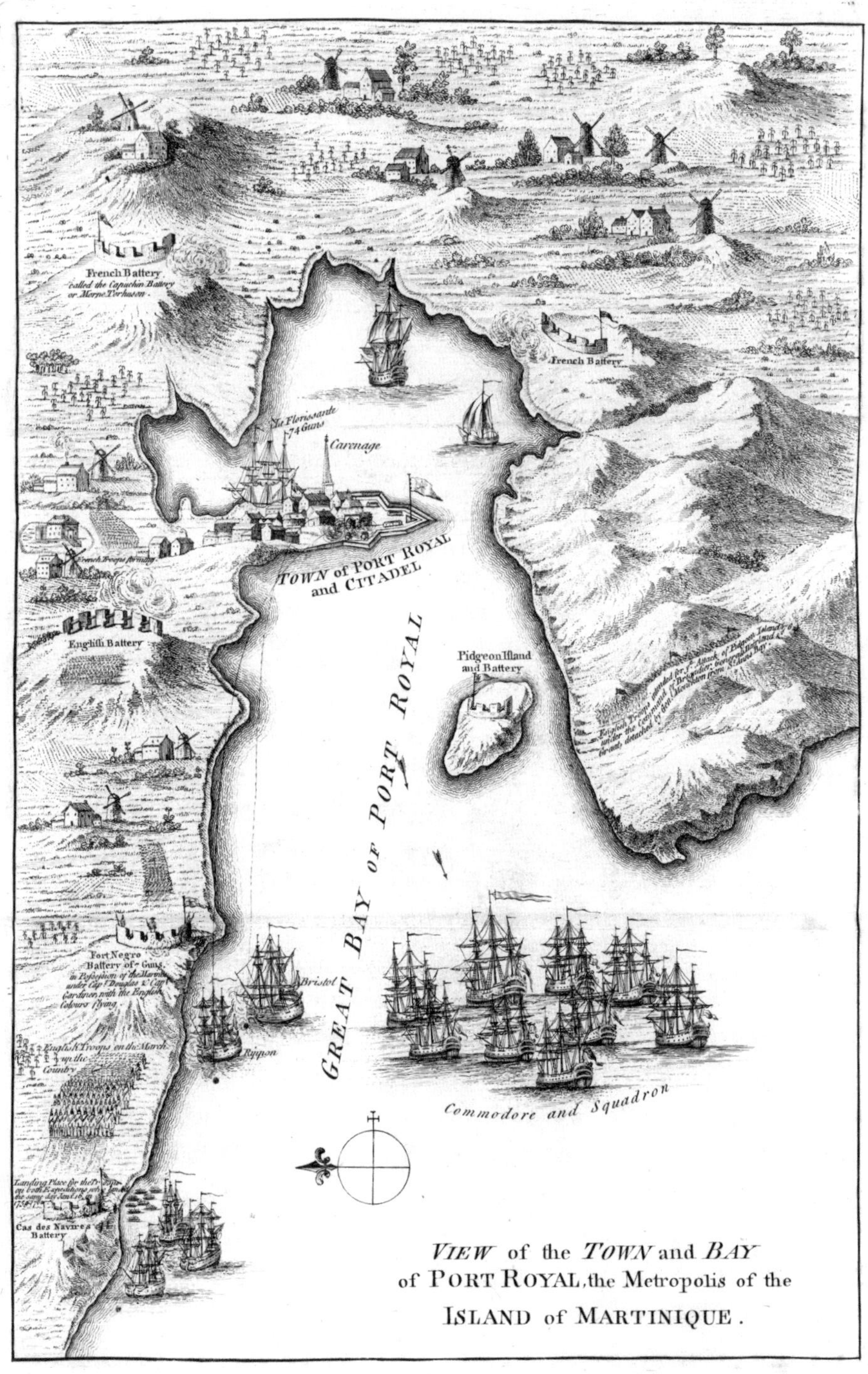

Port Royal and harbour. "View of the Town and Bay of Port Royal, the Metropolis of the Island of Martinique." Drawn by a Marine officer, Richard Gardiner, and published in Birmingham by John Baskerville, 1762. (JCB 02124-2)

The French regulars and black militia saw the new threat created by the arrival of the Highlanders on their flank and fired a volley at them, the musket balls tearing "the ground at our feet," according to Grant, "but we pushed on and received another fire." The 42nd Foot and the Royal Americans, before their enemy could reload, gave them a volley then instantly charged, whooping and uttering bloodcurdling cries. The French did not wait to receive the charge but broke and ran down the hill into a wooded ravine. The Highlanders did not follow at first, but seeing that the enemy was retreating back towards the fort and not to the high ground from whence they had come, immediately exploited forward and established themselves on the plateau of Morne Garnier.

Elsewhere, on another spur of Morne Tartenson, the Light Infantry corps, including 150 men drawn from the three Highland battalions, had been eating their dinner when the surprise attack came and they had reacted as swiftly as Grant's battalion. "About 6 or 7,000 of them made a general attack upon our advanced post," recalled Captain Pringle, but it was soon repulsed by the elite soldiers' counter-attack, the French retreating in "such confusion that we took advantage of their panick [*sic*], pursued them across the most difficult ravine in the Country & up this hill, which we were all obliged to crawl up on all-fours, and took possession of their principal redoubt & all their Cannon which they had not time to spike."[228]

The next morning, British colours flew over the Capuchin and Morne Garnier redoubts for all the army and navy, as well as the French in Fort Royal, to see. British gunners turned the French guns around and kept a constant fire upon the fort while additional batteries were visibly constructed on the higher ground. Before the potential combined firepower of the new batteries could be brought to bear, the French governor asked for terms on 3 February 1762, and Monckton's army took possession of the fort and town the next day.

For the Highland battalions, casualties for the 27 January surprise attack, and the subsequent rout of their French attackers, were light. The 1st/42nd had one private killed and two wounded while the 2nd/42nd had Lieutenant George Leslie and a private wounded. Summing up the campaign, Monckton was careful to give his strongest praise to his elite soldiers, the grenadiers, the light infantry and the rangers, "the Warmest part of the Service having fallen to their lot."[229]

After Martinique was taken, there was much reorganization in the Royal

---

228. **Surprise attack.** Henry Pringle to Robert Pringle, 5 February 1762, Fort Royal in Martinique. *Pringle's Letterbook.*

229. **Casualties.** "Return of Killed, Wounded, Missing" 27 January 1762, WO 17/1489, LAC Microfilm Reel B-1566; Monckton to the Earl of Egremont, 9 February 1762, Fort Royal, Martinique. *Gentleman's Magazine* (March 1762), 126; TNA WO 34/55: f. 60.

Highlanders as several officers resigned their commissions or exchanged into other units. The month of May 1762 also saw the first Royal Highland officer succumb to disease since leaving Staten Island. John Charles St. Clair, who had been promoted lieutenant "in room of" David Barclay, who was killed in the assault on Morne Tartenson in January, died from the "yellow jack" on 15 May. His death was a harbinger of things to come.

* * *

We embarked in transports under the command of Major General Monckton, 11 Regiments strong, about 5 or 6,000 men.[230] We had a convoy of Men of War. It was [the] beginning of November. We sailed on Smoothly, enjoying the change of climate 'till the 7th of December '61. A tremendous hurricane overtook us, the morning was dark and sultry, a small cloud appeared on the horizon, which the Captain observing prognosticated a hurricane. In an instant it came on, and before the crew who were at dinner could be called up, the vessel was on its beam ends.[231] I was officer of the watch, called up to the Captain if the soldiers, a third of whom were on deck, to say if they could be of service. He said they could.

I called out to them to assist but they all clung to the sides like cats. Knowing example was better than precept or order when danger was alike to all, I jumped forward & seized a rope. They joined me and we soon lower'd and bailed up the sails, but in a few minutes they were torn to pieces by flapping on the masts.

The sea was like a sheet of foam. Through the intervals of the sea rift we could see the vessels tossing about in every direction, their sails like ribbons. Wonderfully they did not run foul. It lasted 3 hours, no vessels were lost tho' they all lost a suit of sails.[232] But 60 men were shaken into the merciless deep from the Main top yard[233] in attempting to haul the mizzen. The yard was blown into the ocean.

---

230. **Regiments.** 15th Foot, 17th Foot, 22nd Foot, 27th Foot, 28th Foot, 35th Foot, 40th Foot, 42nd Foot (two battalions), 43rd Foot, 46th Foot, and the 3rd Battalion 60th Foot. Figures for the two 42nd battalions were: 1st Battalion, 688 all ranks; 2nd Battalion, 657. The total force number coming from New York was 6,667 all ranks. Embarkation Returns, New York, 19 November 1761, TNA WO 1/5, p.417.
231. **On its beam ends.** A nautical phrase that has come to mean impending doom, or to imply a dangerous life-threatening situation. The beams were the horizontal transverse timbers of ships. Therefore, if the beam ends of a ship were touching the water, it was in imminent danger of capsizing and sinking.
232. **Suit of sails.** Nautical term meaning one complete set of sails needed to sail a particular sailing vessel.
233. **Main top yard.** John Grant must have meant the "main topsail yard," the yard just above the main top. The "top" is the semicircular platform that rests upon the crosstrees at the

In attempting to avoid the crowd of vessels we got so far to leeward that 71 being a heavy sailor, we could not recover our lost ground, and the fleet was out of sight next morning.

We shaped our course for Barbados. Saint Lucia[234] was the first land we met after 10 days sailing and, in consequence of the wind proving contrary, we did eat our Christmas dinner the day of our arrival at Barbados. We had been given up as foundered and some hopes of promotion were blighted by our appearance.

Some Regiments arrived from England making us to 8,000 men. We remained at the agreeable Island of Barbados about a fortnight, so as to revisit my old acquaintances of 1758.[235]

I was ordered with another officer to make a report to Brigadier General Grant.[236] We were equipped in jackets without lace made to resemble [the] soldiers', with a haversack with provisions on one side and a canteen of liquor on the other. Our few change of shirts &c. wrapped in our plaid which was wound round our chest.

We did not cut gay figures. We took off our bonnets in giving our report. The general returned [the salute]. We afforded a good deal of mirth [to the] Belleisle Gentry[237] near whose Regiment the Camp was, but he very properly said, "I own you will regret you have not followed their example."[238]

[Rear Admiral] Sir [George] Brydges Rodney found us with some Men of War from England and took command of the Fleet. We left Barbados early in January and arrived off Martinique in 3 days.

---

head of a lower mast. Tops are named after the mast to which they belong, e.g., foretop, maintop, mizzentop.

234. **Saint Lucia**. An island country in the eastern Caribbean Sea, Saint Lucia is located north-northeast of Saint Vincent, northwest of Barbados and south of Martinique. The French first established a permanent settlement on the island in 1643. During the 18th century, control of the island changed hands between France and Britain many times, with Britain taking definitive control in 1814. During the Seven Years' War, Britain occupied the island for a year, handing it back to the French at the Treaty of Paris in 1763.

235. **Barbados, 1758**. See folio page 29 for John Grant's earlier experiences on the island of Barbados.

236. **Editors' note**. The next two paragraphs, originally appearing in one of the four loose quarto sheets, were placed here in the narrative.

237. **Belleisle Gentry**. The 76th Foot was one of the British regiments that had participated in the capture of Belleisle (Belle-Île-en-Mer), off the coast of France, in 1761, and its officers landed at Barbados for the Martinique campaign wearing their regulation uniforms complete with sashes, gorgets and spontoons. By contrast, the veteran regiments of the "American Army," including John Grant's, wore a more relaxed campaigning dress and thus jokingly referred to the officers of the 76th as the "Belleisle Gentry."

238. **Followed their example**. In other words, Brigadier General Grant was telling the "Belleisle Gentry" that they would soon regret not following the relaxed clothing example of the 42nd Foot.

Upon leaving Barbados, a run of a few hours brought us in sight of Martinique.[239] We soon approached the windward side of it and turned along its beautiful shore for Saint Pierre.[240] In the morning we were opposite to it. We landed at this beautiful town. Many of the houses are built of stone, and along the principal streets are rows of trees after the French fashion. In the middle runs a stream of water.

Most houses in the West Indies are of wood, gaily painted, of two stories with galleries and verandas round. The Masters and mistresses lounging in them gave an air of population which strikes a stranger, struck with seeing the markets on Sunday and the Negro dancers. Markets, from the variety, produce curious scenes.

August, September and October are the Hurricane months. These hurricanes, however disastrous in their effects, benefit the Islands by making them more healthy. Good many dangerous snakes on Martinique as well as centipedes and scorpions.

It is a fine picturesque Island seen from a distance. We came to anchor off the Island and the whole army landed [the] next day amidst a low hilly country cover'd with brushwood and every regiment bivouacked and constructed the best shelter they could, no tents being landed and no houses near.

We remained 3 days in this uncomfortable position when our Regiment, Montgomery's [Highlanders, 77th Foot] and the 76th were ordered under the command of Brigadier General [Francis] Grant to embark and land on the opposite of the Bay that runs up to Fort Royal, to attack Pigeon Island,[241] a rock which had heavy guns on it 72 and which defended the approach to Fort Royal, so that ships could not work up to attack the fort. The trade winds generally blowing down would have caused ships to beat up and be exposed to the raking fire of Pigeon Island.

We landed with an order for officers and men to carry ten day's provisions

239. **Editors' note**. The next three paragraphs, originally appearing in one of the four loose quarto sheets, were placed here in the manuscript.

240. **Saint Pierre**. Founded in 1635 by Pierre Belain d'Esnambuc, a French trader and adventurer, Saint Pierre was the first permanent French colony on the island of Martinique. Before its destruction in 1780 by a hurricane "which inundated the city, destroying all houses" and killing 9,000 people, it was Martinique's most important city, culturally and economically. The city was destroyed again in 1902 when the volcano Mount Pelée erupted, killing over 30,000 people. Today the town is the district capital of the Caribbean North district of Martinique.

241. **Pigeon Island**. Also known as Islet à Ramiers, Pigeon Island was essentially a fortified rock in Fort Royal Bay, Martinique, due south of Fort Royal. Key features included five cannon batteries, a mortar battery, three barracks (soldiers', artillery's and officers'), a kitchen, a small magazine and a crane "to draw up provisions." The only way to the top of the rock was a winding path easily defended by its garrison. The island, though engaged by British warships, was never attacked by the army during the campaign.

(no bat horses).[242] The [officers of the] 76th who had lately arrived [at Bridgetown] from the taking of Belleisle landed in White Spatterdashes, Gorgets, spontoons & sashes and trusted their provisions to their Servants. We older campaigners, accustomed to backwood expeditions, took care to equip ourselves with haversacks containing our provisions and were ridiculed by the gay gentlemen for so doing, but in 2 days the note was changed. Their Servants lightened their burdens & they were glad to partake of our fare.

We found it impracticable to attack the Island [Pigeon Island], from its rocks & steep nature, and impossible to batter it with effect from its distance from the shore, about half a mile. But we did not suffer from its fire, being out of sight behind a hill, but we were occasionally visited by a few Ricochet shots.

We were sitting down around a spring with our provisions spread out when a shot pitch'd into the centre and in a moment covered the whole Party with mud and water.[243] We threw ourselves instantly on our faces to save ourselves and our provisions, and some of the Belleisle Gentry who had lost their provisions and whom we had invited to partake of ours, some with their gayness and gilt all besmirched from their muddy bed.

A long backed hill ran from the water's edge into the country. Upon this 6 Companies of Light Infantry, that also accompanied us, was [*sic*] posted. I was posted the second day in charge of the well which served as a watering place, with 20 men. I was alarmed at night as of 73 course we were upon the alert for fear of a surprise – by the noise of feet ascending the hill not far from me, amidst loose pebbles. I was posted and could not move, my alarm would have been of no use. My situation was not pleasant; I was half a mile from the rest of the detachment.

I heard them distinctly saying: "*Allons, Allons, Met ces Bayonets. Il faut donner les Anglais un coup de Bayonet pour l'honneur de France!*"[244]

Waiting in breathless expectation we heard a single shot, and then, the fire of a platoon. Then a confused noise of voices and a noise like thunder rushing down the hill plainly told of the defeat of the [French] detachment and the fire from above continued 'till the noise dissipated and we could hear the feebly cry of: "*quartier pour l'amour de dieu!*"[245]

That night the General [Francis Grant], fearing a more serious attack, order'd

---

242. **Bat horses.** Partial translation of French *cheval de bât*, or packhorse. In the 18th-century British army, an officer's horse used primarily to carry his baggage (i.e., tent, camp furniture, rations, etc.).

243. **Editors' note.** This paragraph, originally appearing in one of the four loose quarto sheets, was placed here in the narrative.

244. **Translation**: "Let's go! Let's go! Fix bayonets! We must give the English cold steel for the honour of France!"

245. **Translation**: "Quarter for the love of God!"

all guards and the Light Infantry to be called in and to march for the place of embarkation. I was neglected and would in all probability have been left and taken prisoner in the morning. But the Army were already on [the] march when the Adjutant, seeing but half of my Company by mere chance in the dark, enquired where I was. Nobody knew and accordingly the party was sent in search of me. After the noise had ceased I was alarmed by the noise of the steps and by the light of a starlyht [*sic*, starlit] night I could observe a small party marching down the road which led to the well.

I immediately formed 74 my small party on either side of the road with orders to charge and surround them, taking them for French as they had wandered out of their way and were coming in an opposite direction from their [*sic*] usual route of our men. The [call], "Stand, who comes there," and the answer, "Friend," soon dispelled our hesitation and we were informed of their errand.

We re-landed [the] next day with the rest of the Army on the same side as Fort Royal who were in the same position we had left them in. On the 24th January we were formed to attack Morne Tartenson, a strongly fortified hill at about 2 miles from our position but separated from it by a ravine. Our Brigade formed the left of the Line and were order'd under Brigadier Haviland to turn the right flank of the hill and leaving the works, we were at some distance from the other 4 Brigades.

We had to descend into the ravine by a very steep descent & narrow path but it was out of fire and to make somewhat a circuitous route to reach our destination. Just as we ascended the shoulder we heard the fire of the Howitzers, 6 of which played on the works. We heard a heavy firing, firing to our right, and could distinctly see our line through the smoke carry several advanced works.

We pushed on to the crest which open'd [onto] a Plateau, where to our consternation we saw our line in full retreat. We were order'd to halt, and as our Brigadier [Haviland] was whisper'd to be not over valiant, 75 the men were most abusive and impatient to advance and take off the enemy's attention and thus give others time to rally. The General still hesitated, but the clamour became so great that he was forced to advance.

At the same moment we saw the part of the line reform and advance again, and with a cheer we rushed on. Before however we got under the reach of musketry, the works were abandoned, but on scaling them we saw the enemy in full retreat. The part of the Army which performed this consisted of the 42nd and the Grenadier Companies of the Army, who gallantly stormed the breastwork with the bayonet. They were the support or the reserve and when the rest retreated, they advanced and singly took it. We lost a number of men killed and wounded.

From Morne Tartenson we could see the Fort below us (the cause of the retreat was imputed to a drum beating the retreat, but it could never be discover'd who did it). General Monckton however rode up under a heavy fire and rallied them, but the Works were taken before they arrived.

We marched the same night to take post on a neighbouring hill about 2 miles to the right, which rose above the rest of the ridge and only separated from Morne 76 Garnier, another hill on the opposite side of the town, strongly fortified by a ravine similar to that that [*sic*] separated us from Morne Tartenson. Our Detachment consisted of [the] 2nd Battalion 42nd, Montgomery's 77th Highland Regiment & part of the 60th [Royal Americans].

There was a house on it and the general, Haviland, selected it as his quarters. We remained lying on our arms until the 27th which in this climate was not agreeable during the day from the heat, but at night our ample plaids shelter'd us.

On the 27th our tents arrived and we were order'd to form our camp on the banks of a rivulet which ran through a ravine on the other side of the ridge which bounded the ravine behind us. We had pitched our tents & our women had arrived and were coming to wash when three shells were fired quickly about 12 o'clock of the day, and falling in the pebbly bed of the river, caused in their explosion such a noise as put the whole melee to instant and screaming foment. We could not imagine the meaning of this.

Within a quarter of an hour, we saw our Adjutant who had been at headquarters, rushing down the hill and calling out: "Turn out Highlanders, 77 the French are attacking the General's house." We instantly seized our arms and the Colonel, commanding us to form as we advanced, we ran on.

In coming to the brow of the hill, we saw a large body of French immediately opposite to us, driving in the 60th who were slowly retiring before them to our right down the hill. We instantly gave the Indian "Halloo," part of our Backwoods acquirements. The brave fellows of the 60th instantly stood as if riveted to the spot and advanced with us. The French immediately fired and

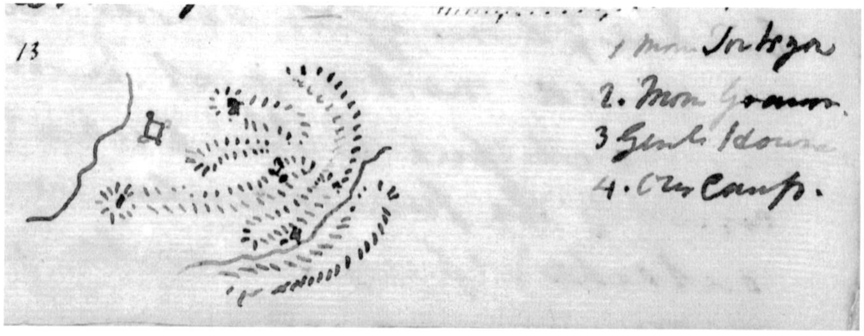

Sketchy memory. The sketch on page 77 of the manuscript journal shows the area around Fort Royal, Martinique. The editors have been unable to match the features of this sketch to modern contemporary maps. (Editors' photo)

we heard the Balls tear the ground at our feet [but] we pushed on and received another fire. We began to ascend the hill and received a third at about 100 yards from them. Before they could reload, we gave them a volley and instantly charged. They did not [wait to] receive it but broke and ran down the hill into a wooded ravine.

We did not follow them, but on seeing them retreat towards the Fort Royal, we crossed a hollow and established ourselves on a plateau of the ridge of Morne Garnier to the right of our former position.

78 We remained there all night. I was then on the General's Guard and as I was well acquainted with him, I ventured to suggest that if we did not advance, that General Grant with the Grenadiers who was on a neighbouring height would occupy it in the night, as the enemy after the repulse would perhaps retire, and at any rate, would be dispirited beside make no resistance as they were unsupported by any troops. He did not take my advice, tho' he was authorised to act independently.

Before day however, we advanced. I was in the advance with the general when we heard the Scotch reveille.[246]

I said, "General, Brigadier Grant has anticipated us."

"No [said the General], it is a Sco[tch]-Irish Regiment in the French Service."

We marched on and at dawn saw the British flag flying. They had occupied it during the night. They, on our arrival, marched to their former position and we were left in possession of the redoubt which, notwithstanding its formidable appearance, we found weak. We found two 13 inch mortars in the Work. We had no artillery men with us. One of the mortars was loaded, left in the hurry. Some of us said, "'Tis a pity we could not fire it into the town. I will set fire to the fuse (which according to the French custom, was on the outside) if anyone will fire the 79 powder."

We turned it to the town. I set fire to [the] fuze, it made a terrible hissing. The other man was frightened. We both set off and the shell burst in the mortar. There were some cannon but no ammunition.

From the steep sides we looked down upon the Fort Royal from a considerable height, and completely commanded it, and the Redoubt had been built to fire upon [the] shipping. When they saw us they fired some shells at us. One fell into the redoubt. As usual on such visits where we could do it, some of us lay down or ran away. But one officer who was lying in a sort of hut of branches erected by the French in which was left a thick cotton mattress, thought by

---

246. **Reveille**. A bugle, trumpet or bagpipe call, chiefly used to wake military personnel at sunrise. The name comes from the French *réveille* (or *réveil*) meaning "wake up."

Killed in a duel. Colonel George Scott (c.1725-67) was considered by some to be the father of the first true British Light Infantry, and commanded the *ad hoc* light infantry corps for Major General Jeffery Amherst at Louisbourg in 1758, and for Major General Robert Monckton at Martinique in 1761/62. He was killed in a duel on Dominica in 1767. This portrait shows him wearing some of his own proposed dress modifications along with some of the equipment he proposed for the new experimental corps: a cut down frock coat; a hardened leather cap to ward off the blows of tomahawks; a bandolier for paper cartridges; a powder horn to carry priming powder like those used by the rangers and Indians; and a shortened carbine musket with a short knife bayonet instead of the long regular issue. (Private Collection)

turning it over him to escape. 'Tho the shell was near, it burst and a fragment falling on his leg disabled him during the campaign.

Next morning, I was order'd to join the Light Infantry under Colonel Scott[247] to replace a wounded Lieutenant [George Leslie], about 600 strong, composed of the Light Company's [*sic*] of the different regiments. The Company I was attached to was composed of 50 of [the] 42nd and 50 of the 44th Regiments. We occupied the extremity of the ridge of Morne Tartenson towards the country, rather lower than the rest. At its extremity was seated the Store and house of a maker of the famous *Noyau de Martinique* – Madame Manfou by name.[248] We had received strict orders to respect private property and to prevent all marauding.

Accordingly, I happened 80 soon after my arrival to stroll near the house

247. **Major George Scott** (c.1725-67). British army officer. Scott had been a captain in the army since 1746. He succeeded Colonel Robert Monckton in the command of Fort Lawrence on the isthmus of Chignecto in 1753. In 1755 he was appointed to command a battalion of Massachusetts troops raised for the siege of Fort Beauséjour, with the provincial rank of lieutenant colonel. Scott likely impressed his superiors as a useful commander of light and irregular forces, and when the expedition against Louisbourg was planned in 1758, he was given command (with the local or temporary rank of brevet major) of the *ad hoc* light infantry corps raised for the occasion, "a corps of 550 men, chosen as marksmen from the different regiments." He served with distinction at Louisbourg and was given the rank of major "in the army" effective 28 December 1758. He served with distinction at Quebec in 1759 and was appointed lieutenant colonel "in the army" on 11 July 1761. He served with Major General Robert Monckton at Martinique, again commanding a unit of light infantry. He was first appointed governor of Grenada in 1762, but later became lieutenant governor of Dominica, where he was killed in a duel in 1767.

248. ***Noyau de Martinique***. Noyau is a brandy cordial or liqueur flavoured with the kernel of the bitter almond or the peach stone.

when out rushed madame, calling: *"Ah, Monsieur L'Officier. Je suis perdu!"* [249] I recognised what was the matter. "The soldiers are breaking open my stores and destroying my *Noyau*."-

I immediately ran forward to where she pointed and found some Irishmen of the 44th of the [composite light] Company I was attached to, discussing the contents of two bottles whose tops they had broken off. I drove them out and got an order issued to protect her. Her gratitude was unbounded as I had reason to know when [I became] ill afterwards.

We now got our tents and bell tents erected for the men's arms but which, as there was a body of French on the opposite hill, the men had grounded their arms in line to be ready to fall in at a moment's notice. It began to rain and the men were order'd to fall in and place their arms under cover. I happened to be the officer on duty and was the first who order'd the Company to take up theirs. They hesitated and called out, "Rum!"

I had known that rum from some accident had not been deliver'd for some days, but as I made it a rule of strict obedience, I again order'd. There was the same answer.

I then addressed the Highlanders in *Erse*,[250] [that] I did not expect such conduct of greed. They should be redressed. The magic language brought back feudal obedience and upon the third order they took up their arms. I immediately order'd out a Sergeant and 6 men and approached the other half [of the composite light company] and again repeated the order.

81 They called out "Rum!"

I seized the first man and gave him a charge[251] [and the next] 5 were treated in the same manner. During this, the other officers had approached their companies and received the same answer of "Rum!" to their order. Seeing, however, my proceedings, they stood to, as well as the men, to see the result of my experiment. When they saw that I had seized 5, they [were] again order'd and the whole instantly took up their arms.

I carried my 5 [men] to Colonel Scott. A Court Martial was held on the spot. They were punish'd and sent [back] to their Regiments and I was thanked. I had acted thus from recollecting my former conduct on a like occasion in America.[252]

---

249. **Translation**: "Mr. Officer. I am lost!" In other words, financially ruined.
250. ***Erse***. The prevailing term in the 18th century for the Gaelic or "Irish" language.
251. **A charge**. In other words, John Grant put some of the men on report, likely charged with insubordination.
252. **Editors' note**. This is a reference to the mutiny that John Grant had quelled two years earlier while working with another composite company of soldiers on the bateaux service between Fort Stanwix and Oswego, October–November 1759.

Three days afterwards the Town and Fort surrendered. We had occupied all the surrounding heights; it had become untenable.

Immediately afterwards 600 Light Infantry and a detachment of the line were embarked on board of Transports under convoy of Commodore Swanton[253] and some Men of War. We arrived off the Island [of Grenada][254] with the Trade Wind. In the course of a few days, and as we sailed slowly along close in the shore, we could see the people galloping about and we expected a defence. We anchor'd within sight of the fort,[255] abreast of a Battery, but out of Shot. In the morning we were order'd to get into flat bottomed boats and land. We all expected hard work, 'till we saw Colonel Scott landing in a Man of War boat. He was suspected of being not over valiant and, as soon as this was done, 82 the soldiers called out from boat to boat, "Hurrah, pull away, the Colonel's in front. There will not be a shot fired today."

It so happened that the battery was deserted, perhaps because of the fear of being batter'd by the fleet, or from not having [enough] troops to defend it and the Fort. We landed and got quarters in some houses in the town of which we took possession. The Battery was on a hill higher than the fort and completely commanded it, being separated only by a ravine.

We summoned the Fort, the Commandant said he would not surrender whilst one stone lay upon another. However, we were not fired upon and next day he surrender'd.

---

253. **Commodore Robert Swanton** (c.1730-65). Royal Navy officer. Enlisted in the Royal Navy as a lieutenant in 1742, promoted to captain in 1745 (commanding HMS *Mary Galley*, 44 guns). Commanded HMS *Vanguard* (70 guns) from September 1757 to January 1763. Present with his ship at the siege of Louisbourg, 1758, and at the surrender of Quebec, 1759, after which he returned to England. He returned to Quebec in command of the squadron sent to relieve the garrison and raise the French siege, the first ship (HMS *Lowestoft*) arriving off Quebec on 9 May 1760. Commodore at Martinique, 1762, but before Fort Royal surrendered on 3 February he was ordered away to take the island of Grenada. He died in 1765.

254. **Grenada**. Formed as an underwater volcano, Grenada is located at the southern end of the Grenadines in the southeastern Caribbean Sea, southwest of Barbados. A permanent French settlement was founded in 1649, its economy initially based on sugar cane and indigo. Its principal town was Ville de Fort Royale ("Fort Royal Town"), which overlooked a natural horseshoe-shaped harbour where French ships would often take refuge from hurricanes. When the island was ceded to Great Britain by the Treaty of Paris in 1763, the new administration renamed the town Saint George's, after the patron saint of England, and Fort Royal was renamed Fort George, after George III.

255. **Fort Royal, Grenada**. A small bastion tracer fort, meaning that each level can give covering fire to the other level. Situated on a volcanic spine 175 feet (53 m) above the harbour of Ville de Fort Royale, capital of Grenada, Fort Royal was built by the French between 1706 and 1710 on an earlier battery position erected in the 1600s. Renamed Fort George in honour of George III when the British took possession of the island, today it houses the Royal Grenada Police Force. Despite severe damage by a hurricane in 2004, Fort George remains one of the finest examples of Vauban-style masonry fortresses in the world.

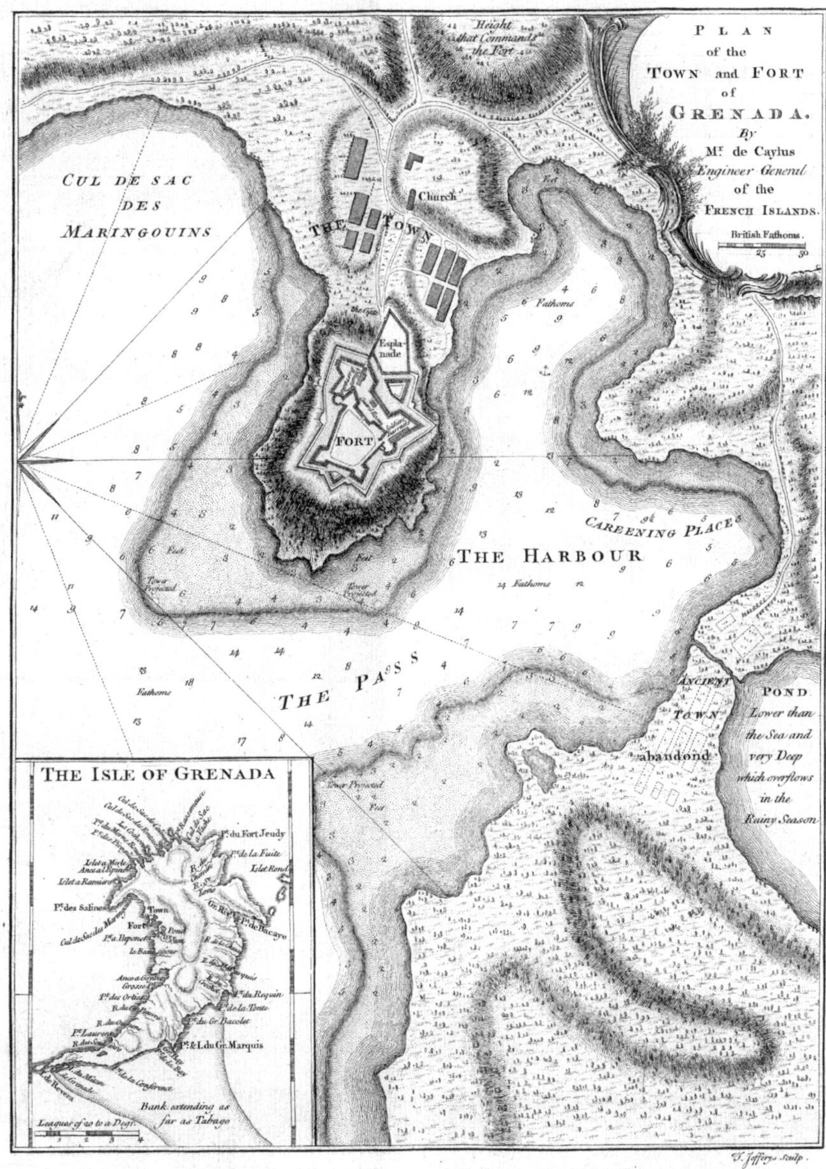

Grenada. "Plan of the Town and Fort of Grenada by Mr. de Laylus, Engineer General of the French Islands." John Grant and his fellow Highlanders participated in the bloodless capture of Grenada on 4 March 1762, part of an amphibious force commanded by Commodore Robert Swanton. The island was formally ceded to Britain by the Treaty of Paris on 10 February 1763. Published by the *London Magazine*, 1762. (LOC 2010593380)

Six days after our landing a fast sailing vessel came to order the Light Infantry back to Martinique, as it was reported that a French fleet with 3000 men were coming to endeavour to retake the Island [Martinique].

Instead of putting us on board Men of War they re- embarked [us] on board of our tubs of North Country Merchantmen, and we were 8 or 9 days getting to Guadeloupe*(having been driven to Leeward and past Martinique)[256] where the Master insisted upon entering in order to avoid being driven down to Saint Eustatius [*sic*]. We remained a week at Martinique[257] [*sic*] (the rest of the convoy we had lost sight of). At last we set sail.

We [had] lost sight of Guadeloupe in the evening but were making but little way when luckily we fell in with Admiral Rodney and told him our plight. He said he would remain by us 'till morning.

In the morning 83 he saw a frigate and signalled him to come up. He then gave us in charge to [the] Honourable Captain Montague[258] with orders to tow us into Saint Pierre in Martinique.

We were accordingly attached by a hawser to the Frigate. The motion is most unpleasant. The rope slack, the frigate shot ahead and we got a jerk that almost pulled our bows out. We then shot ahead and the same thing occurred. As soon as the Admiral was out of sight, He [the frigate captain] called out to let go the hawser. The master [of the Merchantman] said to us, "If we do, I do not know when she will get in."

I went down to my Captain and reported the order. He said, "We must obey."

I said, "No, the Admiral order'd him to convey us in and if we do let go, we shall never get in."

"Well, I will not appear and you can manage it."

The order was repeated [by the frigate captain].

I called out, "Cut it".

Montague then came up in a violent passion, order'd us again [to let go of

---

256. **Grant's footnote**. The asterisk marks an original footnote to the manuscript that appears near the bottom of the page.

257. **Martinique**. John Grant's memory was hazy when he dictated this paragraph, as he definitely meant to say Guadeloupe. His ship was ordered back to Martinique (from Grenada) but was blown off course to Guadeloupe, where they spent a week refitting. His next sentence shows that he was leaving Guadeloupe when they ran into Admiral Rodney's squadron.

258. **Editors' note**. While this incident with the frigate captain may have taken place in the spring of 1762, the naval captain in question was certainly *not* the Honourable William Montague (c.1720-57) (whose eccentric behaviour earned him the name "Mad Montague" in the Royal Navy) for he had died five years previously. A search of naval records and historical documents reveals no frigate captains named Montague serving in Rodney's West Indies fleet or adjacent squadrons during this campaign, though a Captain John Montague had commanded one of the ships of the line, HMS *Raisonnable*, the previous year, 1760, before returning to England in 1761 to take command of HMS *Newark*, 70 guns. He commanded several more men of war, each larger than the last, before finally becoming an admiral. Why John Grant chose to embellish this story and change the frigate captain's name to Montague is uncertain.

the hawser]. I said he had been order'd by the Admiral to convey us to Martinique, and it should not be cast off. Montague, commonly known by the name of Mad Montague, became furious. He did not choose to cut the hawser as our retaining it might have subjected him to a reprimand. But he swore and said, if we did not cut it off, he would not fire a broadside into us. I laughed and said I hoped he would not do so to an unarmed vessel, but that if he would let us come alongside, and let his crew only use the same arms as ours, that we would soon get into Saint Pierre by taking his vessel.

He became still more outrageous and abusive to our notions. This is a subject 84 which no Scotchman, as national antipathy then ran high, could suffer, and I thought it high time to put a stop.

"Captain Montague," I said, "Let us, if you please, talk like Gentlemen. I now beg to tell you that if I or any other officer of the 42nd ever meet you, you may depend upon it that they will make you eat your words."

Nothing more was said. We were towed for 12 hours longer when the Master, thinking he could make Saint Pierre, cast off the Hawser, to the great delight of the Frigate whose crew had favour'd us all along with curses both loud and deep. We arrived at Saint Pierre that evening.

There was a public sort of Caffé at Saint Pierre where both services used to meet.[259] I have heard Captain O'Brien, called Skyrocket Jack, say that he had misbehaved, that he had suffered and forced to escape. That he cared not who heard it as he knew there were some of Sir B['s] creatures[260] about the room.[261]

---

259. **Editors' note.** This paragraph, originally appearing in one of the four loose quarto sheets, was placed here in the narrative.

260. **Sir B's creatures.** Likely, the supporters or informants of Rear Admiral George Brydges Rodney, the naval commander at Martinique in 1762.

261. **Skyrocket Jack.** The story of "Skyrocket Jack" O'Brien seems to be one of those floating yarns that is applied as the fancy of the narrator dictates. One tale involves Lieutenant John (Jack) O'Brien, RN, who was launched into the sky when his ship, HMS *Edgar*, accidentally blew up at Spithead on 15 October 1711. The other version involves Lieutenant (or Midshipman) John O'Brien, RN, (a descendant of the 8th Earl of Inchiquin, Irish peerage) who was also launched into the sky when his ship, HMS *Dartmouth*, exploded on 8 October 1747, while engaged with a Spanish warship off Cadiz. In both yarns, the shaken but determined survivors are allegedly retrieved from the wreckage and brought before their respective commanders. In both cases, the rescued O'Brien's are reported as saying: "Sir, you will excuse me for appearing before you in such a dress; for I left my ship with so much precipitation, that I had not time to put on better clothes." In either case, both officers "went afterwards by the appropriate name of *Skyrocket Jack*." For Jack O'Brien of the *Edgar*, see: *Letters and Papers of Admiral of the Fleet, Sir Thomas Byam Martin*, edited by Admiral Sir Richard Vesey Hamilton, vol 3 (Navy Records Society, 1901), 302-304. For John O'Brien of the *Dartmouth*, see: *The Irish Builder* (Dublin, 1893), vol XXXV, 186; *Dublin Chronicle*, January 1788; Robert Beatson, *Naval and Military Memoirs of Great Britain from 1727 to the Present Time* (London, 1790), 353.

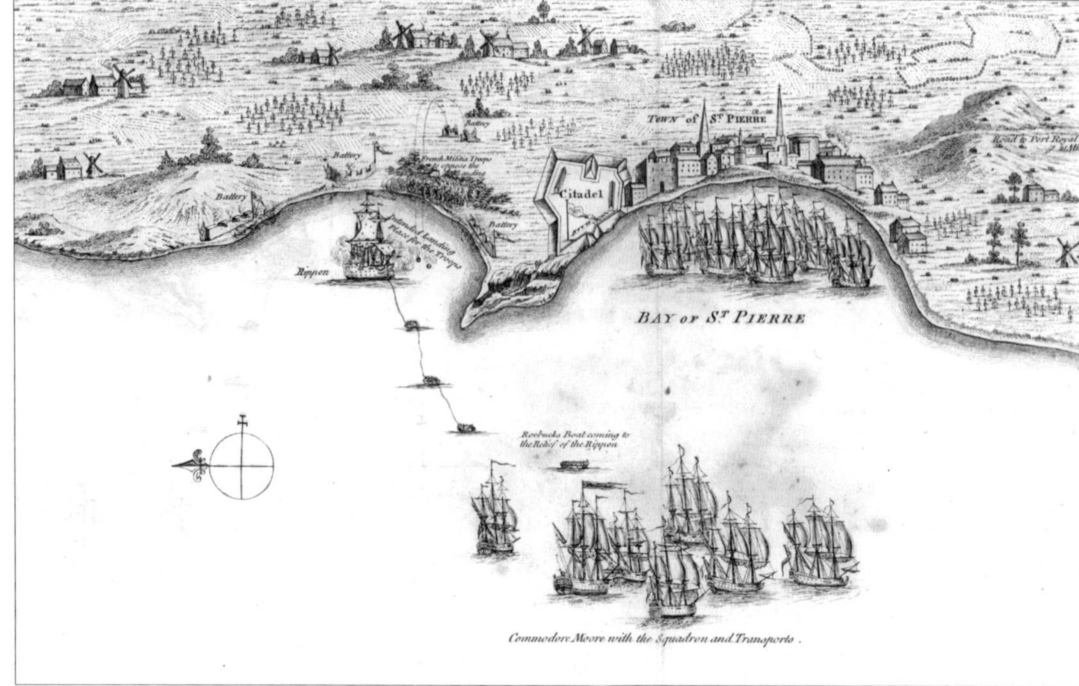

"Island of Martinico." A detail of St. Pierre drawn by a Marine officer, Richard Gardiner, serving aboard HMS *Rippon* during the 1759 campaign. This drawing appeared in his book entitled *An Account of the Expedition to the West Indies…* published by John Baskerville in 1762. (JCB 02124-1)

We remained a few days at Saint Pierre, then embarked for Fort Royal where we remained some time.

The yellow fever[262] raged in the Town and many of the men and officers died of that terrible disease. **Severe headaches and insupportable lassitude compelled me to have medical advice.**[263] **It was discovered I had had the fever on [edge of page missing] 24 hours, in a few hours more I became [edge of page missing followed by illegible word]**

[Section of page missing] I[,] conscious, but so far recovered [edge of page missing followed by illegible words] bed, tho' not without pain [edge of page missing].

262. **Yellow fever.** A disease caused by the yellow fever virus and spread by the bite of an infected female mosquito. Most cases only cause a mild infection with fever, headache, chills, back pain, fatigue, loss of appetite, muscle pain, nausea and vomiting. In these cases, the infection lasts only three to four days. In 15 per cent of cases, however, people enter a second, toxic phase with recurring fever, this time accompanied by jaundice due to liver damage, as well as abdominal pain. Bleeding in the mouth, the eyes and the gastrointestinal tract will cause vomit containing blood, hence the Spanish name for yellow fever, *vomito negro* ("black vomit").
263. **Editors' note.** The next two paragraphs, originally appearing in one of the four loose quarto sheets, were placed here in the narrative.

There were 8 officers ill in the house with me, 4 of them died. The crisis generally took place in 3 days. I was 4 and was cured by vomits of Tartar & milk but was so reduced that I could not move; the fatal blackning [*sic*] had even appeared round my neck.

I was a month before I could move but Madame Manfou sent me in gratitude, what I wanted particularly, soup and good bread, which were difficult to procure and materially improved my health.

I was order'd to go as an Invalid to America, but would not and was carried on board to my company. We were two Companies on board, the Grenadiers & Light Infantry, fortunately a better vessel than the former one. Before we sailed Lord Albemarle[264] arrived to take the command of the [Havana] expedition with some Regiments from England.[265]

Upon arriving at Fort Royal and seeing the sickness at 85 Martinique he began to be alarmed and to enquire into the state of the Medical Staff for the General Hospital he brought out. He found that they were chiefly London Apothecaries, and the Mates were merely their apprentices, so difficult was it at that time to find men ready to go out in expedition to the West Indies.

The Director General, Sir Clifton Wintringham,[266] was a very unfit person. Ten Thousand Pounds were granted for medicines and when examined into, it

---

264. **Lieutenant General George Keppel, Earl of Albemarle** (1724-72). British army officer. Oldest son of William Keppel, 2nd Earl of Albemarle. Ensign, 1 February 1738, captain and lieutenant colonel 27 May 1745, aide de camp to the Duke of Cumberland at Fontenoy and Culloden, major general, 1756, and lieutenant general, 1759. He commanded the land forces sent to take Havana from the Spaniards in 1762 and was the elder brother to Commodore Augustus Keppel, second-in-command of the naval forces that accompanied that expedition. A third brother, William, also served on the expedition as a major general, so that when Havana finally surrendered in August 1762, yielding prizes and booty estimated at $10 million, more than half the prize money fell to the three Keppel brothers.

265. **Havana expedition.** While British soldiers had been engaged in the campaign against Martinique, George III and his ministers had been busy planning the conquest of Havana, the capital of the island of Cuba, controlled by Spain since Christopher Columbus had claimed the island in 1492. Havana was an important Spanish naval base with one of the finest harbours in the West Indies. The regiments arriving from England with Lord Albemarle were 9th Foot, 34th Foot, 56th Foot and 72nd Foot.

266. **Sir Clifton Wintringham** (1710-94). Military and civilian physician. Born at York in 1710 and educated at Trinity College, Cambridge, taking his doctor of medicine's degree in 1749. He later became a fellow of the College of Physicians and settled in London, where he was appointed physician to the Duke of Cumberland. In 1759, appointed physician extraordinary and subsequently physician-general to the army. In 1762, at the height of the Siege of Havana, he became personal physician to George III, by whom he was knighted and created a baronet in 1773. He had a large practice and was much respected both in public and private life. In 1782 he published some essays on various departments of medicine under the title "De Martiis quibusdam Commentarii," 2 vols. He also published an edition of his father's works and edited Mead's "Monita et Prsecepta Medica," to which he added numerous annotations. He died at Hammersmith on 9 January 1794.

was found that no selection had been made as to medicines for the West Indies, that in short, the contents of an Apothecary shop had been taken as a model. There was very little basic or staple medicine for that climate. He made a regulation.

[A blank space follows equivalent to about seven lines.][267]

The sunsets in the rainy season are finer than in the summer months from the clouds which encircle it and send such a variety of glorious tints from its rays. Passed close to the fine Island of Guadeloupe, richly cultivated & beautiful plantations of sugar and coffee, stretching from the shore to the upland heights and fine houses and cottages enlivening the scene.[268]

Chapter 7 | The Havana Campaign, 1762 – "To the Astonishment of the City"

At dawn on 6 June 1762, a sharp-eyed Spanish lookout atop the tallest tower of Havana's harbour fortress, El Morro, espied a white cloud of sail crowning the horizon 20 miles (32 km) to the east-northeast and sounded the alarm. Senior officers summoned to the spot decided, after much discussion, that it was merely an English convoy bound for Jamaica and garrison gunners were allowed to stand-down and go to breakfast.

Havana, population 35,000, was the principal Spanish city of the New World, with a fine deep-water port and shipyards for supporting a substantial fleet. Lining its harbour were numerous commercial warehouses used for stockpiling the rich exports of sugar, tobacco and hides that were much in demand back in Europe. The city's defences consisted of a strong, bastioned perimeter wall encircling the city on the land side, with larger masonry forts sited on both sides of the harbour entrance. The smaller of the two, the Punta, guarded the lower western side, while El Morro, on the eastern heights, overlooked the city and harbour as well as guarding the seaward approaches.

The Spanish governor's (Field Marshal Don Juan de Prado) forces to defend such a strategic prize were substantial, his land forces comprising some 3,500 Spanish infantry regulars (the Havana Regiment and the 2nd Battalions of the

267. **Editors' note.** It is assumed that space was left for the insertion of the referred to Regulation in John Johnson Jr.'s next more polished draft.

268. **Editors' note.** Embarked for the Havana expedition, John Grant had left Martinique first, passing Guadeloupe on his way to Saint Domingo (Dominican Republic), where the fleet would wait for ships from Jamaica. This paragraph, originally appearing in one of the four loose quarto sheets, was placed here in the narrative.

Aragón and España Regiments) as well as an artillery detachment of 300 gunners augmented by the city's numerous militia (6,000 men but only 2,000–3,000 equipped with muskets). His small cavalry forces comprised a squadron of the Havana Dragoons and four squadrons each of the Aragon Dragoons and the Edinburgo Dragoons (a total of about 810 troopers). Another four militia cavalry regiments of approximately 3,000 men (700 of them lancers) could be raised from Havana's outlying districts. Finally, a further 750 marines and 5,500 sailors and gunners were available from Admiral Gutierre de Hevia's fleet of eighteen warships at anchor in the harbour.[269]

The British fleet bearing down on Havana was a formidable armada of forty warships and some 160 transport, supply and hospital ships. The transports carried the Earl of Albemarle's 12,000-man army, consisting of the 2nd/1st, 4th, 9th, 15th, 17th, 22nd, 27th, 28th, 34th, 35th, 40th, 1st/42nd, 2nd/42nd, 43rd, 48th, 56th, 3rd/60th, 65th, 72nd, 77th, 90th and 95th Regiments of Foot. There was also a Royal Artillery train of 380 experienced gunners and a Pioneer Corps of 600 black slaves. With their grenadier and light infantry companies brigaded and separate, the Highland battalions of the 1st/42nd, 2nd/42nd and 77th Foot numbered 558, 562 and 587 all ranks respectively for the upcoming siege.[270]

The fleet had sailed from Martinique on 6 May 1762 to arrive off Cape Saint Nicolas at Haiti, 13 May 1762. Instead of taking the safer, longer route through the Windward Passage, then sailing along the southern side of Cuba to Cape Saint Antonio and around to Havana, Admiral Sir George Pocock[271] chose instead to take the more direct Bahama Passage, which "was little known and deemed dangerous," according to David Dundas, a Scot who was aide de camp to Lieutenant General George Augustus Elliott, Albemarle's second-in-command.

"We knew of no large ship that had ever taken it," he claimed, "and certainly no such fleet as ours had ever attempted it. But the whole way, the wind was fair

269. **Spanish troop dispositions.** David Greentree, *A Far-flung Gamble, Havana 1762* (Osprey, 2010), 21; David F. Marley, *Wars of the Americas: A Chronology of Armed Conflict in the New World, 1492 to the Present* (Santa Barbara, 1998), 292.

270. **British troop dispositions.** David F. Marley, *Wars of the Americas: A Chronology of Armed Conflict in the New World, 1492 to the Present* (Santa Barbara, 1998), 291.

271. **Admiral Sir George Pocock, K.B.** (1706-92). Royal Navy officer. Joined the Royal Navy as a midshipman in 1718; lieutenant, 1726; commander, 1734; captain, 1738 (commanding HMS *Aldborough*); rear admiral, 1755; and vice admiral, 1758. Commanded the fleet in the East Indies from 1757 to 1760 during which time he vanquished the enemy in three different engagements (Cuddalore, Negapatam and Pondicherry) with an inferior force. Appointed Knight Companion of the Order of the Bath, 23 March 1761. Commanded the West Indies fleet assigned to the capture of Havana in 1762. Appointed admiral on 21 October 1762 and resigned in 1766. He died at Mayfair, Middlesex, on 3 April 1792. He was buried at Twickenham, but there is a monument to his memory in Westminster Abbey.

Spanish soldiers and officer, c.1785. Watercolour by T. Alvarez. (ASKB)

Mounted Infantry. Dragoons of the *Regimiento de Dragones de Edimburgo* (Edinburgh Dragoon Regiment) under the command of Colonel Carlos Caro fought British forces commanded by Colonel Guy Carleton at Guanabacoa during the 1762 siege of Havana. Detail from a larger image, c.1750s. (ASKB, Photo by R. Chartrand)

The Old Straits of Bahama. This engraving after a painting by Dominic Serres depicts the British fleet sailing down the Old Straits of Bahama on 2 June 1762, a somewhat hazardous approach to Havana little used by regular commercial shipping because of numerous shoals and reefs. Using it, therefore, gave the British fleet and army a better chance of surprising the Spanish. (LOC 2003674383)

along the [north] side of Cuba, and leading through the Old Straits of Bahama, we could at once arrive off of Havana.... We arrived on the 6th of June to the windward of the Havana, and to the astonishment of the city, who as yet had no knowledge of our expedition or even of the war."[272]

On 6 June 1762 the Spanish governor issued a general alert and the Spaniards spent the afternoon and evening reinforcing all outlying fortresses and batteries with the grenadier and picket companies of their regular regiments. However, they failed to reinforce the tiny outposts at Bacuranao and Cojimar, about 6 miles (10 km) east of the city, where the British commander actually intended to land. That night, the fleet anchored off Havana and prepared for the assault landings the next morning. At midnight the grenadiers of the army, light infantry and the other troops directed for the first embarkation were ordered into their boats to await first light.

At dawn, signal flags triggered the commencement of the shore bombardment and the ships of the fleet began battering the shore defences into rubble with broadside after thundering broadside. Six hundred light infantry, 150 of them Highlanders, went in first, followed closely by the 1st and 2nd Grenadier Battalions of the army, totalling 1,176 men (of which 200 were Black Watch), under the command of Colonel William Howe.

272. **Bahama Passage.** "Lieutenant General David Dundas' Memorandum on the Capture of Havana," *The Siege and Capture of Havana 1762*, David Syrett, ed. (London, 1970), 315. Hereafter, *Dundas Memo.*

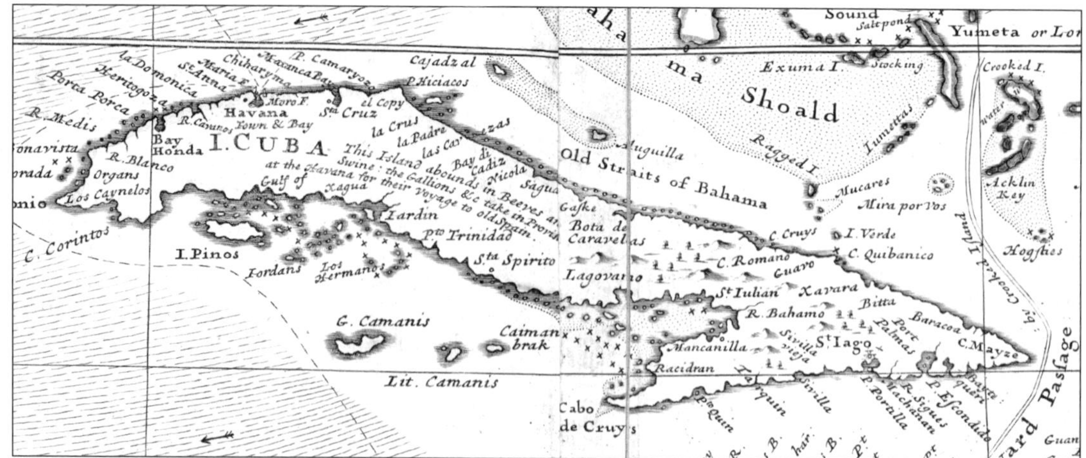

Cuba. Detail from "A map of the West-Indies or the islands of America in the North Sea; with ye adjacent countries; explaning [*sic*] what belongs to Spain, England, France, Holland, etc..." by Herman Moll. (LOC 71004474)

This wave was followed by the 1st Brigade, commanded by Brigadier General William Haviland and comprising the Royal, the 35th and 58th Regiments of Foot. Commanding the reserve was yet another veteran of campaigning with Wolfe, Colonel Guy Carleton, with the 3rd Grenadier Battalion and six light pieces of the artillery train with their crews.

The Spanish redoubts covering the shore were abandoned by the defenders without a fight, and by the afternoon twenty-two British infantry regiments with units of artillery and engineers, 11,800 in all, had landed without the loss of a single man. They encamped for the night with strong pickets posted on the perimeter and in the morning, 8 June 1762, advanced inland in three separate columns towards the Spanish village of Guanabacoa.

It was there the British believed that the Spanish would concentrate their land forces for a major counter-attack. As the British main column emerged from the woods on the heights of La Cabaña on the eastern side of the Cojimar River, they had "for the first time a full and noble view of the Havana, and of the extensive fertile and open country that surrounds it."[273]

Two smaller columns had marched as flank protection. Colonel Carleton, with about 1,200 grenadiers and light infantry, marched on the west side of the Cojimar River abreast of the main column, with Guanabacoa also as their main objective. Lieutenant John Grant, then posted to a light infantry company consisting of fifty Royal Highlanders and fifty men of the 44th Foot, went with them. Colonel Howe, with the other two battalions of grenadiers, pushed

273. **Terrain.** *Dundas Memo*, 316.

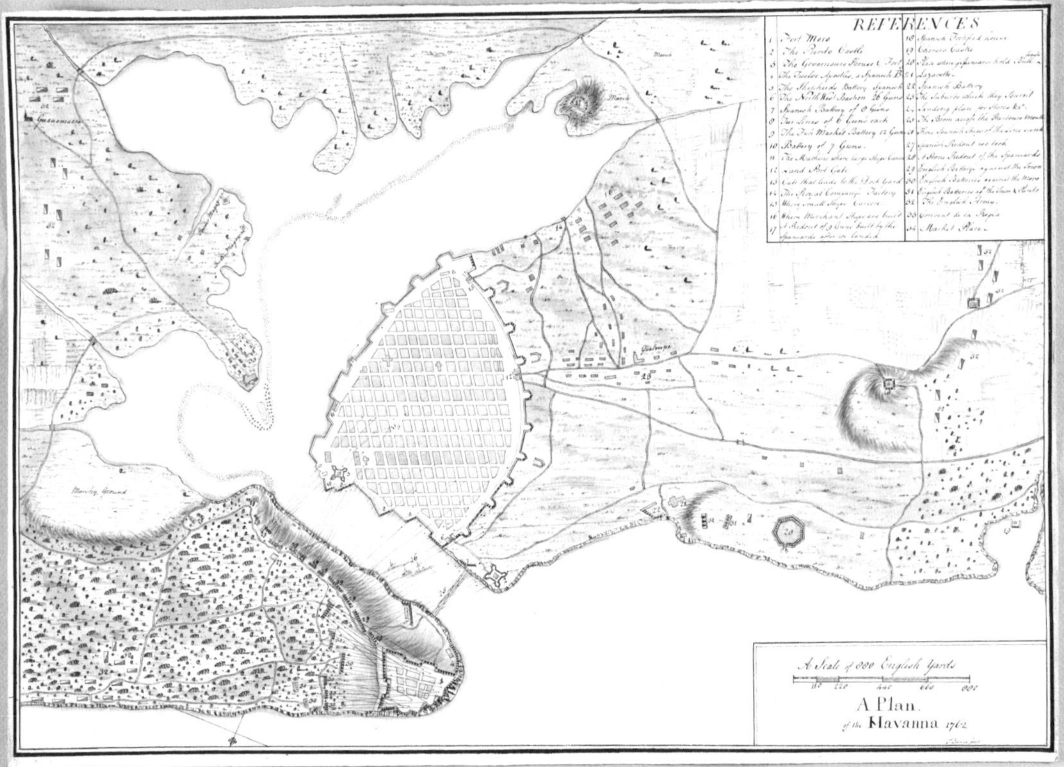

Havana. The artillery officer, Thomas Davies, who painted the watercolour that graces the cover of this book, was also an excellent cartographer who executed several maps of each of the various campaigns on which he served. Here is his "A Plan of the Havanna 1762." (JCB C-7001-000)

out to the right flank and sent his reconnoitring parties probing towards El Morro, "a service which," Dundas noted, "the troops from America could well perform."[274]

The village of Guanabacoa was immediately occupied by a brigade of infantry, who dug in, their mission now to guard the southern approaches to the siege operations planned for El Morro some 6 miles (10 km) to the north. The enemy were found to be constructing a strong redoubt on La Cabaña to help defend the approaches to El Morro. That became a principal objective for Colonel Howe's grenadiers and light infantry. John Grant of the 2nd/42nd light infantry company remembered being shaken awake by an orderly before daybreak on 11 June 1762 and being told to have his company under arms for a projected assault on the Cabaña redoubt.

The Spanish redoubt was captured at dawn and, according to John Grant, renamed the "Light Infantry Redoubt" in honour of the corps' gallant assault.

274. **Light Infantry.** *Ibid.*

Facing page: **Triptych of the Siege**

Top: **Landing at Havana.** Detail from "Perspective View of Landing the Cannon, Bombs, Provisions and Water for the Army, June 30th [1762]…." Hand-coloured engraving by James Mason. (LOC 2003671688)

Middle: **Storming Morro.** Detail from "Perspective View of Entring [*sic*] the Breach of the Moro Castle by Storm the 30th of July 1762…." Hand-coloured engraving by Pierre-Charles Canot. (LOC 2003670600)

Bottom: **Bombardment of Havana.** Detail from "Perspective View of the Grand Attack of that City [Havana] and Punto Castle… August 13, 1762…." Hand-coloured engraving by James Mason. (ASKB)

All three illustrations are details of larger paintings executed by marine artist Dominic Serres from original sketches drawn "on the spot" by Lieutenant Philip Orsbridge, Royal Navy. The vantage point of the three images is as if the viewer was positioned in the crow's nest high on the mast of a ship, where Orsbridge very well may have been at the time.

Possession gave the British the opportunity of erecting gun batteries that could fire across to the harbour, the city and the Punta fortress, but safely, in dead ground and out of site of the Morro's numerous gun batteries. El Morro was now effectively cut off from the land, so resupply and reinforcement efforts from the city were restricted solely to the water.

After this successful assault, Colonel Howe received orders to place the city of Havana under siege from its land side. On 15 June 1762 he landed with two battalions of grenadiers, one of light infantry and another of marines, to the west of the town at Chorera Castle, which had been silenced by naval gunfire the night before. They seized the heights of San Antonio and strengthened their position by building several redoubts in an effort to choke off all routes leading into the walled city. They cut the city's main water supply, then attempted to block off all main roads leading into the city. One of these roads was assigned to Lieutenant John Grant's company, and his previous experiences in Martinique and Guadeloupe would stand him in good stead.

While Grant and his Highlanders' experiences on outpost duty were undoubtedly stressful, they were not as arduous as the boring and backbreaking work of digging trenches before El Morro, the thankless task of the bonnet companies of Brigadier General Francis Grant's brigade. Water was rationed, and the men's diet of salt pork augmented by a daily issue of rum (the latter more cheerfully accepted than the former) was not very conducive to their health. Grenadier James Miller, a Scot serving with the 15th Foot, remembered that "bad water brought on disorders that were mortal" and that "you could see the men's tongues hanging out like a mad dog's." Men and officers would pay a dollar for a quart of water and Miller recalled that, when they couldn't find

The Keppel effect. Lieutenant General George Keppel, 3rd Earl of Albemarle, (1724-72), styled Viscount Bury until 1754, was a British soldier and nobleman. He is best known for his capture of Havana in 1762 during the Seven Years' War. His younger brothers, Commodore Augustus Keppel and Major General William Keppel, also took key parts in the expedition as well, which meant that the three brothers received the lion's share of the substantial prize money for Havana, causing an uproar in Parliament and charges of corruption and nepotism. Mezzotint engraving by Edward Fisher after a painting by Joshua Reynolds. Published in 1762. (ASKB)

water, it was quite common to find "Officers and soldiers drunk every hour of the day."[275]

There were other hazards. Henry Pringle, a light infantry officer like Grant, noted that an aggressive enemy, the lack of good water and food, and the excessive heat were not always one's chief concern in the Cuban jungle. "During the whole campaign encamped in the Wood … we had the opportunity every day of being pleased or frightened with the surprising operations of Nature in the Animal World," he noted. "We grew familiar with the Scorpions, Toads, Santipieds [*sic*] & Tarantulas, or rather Spiders as large as my hand, but among the lesser species, the variety was without end."[276]

Throughout July 1762, along with their comrades in Albemarle's army, the Highlanders of all three battalions began to sicken and die at an alarming rate. A month into the siege, Lord Albemarle lost a third of his force, a thousand men rotting in their shallow graves while another 3,000, too sick to work, lay incapacitated in their tent lines. The prescient pronouncement of a concerned Dr. Richard Huck to a friend from Martinique that "a Spanish war" would mean that the "American Army" would "broil long in the Torrid Zone" had come to pass.[277]

As the siege works moved inexorably closer to El Morro, the desperate Spanish sent several sallies in force to disrupt the progress of the works. Fresh troops commanded by Brigadier General Ralph Burton arrived from New York to

275. **Shortages.** James Miller, "Memoirs of an Invalid," Kent History and Library Centre (formerly Centre for Kentish Studies), U1350/Z9 & Z9A.

276. **Jungle insects.** Henry Pringle to Robert Pringle, 26 October 1762, Havana. *Pringle's Letterbook.*

277. **Torrid Zone.** *Return of the Surgeons …* dated 21 July 1762, *James Grant Papers* (microfilms), Library of Congress; Dr. Richard Huck to Captain Dalyell, 14 February 1762, Fort Royal, Martinique, quoted in Stephen Brumwell, *Redcoats: The British Soldier and War in the Americas, 1755-1763* (Cambridge University Press, 2002), 156.

Fighting Peacock. Admiral Sir George Pocock (1706-92) was the British naval commander at the 1762 siege of Havana, his share of the prize money on its fall a whopping £122,697 10s. 6d! Upset that an officer junior to him (Sir Charles Saunders of Quebec fame) was promoted over his head to First Sea Lord in 1766, he resigned his flag in a fit of pique, but retired to his estates a wealthy man. Mezzotint engraving by James McArdell after a painting by Thomas Hudson. Published in 1762. (ASKB)

relieve the exhausted and sickly army. Even the brigade stationed at Guanabacoa in a static defensive posture, with no work to do, had sickened and had been withdrawn to La Cabaña.

Since 20 July 1762 engineers had been mining under the walls of El Morro. On 30 July 1762 mine shafts packed with explosives were set off under the walls and the assault party of the 2nd/1st Foot (Royals) moved forward, supported by the 90th Foot and 35th Foot. First into the breach was a band of twenty volunteers known as the "forlorn hope," led by Lieutenant Charles Forbes of the Royals, a veteran of Culloden and Flanders. If he survived the day, army tradition dictated that he would be promoted to the next rank without purchase and rewards would be given to each of his surviving men.

The "forlorn hope" crept across a narrow ledge of rock, scrambled up a difficult slope of blasted rubble and then gained the platform of the enemy gun bastion. Forbes and fifteen of his men were up before the Spaniards spilled out of the bomb-proof casemates in which they had been sheltering, afraid of another massive mine detonation. The fighting was fierce and hand-to-hand, but the "hope" was quickly reinforced as fast as their comrades in the assault brigade could follow.

El Morro's garrison, mostly naval gunners and militia, were no match for the Royals and Colonel Francis Grant's 90th Foot, and they were quickly driven back into the fort's interior, then down into their casemates or out through their gun embrasures facing the sea. The British now controlled the entire length of high ground along the eastern side of Havana's harbour.

"We therefore with renewed zeal and vigour in the army and the fleet, immediately resumed our labours on La Cabaña to complete the necessary batteries," wrote Dundas. At daybreak on 11 August 1762, British batteries consisting of forty-four pieces of ordnance and eight mortars opened against the city and in six hours silenced its fire. They also made several breaches in the Punta fortress, destroyed its defences and disabled most of the guns on its northern bastion. The overwhelming fire superiority of the British "obliged the besieged to propose terms of capitulation, which were signed the 13th, and full possession was taken of the city on the 14th August," wrote Dundas.[278]

Celebrations were muted throughout the camps on La Cabaña, however, where the survivors of Francis Grant's brigade lingered on in misery. Any Highlander dying in August–September 1762 did so without the comfort of last rites. The Reverend Lachlan Johnston, the 42nd chaplain who served both battalions, had been dead of yellow fever since early August. The sufferings of the British troops were well portrayed by an eyewitness, the chaplain of the 1st Connecticut Regiment:[279]

> … had but little rest – my Ears constantly accosted with the groans and outcrys of the Sick and distressed: that the Camp is no other than a constant Scene of Woe … who are these – behold a Number, straggling along the road – awful, how they look? what appearance do they make? not unlike walking ghost, just come from the Shades – but viewing more narrowly find them to be men. Crawled out of their Tent, wasted with Sickness: their flesh all consumed, their bones looking thro' the Skin, a Mangie and pale Countenance, eyes almost sunk into their heads, with a dead and downcast look – hands weak, knees feeble, joints trembling – leaning upon Staves like men bowed and over loaded with old age, and as they Slowly move along Stagger and Reel, like drunken men – pitiful objects … Just by, six Soldiers take up their Captain upon their Shoulders as he lies pale and helpless in his bed, his bedstead serves as a Brier, and his Curtains waving in the wind, as a pall, in this manner conveyed from his Tent in Camp to a neighbouring room, if possible to prevent the extinction of the remaining Sparks of Life. There is one, two, three Graves open'd, here they come with as many Corpses, their blankets both their winding sheet and Coffins; scarce have they finished the interment of these, but a messenger comes in hast to tell them they must open a grave or two more, for Such a one is dead, and another is dying.

According to another account, "suffice it to say that perhaps those were happiest who died and left their bones around Havana, for those who returned home, took with them broken strength, and a languor which lasted to their life's end."[280]

Two weeks after the surrender of Havana, the remnants of Grant's brigade

---

278. **Capitulation.** *Dundas Memo*, 321-2.

279. **1st Connecticut Regiment.** Entry, 28 September 1762, *Extracts from the Journal of the Reverend John Graham, Chaplain of the 1st Connecticut Regiment, September 25th to October 19th 1762, at the Siege of Havana* (New York, 1896), 10-11. Almost 1,000 men strong when they had shipped out of New York, 423 had died in Cuba or on the return voyage.

280. **Another account.** Robert Burton, "Siege and Capture of Havana in 1762," *Maryland Historical Magazine*, vol IV (Baltimore, 1909), 334. Burton's account was written in 1899.

were placed in "transports, 9 of which had the two battalions of Royal Highlanders on board, 3 had the 17th Regiment and 5 the 77th" and were sent back to New York. Many would not survive the voyage. When the convoy carrying Grant's brigade dropped anchor at New York on 5 September 1762, General Jeffery Amherst "ordered Surgeons immediately to examine the men on board who were in general in a most deplorable state, and made dispositions for the sick to be taken into the Barracks at Elizabeth Town, Amboy, and New York, which we were forced to convert to Hospitals."[281]

Surgeon John Adair, reporting back to Amherst, described the Highlanders as "being reduced to the lowest State with dangerous Fevers, and Fluxes; Many of whom are too far gone to be recovered." It was his medical opinion that the entire brigade, which included the remnants of the 17th Foot, did not contain above thirty men "fit for service."[282] Adair proved correct in his observations, as he recorded on 25 October than 198 men from the four regiments had died in hospital over the previous month.[283]

Deaths in the two 42nd battalions by shot and shell at the siege of Havana had amounted to only two drummers and six privates killed and four privates wounded. By comparison, the death toll from disease was staggering. No fewer than seventeen Black Watch officers died during the siege or in the weeks that followed the capitulation.

When the nine companies of Montgomery's Highlanders and the two battalions of Royal Highlanders had set out from Barbados to take Martinique and Havana, they had mustered 2,075 all ranks, exclusive of officers, but by November 1762, they mustered only 795 men and many of these would die over the next few months. With the known numbers killed in action and missing subtracted from this total, it is apparent that a staggering 1,245 sergeants, corporals, drummers and private men of the Highland battalions died of yellow fever, malaria and other diseases.

Once ashore in New York, the two Royal Highland battalions could only muster 480 men, requiring another 231 just to complete the 1st Battalion to the new "reduced" establishment. Amherst recorded in his Journal on 26 October 1762 that he had sent home that day the invalid "officers, Sergeants, Corporals and Drums of the 2nd Battalion, Royal Highlanders" on transports, remarking that even after he had drafted all "the men into the first, the two Battalions

281. **Hospitals**. Entry, 5 September 1762. *Amherst's Journal*, 291-2.

282. **Fit for service**. "A Report of the State of the Men of the 17th, two Battalions of the 42nd, and 77th Regiments," 18 September 1762, in Kent History and LIbrary Centre (formerly Centre for Kentish Studies), U1330/042: f.8A; see also TNA CO 5/62, fol. 320.

283. **Adair's observations**. TNA WO 34/64, fol. 55.

The world's greatest diarist? Scottish biographer and diarist James Boswell (1740-95), who wrote *The Life of Samuel Johnson, LL.D.*, published in 1791, is considered by some critics to be the greatest biographer in the history of Western literature. All agree he changed the literary genre forever and that his private papers reveal him to be a most distinguished diarist. Oil on canvas, studio of Sir Joshua Reynolds, 1785. (NPG 1675. Editors' photo)

would only furnish two parts in three of [the] sergeants and corporals that were able to go and not a Drum to each company."[284]

Perhaps the saddest episode to end the year would take place inside a London theatre when in December 1762 some of returned officers of John Grant's battalion, on their way home to the Highlands, attended a play dressed in their Highland uniform. Unbeknownst to them, much political ill will and unrest had been stirred up by the young King George's choice for Prime Minister, John Stuart, the 3rd Earl of Bute. Instead of being cheered by the crowd at Covent Garden for their successes and sacrifices in the Caribbean, the two Highland officers were pelted with apples, the anti-Scottish crowd chanting, "No Scots! No Scots! Out with them!"

The diarist James Boswell was present and went to offer the Scots his moral support. One of the Havana veterans remarked angrily to him: "And this is the thanks we get – to be hissed when we come home!" The other, more irate, growled: "If I had a grup o yin or twa o the tam'd rascals, I sud let them ken what they're about!"[285]

But, of course, most of those "tam'd rascals" lay in unmarked graves in Cuba or had their corpses dumped unceremoniously over the sides of the hospital ships and transports as they had made their sorry way back to New York, trailed by schools of scavenging sharks. Scottish merchant John Watts witnessed the return of the survivors to New York city and, grieving for the many friends lost, spoke for many when he hoped that the "wofull [*sic*] reduction of the Havanna" would secure a long-lasting peace, as it had "entirely broke the heart of the stoutest little Army in the world."[286]

---

284. **Amherst's comments**. Entry, 26 October 1762. *Amherst's Journal*, 296.
285. **"Tam'd rascals."** Quoted in James Boswell, *London Journal, 1762-1763*, F.A. Pottle, ed. (New York, 1950), 71-2.
286. **"Stoutest little army."** John Watts to Moses Franks, 27 October 1762, New York, quoted from "The Letter Book of John Watts, Merchant and Councillor of New York, January 1,

The third Hanoverian monarch. George III (1738-1820) was King of Great Britain and Ireland from 25 October 1760 until the union of the two countries on 1 January 1801, after which he was King of the United Kingdom of Great Britain and Ireland until his death. Three years older than John Grant (born 1741), George III succeeded to his father's throne while John was spending the winter on the island of Montreal as a young Black Watch lieutenant. Mezzotint engraving by William Pether after a painting by Thomas Frye. Published in 1762. (LOC 2008675400)

* * *

We were some days getting to Saint Domingo[287] and cruised off that Island for some weeks, aweather,[288] [with] a distant view of it, high land, waiting for the Men of War that were coming from Jamaica. At last they found us, 7 Sail of the line and some frigates. We were in all, 24 Ships of the line, 36 frigates and 400 transports [and] 10,000 troops, one of the finest expeditions that ever sailed from England.[289] We were divided into 3 divisions.

At night a signal was hauled to shorten sail and all the fleet closed in to the Admiral, Sir George Pocock, who, like a hen, gather'd us under his wings, the lighter vessels keeping outside to make the transports avoid the Shoals of which there were many in the Straits of 86 Bahama,[290] through which we had to pass, and not one vessel was lost. The only accident that occurr'd was the running down of one small sloop with 70 men on board. It was never found out who did it, but the vessel was missing and no accounts were ever heard of her.

1762–December 22, 1765," *Collections of the New York Historical Society* (New York, 1928), 92.

287. **Saint Domingue**. A French colony on the Caribbean island of Hispaniola from 1659 to 1804 (today the island is divided between Haiti and the Dominican Republic). Also known as Santo Domingo or San Domingo.

288. **Aweather**. Upon or toward the weather side of a vessel; toward the wind.

289. **Expedition statistics**. Statistics vary. Thomas Mante, *History of the Late War in America*, 409-10, claims a total force of 11,353, with twenty-two ships of the line, twenty frigates, plus transports, supply and hospital ships, as well as ships for "negroes, horses and baggage for the general officers," making a total of over 200 ships. An *Abstract of the General Return of His Majesty's Forces Under the Command of Lieut. General Earl of Albemarle dated on board the Namur off Cape St. Nicholas* [Saint Domingue] shows: 543 commissioned officers, 578 non-commissioned officers, and 10,998 rank and file for a total return of 12,119, TNA CO 117/1.

290. **Old Bahama Channel**. A strait off the northern coast of Cuba and south of the Great Bahama Bank, it is approximately 100 miles (160 km) long and 15 miles (24 km) wide. The Spanish colonial trade routes, which originally favored the Old Bahama Channel, shifted to the Straits of Florida (the New Bahama Channel) as it was a safer alternative.

We enjoyed the Trade Wind, a gentle gale carrying us along at the rate of 5 knots an hour. We coasted along the Island of Cuba which appeared mountainous and but little cultivated. We anchored after 6 weeks off the mouth of the harbour [Havana] about a mile from the land. **(Monday, 12th January [1824]. Last day of personal dictation.)**

We landed to the eastward of the town without opposition, the works however of a perforated and worn nature – looked much like men drawn up to receive us. We halted and bivouacked that day in low hilly ground cover'd with brushwood.

The next day, at day break, the light infantry companies of each Regiment[291] were brigaded under Colonel [William] Howe and were formed and marched forward in the direction of *the Moro*[292] [*sic*]. We met with no opposition, the Inhabitants having fled from the few scatter'd houses into the Towns.[293]

We were quartered for the night in the different houses, the men as they best could who could not find a place. We were much plagued with mosquitoes. I was on picquet, the night was lovely and serene. One could scarce imagine that the stillness around was to be soon disturbed by the thunder of war. We had seen Colonel Howe and some General Officers reconnoitring a work[294] which crested [a] hill on the same ridge as *the Moro* and we expected some work for the next day.

Before daybreak, an orderly Sergeant had warned each Company to be under arms and when 87 I entreated [*sic*] at daybreak, I found the whole [of the Light Infantry Corps] under arms. Colonel Howe addressed us and told us that we were to carry the redoubt in front, that as we approached, was flanked by some guns from *the Moro*. He recommended us to pass the spot quickly, but not in disorder, and instantly to rush in and scale the Works.

As we advanced some shots were fired from the redoubt, which tore the ground but without effect. We had just reach'd the dangerous pass and there was a moment's hesitation. A dash was made by the head of the column and [at] the same moment a salvo from *the Moro* sent 5 poor fellows beyond the column, shatter'd corpses.

---

291. **Light infantry.** Similar to the light infantry organization at Martinique, six (composite) light infantry companies were formed into an *ad hoc* light infantry battalion for the landing at Havana. "Return of the Killed, Wounded and Missing…." 13 July 1762, TNA CO 117/1 f.81.

292. **The Moro.** Morro Castle.

293. **The towns.** One of these towns was Guanabacoa, about 3 miles (5 km) southeast of Havana. After landing, the first objective of the British infantry was to occupy Guanabacoa, prior to commencing operations against Morro Castle.

294. **La Cabaña redoubt.** The reconnaissance took place on 9 June 1762. To defend Morro Castle from a flanking attack, the Spanish had begun to construct a redoubt on the unfortified heights of La Cabaña.

No time was to be lost. The next half platoon pushed on before the guns could be reloaded. The ground was tangled and difficult, and there was some little lengthening of the column, inseparable from rapid movements over broken ground. The Spaniards now changed their mode and kept up a running fire, so that we all had to pass the ordeal.

I never made better use of my legs, which were much lengthen'd by the hiss of a twenty-four pounder over my head. The whole column pushed on with what speed they could and before the Spaniards could fire a second volley, the leading files were in the ditch cutting out the pallisades[295] [*sic*], whilst the constant fire of the others drove the Spaniards from the parapets.

88 (In advancing to the attack a drummer immediately in my rear, roared out he was shot. As the firing of musketry was only directly in front, I called him a fool as it must have passed through my body to reach him. I took no more notice. After all was over I saw my friend come limping into the redoubt. I again taxed him with [a] falsehood, but he pulled down his breeches about the hip [and] showed it was true. Upon examination, [a] ball had made a circular movement and remained under the skin. I cut it out with a penknife. Upon looking at my own dress, I found the mark of a ball right through my Kilt, a little above the knee.)

(There were several cannon in the redoubt which they had not time to spike and their retreat was so rapid that they were out of fire and under [the protection of] *the Moro* before we could reach them. It was called in honour of us, the Light Infantry Redoubt.) It was immediately fortified but *the Moro*, which was through an error, too distant materially to damage it. But a fuse was constantly kept ready to use if the enemy, chiefly Negroes & Mulattoes, were sent out to harass us by a dropping fire. A division was left to garrison it and the remainder fell back, in readiness however to support it.

The [siege] Trenches [for Morro Castle] were commenced [the] next day [12 June 1762] and whilst the Battalion companies were making fascines, we were sent out to forage. This was no easy matter. Tho' there were plenty of wild cattle, yet the thickness of the brushwood and Bush, and the heat of the day, made 89
it a difficult matter. Yet still, it was more agreeable from a spirit of romance in it than the hewing of wood and culling of water of the rest. Water was scarce and procured on a distance on Mules' backs.

After a few days,[296] we were marched round the head of the harbour and

---

295 **Palisade**. A high fence made of stakes, poles, palings or pickets, supported by rails and set endwise in the ground 6-9 inches (15-23 cm) apart.

296. **Expansion of siege**. On 12 June 1762 Colonel William Howe was sent "round on the other side" (i.e., around the harbour on the land side) with two grenadier battalions, a detachment from the composite light infantry battalion and some marines. The other grenadier

took a position to the westward of the town [Havana], on the main road, to prevent provisions entering. We took post on a hill, overlooking the flat space between us and the town and had a large Sugar House as a barrack. One half of the detachment being posted there, and the other half occupied in procuring provisions and scattered in small posts to prevent the entry of supplies for the Town. That part of the country around was in some parts richly cultivated with gardens for the use of the Town, in others dotted with thick and matted woods, and a number of houses and small villages were around.

Bamboo beehives. In the West Indies, farmers still use bamboo as beehives, their segmented sections (internodes) well suited to housing wild honey bees. A closed piece of large bamboo is suspended horizontally under the roof of a house or shed and a small entrance/exit hole drilled in one end. Bees can fill a section in 4-6 weeks. (Private collection)

Numbers of mules were loose, left behind by their Masters who had fled into the Town, so that we had no lack of cavalry. And numbers of cattle in an almost wild state were in the woods and both necessity and amusement made us endeavour to kill these animals. From my length of limb and activity, I was often excused other duty, to go out on hunting parties. These required some address and no inconsiderable degree of fatigue and danger, both from the animals themselves & 90 from the enemy, usually of Creoles & Mulattoes who, from the enclos'd nature of the country were enabled to lurk about unperceived, could get out of the town upon us and also from the interior.

On one of these excursions we had entered a small cluster of houses, apparently deserted. In the Gardens I was attracted by the appearance of a number of large bamboos, from which bees were issuing.[297] I found they were regular beehives and of course [I] wished to get the Honey.

It was no sinecure to attempt the seizure by main force, but perceiving that one bamboo appeared to be fixed on the other, we took one off and found that it was full of honey.

It is the custom as soon as the first is full to place it above another empty

battalion and the remainder of the light infantry were under the command of Colonel Guy Carleton, then conducting siege operations against Morro Castle. Major Alexander Monypenny to governor of New York, Havana, 14 October 1762.

297. **Bamboo beehives.** In the West Indies, farmers often use bamboo as beehives, their segmented sections (internodes) well suited to housing honey bees. A closed piece of bamboo is suspended horizontally under the roof of a house or shed, and a small hole is made in one node at one end enabling the bees to enter. The bees will then create a densely packed matrix of beeswax inside the bamboo. After about four to six weeks, honey can be harvested from the bamboo internode by splitting it lengthwise with a machete.

one. This had been done but the flight of the inhabitants had left them there, tho' ready for removal. We got several and were carrying them off when my companion called out: "The Spaniards, the Spaniards!"

I dropped my prize and ran to the front door. I saw six armed men close to it. I alas, returned back, but saw a man within the house levelling a musket at me. He fired – the house was filled with smoke.

I intuitively thrust in his direction with my fusee which had a small bayonet attached. I found that I [had] impelled [*sic*, pushed] some heavy body before me. An agonised groan soon inform'd me that my aim had been too fatal. I found my fusee grasped [*sic*, held tight] when attempting to withdraw it, and the smoke clearing, I found I had run my opponent through the body [91] and fairly pinned him to the wall, whilst his face glaring with rage and pain was close to me.

I wrenched my fusee from him by a violent effort and darted out of the house. New dangers awaited me. I saw two men at no distance who instantly fired without effect. A moment convinc'd me that unless I could clear a deep ditch at the end of the house which surrounded the yard, I was a dead man or a prisoner. I made the attempt.

I succeeded and ran towards where I had last left my party. I found them running up on hearing the shots. The Spanish party had [also] run towards the spot. We instantly pushed on to the house, but the enemy had retired under cover of the woods. I found my opponent, a fine looking Spanish Creole, killed dead on the floor, but there was no time for sympathy. We feared an attack by [a] stronger force, and seizing upon our honey, we retreated out of the enclosed ground around us. We shot however several cattle and after embowelling them, placed them over the mule's backs we brought for the purpose and returned to our position. All this was very agreeable, to a youth, than the more formal work of the other branches of the army. But it was fatiguing and many of our men suffer'd under it.

Our duty on outpost was very harassing, the nature of the country making surprise easy and the strict order we had receiv'd to prevent any supplies from the country from entering [the town] [92] made [us] always on the alert. The flies also, and venomous reptiles when we could not get shelter, also tormented us – and the want of good water. What we had was carried in skins or barrels [and] was boiling before it reached us. Whenever we apprehended a string of mules in their attempts to get in, with the negroes who were their attendants, after helping ourselves, we sent them to headquarters, where both were employed in carrying water, &c.

On one attack we made on a Village near the suburbs I happen'd to be on the advance, and after pushing the enemy through it, we received orders to return and occupy it. On so doing we found that it had been ransacked by the rest of the troops. It contained many *Don* houses,[298] and trunks &c. were thrown out of the windows. Fine brocaded dresses, velvet suits &c. were seized upon by the soldier's wives and camp followers who were soon seized upon and, equipped most amusingly in their borrowed plumes.

Of course we endeavour'd to stop wanton plunder, but I could not resist seizing on some excellent shirts which lay dispersed amidst the fine dresses, and some bundles of Legume [vegetables] and sticks of Chocolate (mind, this happen'd on our first landing. Strict orders were afterwards not to plunder in a wanton manner, but merely to take [the] necessaries of life).[299]

On one occasion my Captain, an Irishman of the name of Morris,[300] was order'd with his company

[The narrative abruptly ends at this point.][301]

---

298. ***Don***. A Spanish courtesy title placed before the first name of a distinguished nobleman or gentleman. From *dominus*, master.
299. **Editors' note.** This entire paragraph describing looting refers to an earlier incident that occurred during the first landing of the light infantry to secure the inland heights around Morro Castle. John Johnson Jr. probably intended to place it earlier in his narrative in a more polished draft. It is also the last page of the numbered memoir folios.
300. **Captain Morris**. Apollos Morris, 44th Foot, commanding the composite light infantry company in which John Grant served at Martinique and Havana. Born in Ireland 1729, Morris became major of the Enniskillen Regiment (44th Foot) on 28 November 1771. Strongly opposed to the war against the American colonies, he retired from the army in October 1775 when his regiment was in Boston. Although George Washington briefly contemplated making Morris adjutant general of the Continental Army in January 1777, Morris's avowed neutrality and many attempts to seek a reconciliation between America and Great Britain led Washington to reject the idea. Several months later, Morris was put under house arrest by the Americans, but he was later paroled and permitted to leave the Colonies.
301. **Ending of journal**. Based on a careful inspection of folio page 92, the editors believe that the narrative continued on at least one more folio page but this part of the memoirs is lost (in much the same fashion as the missing folio sheet containing pages 55 and 56). In any case, folio page 92 ends chronologically on or about the end of June 1762.

PART THREE

BIOGRAPHICAL NOTES

The many people listed in these biographical notes, from colonial governors to members of parliament to army officers and extended family members, are those who had a significant impact on John Grant's life and military career, a career spanning some fifty years of service to the British Crown, in Scotland, North America and the Caribbean. They are presented alphabetically and all officer entries are accorded their rank at the time of their first appearance in Grant's memoirs.

"To prevent untruths...." Major General Jeffery Amherst (1717-97) wrote his own obituary for the newspapers before his death "to prevent untruths." It was, he claimed, "void of any ostentation" and "contained only dates & Appointments without any claim of Merit from Services and made short as I could do it." (Private Collection)

Major General Jeffery Amherst (1717-98), *British army officer.*
Jeffery Amherst was born on 29 January 1717 at "Brooks Place" in the town of Riverhead, Kent. He was the second son of a well-to-do barrister and his wife, Jeffery and Elizabeth Kerrill Amherst. Gazetted an ensign in the 20th Foot, he transferred two years later as a cornet in the 9th Dragoons. His rise in rank was swift due to the patronage of the Duke of Dorset and his lifelong friend and first commanding officer, General John Ligonier. He served in the War of the Austrian Succession on the staffs of Ligonier and the Duke of Cumberland and in 1756 became colonel of the 15th Foot.

In 1758 he was sent to America as a major general to command the attack upon the crucial French stronghold of Louisbourg on Cape Breton Island. The capture of the French fortress gave Britain her first important victory in the war, and the victorious Amherst replaced the unfortunate James Abercromby as commander-in-chief in North America. In the late summer of 1759 Amherst pushed northwards from Albany and took Ticonderoga and Crown Point with minimal resistance from the French. He then halted cautiously to consolidate his gains by building a massive fort at Crown Point. The season being too far advanced to push on to Montreal to relieve pressure on Major General James Wolfe's army besieging Quebec, Amherst dispatched Robert Rogers and a force of chosen men to penetrate into French territory and destroy the Abenaki village of St. Francis near present-day Drummondville, Quebec.

The next year, with John Grant's regiment as part of his expedition, he led one of three forces against Montreal. Launching from Oswego, where he had ordered Fort Ontario rebuilt, his force crossed Lake Ontario, descended the St. Lawrence River, captured Oswegatchie (La Galette) and besieged Fort Lévis. He arrived at Montreal on 6 September 1760 as did his other two armies and accepted its surrender on 8 September 1760.

From his headquarters in New York, Amherst's next mission was to deal with a series of Indian uprisings and rebellions in the Carolinas and western Pennsylvania while simultaneously supplying regiments of his experienced "American Army" for the campaigns to wrest the West Indian sugar islands and the port of Havana from French and Spanish control. The Cherokee Wars in 1759-61 were followed by the so-called Pontiac uprising of 1763-64 that saw the western frontiers of Virginia and Pennsylvania go up in flames as the native tribes rebelled. Most of the French forts ceded to the British in 1763 were captured and their garrisons butchered, the only exceptions being Fort Pitt and Fort Detroit.

Amherst was recalled for his alleged misreading of Indian affairs in late 1763 and he gladly handed over his responsibilities to his subordinate, Brigadier General Thomas Gage. With the onset of the American Revolution, Amherst was asked twice (once in 1775 and again in 1778) by King George III to reprise his role as commander- in-chief in North America but refused. He agreed, however, to be commander-in-chief of forces in Britain and thus was responsible for the bloody suppression of the Gordon Riots.

Amherst was created a baron in 1776, styling himself "Amherst of Montreal." In July 1796 he was made a field marshal and he died the following year on 3 August 1797, having written his own obituary for the newspapers beforehand "to prevent untruths." It was, he claimed, "void of any ostentation" and "contained only dates & Appointments without any claim of Merit from Services and made short as I could do it."

J.C. Long, *Lord Jeffery Amherst: A Soldier of the King* (New York, 1933); Jeffery Amherst, *Journal of Jeffery Amherst: Recording the Military Career of General Amherst in America from 1758 to 1763*, J.C. Webster, ed. (Toronto, 1931); R. Whitworth, "Field Marshal Lord Amherst, a military enigma," *History Today*, IX (1959), 132-7; *DCB*, IV, 20-26; Jeffery Amherst, *The Journals of Jeffery Amherst 1757-1763*, R.J. Andrews, ed., 2 vols (East Lansing, 2015).

Captain William Anstruther (1738–1805),
British army officer.

William was born 27 July 1738, the fifth son of Sir Philip Anstruther of Balcaskie, 2nd Baronet (1688-1753), and Catherine Hay, daughter of Lord Alexander Hay of Spott. On 8 August 1755, at the age of seventeen, he was commissioned an ensign in the 26th Foot (Cameronians), then stationed in Scotland, his older brother John having been commissioned in the same regiment four years earlier. He purchased a lieutenancy in 1757, the same year his unit was sent to garrisons in Ireland for the next ten years.

While in Ireland, William purchased a captaincy with seniority from 1 January 1766 (26th Foot) and in May 1767 his regiment was ordered to North America. In 1772 he was given command of the fortresses of Ticonderoga and Crown Point on Lake Champlain, guarding the lines of communication between New York and Montreal, and made his headquarters at the latter fortress. On 21 April 1773 the barracks inside Crown Point caught fire, the destruction spreading from building to building over a period of two days until all was consumed.

"The conflagration," wrote the investigating engineer, Captain John Montresor, "rendered it an amazing useless Mass of Earth only; it's Frame Work or Casing which was Pine Wood, caulked with Oakum, and paid with Spanish Brown and Tar facilitated its destruction, the Casemates being composed of the same materials, and contiguous to the Barracks and Laboratory completed its Destruction." It was never rebuilt.

The next step in the drama was the recalling of all officers to Canada, where, at a Court of Inquiry, Anstruther's second-in-command, Lieutenant Joyce Feltham, took the stage, not only as accuser but actually as prosecutor of his captain, bringing charges and examining the witnesses. However, due to deteriorating relations between colonists and British authorities, the enquiry was never completed. No reprimand or reproof was administered, but Anstruther was removed from command and replaced by Captain William Delaplace of the same regiment, who set up his headquarters at Ticonderoga.

On 11 May 1775 Anstruther's replacement had the extreme misfortune of being the first British officer to surrender a fortress to the enemy in the American War for Independence. The forts at Crown Point and Saint John's, all manned by the 26th Foot, fell in quick succession to the rebels and Anstruther became a prisoner of war with his men at about the same time as John Grant. He and his men were sent to Reading, Pennsylvania. After being released in an exchange of prisoners, William Anstruther retired from the army on half-pay in 1777 and in 1779 was living at Bergen, New Jersey.

Fortune shined on the old half-pay officer when Sir Henry Clinton, the commander-in-chief, made him a major in the provincial Garrison Battalion on 26 October 1779, over John Grant's head, perhaps through the influence of his older brother, Lieutenant Colonel John Anstruther, who was then commanding the 62nd Regiment of Foot. Anstruther joined his unit in Bermuda, where he remained until its disbandment in 1783. His surviving correspondence from Bermuda shows that he busied himself importuning Sir Guy Carleton and others for military appointments for his two sons, one of them, Philip, being then at school in Glasgow. He stated that he was an unfortunate old officer who had to purchase every step of his promotion and had "losed" his limbs or the use of them in the service and, moreover, had lost three brothers and great property in lands, so that his sons had nothing to expect from their "much reduced father."

At the conclusion of the war he retired to St. Andrews, Charlotte County, Nova Scotia, as a half-pay major and was appointed a magistrate in 1785. In 1787 he married Isabella McLeod, and shortly afterwards he seems to have left the province for the Channel Islands. On 25 June 1790 he returned to active service as captain of one of the companies of Royal Invalids, stationed first on the Island of Jersey, then was made lieutenant colonel commandant in 1794 of all the invalid companies in Guernsey, and then colonel in the Army in 1795. His surviving son, Philip, eventually went into the Royal Navy. He was on full pay at the date of his death in 1805.

CBs, SBs, BALs, TNA, CO 5 vol 91.

Juan Manuel Cagigal y Monserrat (1738–1808), *Spanish army officer, colonial administrator.*

Sometimes written as "Cajigal" and not to be confused with his cousin Juan Manual de Cagigal y Niño, also governor of Cuba from 1811, Juan Manuel was born in Santiago de Cuba in 1738, the son of General Juan Francisco Antonio Cagigal de la Vega, Marquis of Casa Cagigal, commander-in-chief of Venezuela, and the governor of Cuba. Under the influence of his father, he obtained a commission in a prestigious Havana infantry regiment, quickly rising to captain. In 1760 he travelled to Mexico as an

"The love of the people and the soldier." Detail from an anonymous sketch found in a private library in England, the only known portrait of Juan Manuel Cagigal y Monserrat (1738-1808). It is inscribed by Francisco de Miranda, a former officer under his command: "sacrificing his life to his country, the state, Cagigal is the love of the people and the soldier." (Private Collection)

official assistant viceroy of New Spain, participating in the expeditions to Argil (1775) and Santa Catalina (1776) when he was promoted to brigadier general.

In 1778 he returned to Spain, where he participated in the blockade and siege of Gibraltar. During the Louisiana campaign (1781), he was second-in-command to General Bernardo de Gálvez, Spanish governor of Louisiana, and was reported as "the first to storm the breach at the walls of Pensacola." After the battle he was promoted to lieutenant general and named captain general of the Island of Cuba and governor of Havana.

While in Havana in 1782, he was placed in charge of the Spanish invasion of the Bahamas, leaving his commander (Gálvez) to focus on the more important expedition at that moment, Jamaica. These plans were upset when British Admiral George Rodney's fleet defeated the Comte de Grasse's French fleet off the island of Guadeloupe in the Antilles in one of the key battles of the war, giving the British undisputed naval superiority in the Caribbean. However, knowing of Rodney's victory and his intention to sail west to stop the Franco-Spanish invasion of Jamaica, Cagigal realized that the opportunity to undertake the expedition to the Bahamas was perfect.

On 22 April 1782, without the express permission of his commander, Cagigal set sail for Nassau with eight American ships of the line under Commodore ALEXANDER GILLON, who had been hired to protect the fleet of Spanish transports carrying 2,500 soldiers. On 6 May Cagigal sent his then-obscure aide de camp, Pensacola veteran and lieutenant colonel of the Aragon Infantry Regiment Francisco de Miranda, to parley at Nassau with John Maxwell, British governor of the Bahamas. (Miranda would later become famous in the struggle of the Spanish colonies in Latin America for independence.) Maxwell quickly realized his position was hopeless and opted to surrender to avoid unnecessary bloodshed. The capitulation was signed on 8 May 1782, the British surrendering a garrison of 612 regular soldiers and militia, including Captain John Grant and his two invalid companies of the provincial Garrison Battalion.

After his surprising victory – Nassau had been well defended – Cagigal wrote a letter to his commander, Gálvez, attaching the terms of capitulation as well as his battle diary and maps, to be carried personally by Francisco de Miranda. He left a token garrison to protect the Bahamas and ordered the rest of the expedition back to Cuba. He had obtained a notable victory for Spain in spite of the odds, but subsequent events made him pay a heavy price for his success. In December 1782, not long after he had returned to Havana, he received word of his replacement as captain general by Luis de Unzaga, Gálvez's brother-in-law, in spite of only having completed a short period of the customary five-year tour of duty.

His removal was due to a variety of factors, one being that Miranda, after the fall of Pensacola, had gone to Jamaica to arrange a prisoner exchange. Miranda accomplished this task, but while on that island he apparently engaged in a contraband operation for which he was later indicted, along with Philip Allwood of Jamaica and other prominent Spaniards. Another reason for his replacement was the traditional Gálvez nepotism, Bernardo wanting his brother-in-law to assume that important

Cuban post. Not only was Cagigal relieved of command but a short time later in 1783, he was arrested and shipped back to Spain as a *reo de estado* (prisoner of state) to stand court martial for the Bahama expedition, contraband and failure to arrest and send Miranda to Spain.

Back in Spain in the Santa Catalina military prison on Cadiz Bay, Cagigal's court martial brought up old (and new) wounds in the ongoing rivalry among Spanish Caribbean military officers. After a lengthy legal proceeding and a spirited defence, Cagigal was judged guilty of the charges and sentenced to four years in prison. To make matters worse, the United States Congress passed a resolution in May 1784 on behalf of the South Carolina delegation demanding "adequate compensation for that state [South Carolina] for the service performed by the South Carolina Frigate, in cooperating with the Spanish general [Cagigal] and forces in the Expedition against the Bahamas...." As a result of the investigations (conducted partially by the Count de Gálvez [Bernardo], who had been recently appointed as captain general of Cuba, Louisiana and the Floridas), part of the Spanish compensation for American services rendered in the war included "two burros from Carlos III for George Washington," then at Mount Vernon. At the end of 1785 a grateful Washington wrote to the Spanish minister of State, Count de Floridablanca, asking him to convey to "the King, my thanks for the Jack Asses...." This unique Spanish gift "concluded some of the final details of the last true battle of the American Revolution."

In 1789 Cagigal was fully exonerated by His Majesty, Carlos III. When war broke out against the French Republic (1793-95), he returned to active duty, participating in the battles at Navarre and Guipuzcoa. After the peace, and having become one of the most brilliant Cuban military leaders of his time, he retired to the city of Valencia, where he died in 1811.

Eric Beerman, "The Last Battle of the American Revolution: Yorktown. No, the Bahamas," *The Americas* 45 (1988), 79-95.

Major John Campbell, 7th of Glenlyon (1715–84), *British army and marine officer.* Born in 1715 at Fortingall, Perthshire, John was the eldest son of John *Iain Buidhe* (yellow-haired John) Campbell (c.1675-1746), 6th of Glenlyon and Fortingall, and his wife, Katherine Smythe. His grandfather, Robert Campbell (1630-96), 5th of Glenlyon, was the commanding officer of government troops at the Massacre of Glencoe in 1692. John's father fought for the Stuart cause at Sheriffmuir in the 1715 Rebellion and once again in 1745, at the age of seventy, risking all that he had by declaring once more for the Stuarts. He died exiled in Bruges, leaving behind a "plethora of debts," his remaining lands forfeited, as well as an obligation which his descendants "found unredeemable, and which they called *the curse of Glencoe.*"

John, *Iain's* eldest son and heir, was very different from his father. A tall, serious young man, he had no time for the Jacobite cause and his strongly held Hanoverian sympathies caused an irreparable breach between him and his father. His younger brother, Archibald *Roy* Campbell (1728-79), fought as an eighteen-year-old lieutenant in the Jacobite army at Culloden but was pardoned and later served honourably and with distinction with the 78th Foot (Fraser's Highlanders) in North America during the Seven Years' War. John's foster brother, John Campbell (1717-58), a captain lieutenant in the 42nd Foot, would be killed at Ticonderoga on 8 July 1758, leading the only group of soldiers to penetrate the French defensive works.

On 25 December 1744 John was commissioned a lieutenant in one of the three new-raising companies formed to augment the 43rd Foot (soon to be renumbered as the 42nd), all of which served in Scotland during the 1745 uprising. The aftermath of the Rebellion was a sad time for young John as he and his Black Watch soldiers were ordered to burn the houses and remove the cattle from the Jacobite lairds of Perthshire, most of whom he knew personally. He went out on lieutenant's half-pay 31 May 1749, but returned to active service as a captain in the new-raising 19th Company of Marines, 22 February 1755. He obtained his majority (brevet) 19 October 1758 and was part of the Marine force which landed at Guadeloupe in spring 1759, helping Lieutenant John Grant of the 42nd Foot aim and fire an artillery piece during the siege of Fort Louis. He exchanged to the 2nd Company of Marines during the 1763 peace reductions because of his seniority. He was promoted major 13 February 1764 and brevet lieutenant colonel 4 March 1767, retiring onto half-pay in 1771.

During the American Revolution, John was recalled from half-pay, but once again *the curse of Glencoe* travelled with him. Colonel DAVID STEWART in his *Sketches...* relates the story: "In 1771, Colonel Campbell was ordered to superintend the execution of a soldier of marines condemned to be shot. A reprieve was sent, but the ceremony was to proceed until the criminal was on his knees with a cap over his eyes. It was then he was to be informed of his pardon. No person was to be told, even the firing party who were warned that the signal to fire would be the waving of a white handkerchief by the commanding officer. When all was prepared, Colonel Campbell put his hand in his pocket for the reprieve, and in pulling out the packet, the white handkerchief accompanied it and the unfortunate prisoner was shot dead. The paper dropped through Colonel Campbell's fingers and clapping his hands to his forehead he exclaimed, 'The curse of God and Glencoe is here: I am a ruined man.' Soon after, he retired from the service, though great efforts were made to persuade him to change his mind."

Perhaps this anecdote is the reason he became widely known by the nickname, *An Coirneal Dubh* (The Black Colonel). John returned to Glenlyon and set about regaining the lands that had been lost by his grandfather but ironically there would be no male heirs to carry on the family name or to live on those lands. John *Coirneal Dubh* Campbell died unmarried at the age of sixty-nine on 4 April 1781. His younger unmarried brother Archie *Roy* had suddenly pre-deceased him at Armaddy, Scotland, from old wounds sustained at Quebec opening up. A third brother, David, also died unmarried.

CBs; SBs; Perthshire Diary, 4 April 1781, <http://www.perthshirediary.com/html/day0404.html> (assessed 4 July 2016); Clan MacFarlane, Descendants and Associated Families, <http://www.electricscotland.com/history/glenlyon/Clans Genealogy> (assessed 4 June 2016); John Prebble, *Glencoe: the story of the massacre* (New York, 1966), 258-9.

Colonel Guy Carleton, later first Baron Dorchester (1724–1808), *British army officer, colonial governor.*

Guy Carleton was born 3 September 1724 at Strabane, Ireland, the third son of Christopher Carleton and his wife, Catherine Ball. Commissioned an ensign in the 25th Foot (Rothes) on 21 May 1742, he transferred three years later by purchasing a lieutenancy in the prestigious 1st Foot Guards and was promoted captain in the army 22 July 1751. By 1757 he had become lieutenant colonel in the army and was appointed to command the newly-raised 72nd Foot in 1758.

A close personal friend of James Wolfe, Carleton was a solemn, competent and thoroughly professional officer and not averse to criticising Hanoverian soldiers serving on the continent. Not surprisingly, he incurred the personal disfavour of England's ultimate Hanoverian soldier – King George II. It would take three attempts at persuasion on William Pitt's part, and James Wolfe's threat to resign, before the King would sign Carleton's commission as the

1759 Quebec expedition's quartermaster general.

He was wounded in the head at the Battle of the Plains of Abraham, 13 September 1759, while leading the Louisbourg Grenadiers and returned to England in October to recover. He returned to action with the amphibious assaults on Belleisle off the coast of France in 1761 and the siege of Havana 1762. Carleton again suffered life-threatening wounds in both campaigns and was promoted colonel on 19 February 1762 and given the 93rd Foot, which was disbanded the following year at the peace.

In 1766 he was promoted "Brigadier in America" and appointed lieutenant governor of Quebec after Governor James Murray's recall. When Murray did not return, he assumed the title of governor-in-chief two years later on 12 April 1768. During this time Carleton returned to active military service from half-pay as the colonel of the 47th Foot (2 April 1772). Carleton's term of office as governor spanned some ten years until his departure 27 June 1778, during which he successfully defended Quebec from the American invasion of 1776-77, but he resigned his post a year later after continual disagreements with Lord Germain over the conduct of the war and the latter's criticism of his governance style.

Carleton's military career progressed in tandem with his political appointments. Promoted major general on 25 May 1772 and lieutenant general on 29 August 1777, he became a general of the army on 12 October 1793. After his colonelcy of the 47th Foot on 2 April 1772, he progressed to several colonelcies in the cavalry: 15th Dragoons, 16 July 1790; 27th Dragoons, 18 March 1801, and 4th Dragoons on 14 August 1802.

In 1782 Carleton was sent back to North America as commander-in-chief of all forces in North America, tasked to supervise the orderly withdrawal of British and Loyalist forces from the former Thirteen Colonies. On his return to England, he strongly recommended the creation of a governor general of all the provinces in British North America. Instead, he was appointed "Governor-in-Chief," with simultaneous appointments as governor of Quebec, New Brunswick, Nova Scotia and St. John's Island (present-day Prince Edward Island). As a sop for not having his recommendation accepted by the administration, and agreeing to take the post anyway, Carleton was raised to the peerage in August 1786, taking the name Lord Dorchester, Baron of Dorchester in the County of Oxford.

The King's disfavour. Colonel Guy Carleton, later first Baron Dorchester (1724-1808), was a solemn, competent and thoroughly professional officer and not averse to criticising Hanoverian soldiers serving on the continent. Not surprisingly, he incurred the personal disfavour of England's ultimate Hanoverian soldier – George II. He served as Wolfe's quartermaster general for the Quebec campaign in 1759, served with John Grant at the Siege of Havana in 1762, then interviewed him after he had escaped from American rebels who had imprisoned him at Crown Point in 1775. (LAC 1997-8-1)

He arrived at Quebec on 23 October 1786

and quickly found, as he had feared, that his new position as "Governor-in-Chief" was mostly ignored. His authority in any of the provinces, other than Quebec, was only effective when he was physically present in the province in question. He remained in Canada for another fourteen years though, returning to England 9 July 1796, worn out by all the political infighting in Canada and at home.

In retirement, with an annual pension of £1000 for life, Carleton lived mostly at Greywell Hill, adjoining Nately Scures, in Hampshire. After 1805 he moved to Stubbings House at Burchett's Green, near Maidenhead, where on 10 November 1808 he died at the age of eighty-four. He is buried in the parish churchyard of St. Swithun's, Nately Scures.

CBs; SBs; BALs*; DNB; DCB*; A.G. Bradley, *Sir Guy Carleton* (Toronto, 1907); P. R. Reynolds, *Guy Carleton: a biography* (Toronto, 1980)*;* Jeffery Amherst, *The Journals of Jeffery Amherst 1757-1763*, R.J. Andrews, ed., 2 vols (East Lansing, 2015), II, 63.

Brigadier General Sir John Clavering (1722–77), 6th Baronet, *British army officer and diplomat.*

Baptized on 31 August 1722, at Lanchester parish church, County Durham, England, the third son of Sir James Clavering of Axwell and Greencroft, John was commissioned as an ensign in the 2nd Foot Guards on 10 February 1735 and was a lieutenant and captain commanding the grenadier company by 1741. He became a captain lieutenant and lieutenant colonel in the 2nd Foot Guards on 23 December 1752. A death in the regiment paved the way for a free promotion to captain and lieutenant colonel on 7 June 1753. He married Lady Diana West, the youngest surviving daughter of the First Earl De La Warr, in 1756. Clavering and Lady Diana would have five children: two sons and three daughters. Lady Diana died in 1766.

In 1759 he commanded a brigade under Major General John Barrington in the expedition against the island of Guadeloupe, where he led the attack in person, Horace Walpole writing that he was "the real hero of Guadeloupe." As a mark of appreciation for his services, he received a brevet promotion to colonel on 14 June as aide de camp to George II, and in 1762 he was appointed to the colonelcy of the 52nd Regiment, which he retained until his death.

His connections at court and in the political sphere made him a man of some consequence. In 1770 he was promoted to lieutenant general and in that same year was appointed governor of Landguard Fort in Sussex. Clavering married his cousin, Catherine Yorke, in 1772, his second marriage producing no children.

In 1773 John was selected for the command of the Bengal Army with a seat on the council

"The real hero of Guadeloupe." Brigadier General John Clavering (1722-77) commanded a brigade under Major General John Barrington in the expedition against the island of Guadeloupe and was always in the forefront of the fighting, causing Horace Walpole to observe that Clavering was "the real hero of Guadeloupe." Attributed to Gilbert Stuart, the painting shows Sir John wearing the scarlet frock coat of a lieutenant general prior to his leaving England to command the Bengal Army in India. (Illustration from Leslie, *The History of Languard Fort*)

of the government of India, ranking next to the governor general. He was made a Knight of the Bath in 1776 but his health deteriorated in India's hot climate and he died at his home in Mission Row, Calcutta, on 30 August 1777. A monument over his grave in South Part Street Cemetery in Calcutta reads: "To the Memory of Sir John Clavering. Knight of the Most Hon. Order of the Bath, Lieut. Gen. in his Britannic Majesty's service, and Colonel of the 52nd Regiment of Foot, second in the Supreme Council of Fort William in Bengal, and Commander in Chief of all the Company's forces in India; Died Aug 30th 1777 in the 55th year of his age, and was interred here." While "not a man of great mark as a statesman, he was, nevertheless, an honourable, straightforward, and energetic soldier, and though … of an impetuous and combative disposition … a man of sterling integrity."

CBs; SBs; BALs; Major John Henry Leslie (RA), *The History of Languard Fort* (London, 1898), 106-8.

Controversial commander. General Sir Henry Clinton (1730-95). While some believed Clinton to be "fool enough to command an army when he is incapable of commanding a troop of horse," the experienced Guards officer was actually a capable field commander. Clinton resigned his command of the North American theatre in 1781 and on his return to England found that his subordinate, Lieutenant General Charles Cornwallis, was viewed with a great deal of sympathy and he himself was blamed for the Yorktown defeat. His *Narrative of the Campaign of 1781 in North America* published in 1783 to set the record straight only served to provoke an outraged reply from Cornwallis and more political fallout. Engraved by Francesco Bartolozzi after the oval bust portrait by John Smart. Published in London, 1780. (ASKB)

Major General Sir Henry Clinton (1730–95), *British army officer.*

Henry Clinton was born, probably on 16 April 1730, to Admiral George Clinton, a future governor of New York, and Anne Carle, the daughter of a general in England. Most histories claim his birth year as 1738, a date widely propagated even in modern biographic summaries, but Clinton himself claimed to have been born in 1730. He would have grown up in Newfoundland, where his father was stationed from 1732 to 1738, then moved to New York, where his father, the Honourable George Clinton, served his term as governor of New York colony.

It was there that Henry started his military career as a fifteen-year-old lieutenant in a New York independent company commanded by Captain Hubert Marshall and he was present at the capture of Louisbourg in 1745. He then transferred on promotion to the command of the Governor's (his father's) Independent New York Company as its new captain lieutenant the same year. In 1750 his father purchased him a commission as lieutenant and captain in the 2nd Foot Guards, and eight years later Henry transferred to the 1st Foot Guards, purchasing a commission as captain and lieutenant colonel on 6 May 1758.

He was made colonel of the 12th Foot on 28 November 1766 and promoted major general on 25 May 1772. Three years later, on the outbreak of hostilities with the colonies, Clinton went to North America as the second-in-command to Sir William Howe with the rank of lieutenant general "in America only."

Clinton fought with distinction at Bunker Hill and Long Island and was left in command at New York when Howe went south to Pennsylvania. He attacked and carried Forts Clinton and Montgomery in October 1777 and in May 1777 was made a Knight of the Bath. In January 1778 he replaced Howe as commander-in-chief of all British forces in North America with the rank of general "in America only" and in 1779 became colonel of the 7th Foot.

Under his command, British forces took Savannah and Charleston, 1779-80. After Charleston fell, he returned to New York, leaving Lord Cornwallis, his second-in-command, in charge of the subsequent operations that led to the capitulation at Yorktown and the peace treaty recognizing American independence. Clinton resigned his command in 1781 and went back to England, where he found his subordinate Cornwallis viewed with some sympathy and himself blamed for the Yorktown defeat. *His Narrative of the Campaign of 1781 in North America*, published in 1783, provoked an angry reply from Cornwallis. On 12 October 1793 he was promoted full general and the following July he was appointed governor of Gibraltar, but he died at Portland Place before he was able to assume that post. He was buried in St. George's Chapel, within Windsor Castle.

CBs; SBs; BALs; *DNB; DCB*; William Willcox, *Portrait of a General: Sir Henry Clinton in the War of Independence* (New York, 1964).

Major Gavin Cochrane (1726–86), *British army officer.*

Gavin Cochrane was born in 1726 in Scotland and was commissioned an ensign in the 31st Foot at the age of eighteen, 25 June 1744, and lieutenant in the same regiment 26 November 1751. When the 60th Foot (Royal Americans) was stood up for service in North America, he secured a captaincy dated 15 January 1757. Serving with the 1st Battalion at Ticonderoga, 8 July 1758, he was wounded in the attack. He spent most of his North American service on the Great Lakes at Niagara, Fort Presque Isle (present-day Erie, Pennsylvania) and in the back country. In 1764, after the peace, Cochrane wrote a surprisingly frank and humane "Treatise on the Indians of North America" and sent it to the Board of Trade and Plantations.

Stationed at Crown Point from 1768 to 1772, Cochrane was finally relieved by Captain William Anstruther of the 26th Foot. Cochrane's troops had spent most of their time making repairs to the fortress as the British government was reluctant to spend money on fortifications in peace time. Cochrane reported: "a side wall of the Bakehouse rebuilt, which was tumbling down and could not get it done for less than a Dollar a day by the Bricklayer," "the Gate of the Fort being wore out and gone to pieces, I ordered a stout new one to be made," "the Bridge of plank which was the only way to go upon the Ramparts has fallen down, but nothing can be done 'til the frost is gone." He was referred to in the *New York Mercury* of 1772 as "a very respectable gentleman" and "hopes he will get the vacant majority in the regiment."

Cochrane's hopes were answered and he was made major "in the Army" on 23 July 1772, returning to England, where the following year he was made major to the 69th Foot, 14 August 1773. In London he met John Grant socially and used his influence with Lord Dartmouth to try to obtain John Grant a personal interview. In 1777 he was promoted lieutenant colonel of the 58th Regiment, then stationed at Gibraltar, and subsequently colonel "in the Army," 20 November 1782.

He died 23 March 1786, the *Scots Magazine* noting: "23 March, Edinburgh, Lt. Colonel Gavin Cochran [*sic*], buried in Abbey-church with military honours."

SBs, CBs, BALs; *St. Andrews Roster;* W. Legge, *Manuscripts of Lord Dartmouth* (London, 1887); *Scots Magazine* 48 (March), 155; TNA, WO 34/100, f.8; Jeffery Amherst, *The Journals of Jeffery Amherst 1757-1763*, R.J. Andrews, ed., 2 vols (East Lansing, 2015), II, 2.

Lieutenant Thomas Davies (1737–1812),
British artillery officer and artist.
Davies entered the military academy at Woolwich, England, on 17 March 1755, a training school for future artillery officers where cadets were introduced to drawing and watercolour painting, not to encourage fine art but so they could draw readable pictures of forts, gun redoubts and details of military operations. Drawing classes were an important part of the curriculum, and there is no doubt that this is where he received much of his artistic training. He was commissioned as a lieutenant fireworker in the Royal Artillery on 1 April 1756. He first came to America in 1757 as a 2nd lieutenant, and he was at Halifax as part of Loudoun's aborted Louisbourg campaign – a watercolour drawing of Halifax that year is Davies's earliest dated picture. He was back at Louisbourg the next year, this time as part of Amherst and Wolfe's well-managed, successful campaign. He was promoted to 1st lieutenant on 1 January 1759 and was an active participant in Amherst's expedition that resulted in the capture of forts Ticonderoga (Carillon) and Crown Point (Saint Frederick) on Lake Champlain. In 1760 Davies was part of General JEFFERY AMHERST's division in the three-pronged campaign against Montreal, where he commanded a row galley, taking part in the siege of Fort Lévis on Île Royale. On the way to Montreal, he would have first traversed the rapids at Long Sault, just north of the modern community of Massena, New York, and then the much more dangerous rapids at the Cedars, closer to Montreal at the eastern end of Lac Saint-François. Davies was obviously impressed by the rapids, executing the monochrome wash painting which appears on the cover of this book, most likely depicting the rapids at the Cedars. When Montreal fell in September 1760, Davies was almost certainly the officer who first hoisted the British flag over the city, an honour traditionally awarded to an artillery officer. He was promoted to captain lieutenant on 10 March 1762.

"The Military Caricaturist." The title of an unflattering caricature depicting Thomas Davies (c.1737-1812), the artist-soldier, in much later life, now a lieutenant general and colonel commandant of the Royal Artillery. Apparently, he slighted the well known cartoonist James Gillray, who countered with this fairly scurrilous portrait. Inscribed under the print were the words: "... his Satires are as keen as the Back of a Rasor; – and having but Three Ideas in the World, Two of them borrow'd, – & the Third, nobody else would own." (British Museum 1851,0901.1004. Editors' photo)

Davies made regular use of his painting skills throughout the war, producing a number of scenes that are remarkable for their artistic merit and their historical accuracy. One of these, a view of Amherst's camp at the foot of Lake George in 1759, contains what is probably the only contemporary view of a Rogers' Ranger. This original is now in the collection of Fort Ticonderoga. He returned to England at the end of the Seven Years' War, but he was back in America with his artillery company in 1764 where he produced a series of watercolours which "mark the beginnings of a personal style characterized by strong compositions and glowing colours." He returned to England in 1767 and was promoted to captain, 1 January 1771. In 1773, on the eve of the American revolution, Davies again sailed for Halifax, moving to Boston the following year, where he doubtless saw action at Bunker Hill in June 1775. By mid-1779 he was back at Woolwich and in 1780 served as Amherst's aide de camp, "making charming drawings of ladies and gentlemen strolling among the troops stationed in the London parks during the Gordon riots." Over the years he had been cultivating an interest in birds, and he now began to win recognition for his work as a naturalist. In 1781 he was elected a fellow of the Royal Society of London. He was promoted brevet major on 7 June 1782; major, 1 December 1782; and lieutenant colonel, 21 November 1783.

He returned to America in 1786, assuming command of the artillery at Quebec. It was during this peacetime posting that he executed his best watercolours, mostly of Quebec and region, and developed his style "to its highest point of excellence," far removed from the competent but narrowly topographical style of the 1750s. He returned to England in 1790 and rose in rank to brevet colonel, 1 March 1794; colonel, 14 August 1794; and major general, 3 May 1796. He was appointed colonel commandant of the Royal Artillery on 13 July 1799, the highest position within his own branch of service. He was promoted lieutenant general on 25 September 1806. His last work, and probably his finest, was a masterly panoramic view of Montreal dated 1812, the very year of his death.

Davies was the most talented of all the early topographical painters in Canada, "surpassing his predecessor Richard Short, his contemporaries Hervey Smythe and James Peachey, and his successors George Heriot and James Pattison Cockburn." Because his work was hidden away in private collections, he had no direct influence on later Canadian artists. According to the *Dictionary of Canadian Biography*, "the brilliance, breadth, and clarity of his landscapes would not be found again until the advent of the Group of Seven." In the 1950s the National Gallery of Canada acquired most of his watercolours of Canadian subjects and this acquisition stirred renewed interest in the painter. Thomas Davies was certainly one of the most well rounded men of his generation – an extremely talented soldier, an artist with an exceptional eye for accuracy and detail, and a gifted naturalist was well. He died in in Blackheath, England, on 16 March 1812.

SBs, CBs, BALs; *DCB;* Stephen Sears, "The Lion's-eye view: A British officer portrays colonial America," *American Heritage*, vol 29, no 4 (June/July 1978), 98-107; C.P. Stacey, "Thomas Davies – Soldier and painter of 18th-century Canada," *Canadian Art*, 13.3 (1956), 275.

Lieutenant Alexander Donaldson (c.1738–94), *British army officer.*

Alexander Donaldson was born about 1738, the second son of Robert Donaldson of Ayr and his wife, Katherine Brodie. He joined the newly-raised 2nd/42nd as an ensign in the summer of 1758 and saw service at Martinique and Guadeloupe, 1759. Served on all major campaigns and, as the experienced adjutant of both the 1st and 2nd Battalions of the regiment, talked down mutinous soldiers at Fort Pitt in August 1764 prior to the Muskingum expedition. Alexander was listed as a participant in peace talks with Shawnee, Delaware and Iroquois Indians at Fort Pitt, 9-10 June 1766. He married Anne, the daughter of Lieutenant Colonel Gordon Graham of Drainie, his commanding officer, in May 1773.

After the outbreak of the American Revolution, and failing to get promotion within his own regiment, he was appointed first major of the new-raising 76th Foot (Macdonald's Highlanders) in 1777, "an officer admirably calculated to command and train a body of young Highlanders" according to Colonel DAVID STEWART (later Stewart of Garth) as he was "a native of the country and, having served 19 years as adjutant and captain in the 42nd Regiment, he had full knowledge of their characteristics and habits." The newly-designated commanding officer, Lieutenant Colonel John Macdonell of Lochgarry, a former Fraser Highlander had been captured by the Americans at sea while returning from America to Scotland. Donaldson spent a year in command of the regiment at Fort George, but became ill from a growing tumour on his back. Daily command thus passed to the arrogant second major, John Sinclair, Lord Berrisdale.

When the ailing Donaldson marched the regiment down to the Lowlands, his Highlanders mutinied at a town near Edinburgh over outstanding pay matters and other petty grievances nursed during his absence. Through his consultations and persuasion, the men returned to duty after being promised their bounty money and assured they were not bound for the West Indies. When the 76th sailed for New York, however, their well-liked, but very ill, senior major remained behind for an operation to remove the tumour from which he recovered very slowly.

The commander-in-chief for North Britain, Lieutenant General Sir James Adolphus Oughton, relayed to the War Office on 1 May 1779 that he feared "we shall lose poor Major McDonald [*sic*] of the 76th who has been dangerously ill since the Operation was performed: I have found him a very excellent Officer; of which he has given evident Proofs in the forming and raising that Regiment without the least Assistance." Donaldson became too ill to continue with the regiment and retired on half-pay 10 August 1780.

With the threat of a French invasion in the fall of 1782, several volunteer corps began to organize and the *Scots Magazine* noted that on: "Thursday, Sept. 5. There was a meeting of several noblemen and Gentlemen at Edinburgh, to Consider of a plan for raising a volunteer corps of ten companies, to serve without pay, (until called out on actual service), on Lord Shelburne's plan. They are to be clothed in the highland dress, and called the CALEDONIAN BAND. The meeting agreed to associate immediately, and appointed the following officers, viz, the marquis of Graham, colonel; the earl of Buchan, Lieutenant Colonel; Maj. Alexander Donaldson, late of the 42d regiment, Major.... The officers' names are to be transmitted to Lord Shelburne, for his Majesty's approbation, with a request of arms and accoutrements. Near 300 have already given in their names to serve in the corps."

However, before the commissions could be issued, the preliminary articles of peace with the French were signed and the government no longer required any volunteer corps. But Donaldson was not finished following the colours. In June 1793 he was appointed major in the West Lowland Fencibles raised by Colonel Hugh Montgomerie, an old "American Army" friend and a veteran of Montgomery's and Fraser's Highlanders. A month later Donaldson was promoted to lieutenant colonel of the Fencibles and served with them just under a year. The *Scots Magazine* for 1794 recorded his death on 17 June: "At Edinburgh, Lieut. Col. Donaldson, of the West Lowland regiment of fencibles." His wife, Anne Graham, died the following year at Bankfoot, 5 August 1795. Their only son, Alexander Donaldson Jr., commissioned a lieutenant in the Black Watch during the Napoleonic Wars, died of wounds received at the Battle of Alexandria in Egypt, 1801.

CBs; SBs; BALs; Stewart, *Sketches*, I-II; Croghan to Gage, 15 June 1766, WLCL, *Gage Papers*, American Series, vol 52, Reel 10; Jeffery Amherst, *The Journals of Jeffery Amherst 1757-1763*, R.J. Andrews, ed., 2 vols (East Lansing, 2015), II, 101.

Lieutenant Colonel Robert Donkin (1728–1821), *British army officer.*
Robert Donkin was born in 1728 in Morpeth, Northumberland, England, son of Aynsley Donkin (1691-1750) and Elizabeth Todd. He started his career as an ensign in the 2nd Foot (Fowke's), commissioned 21 July 1747 at the start of the War of Austrian Succession. He served initially with his regiment at Gibraltar. He served with a young James Wolfe in Flanders on the staff of his regimental colonel, General Thomas Fowke, and of Lord Granard when the latter was commander-in-chief in Ireland, the first of many staff appointments. He is stated to have been a personal friend of David Hume, the historian, and to have written at the suggestion of the latter an account of the famous siege of Belleisle off the coast of France, at which he was a spectator.

He was promoted lieutenant in the 2nd Foot on 4 September 1754. On promotion to captain (13 December 1759) he transferred to the 76th Foot (Rufane's), then stationed in Ireland. In 1761 his regiment was sent to join Major General Robert Monckton's expedition at Barbados to take French Martinique and he subsequently served as aide de camp and secretary for Brigadier General William Rufane, the regimental colonel of the 76th Foot and the governor of Martinique after the capture of the island until July 1763.

He went on captain's half-pay on 1 December 1763 but returned to active service as a captain in the 23rd Foot (Royal Welch Fusiliers). Brevetted a major "in the Army" on 23 July 1772, Donkin went to North America with the Royal Welch in 1773, reportedly serving as an aide de camp to General Thomas Gage, and was promoted brevet lieutenant colonel "in the Army" on 29 September 1777. For his services to Gage he was made major of the general's own regiment, the 44th Foot, 5 October 1777.

In that same year he wrote a book entitled *Military Collections and Remarks* and published it for "the children and widows of those valiant soldiers inhumanly and wantonly butchered when marching peacefully to and from Concord on April 19th, 1775." In it he professed his hatred of the rebels and showed few qualms about the tactic of infecting the general civilian population as well as the enemy army with smallpox. He suggested: "Dip arrows in matter of smallpox, and twang them at the American rebels, in order to inoculate them; this would sooner disband these stubborn, ignorant, enthusiastic savages, than any other compulsive measures. Such is their dread and fear of that disorder."

He was Sir Henry Clinton's choice on short notice to replace the discredited major commandant of the Royal Garrison Battalion in Bermuda who had fallen afoul of the authorities and was recalled. Made

"Doomed to retire upon half pay." Major Robert Donkin (1728-1821), 44th Foot, was Sir Henry Clinton's choice, at short notice, to replace the discredited major commandant of the Royal Garrison Battalion in Bermuda in 1779. As the war wound down and peace loomed, the Northumbrian officer tried hard to obtain full pay for his invalid officers on the pending disbandment instead of the customary half pay. The sketch executed by Robert Dighton (no date) is entitled "General Donkin of Bath." (Royal Collection Trust 990860. Editors' photo)

the lieutenant colonel commandant of the provincial unit on 25 October 1779, he was still commanding it in December 1782 when it was brought onto the regular establishment, thereby making him a substantive lieutenant colonel in the regular army.

As the war wound down and regimental reductions loomed, Donkin lobbied on behalf of the many invalid officers in his unit, arguing they should receive full pay on the pending disbandment of regiments. He wrote: "That, from Age, wounds or Infirmities, the Officers of the Royal Garrison Battalion can have no Prospect of ever returning into the Service. And that consequently, as these Circumstances and the Habits of their past Lives must render them incapable of adding to their Incomes, they will be exposed, during their remaining Existence, to all the Miseries of Poverty and Distress, should they be unfortunately doomed to retire upon half Pay." He noted that "it has been hitherto the usual custom, upon the Reduction of Invalid Corps, to continue Officers thereof upon full Pay, until opportunities might occur of providing for them in the Standing Invalids, or they should be otherways [*sic*] disposed of."

He was unsuccessful and went out with his regimental officers on half-pay 25 October 1783. Brevetted colonel "in the Army" on 18 November 1790, he was subsequently promoted major general, 1794; lieutenant general, 1801; and full general, 1809. He died in Bath on 6 March 1821 at the age of ninety-three. He was buried in Saint Mary Redcliffe Churchyard, Bristol, England.

His obituary in the *Gentleman's Magazine* stated: "General Donkin passed a long life of the most unsullied honour and with the greatest respectability, without sickness and apparently without uneasiness of any sort and although he served in a variety of climates and had been engaged in nine actions and in seven sieges, he was never absent from his duty either from illness or wounds." He was married to Mary Collins (1746-1816) of Bristol in 1772 and had one son and two daughters (Jane Ann and Laetitia). The son, Sir Rufane Shaw Donkin (1773-1841), became a general like his father.

BALs; CBs; SBs, *Gentleman's Magazine*, 1822.

Surgeon Robert Drummond (1730–c.1788), *British army surgeon.*

Educated at King's College in Aberdeen, Robert Drummond's family origins are unknown but his connections and influence were such to obtain the surgeon's commission with the newly-raising 2nd/42nd Foot (5 August 1758). He served with John Grant at Martinique and Guadeloupe in 1759, Montreal in 1760 and the Caribbean again in 1762 for the Martinique and Havana campaigns. He is shown on a return of surgeons at Havana, August 1762, as "ill in camp." He survived the "boneyards of the Caribbean," however, and spent all of 1763 administering to the sick of both Black Watch battalions at New York.

Drummond exchanged to half-pay on 24 October 1763, as he was the junior of the two battalion surgeons, and returned to Scotland. In 1768 he petitioned the Board of Forfeited Estates in 1768 for a residence and farm at Corriehumain on the Strowan estates, noting that the area of Rannoch was large and populous with no resident surgeon within 30 miles (48 km). If successful, Drummond vowed to live and practise there as a surgeon with his wife and children. Three years later, records show him as the "Tenant of Corroghtinan" for which the Commissioners gave him a forty-one-year lease.

CBs; SBs; BALs; "List of the Officers of the 42nd or Royal Highland Regiment according to seniority dated December 29th, 1762," BL Add. MSS 21,634: f.178c; Alexander Hastie Millar, *A Selection of Scottish forfeited estates papers* (Edinburgh, 1909), 244.

Commodore Alexander Gillon (1741–94), *South Carolinian naval officer, merchant, landowner, politician.*
Alexander was born in Rotterdam, Holland, on 13 August 1741, to Alexander Gillon, a Scots sea captain who had immigrated to Holland in 1726, and his second wife, Mary Harris. Well educated in London, England, where he lived for some time, young Alexander became proficient in at least four languages – English, Dutch, French and German – and could write in the first three. After the death of his father in 1764, he followed in his footsteps and became a sea captain. In 1766 he married a wealthy widow, Mary Cripps, in Charleston, South Carolina, and with her money quickly established a large and profitable mercantile business along Broad Street in that city. He soon became one of the wealthiest men in South Carolina, owning at the outset of the Revolution a waterfront residence in Charleston, along with an adjacent lot and a wharf, as well as fifteen other lots, with an estimated valuation of £30,000 pounds.

As a merchant and owner of shipping, he was well placed to procure arms and munitions for the rebel cause, and on 8 November 1775 he became a delegate to the Second Provincial Congress of South Carolina and subsequently the South Carolina House of Representatives. On 20 November 1778 he was appointed a commodore in the Colony of South Carolina's Navy, tasked to procure suitable warships from France. In 1780 he successfully chartered the frigate *L'Indien*, 40 guns, from the Duke of Luxembourg on behalf of the colony for a quarter-share of her prizes, renaming the vessel *South Carolina*. In August 1781 the *South Carolina*, commanded by Alexander and manned by American officers and a group of European seamen and marines, sailed across the Atlantic, eventually reaching Charleston. When he found that the British had already occupied that city, he sailed on to Cuba, arriving at Havana on 13 January 1782.

Frigate captain. Alexander Gillon (1741-94), a successful merchant and ship owner in Charleston, was appointed a commodore in the Colony of South Carolina's Navy in 1778 and tasked to procure suitable warships from France. In 1780, he successfully chartered a 40-gun frigate which he renamed *South Carolina* and two years later, in 1782, joined a Spanish force sent from Havana to capture the British colony of New Providence in the Bahamas. Executed by Gilbert Stuart, 1873. (FARL)

At Havana, after negotiations with the Spanish, the *South Carolina* joined a force of sixty-three vessels sent to capture the British colony of New Providence in the Bahamas. The expedition sailed on 22 April and by 5 May the fleet had reached New Providence. On 8 May, outnumbered six to one, the British defenders, including Captain John Grant's two companies of invalid veterans, surrendered to the Spanish commander, JUAN MANUEL CAGIGAL Y MONSERRAT, captain general of the island of Cuba, and governor of Havana. After the war, the remainder of Alexander's life was spent in public service. Soon after his return to South Carolina, Alexander was re-elected to the House of Representatives, and in March 1784 he was elected to Congress. Four years later he was a delegate to the State convention which ratified the Federal Constitution.

In February 1789 he married Ann Purcell, the daughter of Reverend Henry Purcell, rector of St. Michael's Church in Charleston, and was elected to the Third Congress, serving from 4 March 1793 until his death at his plantation on 6 October 1794. Alexander was interred in the family burial ground at "Gillon's Retreat."

Biographical Directory of the United States Congress, 1774 – Present, <http://bioguide.congress.gov/scripts/biodisplay.pl?index=G000211> (accessed 18 July 2016); James A Lewis, *Neptune's Militia: the frigate South Carolina during the American Revolution* (Kent State University Press, 1999); D.E. Huger Smith, "Commodore Alexander Gillon and the Frigate South Carolina," *The South Carolina Historical and Genealogical Magazine*, vol 9, no 4 (October 1908).

Major Gordon Graham (1718–c.1786),
British army officer.
Gordon Graham joined the Black Watch as an ensign on its formation as the 43rd Foot in 1739 and rose to the rank of captain by 1747, before retiring onto the half-pay list in 1749. He returned to active service in June 1752, purchasing the captaincy of John MacLeod, younger of MacLeod, in June 1752.

When the regiment sailed for North America in 1756, Graham was a "Flanders" veteran, the senior serving captain and the regimental paymaster. When the three so-called "additional companies" were added to the regiment's establishment in 1757, Graham made the case for a second major to be appointed within the regiment, similar to the wartime establishments of the two new Highland battalions raised for North American service, the 77th (Montgomery's) and 78th (Fraser's) Regiments of Foot.

In a memorial, he sketched out his previous service: "Your Memorialist hath ... upwards of twenty-five years, twelve of which as Captain in the above Regiment, and is now the eldest in that rank. That he hath served in Flanders and elsewhere during all the last war, some part of which he was employed as Major of Brigade, and had a Commission as such from General St. Clair in the Expedition under his command in the year 1746."

Graham was supported in his request by Lieutenant Colonel Francis Grant and Major General James Abercromby. His request was overtaken by events and he was promoted major on the death of Duncan Campbell after the battle of Ticonderoga in July 1758. His arguments for a second major, however, bore fruit, for John Reid, the next captain in seniority, was promoted second major the following year on 1 August 1759. Graham thus handed over his 1st/42nd duties as the second-in-command to Reid as he was given the battalion command as major commandant of the 2nd/42nd when it arrived, sickly and poorly-equipped, from its gruelling ordeal in the Caribbean.

Graham spent the better part of the winter of 1759-60 reorganizing, re-clothing, re-equipping and training the battalion. During the winter of 1760-61, he clashed with Francis Grant over who really commanded the 2nd/42nd and lost out to the latter. The following year he assumed command of the 1st/42nd on Francis Grant's departure to take up his appointment as the new colonel of the 90th Foot, while John Reid backfilled Graham as major commandant of the 2nd/42nd.

Graham returned home to Scotland in January 1764 with a leave granted until 16 July 1766 but never returned to America. Graham instead rejoined the regiment the following year when it returned to Ireland in 1767 having been absent for over three years. He retired three years later in December 1770.

CBs; SBs; BALs; Stewart, *Sketches*, I-II; "List of the Officers of the 42nd or Royal Highland Regiment according to seniority dated December 29th, 1762," BL Add. MSS 21,634: f.178c; TNA, WO 1/1; LAC

MG 23, series K34 (Frederick Mackenzie Papers) Order Book, 1761-62; Jeffery Amherst, *The Journals of Jeffery Amherst 1757-1763*, R.J. Andrews, ed., 2 vols (East Lansing, 2015), II, 145; Frederick B. Richards, "The Black Watch at Ticonderoga and Major Duncan Campbell of Inverawe," *Proceedings, New York State Historical Association*, vol X (1910). Hereafter, *Black Watch at Ticonderoga.*

Alexander Grant, 4th of Dalrachney (c.1660–89), *baron-baillie, landowner, John Grant's paternal great-grandfather.*

Alexander was born c.1660, the eldest of two sons by the second marriage of John (a.k.a. John *Oig* M'Quene) M'Swine Grant (c.1600-1667) who in 1647, was a factor for the Laird of Grant in Glencarnie. His father had, in 1653, a wadset of *Dalrachnie-beg* and married first, Elspet, (daughter of Robert Grant of Glenbeg, by whom he had one son, Donald) and secondly, Janet McPherson. Alexander's older step-brother Donald by the first marriage was the progenitor of the Dalvey Grants.

On his father's death, Alexander succeeded to Dalrachney, while Inverlaidnan passed to his older brother, Donald. He was considered one of the representatives of the Gartinbeg branch of the family in the bond of amity with the Grants of Tullochgorm in 1669. He paid *cess* (land tax) for Dalrachney and half of the Forrigen estates in 1667 and 1668. On 1 March 1673 he arranged with his chief, Ludovick Grant of Freuchie, for a renewal of the wadsets (mortgages) for *Dalrachnie-more, Dalrachnie-beg* and Forrigen; and in 1683 the wadset was again renewed, the amount of the redemption-money being raised to 5,250 merks. He was confirmed executor of his brother Donald on 19 July 1676.

He married Christian Cuthbert of Castlehill in 1680. They had four sons: JOHN *DHU* (John Grant's grandfather), Alexander, David and George.

JGM; W. Fraser, *The Chiefs of Grant*, 526-7.

Lieutenant Alexander Grant (1734–1813), *British naval and army officer, colonial administrator.*

Alexander Grant was born in Glenmoriston, Scotland, second son of Patrick Grant, the 8th Laird of Glenmoriston, and Isobel Grant of Craskie. He served five years with the Royal Navy as a midshipman but on 4 January 1757 accepted a commission in the 77th Foot (Montgomery's Highlanders) as its senior ensign. He survived Major James Grant's botched raid at Fort Duquesne in September 1758 as he had the fortune of being sent back at the height of the battle to request assistance for the survivors. He was promoted lieutenant after the raid "in room of Charles Farquharson," who was moved up to the captain lieutenancy of the 77th.

During the 1759 campaign against Crown Point, Major General JEFFERY AMHERST placed Grant in command of the sloop *Boscawen*, 16 guns, on Lake Champlain and the following year, he gave him command of the snow *Mohawk* on Lake Ontario for the 1760 campaign. After the war Grant was one of several 77th officers who decided to remain in North America, taking up a land grant of 2,000 acres in Orwell, Vermont, between Crown Point and Ticonderoga, but this land remained vacant when he acquired land at Grosse Pointe near Detroit and married Thérèse Barthe (1758-1810) in 1774.

During the American Revolution, Grant became commander of the Provincial Marine on the Great Lakes, based at Detroit, though this 1776 appointment was reduced to Lakes Erie, Huron and Michigan in 1778. He held the appointment until 1812 when he retired with the rank of commodore. He was appointed a Justice of the Peace in 1786 and served on the Land Board of the District of Hesse from 1789 until 1794. He was appointed lieutenant of Essex County in 1799. As a senior member of the Executive and Legislative Councils of Upper Canada, he became administrator-president for a year upon the death of Lieutenant Governor Hunter in 1805.

A contemporary observer of Grant described him as "a large, stout man, not very polished, but very good tempered, (who) had a great many daughters, all very good looking, all very lively, all very fond of dancing and all very willing to get married as soon as possible." In fact, Grant had eleven daughters and a son with Thérèse Barthe, his wife of thirty-six years. He retired as commodore at the age of seventy-eight but did not long enjoy his retirement, dying on 8 May 1813 at his beloved farm, Castle Grant (named in remembrance of his Scottish ancestral home), at Grosse Pointe, Michigan. Grant was buried in St. John's churchyard, Sandwich (present-day Windsor), Ontario.

CBs; SBs; BALs; Stewart, *Sketches*, I-II; General Return, 1757, 77th Officers List, JGP; "Alexander Grant," *DCB*, V, 36364; Gilkison Family Papers: 1786-1910, Archives of Ontario, MSS 497; TNA, WO 34/44: f.182; *Chiefs of Grant*, I, 522-3; Jeffery Amherst, *The Journals of Jeffery Amherst 1757-1763*, R.J. Andrews, ed., 2 vols (East Lansing, 2015), II, 146.

Alexander Grant, 6th of Corrimony (1716–97), *landowner, Jacobite supporter.*
Alexander was born in 1717 in Aberdeenshire, eldest son of John Grant, 5th of Corrimony (1690-1726), and Mary Keith, eldest daughter of Alexander Keith of Kidshill. On 17 April 1727 he was retoured heir to his father, and in 1740, shortly after his marriage to Jean Ogilvie, the only daughter of Lieutenant John Ogilvie of Kempcairn, he built the now old mansion-house of Corrimony, over the door of which is carved the family arms, with the initials AG + JO (Alexander Grant and Jean Ogilvie).

During the '45 Uprising, he was one of the three Urquhart gentlemen known collectively as "the three Alexanders" who actively supported the Jacobite cause. On the landing of Bonnie Prince Charles at Moidart in August 1745, he was sent by Alexander Brodie of Brodie, the Lyon King of Arms, to Ludovick Grant of Grant, to inform him of the fact. When at Castle Grant, Ludovick, not fully trusting Corrimony, appears to have extracted a promise from him that he would not rise in arms without his consent. This he does not seem to have observed very strictly, for soon thereafter he was reported by the factor John Grant to have attended a meeting of the gentlemen and tenantry of Urquhart convened by Alexander Grant of Shewglie, a zealous Jacobite agitating for the Jacobite cause.

Shortly after this, on 14 October 1745, he visited Lord Lovat at Castle Downie, and when there, Simon Fraser, Lord Lovat proposed that Alexander should join the Master of Lovat and the Fraser Clan, which was just then about to march for the Highland army. To this Alexander replied that while he was willing to act without his Chief's approval, he would not join a two-faced person who pretended to be on the side of the government and was actively intriguing on the other. At this Lovat flew into a rage and ordered him to be silent in his house, threatening to inform his brother-in-law, Sir James Grant.

The next day Alexander wrote to Ludovick Grant and informed him of his intention to rise in arms for the Prince, and added that the Master of Lovat intended to come with 300 men and force the tenants of Urquhart to go with him. On 22 October 1745 a meeting of the gentlemen and men of Urquhart was held at Torshee, at which he was present, together with the Master of Lovat and Coll Macdonald of Barisdale. The threats uttered by the Master of Lovat, however, angered the people, and Corrimony vowed if any of the Frasers came into the Glen he would give them a beating.

Finding none of the other Urquhart men would go but those they had already, he set out, accompanied by his wife and Alexander Mackay of Auchmony, for Castle Grant, apparently for the purpose of renewing friendship with the Chief, or, as the factor John Grant put it, "Corremone beleivis his lady will make his piece with you." They were received by Ludovick Grant, who conferred with them, and thereafter they returned home. However, by December 1745, Corrimony finally resolved to join the Jacobite cause, no longer willing to be held in check by John Grant, the factor, causing Ludovick Grant to style him "that mad villain Currymony [*sic*]."

Corrimony joined the Prince at Inverness on 15 April 1746, arriving just as the midnight march on Nairn was starting, and though he had come from Glenurquhart that day, he immediately joined the army and took part in the battle of Culloden the following day, where he received two severe wounds. Carried off the field by John *Garbh* Cameron of Carnoch, one of his tenants, he made his way home to Corrimony, where he hid himself in a cave near the Fall of Morrall. While in hiding, his lands were plundered by Grant militia under the command of Ludovick Grant. A subsequent raid of Glenurquhart in July 1746 by the infamous Major JAMES LOCKHART saw a party of troops despatched to destroy his house, but the officer in charge, whose name was allegedly Ogilvie, spared it on account of his clanswoman, Jean Ogilvie, Corrimony's wife. On another occasion Alexander started out for Strathspey to give himself up to his chief but, receiving warning, had second thoughts and went back into hiding. No further steps were taken against him. He died at Nairn in 1797, aged eighty-one.

JGM; *Chiefs of Grant*, I, 526-7; F.J. Grant, *The Grants of Corrimony* (Berwick, 1895), 516-7. Hereafter, *Grants of Corrimony.*

Alexander Grant, 6th of Dalrachney, later Inverlaidnan (1705–65), *advisor, land tax collector, landowner, John Grant's paternal uncle.*

Alexander Grant was born in Strathspey, Scotland, in 1705, the oldest of three sons of JOHN *DHU* GRANT, 5th of Dalrachney, and Margaret Grant of Knockando. When his father John *Dhu* died in 1735, Alexander inherited the lands of Dalrachney, to which he added the estates of Inverlaidnan and Duthil. He and his father were both baron-baillies in their time, and were both said to have made £3,000 or £4,000 in the exercise of their authority.

As Sir LUDOVICK GRANT's principal advisor during the 1745 Jacobite Uprising, John Grant's Uncle Alexander was a rich and important figure in Strathspey, mentioned as early as 1728 as "Younger of Dalrachnie [*sic*]." In 1738 he was a cautioner in the testament of James Grant of Curr, and in 1739 the fledgling *Scots Magazine* reported in its "Domestick Occurrences" section that "the fine new-built house of Alexander Grant of Delrachney, Esq. was burnt to the ground by accidental fire; whereby the whole furniture, plate about L 170 [*sic*] in cash, and a great many valuable papers, are consum'd." He was appointed collector of cess (land tax) for the Regality of Grant in 1742, and again in 1746. He rebuilt the mansion-house of Inverlaidnan, in which Prince Charles Edward slept on 22 February 1746 on his way to Culloden. In 1751 Alexander Grant was one of the curators of William Grant of Ballindalloch.

He married Helen Grant of Easter Elchies, who bore him two sons, both of whom pre-deceased him: Gregor (1742-59) who died at the age of seventeen, and John Grant, who served in Lord Loudoun's regiment (later the 64th Foot) during the Uprising but was killed serving at the siege of Bergen-op-Zoom in Flanders in 1747. Alexander died in 1765, leaving his nephew, Lieutenant John Grant, late of the 42nd Foot and the hero of our tale, as the last male survivor of the Dalrachney Grants.

JGM; *Chiefs of Grant*, I, 526-7; *Scots Magazine* (September 1739), vol I, 42.

Alexander Grant, 4th of Shewglie, (c.1685–1746), *landowner, Jacobite supporter.*
Alexander took an active part in the 1715 and 1745 uprisings and was described by LUDOVICK GRANT as "a man very remarkable for Highland cunning." Alexander was a staunch Jacobite, his father James Grant of Shewglie having fought for King James at Killiecrankie and been slain at Corribuy in 1691. Alexander's first wife, Margaret, was a daughter of John Chisholm of Comar, and his second, Isabel, a daughter of John (*Iain a' Chragain*) Grant of Glenmoriston. He fathered nine sons and five daughters and was one of the three Urquhart gentlemen known as "the three Alexanders."

At the end of the '45 uprising, sixty-year-old Alexander Grant of Shewglie was made prisoner, accused of being the chief mover in the rebellious actions of the Urquhart men, though he himself did not actually join Prince Charles's Jacobite army. Grant was taken to London and confined in Tilbury Fort, where he died of a fever on 29 July 1746, just as he was about to be brought to trial.

Ironically, John Grant, the hero of this book, married the granddaughter of Alexander Grant of Shewglie, Isobel Grant, daughter of PATRICK GRANT of Lochletter and Redcastle, a son by Alexander's second marriage. This was the same family that had threatened John's family when he was only five years old, causing his father to write to Ludovick Grant requesting that his wife and children be moved to Strathspey for safety.

Chiefs of Grant, I, 515; *Grants of Corrimony.*

Charles Grant, (1740–85), *British army officer.*
Charles Grant was born 13 March 1740, the youngest son of a Jacobite, Alexander Grant, 4th of Shewglie, and his second wife, Isabella Grant (daughter of John Grant, 6th of Glenmoriston. Shewglie is located in Glenurquhart, about 8 miles (13 km) west of Urquhart Castle on Loch Ness. Grant began his service as a volunteer in the 77th Regiment (Montgomery's Highlanders) during the French and Indian War. Volunteer Grant took part in Major James Grant of Ballindalloch's abortive attack on Fort Duquesne (the current site of Pittsburgh, Pennsylvania) in September 1758 and was captured and held prisoner by the Wyandot Indians near Detroit. While in captivity, Charles was commissioned ensign in the 42nd Foot, 28 July 1760, and after being released in a prisoner exchange, he participated with his regiment in the capture of Montreal in 1760 and Martinique in 1762.

He was promoted to lieutenant in July 1762 at the siege of Havana and, instead of going out on half-pay when the battalion was reduced, he opted to revert to the rank of ensign on the peace reductions but retained his seniority as lieutenant. He subsequently participated in the 1764 expedition to Muskingum to subdue the Shawnees and later served as the commander of Fort Loudoun about 70 miles (113 km) southwest of Harrisburg, Pennsylvania, and about 150 miles (241 km) southeast of Fort Pitt.

In 1765 Lieutenant Grant was involved in a series of confrontations with James Smith, the leader of a local paramilitary group of about 300 men, nicknamed the "Black Boys," who darkened their faces prior to engagements and were opposed to traders supplying the Indian tribes with firearms, shot and powder. At one point Grant was captured by Smith but was soon released. A senior officer described Grant's capture in a letter from Carlisle dated 1 June 1765: "I received letters from Lieutenant Grant, commanding at Fort Loudoun, complaining much of some late insult, received from the rioters near that post. He says on the 28th ult. [May], he was taking the air on horseback and about half a mile from his post, was surrounded by five of the rioters, who presented their pieces at him. The person who commanded them, calling to them to 'shoot the bugger' – that one of them fired at him, frightened him and his horse that he ran into the bushes and occasioned his being thrown upon the ground. They then disarmed him, carried him fifteen miles into the woods and threatened to tie him to a tree and let him perish if he would not give them up some arms...."

Grant was released by the "Black Boys" and resumed his command of Fort Loudoun. On the regiment's return to Ireland, it would be another four years until Grant was finally reinstated as a lieutenant on 16 December 1771 (with his seniority retroactive to his first commissioning date) in place of Lieutenant Nathaniel McCulloch. Several editions of the annual Army List incorrectly listed Grant's date of rank as 1771, but the date was corrected to 9 August 1762 by the 1775 publication. Lieutenant Grant then obtained Captain Alexander, Earl of Balcarres', company when the latter was promoted out of the regiment in March 1776 just as the regiment prepared to go overseas to the rebellious colonies. A few weeks before Grant sailed from Scotland for America, his illegitimate daughter was born. The entry of the baptism reads: "3 April 1776, Inverness - Captn Charles Grant of the 42nd Reg^t^ & Jean Steven had a child begotten in fornication baptised by Mr. George Watson called Anne."

Grant's company travelled to America on the transport *Glasgow* and he served as a company commander in one of the line battalions for the entire American war. His service included the New York-New Jersey campaign of 1776-77, the Philadelphia Campaign of 1777-78, the raid on Portsmouth, Virginia, and the occupation of Stoney Point, New York, in 1779, the Siege of Charleston, South Carolina, in 1780, and the relief attempt to rescue Lord Cornwallis in 1781.

During the war, Grant married a "Miss Hunt" from Newtown, Long Island, where the regiment went into winter quarters in November 1778. Captain John Peebles commented on Mrs. Grant in his journal for 17 July 1780 writing: "... paid a visit to Mrs. C. Grant who is in Camp. She looks well & may turn out something." Grant was the senior captain of the regiment in 1784 in Halifax, Nova Scotia, but, contrary to the regimental succession book which shows Grant retiring on 26 August 1785, his tombstone in the St. Paul's Church burial ground in Halifax reads: "Here lies the body of Charles Grant, Esq., late Captain in the First Battalion of His Majesty's 42nd Royal Highland Regiment of Foot, who departed this life the 1st day of February, in the year of our Lord, 1785. Aged 44 years."

SBs, BALs, *Chiefs of Grant*, I, 515; "Descendants of Alexander Grant, 4th Sheuglie," by Marie Fraser, Clan Fraser Society of Canada; *Grants of Corrimony*, 516-7; "Return of the prisoners brought by Lieut. Holmes from Detroit...the 26th December 1760," Bouquet Papers, LAC Q3-61578-B, vol 21655, Reel A-1079, 98-99; Letter, Lieutenant James Grant to Colonel Henry Bouquet, 18 July 1759, *The Papers of Henry Bouquet*, vol III, January 1, 1759-August 31, 1759, Donald H. Kent, Louis M. Waddell and Autumn L. Leonard, eds. (Harrisburg, 1976) 422-42. Hereafter, *Bouquet Papers.*

Brigadier General Francis Grant (1717–82), *British army officer, Member of Parliament.* Francis Grant was born 10 August 1717, the third living son of Sir James Grant of Grant, and Anne Colquhoun of Luss. By the time Francis went to North America, his father had died and his oldest living brother, Ludovick, was the Laird of Grant. Francis was one of three "original" officers of the 42nd still remaining seventeen years after its inception in 1739, the others being Gordon Graham of Drainie and John MacNeil.

Commissioned as a second lieutenant in one of the six independent companies of the Black Watch, Grant was promoted lieutenant when his company was amalgamated in 1739 with the other five and four new companies to form the 43rd Regiment of Foot (Earl of Crawford's). By the time of the '45, Grant had risen to the post of second-in-command of the regiment. Promoted lieutenant colonel in January 1756, he took the first division to North America in April and arrived in New York, 16 June 1756. He was made a "colonel in America" early in 1758 and was slightly wounded at Ticonderoga, 8 July 1758, leading the left wing of the army.

For the 1760 campaign against Montreal, he was placed in charge of the vanguard comprising the brigaded grenadiers and light infantry of Amherst's army. He spent the winter with both battalions of the 42nd on the island of Montreal until ordered to march both battalions south to Staten Island via Crown Point. Once there, he was to take command of all troops assembling there for General Monckton's expedition against Martinique. Grant, now a "brigadier-in-America," commanded the expedition's 2nd Brigade consisting of both battalions of the 42nd, the 77th (less five companies left in Nova Scotia) and the 2nd/1st Foot (The Royal).

Francis was appointed colonel of the 90th Foot in July 1762, a newly-raised regiment sent over from Ireland for the 1762 Havana campaign, and Grant officially handed over command of the 1st/42nd to Gordon Graham. When Grant's 90th Foot was disbanded at the peace he went out on half-pay and returned to England, where he married Catherine Sophia Cox on 17 March 1763, granddaughter of the Duke of Buckingham and the daughter of Joseph Cox of Stanford Vale. This union produced three sons and three daughters.

He was elected Member of Parliament for Elginshire and sat in the House of Commons from 1768 to 1774. In He was made colonel of the 63rd Foot in 1768 and rose to the rank of lieutenant general by his death in 1781. He was buried at Saint Peter's Church in Farnborough, Hampshire. His gravestone reads: "Sacred to the memory of Lieut. General Francis Grant, fourth son of Sir James Grant of Grant Bar[t.] in whom the grave and active soldier the affectionate husband and father and friend were conspicuously united. He quitted this mortal life for a happy immortality universally lamented Dec[r] 29th 1781 aged sixty-three."

CB, SB, BALs, Stewart, *Sketches*, I-II; *Black Watch at Ticonderoga; Chiefs of Grant*, I, 393-441, 449-452; Jeffery Amherst, *The Journals of Jeffery Amherst 1757-1763*, R.J. Andrews, ed., 2 vols (East Lansing, 2015), II, 146-7.

Sir James Grant of Grant (1679–1747), *20th Chief of Clan Grant, 3rd of Grant, Member of Parliament.*

James Grant was born 28 July 1679, the second surviving son of Ludovick Grant of Freuchie and Grant, and Janet Brodie, daughter and heir of Alexander Brodie of Lethen. From his correspondence preserved at Castle Grant, it appears that part of his education was obtained at a seminary in the town of Elgin, but little is known of his early years until his marriage on 29 January 1702 to Anne, the only child and heiress of Sir Humphrey Colquhoun, 5th Baronet of Luss. James was for some time designated as James of Pluscardine, from the abbey and lands of that name which he inherited from his mother. He retained that designation until the death of his father-in-law in 1718 when he was designated Sir James Colquhoun of Luss, Baronet. He held the Luss estate for only a year, as in 1719 he succeeded to the estates of Grant on the premature death of his older brother, Brigadier General Alexander Grant. At this time, he dropped the name and arms of Colquhoun of Luss and changed back to Grant, becoming Sir James Grant of Grant, Baronet, chief of the Clan Grant.

James and Anne had fourteen children, six sons and eight daughters, of which only ten lived to maturity, five sons and five daughters: Humphrey, born 1702, who died unmarried in 1732; LUDOVICK, born 1707, who succeeded to the estates of Luss and afterwards to those of Grant; James, born 1714, who succeeded to the estates of Luss and carried on the line of

Highland laird. Sir James Grant of Grant (1679-1747), 6th Baronet, Grant of Grant, and the 20th hereditary clan chieftain. Bonnie Prince Charlie sent him a letter summoning him and his clan to the Standard in 1745. Grant sent the letter unopened to the Secretary of State. However, he was opposed to the raising of independent companies from the various clans and believed that an entire clan under their chieftain should be the norm and instructed his son to not comply with any piecemeal requests. (Illustration from Fraser, *The Chiefs of Grant*)

the family of Colquhoun of Luss; FRANCIS, born 1717, who became a lieutenant colonel in the 42nd Regiment and afterwards a lieutenant general in the Army; Charles Cathcart, born 1723, who became a captain in the Royal Navy; Jean, born 1705, who became countess dowager of Fife; Anne Drummond, born 1711, who married Sir Henry Innes of Innes; Sophia, born 1716, who died unmarried in 1772; Penuel, born 1719, who married Captain Alexander Grant of Ballindalloch; and Clementina, born 1721, who married Sir William Dunbar of Durn, Banff. His wife, Anne, passed away at Castle Grant on 25 June 1724.

On 12 April 1722 Sir James was elected Member of Parliament for the county of Inverness; he was re-elected in 1727 and 1734 and continued to represent the county until 1741 when he resigned and was elected member of Elgin, which he represented until his death in 1747. His only recorded speech was made on 5 May 1732, asking for leniency for his relative, Sir Archibald Grant. In 1734 he was described as the "hereditary commoner of Inverness-shire," denying an allegation that he was "enslaving the shire" by creating voters, observing: "I always rely entirely on the gentlemen of the shire for their help and assistance." Though seldom at Castle Grant due to his Parliamentary duties, which required him to reside chiefly in London, he still promoted the plantation and improvement of his estate and neighbourhood through his son Ludovick, then acting as resident and virtual Laird of Grant.

During the 1745 uprising he remained in London, advising Ludovick "to stay at home, take care of his country and join no party." He was opposed to the government scheme of forming the loyal clans into independent companies, believing that the best method for securing the effective assistance of his own clan, or any other clan, was to follow the Highland custom – which was to summon each clan to muster under their respective chiefs.

At the end of 1746 or the beginning of 1747, while in London, he was seized with "gout in the stomach" and died there on 16 January 1747. The following character of Sir James was given by one who obviously knew him intimately: "he was a gentleman of very amiable character, justly esteemed and honoured by all ranks of men; his natural temper was peculiarly mild, his behavior grave, composed and equal; and his social conduct was full of benevolence and goodness. To his clan he was indulgent, almost to a fault; to his tenants just and kind; and did not very narrowly look into things himself, but committed the management of his fortune to his factors and favourites. To sum up his character, he was a most affectionate husband, a most dutiful and kind parent, sober, temperate, just, peaceable ... a lover of all virtue and good men ... he was very happy in his children, and they in him." He was succeeded in the estate of Grant by his eldest surviving son, Ludovick.

Chiefs of Grant, I, 371-393; 449-52; W. Fraser, *The Chiefs of Colquhoun and their Country,* vol I (Edinburgh, 1869), 328-31; Sir James Balfour Paul, ed., *The Scots Peerage...* (Edinburgh, 1910), vii. 480-3; George E. Cokayne, *Complete Baronetage* (Gloucester, 1983), ii, 295; *Scots Magazine,* ix, 50.

John Grant of Ballintomb (1707–52), *Chamberlain of Urquhart, Factor, baron-baillie, landowner, John Grant's father.*
John Grant was born in Strathspey, Scotland, in 1707, the second son of John *Dhu* Grant, 5th of Dalrachney and Margaret Grant of Knockando. A tall, well-built, handsome man, "the best looking of his clan," little is known of John's early years until his marriage in 1741 to Mary, the daughter of David Ross of Inverchasley. He followed in his father's footsteps as a baron-baillie and succeeded the Laird's brother, Major George Grant in 1742, as chamberlain, stewart, baron-baillie and factor of Glenurquhart. Thus, during the '45 Uprising he was faced with rebellious tenantry led by some other prominent Grants in Urquhart and was unsuccessful in preventing some from rallying to Bonnie Prince Charlie's standard.

John and Mary had eight children, three sons and five daughters: Isobel, born after 1740; John, born 2 December 1741; Mary, born 22 January 1742; Margaret, born 18 March 1743; David, born 21 April 1745, died 1746; Helen, born 12 May 1747; Alexander, born 13 November 1748; and Eliza, born 1751.

After Culloden he witnessed the harrowing of the glens first-hand and, concerned for the safety of his family, removed them north to the safety of Braelangwell in Ross-shire, the estate of his wife's step-sister, Margaret Ross, and her husband, Charles Urquhart. On 25 December 1752 he died suddenly from a botched medical treatment for severe tonsillitis. As a consequence of John's death, Mary, with four daughters and son John, took up residence in Inverness, where the latter was at boarding school, with financial assistance from her husband's older brother, Alexander Grant of Inverlaidnan.

JGM, *Chiefs of Grant,* I, 526-7.

John *Dhu* Grant, 5th of Dalrachnie (1678–1735), *baron bailie, landowner, John Grant's grandfather.*
Born in 1678, John was the oldest of four sons of Alexander Grant of Dalrachney and Christina Cuthbert of Castlehill. He obtained in 1706 from the Laird of Grant a wadset (mortgage) of Wester Duthil, Beananach and Inchlum, redeemable for 4,466 merks. In 1720 he was a baillie of the Regality of Grant, and he is also said to have also been a baillie for the Regality of Gordon. In 1733 he obtained a charter of parts of the barony of Corrimony. He married Margaret Grant of Knockando, who bore him three sons, Alexander, John (John Grant's father) and Robert. He died in 1735.

JGM, *Chiefs of Grant,* I, 526-7.

Sir Ludovick Grant of Grant (1707–73), *21st Chief of Clan Grant, 4th of Grant, Member of Parliament.*
Ludovick Grant was born 13 January 1707, the second son of Sir James Grant, then of Pluscardine, and Anne Colquhoun, heiress of Luss. In 1719, when his father became Laird of Grant, he succeeded to the Luss estates, becoming Sir Ludovick Colquhoun of Luss, Baronet. On 6 July 1727 he married Marian Dalrymple, second daughter of Sir Hew Dalrymple of North Berwick, Baronet, Lord President of the Court of Session. The wedding was a "somewhat hasty step" taken without the consent of their parents, Ludovick, then age twenty, and Mar-

ian a youthful fourteen. However, a reconciliation was made through the services of Patrick Grant, later Lord Elchies. Their union produced a daughter, Anne, born 1728, who died unmarried in 1748, and another child who died in infancy in 1733.

Sir Ludovick studied law and was called to the Scottish bar in 1728; however he retired in 1732 when he became heir-apparent to the Grant estates on the death of his older brother, Humphrey. He soon turned his energies to the management of the Regality of Grant, which his father had entrusted to him (in return for an annual pension). This accession to the position of Younger of Grant raised a new dispute regarding the lands and barony of Luss, however, and he was eventually forced to "denude himself" of the barony of Luss in 1738 in favour of his younger brother, James.

Marian died on 17 January 1735 and was buried in the Chapel Royal at Holyrood on 21 January. A little over nine months later (31 October), Sir Ludovick married Lady Margaret Ogilvie, eldest daughter of James, 5th Earl of Findlater and Seafield, "a lady not only beautiful in her person, but much more by the singular character she has of good sense and understanding, and of a sweet and angelick temper." This union produced one son and seven daughters: James, born in May 1738, who succeeded him in the title and estates of Grant; Marian (or Mariana), who died unmarried in 1807; Penuel, born London, 1750, who married Henry Mackenzie of the Exchequer in Scotland in 1776; Margaret, born London, 1752, who died unmarried; Helen, born 1754, who married Sir Alexander Penrose Cumming Gordon of Altyre and Gordonstoun, Baronet, in 1773; Anna Hope, born London, 1756, who married Reverend Robert Darly Waddilove in 1781; Mary, who died unmarried in 1784; and Elizabeth, who died unmarried in 1804.

In 1741 Ludovick was elected Member of Parliament for the counties of Elgin and Forres, a seat which he held until 1761. During the

A monument to loyalty. Sir Ludovick Grant of Grant (1707-73), 7th Baronet, Grant of Grant, and the 21st hereditary clan chieftain. Not well liked for turning over tenants that had supported the Jacobite cause to authorities after Culloden in 1746, his oldest son, "Good Sir James" (1738-1811), made up for it by building the town of Grantown-on-Spey. While the old Highland way of life was being swept away, James built an entire town, including schools, mills, factories, a hospital and an orphanage to provide employment and fresh opportunities for his clan. The town is a monument to Sir James's loyalty to his clansmen. (Illustration from Fraser, *The Chiefs of Grant*)

1745 uprising, while remaining a staunch supporter of the House of Hanover, he played "a prudent part," following the advice of his father "to stay at home, take care of his country, and join no party." This did not, however, prevent him from rendering important service to the government, and in February 1746 he received orders from the Duke of Cumberland to raise his clan for the King. Castle Grant was occupied in March 1746 by the Jacobites but was soon evacuated. Sir Ludovick and his men joined Cumberland at Culloden on 11 April 1746, but they were not at the battle.

Sir Ludovick succeeded to the Grant estates on the death of his father on 16 January 1747, becoming the 7th Baronet, Grant of Grant. His wife, Margaret, passed away in London on 20 February 1757. One of the prominent cadet branches of Clan Grant was the Grants of Dalrachney, the branch to which John Grant, the hero of our story, was a direct descendant. In later years John Grant would recall the elderly Laird singling him out by name at a fair at Castle Grant in 1757, the year before he went into the army. In 1772, in a nod to the old Laird, John named his only daughter PENUEL, after the Laird's younger sister.

Sir Ludovick continued to attend to his duties in Parliament until 1761, when failing health forced him to resign his seat. His son, James, was elected Member of Parliament, succeeding his father in representing Elgin and Forres. In 1765 Sir Ludovick employed well known Scottish architect John Adam to remodel and enlarge Castle Grant, originally built as an L-shaped tower house in 1593 (and known as Castle Freuchie until it became the main residence of the Grants in 1693). He died at Castle Grant on 18 March 1773 "after an illness of eight days" and was interred in the family burial aisle at Duthil Parish Church, his death "much lamented, and feeling tributes to his memory were made, both in prose and verse, in contemporary journals." Sir Ludovick had always looked kindly upon John Grant's family, and when he passed away, so did any last ties of loyalty or servitude that might have been traditionally passed onto the new chief by his clansmen.

Sir Ludovick's son, James (1738-1811), affectionately known as "the good Sir James," was thought to be the most capable chief of his long line. He became a dedicated public servant and an ardent improver of his vast estates. He was the founder of Grantown and at various times served as a Member of Parliament, Cashier of Excise for Scotland, Lord Lieutenant, and Sheriff of Inverness-shire. In the last decade of the 18th century, he raised and served as colonel of two regiments: the 1st Strathspey Fencibles and the 97th Inverness-shire Highlanders.

JGM; *Chiefs of Grant*, I, 393-441; W. Fraser, *The Chiefs of Colquhoun and their Country*, vol 1, (Edinburgh, 1869), 331, 334-343; *The Scots Peerage*, Sir James Balfour Paul, ed., vol VII (Edinburgh, 1910), 483-5; George E. Cokayne, *Complete baronetage*, vol II (Gloucester, 1983), 295.

Patrick Grant of Lochletter and Redcastle, (1723–1800), *landowner, father-in-law of John Grant.*

Patrick Grant was born in Urquhart, Scotland, in 1723, the fourth son of Alexander Grant, 4th of Shewglie and Isabel, daughter of John Grant, 6th of Glenmoriston. He was the older step-brother of Charles Grant who served alongside John Grant in the 42nd Foot. Patrick married Katherine Bailie of Glenmoriston and had four sons and three daughters, their eldest daughter, Isobel, was born 2 March 1751. Isobel married John Grant in Glenurquhart in 1771, the union producing only one daughter, PENUEL. Patrick's obituary notice in *The Gentleman's Magazine,* dated 3 June 1800, simply stated: "At Lochletter, Urquhart, near Inverness, aged 77 years, Patrick Grant, Esq."

JGM; *Grants of Corrimony; Gentleman's Magazine*, vol LXX (June 1800).

Penuel Grant (1772–1847), *daughter of John Grant.*

Penuel was born 28 April 1772 in Urquhart, Inverness-shire, the only child of John Grant and Isobel, daughter of PATRICK GRANT of Lochletter. In 1793 she married an officer of the Royal Engineers, Captain Lieutenant JOHN JOHNSON, who unfortunately died two years later. Penuel and John had two children: JOHN Jr. (1794-1848) and Isabella Eleanor (1796-1835).

On 10 July 1797, Penuel, then a twenty-five-year-old widow with two small children, married Harcourt Forde Holcombe in Drypool, Hull. Harcourt, born Pembroke, South Wales, 6 January 1778, was a nineteen-year-old junior officer in the Royal Artillery, having attended Woolwich Academy, where he had obtained a 2nd lieutenant's commission on 6 March 1795. His active military career began in 1808 when he embarked to join Sir David Baird's expedition to the Peninsula, almost losing his life to a fever contracted during the Corunna campaign. He was then a captain of artillery having been promoted to that rank on 12 September 1803.

In 1811 Harcourt returned to the Peninsula, where he commanded a company attached to the battering train at the siege of Ciudad Rodrigo and was made brevet major on 6 February 1812. Three months later he was made a brevet lieutenant colonel for "gallant conduct at Badajoz." For his distinguished services during the Peninsular War, Harcourt was made a Companion of the Most Honourable Order of the Bath.

After Badajoz, Harcourt was placed in command of several companies of British and Portuguese artillery and sent to the Mediterranean where he joined the Army from Sicily and took part in the actions on the east coast of Spain. He was commanding officer of artillery at Lisbon in 1813 and remained there until 1815 to supervise the dismantling of all the ordnance depots in Spain and Portugal. He became a substantive major in the army on 29 July 1825, and a lieutenant colonel one month later. During the years 1826-27, he was stationed at Woolwich.

Between his military exploits, Penuel and Harcourt managed to have two sons and five daughters. When Harcourt resigned his commission in 1827, they took up residence in Aberdeen, but relocated to Banchory in Kincardineshire the following year. In 1832, "finding a great want of occupation," Harcourt and Penuel purchased a small estate, called Riemore, near Dunkeld, Perthshire, where Penuel's mother, Isobel, now living with them, died in 1835. Three years later, they sold this estate and relocated to Edinburgh to be nearer to a "proper church" and "better medical facilities." Harcourt passed away at Pembroke Lodge in Murrayfield on 6 March 1847. Penuel died five months later on 31 August. They were both buried in Dunkeld Cathedral churchyard, just north of Perth, next to Penuel's mother.

JGM; CBs; SBs; BALs; J.A. Gilbert, *The Change, or The Passage from Death unto Life, A Memoir of Lieut.-Col. Holcombe* (Binns and Goodwin, 1847).

Captain David Haldane (1722–unk),
British army officer. John Grant's maternal 1st cousin.

David Haldane was born 1722, the only son of John Haldane, 2nd of Aberuthven and Anne Ross, daughter of David Ross, 1st of Inverchasley, and sister to Lord Ankerville. David's name first appears in a disposition of lands, dated 16 December 1743, in favour of Captain George Haldane (3rd Foot Guards, his

The cartoon colonel. Brigadier General George Haldane (1722-59), the governor-designate of Jamaica, participated in the 1759 expedition against Martinique and Guadeloupe commanding a brigade. He was probably instrumental in securing his cousin, Captain David Haldane, a company command in the 2nd/42nd Foot bound for the Caribbean. John Grant was also a cousin by marriage. Pencil sketch by George Townshend, c.1755. (NPG 4855(60). Editors' photo)

first cousin, once removed). In this document, he is designated "Ensign David Haldane of Aberuthven." A David Haldane is shown on the passenger list of the *Everly* transport arriving in Halifax in 1749 as a member of Governor Edward Cornwallis's staff. The entry reads: "David Haldane, Lieutenant, 1 Male Servant, Total 2." David Haldane appears as one of five signatories along with Edward Cornwallis requesting the establishment of one of the earliest Masonic Lodges in Canada. While in Halifax, he was commissioned lieutenant and adjutant in William Pepperell's new-raising 51st Foot and his name appears on a list of officers who surrendered at Fort Oswego in 1756.

On the disbandment of the 51st Foot and his release from captivity, he exchanged to the new 2nd Battalion of the 19th Foot in the Great Britain. In 1758, as forces were gathering for an expedition against Martinique and Guadeloupe under Major General PEREGRINE HOPSON, he secured the last captain's position in the newly-raised 2nd/42nd Foot when one of its seven company commanders, Robert Arbuthnot, suddenly died in London before boarding ship. His cousin mentioned above, now Brigadier General George Haldane, the governor-designate of Jamaica, was participating in the same expedition and may have been instrumental in securing his cousin the last-minute promotion.

David commanded John Grant's company, one of two blown off course and thus late for the Martinique expedition. His company helped capture Fort Saint Louis and, once reunited with the rest of their battalion, captured Guadeloupe in a short campaign. David also served at the capture of Montreal 1760 and Martinique in 1762.

In April 1762, after the capture of Martinique, he was appointed brevet major to the 100th Foot (Campbell's Highlanders) under bizarre circumstances. He replaced the major commandant, Colin Campbell of Kilberrie, who was accused of murdering one of his own officers. David reverted to the rank of captain at the Peace and exchanged to half-pay, 18 November 1763. In subsequent petitions for land grants dated 22 April 1765, Haldane is shown as a 42nd captain on half-pay, requesting 10,000 acres, and eventually granted 5,000 acres, in what is now Vermont.

He appears, however, to have taken up residence in Princeton, New Jersey, as Home Office papers show a "Captain Halden of Princetown" who, with others, was "charged therein with overt acts of high treason in levying war against His Majesty on 26 August 1774, Captain Wilder, of Templeton, and Captain Halden, of Princetown, on 28 Aug. 1774...." The only acts of war during 1773 and 1774 the editors have been able to trace that were considered "high treason" by British authorities were the Tea Party actions in Boston and other ports. His unexplained removal from the Army List of half-pay officers, effective 10 March 1777, was probably due to his rebel sympathies. No other traces of Haldane can be found.

CBs; SBs; BALs; "List of the Officers of the 42nd or Royal Highland Regiment according to seniority dated December 29th, 1762," BL Add. MSS 21,634: f.178c; Stewart, *Sketches*, I-II; TNA, *Journal of the Commissioners for Trade and Plantations*, vol XII, January 1764 - December 1767, 818; TNA, Home Office Papers, 1773-5; J.A.L. Haldane, *The Haldanes of Gleneagles* (Edinburgh, 1929), 291-2.

Lieutenant Elbert Herring (1737–62), *British army officer.*

Elbert was born in New York, 7 April 1737, the second surviving son of Dutch parents, Elbert Haring, and his wife, Catherine Lent. He was one of the original ensigns, commissioned on 3 April 1758, to serve in North America with the 1st Battalion, 42nd Foot. He was promoted lieutenant in the 2nd Battalion on 14 November 1759, "in room of" Robert Robertson, who died of fever contracted while serving at Guadeloupe. Herring went on to participate in the capture of Montreal in 1760 and in the Caribbean campaigns of 1762.

Herring came down with the fever at Havana like many of his brother officers and was invalided back to New York in October 1762. On 1 December 1762, knowing he was dying, he wrote to Lieutenant Colonel John Reid, then the acting commanding officer: "My bad state of health and little prospect of my recovery in a long while, so as to be fit for duty, has made me take the resolution of disposing of my Commission if I can obtain leave. I shall take it as a particular favour, if you'll apply to Sir JEFFERY AMHERST for that purpose, and at the same time recommend a brother of mine, who is desirous of being in the Army, to succeed to the Ensigncy."

On 7 December 1762, he resigned his commission in favour of Ensign Alexander Graham, an absentee relative of the commanding officer and who never came to America, but his step up from ensign ensured that Elbert secured an officer's vacancy for his younger brother, Peter, then serving as a gentleman volunteer in the regiment. Elbert, according to a family genealogy, died the following day, 8 December 1762, his duty done to King, country and family.

CBs; SBs; BALs; TNA, WO 25/209, fol. 158; "List of the Officers of the 42nd or Royal Highland Regiment according to seniority dated December 29th, 1762," BL Add. MSS 21,634: f.178c; Stewart, *Sketches*, I-II; Jeffery Amherst, *The Journals of Jeffery Amherst 1757-1763*, R.J. Andrews, ed., 2 vols (East Lansing, 2015), II, 167.

Major General Peregrine Thomas Hopson (1685–1759), *British marine and army officer, colonial administrator.*

Peregrine Thomas Hopson was born in 1685, probably in England and likely a son of Admiral Sir Thomas Hopson. He started his career as an eighteen-year-old 2nd lieutenant of Marines in 1703, and by 1738 he was a major in the 14th Foot (Clayton's). He was promoted lieutenant colonel in Cholmondeley 's regiment (48th Foot) in January 1740/41 and went to Gibraltar during the siege of 1727. With exception of a brief stay in England from 1741 to 1743, Hopson was stationed there until 1745. Seeking promotion in 1746 he claimed, in a letter to the Duke of Newcastle, to have more than 35-years of continuous service in the army.

In the spring of 1746 Hopson arrived at Louisbourg from Gibraltar, the senior officer in Fuller's regiment (29th Foot) which had been sent to reinforce the garrison. Louisbourg had been captured from the French the previous year by a joint New England and British force under William Pepperrell and Peter Warren. Hopson took command of the colony in September 1747 as its lieutenant governor, succeeding Governor Charles Knowles, and later became governor. Hopson was promoted colonel of the 40th Foot on 6 June 1748. In October the treaty of Aix-la-Chapelle returned Louisbourg and Cape Breton Island to France. Hopson took the British troops and supplies to the new English settlement at Halifax (Chebucto) and then returned to England.

In 1752 he returned to Halifax as governor of Nova Scotia, taking office on 3 August. He recognized the importance of the Acadians to the success of the area and pushed his superiors to reject the need for the Acadians to pledge their allegiance to the British Crown with a formal oath. As internal issues developed between the English and North Americans living in the colony, he attempted to be a peacemaker to ensure both sides worked together for the common good. He did however reject the plan to bring "foreign Protestants" to the colony and instead obtained supplies so that these new immigrants could start their own colony at Mirliguèche (later named Lunenburg).

Severe eye trouble forced Hopson to hand over the governance of Nova Scotia to Charles Lawrence. Hopson left for England in November 1753 and resigned two years later. He was promoted major general on 11 February

1757 and was sent to Halifax with reinforcements for Lord Loudoun's army preparing to mount an expedition against Louisbourg that summer. As a former governor of Louisbourg, Hopson was expected to provide detailed information and advice to Loudoun. When Loudoun decided to abandon the expedition because of the late arrival of British troops and the superior strength of the French fleet at Louisbourg, Hopson concurred with his commander's decision to abort the mission.

Loudoun returned to New York in August 1757, leaving Hopson in command of all troops in Nova Scotia and earmarked him to lead a new expedition against Louisbourg the following summer. Hopson, however, was recalled to England before the 1758 campaign commenced, allegedly on grounds that the government feared for his health. On his arrival, however, he was placed in charge of the secret expedition assembling to attack the French sugar islands of Martinique and Guadeloupe.

After an initial landing in Martinique in January 1759, Hopson's first objective, the expedition withdrew and took up a position at Basse Terre, Guadeloupe. Hopson was already seriously ill and died a month later on 27 February 1759. John Barrington, his second in command, completed the conquest of the island. Hopson's age and health, as well as the different qualities required in the two situations, seem to explain the differences in his performance as governor of Nova Scotia and as leader of this expedition.

CBs; SBs; BALs; "Peregrine Thomas Hopson," *DCB*, III (1741-1770); Jeffery Amherst, *The Journals of Jeffery Amherst 1757-1763*, R.J. Andrews, ed., 2 vols (East Lansing, 2015), II, 172-3.

Colonel William Howe (1729–1814), *British army officer, colonial administrator, Member of Parliament.*

William Howe was born 10 August 1729, the third son of Emanuel Scrope Howe, 2nd Viscount Howe, and Maria Sophia Kielmansegge,

"Best trained battalion in all America." William Howe, 5th Viscount Howe (1729-1814), was best known as the commander in chief of the British army in North America (1776-78) during the War of Independence and was the youngest of the three famous Howe brothers. William's oldest brother, George Augustus, Lord Howe, "The Idol of the Army," was killed at Ticonderoga in 1758. His second oldest brother was Admiral Richard "Black Dick" Howe. James Wolfe, a commander of William's at Quebec in 1759, considered him an outstanding officer "at the head of the best trained battalion in all America" and made him commander of his *ad hoc* light infantry corps. At Havana Howe commanded the light infantry corps again, and John Grant remembered him addressing the assembled troops before the assault on La Cabana: "Colonel Howe ... told us that we were to carry the redoubt in front" and that as they approached the objective to remember it "was flanked by some guns from the Moro. He recommended us to pass the spot quickly, but not in disorder, and instantly to rush in and scale the Works." A rather fanciful coloured mezzotint drawn and engraved by Richard Purcell and published by John Morris, 1777. (ASKB)

and brother to 3rd Viscount, George Augustus Howe, killed at Ticonderoga, 6 July 1758, and Admiral Richard Howe. Schooled at Eton, William followed his two elder brothers into the services when his father purchased him a commission as a cornet in the Duke of Cumberland's Light Dragoons, 18 September 1746.

He was promoted to lieutenant the following year and briefly went out on half-pay in 1748 but returned to active service in the 20th Foot, the same regiment in which James Wolfe, a friend and future commander served. Made captain lieutenant of the 20th Foot on 20 January 1750, and captain the same year (1 June 1750), he served with Wolfe for five years before leaving in 1756 to take up the majority of Anstruther's 60th Regiment of Foot (subsequently re-numbered the 58th Foot). William became the lieutenant colonel of the 58th Foot in December 1757 and commanded it during the Louisbourg 1758 campaign. While in America, he was elected MP for Nottingham in 1758. Wolfe handpicked him the following year to lead the combined light infantry of his army during the siege of Quebec in 1759. Wolfe, a firm believer in training at all times, considered Howe to be an outstanding officer "at the head of the best trained battalion in all America."

Howe returned to England after the fall of Quebec in October 1759 to recover from a light wound but more probably to attend to his Parliamentary duties. He returned the following summer 1760, and as a "colonel in America," led one of the brigades under James Murray's command up the Saint Lawrence River to participate in the capture of Montreal with Amherst's army. At the end of the campaign, he returned to England to serve as the adjutant general of the force that assaulted Belleisle off the coast of France in 1761, then joined the forces sent to assault Havana in 1762. There he was active in commanding the light infantry of the army during the siege, including John Grant's company. After the fall of Havana, he returned to England and in 1764 was appointed colonel of the 46th Foot, then stationed in Ireland. In 1768 he was appointed governor of the Isle of Wight, where, promoted to major general in 1772, he supervised the training of the British army's light infantry units.

Representing a largely Whig constituency in Parliament, Howe opposed the Intolerable Acts and preached reconciliation with the American colonists as tensions grew in 1774 and early 1775. His feelings were shared by his brother, Admiral "Black Dick" Howe. Though publicly stating that he would resist service against the Americans, as well as openly critical of Thomas Gage's abilities as a commander, he accepted the position as second-in-command of British forces in America, stating that "he was ordered, and could not refuse." Howe sailed for Boston with Major Generals HENRY CLINTON and John Burgoyne, as well as reinforcements, for the British forces already stationed in the colonies.

Under siege in the city, the British were forced to take action when American forces fortified Breed's Hill on the Charlestown Peninsula overlooking the harbour. While Clinton favoured an amphibious attack to cut off the American line of retreat, Howe advocated a more conventional frontal attack. Taking the latter course of action, Gage ordered Howe to attack 17 June 1775. Commanding the right of the line, Howe and his men succeeded in driving off the Americans, most of whom escaped, but sustained over 1,000 killed or wounded in doing so. This one action, though a small tactical victory, deeply influenced Howe at the strategic level, crushing his initial belief that the rebels represented only a small misguided part of the American people. He was a light infantry commander full of vim and *élan* earlier in his career, but the high casualty rate of Breed's Hill tempered Howe's future use of manpower and made him a more cautious and conservative commander. Knighted that same year, Howe was temporarily appointed commander-in-chief on 10 October 1775 (it was made permanent in April 1776) when Gage returned to England, never to return.

Two years later, he was made lieutenant

general (29 August 1777), in spite of American victories at White Plains, Brandywine and Germantown. When news of John Burgoyne's surrender at Saratoga reached him, compounded with charges at home in Britain that he and his brother, Admiral Howe, were too conciliatory with the rebels and not prosecuting the war with sufficient vigour, he resigned as commander-in-chief, but did not leave America until 24 May 1778.

Howe arrived back in England on 1 July 1778 where he and his brother faced widespread censure for their actions in North America. In 1779 William and his brother Richard demanded a parliamentary inquiry into their actions, which was unable to confirm any charges of impropriety or mismanagement levelled against either of them. Because of the inconclusive nature of the inquiry, attacks continued to be made against the Howe brothers in pamphlets and the press, accusing them of deliberately undermining the war effort for the benefit of the anti-war Whig faction in Parliament.

In 1780 Sir William lost in his bid to be re-elected to the House of Commons. However, in 1782 he was named master general of ordnance and appointed to the Privy Council. His colonelcy was transferred from the 23rd Foot to the 19th Light Dragoons in 1786 and he resumed a limited military role in 1793 when he was promoted full general and given the command of the Northern District and, subsequently, the Eastern District and the governorship of Berwick-on-Tweed in 1795. When his brother Richard died in 1799 without any surviving male issue, William inherited the Irish titles and became the 5th Viscount Howe and Baron Clenawly. In 1803 he resigned as master general of the ordnance, citing poor health. In 1805 he was appointed governor of Plymouth, and he died at Twickenham near London in 1814 after a long illness. Married in 1765 to Frances Connolly after his return from Havana, his marriage was childless and the Howe family titles died with him.

CBs; SBs; BALs; "William Howe," *DNB*, XXVIII, 490-3.

Captain Lieutenant John Johnson (1753–95), *Royal Engineer officer.*
Born in London in 1753, John was the only son of John Johnson (died 1772) and Eleanor Whittingdale (died 1800), who had married at St. Anne's, Soho, London, on 19 August 1752, the family living at the Tower of London. John was admitted as a practitioner engineer in the Corps of Engineers on 17 January 1776 (the Corps becoming the Royal Engineers in 1787). He was promoted to 1st Lieutenant on 1 January 1783, and was present at the Great Siege of Gibraltar (1779-83) when Spain and France tried to wrest Gibraltar from the British, the longest siege endured by British forces. He was promoted to captain lieutenant on 16 January 1793, at that time serving with the Duke of York's army in the Low Countries.

Later that year, he arrived in Guernsey, one of the Channel Islands off the coast of France, where he met and married PENUEL GRANT, "an agreeable accomplished young lady of a respectable family," the family connection in his mind being "highly flattering to himself and his family." Penuel was the only child of John and Isobel Grant, her father then commanding the Guernsey Invalid Company. John Johnson returned to the Low Countries, where he remained until 1795, leaving his pregnant wife under the capable care of her parents.

In July 1793 Penuel's father took up command of the Portsmouth Invalid Company and relocated his family to that station. In 1794 Penuel gave birth to their first child there, a son named JOHN after his grandfather and absent father. In June 1795 John returned to England and began to look for suitable accommodation in Portsmouth for his wife and child. Sadly, in November 1795 he passed away in Gosport (a major naval town associated with the defence and supply of Portsmouth naval base), causes unknown. Their daughter, Isabella, was born a few months after his death, and Penuel, with her two infants, remained with her parents.

In 1817 John's unseen daughter, Isabella, married Dr. James Errol Gray at Inverness, Scotland, and they had three children: John James, born 1818; and David and James, both born in 1819, who lived less than a year. Tragedy struck again when Dr. Gray died in 1820, at the age of only thirty. Isabella remarried in 1826 to John Anderson Robertson at Urquhart, Scotland, and they had six children, several of whom settled and established themselves in Australia.

JGM; CBs; SBs; MCA, DJQ.

First Lieutenant John Johnson (1794–1848), later Dr. John Johnson, *Royal Artillery officer, surgeon, surveyor, amateur artist, John Grant's grandson.*

Born in Portsea, Hampshire, 1794, John was the son of Captain Lieutenant John Johnson and Penuel Grant, the daughter of John Grant. On the premature death of his father in November 1795, John was brought up by his grandparents, John and Isobel Grant. Like his father and maternal grandfather, John would join the army, being admitted to Woolwich as a gentleman cadet in the Royal Artillery, 31 October 1808. He seems to have had some medical training while in the Royal Artillery, perhaps serving as an assistant surgeon. He was promoted to 2nd lieutenant on 13 December 1813, and 1st lieutenant on 5 August 1816, at that time stationed in Corfu, Greece. In September of that year, he wrote to his grandfather, John Grant (then residing in Drynie, Ross-shire) asking for twenty-five pounds "for a horse and other expenses."

In 1822 John married Emily Anderson and five of their nine children were born in Forres, Scotland. Forres is about 20 miles (32 km) from Fort George, guarding the approaches to Inverness, so John's artillery command was probably stationed there. He retired on half-pay on 1 February 1827, perhaps terminating his military career to care for his aging grandparents. He was the sole beneficiary of John Grant's will when he died in 1828. Sometime after his grandfather's death, John left Forres to undergo medical training at the Royal College of Surgeons in Edinburgh, obtaining his medical practitioner's licence on 20 January 1834. Two of John and Emily's children were born in Edinburgh. The last child was born 1837 in Gravesend, Kent, but both mother and child died shortly thereafter.

At this time, Scottish medical schools, particularly Edinburgh, produced more practitioners than were needed in Scotland, and many doctors unable to find work in their native land emigrated to Canada, Australia and New Zealand. Now a fully accredited medical practitioner, John went out to Australia in 1839 with three of his sons (John Grant, Alexander and William) to check its suitability, arriving at Sydney, 31 March. He left his younger surviving children (one son and three daughters) with relatives in England. Upon reaching Australia he made his way to New South Wales, where he obtained his medical accreditation from the Medical Board (No. 82), later purchasing a property to farm.

In 1840, when New Zealand came under the jurisdiction of the British Crown, John decided to investigate its potential, departing from Sydney on 19 January. He visited the projected site of Auckland, New Zealand, with Governor William Hobson and was with the first group of officials to settle there in September, making sketches of the first days of Auckland as a settlement. Besides being named New Zealand's first colonial surgeon in 1840, he was also given the posts of coroner, health officer and magistrate. As colonial surgeon, he was compensated thirteen shillings a day, with an added fifty pounds for "lodging money," along with an allowance "for a hospital servant and medicines and incidental expenses."

"The Shop." John Johnson Sr. and his son, John Johnson Jr., were both graduates of the Royal Military Academy at Woolwich, established in 1741 to standardize the training of engineer and, later, artillery officers. Its mandate was not only to provide an education but to produce "good officers of artillery and perfect Engineers." The Academy was commonly known as "The Shop" because its first building was a converted workshop of the Woolwich Arsenal. (ASKB)

In 1843 he was the founder and first president of the Agricultural and Horticultural Society of Auckland, extolling "the very great advantages New Zealand offers to the British farmer in the varieties of its soil, so well adapted to the growth of European grains, roots and grasses." He was one of the trustees of the Auckland Newspaper and General Printing Company which printed the first New Zealand Gazettes. In 1845 John visited England to bring out his daughters, who had finished their schooling, and on his return, visited with his eldest son, then living in Australia.

John became an important explorer and recorder of early New Zealand history and his drawings and watercolours of fledgling Auckland and its environs, as well as the Waikato District, are considered to be important to the historical record as they showed "life on the edge of the New Zealand frontier." He died of tuberculosis in Auckland on 27 July 1848, "much lamented by the inhabitants."

After a detailed handwriting analysis, comparing surviving journals and letters written by John after he emigrated to New Zealand to the handwriting found in John Grant's "Journal," the editors have concluded that John Jr. actually wrote the manuscript held at the Alexander Turnbull Library and not John Grant. In effect, it was a first draft of the dictated memoirs of a Seven Years' War veteran as recorded by a proud grandson. The number of loose papers and the abrupt end of the manuscript are good indications that this collaborative work-in-progress with his ailing grandfather stopped when the latter lost the ability to speak in 1824. Undoubtedly John cherished his grandfather's memoirs enough to bring his copy-book with him when he emigrated halfway around the world.

The manuscript was passed down through Dr. John Johnson's New Zealand descendants along with his other papers, including a collection of his sketches and paintings, mostly sepia wash drawings, all eventually deposited in various collections in New Zealand; his cherished grandfather's manuscript Journal was donated to the Alexander Turnbull Library in Wellington in 1968 by his great-grandson, Frederick Grant ("Mick") Johnson.

"Mick's" great-grandfather, and Dr. Johnson's oldest son, John Grant Johnson, then sixteen years of age, had come to New Zealand with his father in 1840. He quickly learned to speak Maori and entered government service as a clerk. In 1854 he was appointed land purchaser in the Whangarei and Kaipara districts, also serving as a government interpreter engaged in land negotiations. Like his father, he practised watercolour sketching and many of his works survive alongside his father's in the Auckland Institute and Museum Library.

JGM; CBs; SBs; BALs; Una Platts, *19th-Century New Zealand Artists: A Guide and Handbook* (New Zealand, 1980); W.H. Askwith, ed., *List of Officers of the Royal Regiment of Artillery from the Year 1716 to the Year 1899* (London, 1900), 44; MCA, DJQ; Medical Board of New South Wales, Minutes 3 June 1839; Shipping Intelligence, *Sydney Herald*, 1 April 1839 and 20 January 1840.

Lieutenant George Leslie (c.1740–62), *British army officer.*

George Leslie was born in Scotland circa 1740, his family origins unknown. His interest was sufficient to secure a lieutenancy in the new-raising 2nd/42nd Foot on 23 July 1758, and he participated with his battalion in the Martinique and Guadeloupe campaigns of 1758-59. He was wounded in the fighting for Morne Tartenson above Fort Royal on Martinique in January 1759 and sent with other invalids to Albany, New York, to recuperate over the winter of 1759-60. He participated in the 1760 Montreal campaign the following summer, and on his return to Martinique in 1762 was wounded a second time, storming the same hill, Morne Tartenson, on 24 January 1762. His place in a composite light infantry company of the 42nd and 44th Foot, commanded by Captain Apollos Morris, was taken by Lieutenant John Grant. Leslie died of fever on 11 August 1762 at Havana.

CBs; SBs; BALs; Stewart, *Sketches*, I-II, *Miscellaneous Correspondence*, II, (August 1758), 867.

Major James Lockhart (c.1717–60), later Sir James Lockhart-Ross, *British army officer, baronet, Chief of Clan Ross.*

Born at Lockhart Hall, Lanarkshire, in 1717, James was the second son of Sir James Lockhart, 2nd Baronet of Carstairs, and his wife, Grizel, third daughter of William, 12th Lord Ross. On 14 June 1734, at the age of seventeen, James purchased an ensign's commission in the 29th Foot (Fuller's) then stationed at Gibraltar. He became a lieutenant, also by purchase, in the same regiment on 1 February 1740. By the 1745 Jacobite Rebellion, he was a twenty-eight-year-old major in the 34th Foot (Cholmondeley's).

Wounded and taken prisoner at Falkirk in 1745, James violated his parole and was wounded again at the battle of Culloden. In the subsequent harrowing of the glens after Culloden he became notorious for his pillaging of Jacobite estates, historian John Prebble styling him as a "fiery and choleric Scot" and "the greatest reiver in the Army." On 2 February 1747, as a reward for his ruthless punishment of the Jacobite clans, he was given the opportunity by the captain general of the army, the Duke of Cumberland, to purchase the lieutenant colonelcy of the 33rd Foot (Johnson's). He received his third wound while serving with the 33rd Foot at the battle of Laffeldt, 2 July 1747. On his promotion to full colonel on 26 May 1756, he was given his own regiment, the 38th Foot.

On 19 August 1754, on the death of his cousin William Ross, he became the 2nd Baronet Lockhart-Ross of Balnagowan, and thus the hereditary clan chieftain of the Ross Clan through his mother's side of the family, taking the name of Lockhart-Ross (i.e., Sir James Lockhart-Ross). Similarly, on the death of his older brother, Sir William Lockhart, on 28 June 1758, he became the 4th Baronet of Carstairs, a title in the Baronetage of Nova Scotia, first created on 28 February 1672 for Sir James's great-grandfather William Lockhart of Carstairs. He was promoted to major general on 25 June 1759. About this time, he married Elizabeth, the daughter of Major John Crosbie, the union producing a daughter, Joan Elizabeth Ross.

His chieftaincy of the Ross Clan was short-lived however as he died on 30 September 1760 in London at the age of forty-three. The mantle of chieftain (for what it was worth after the clans were broken) passed to his younger brother George and subsequently to the most famous and distinguished sibling of his family, his youngest brother, Admiral Sir John Lockhart-Ross, Royal Navy, and Member of Parliament. His wife, Elizabeth, survived him by some years, passing away in April 1814, at the age of eighty-five.

CBs; SBs; BALs; *Complete Baronetage*, vol IV, 1665-1707 (Exeter, 1904), 286-287; William Mackay, *Urquhart and Glenmoriston: Olden Times in a Highland Parish* (Inverness, 1893), 295-6; John Prebble, *Culloden* (London, 1961); *The London Gazette*, no. 8654, from Tuesday, June 30, to Saturday, July 4, 1747.

Alexander Mackay, 7th of Auchmony (c.1717–89), *landowner, Jacobite supporter.*

The eldest son of John Mackay, 6th of Auchmony, and Elizabeth Grant, daughter of John Grant of Shewglie. He was one of the three Glenmoriston gentlemen known as "the three Alexanders," all active in the '45. He first married Mary Grant, the union producing two daughters, Jane and Elspet (or Isobell). He next married Angusia, daughter of Colonel Angus Macdonell of Glengarry, who commanded the Glengarry men in the '45 and was killed at Falkirk. This second union produced no children.

Mackay was not punished for his part in the Rebellion, nor was his estate forfeited to the Crown; however, "he had the honour of being the only person in the parish who found a place in a great list of "rebels" prepared by the officers of excise for the information of the Government." A short biography in this "great list" states that "he made himself very active in the Jacobite cause in his district, and induced the people of Glenurquhart to join the Rebellion," adding "After Culloden he concealed himself in a cave in Craig-Achtmony [*sic*], and so escaped."

In December 1779 he sold Auchmony to Sir James Grant and settled in Nairn, where he died in 1789 without male issue. His brothers James, Patrick and John all predeceased him without male issue, and he was succeeded as representative of the family by his youngest brother, Donald, who was transported to Barbados for the part he took in the '45 and, escaping, had assumed the name Macdonald.

William Mackay, *Urquhart and Glenmoriston: Olden Times in a Highland Parish* (Inverness, 1893), 295-6, 513; John Prebble, *Culloden* (London, 1961); *A List of Persons Concerned in the Rebellion Transmitted to the Commissioners of Excise … in Obedience to a General Letter of 7th May 1746 …* (Edinburgh, 1890), 330, 386.

John Robert Maxwell (c.1734-91), *British army officer, colonial administrator.*

John was born in Ireland, c.1734, the son of the Venerable John Maxwell of Falkland County, Monaghan, Archdeacon of Clogher, 1762-83, and his second wife, Isabella Leavons. He obtained an ensign's commission in the 15th Foot (Amherst's) 4 September 1754; promoted to lieutenant, 1 September 1756. He participated in the 1757 Rochefort expedition, serving under Sir John Mordaunt, and the following year soldiered with the 15th Foot at the siege of Louisbourg 1758, and at the siege of Quebec 1759, where he was wounded in the battle on the Plains of Abraham. He also participated in the battle of Ste. Foy the following spring in 1760, where he was wounded once again.

He was promoted captain, 4 May 1761 and his regiment participated with others in the capture of Martinique 1762 under Major General Robert Monckton. By September 1762, recovering from illness in New York, he found himself commanding the 1st Company of Light Infantry (a makeshift unit cobbled together from recovered invalids of various regiments serving at Havana) and was sent with an expedition commanded by General JEFFERY AMHERST's younger brother, Lieutenant Colonel William Amherst, to recover Newfoundland from the French. He was promoted to major, 10 July 1771.

He served in the American War of Independence with the 27th Foot, 1776-78, becoming the regiment's lieutenant colonel on 26 October 1775. On 2 February 1776 he married a landed widow, Mrs. Grace Corry (*née* Johnston), with considerable property in Counties Fermanagh, Monaghan and Tyrone, the marriage taking place in St. Mary's Church, Dublin. There was no issue. His marriage to Grace was short-lived. When seeking a divorce in 1779, Grace complained that her husband, in spite of "repeated efforts for the purpose," had "never consummated the said marriage, but appears totally impotent." She also complained that, "in the previous year, he had induced her to re-settle her estate on him, in failure of issue; and that she had subsequently discovered that he had made a will by which he had left his remainder in fee in her estate to his nephews and nieces, leaving to her nothing but a small island on the coast of North America at … [that] time … actually in the hands of the insurgents." It is unclear if she obtained her divorce and reacquired her landed property.

Maxwell, after the Battle of Germantown, transferred back to his old regiment, the 15th Foot, to be its commanding officer on 5 October 1777, passing command of the 27th Foot to newly promoted Lieutenant Colonel WILLIAM MURRAY of the Black Watch. Maxwell retired from the army the following year in January 1778 and, two years later, in 1780, was appointed captain general and governor of the Bahamas. The Spanish occupied the island on 8 May 1783 and Governor Maxwell became a prisoner of war until 19 April 1783. When the Bahamas became a British possession once again in 1783, he resumed his post as governor for the second time, serving until 1784. He died in 1791. As he had no children, almost all of his property was passed to his sister's son, John Waring.

CBs; SBs; BALs; R.J. Jones, *A History of the 15th (East Yorkshire) Regiment …* (Beverly, Yorkshire, 1958); Public Record Office of Northern Ireland, Perceval-Maxwell Papers, D/1556/17/4, Statement of Mrs. Grace Maxwell's case, 12 February 1779.

Colonel Lord John Murray (1711–87),
British army officer, Member of Parliament, landowner.

"Lord John" was born on 14 April 1711, a godson of Queen Anne and the first son of the 1st Duke of Athol by his second marriage to Mary Ross (daughter of William, Lord Ross of Haukhead). He was also half-brother to Lord George Murray, who had commanded Bonnie Prince Charlie's army at Culloden, and John, Marquess of Tullibardine, both hardcore Jacobites. Their father, according to one historian, had felt keenly the defection of his elder sons in 1715 and thus was careful to bring up his younger children by his second marriage as Whigs. Lord John was educated at a private school at Chelsea and, later, at Leiden University in the Netherlands.

On 10 April 1727 General George Wade, who was responsible for the building of military roads in the Highlands, wrote to Secretary of State Viscount Charles Townshend recommending a commission for Lord John indicating that "I must likewise put your Lordship in mind of two persons I had the honour to men-

"Lord John." Major General John Murray (1711-87). Colonel of the 42nd Foot (Royal Highland Regiment), he was a younger son of the 1st Duke of Athol by his second wife. Lord John began his military career as an ensign in the 3rd Foot Guards in 1727 on the recommendation of General George Wade. An aide de camp to George II, Murray was gazetted colonel of the 42nd in April 1745, an appointment he would cherish for the next forty-two years. (BWCM. Editors' photo)

tion to you, the [first] is the Lord John Murray, the eldest son of the Duke of Athol by his second marriage; he has been educated in England, is a youth of good parts, very desirous to serve in the army, and will be very pleased with a Colours in the Foot Guards having very little to depend on...."

Lord Murray was thus commissioned ensign in the 3rd Foot Guards (later, the Scots Guards) on 7 October and promoted to lieutenant (and captain) in that regiment in 1733. After John came of age in 1734, his half-brother James, the 2nd Duke of Athol, helped him secure a seat in the House of Commons as MP from Perthshire, a seat he retained until 1761. By 1743 Lord John was a lieutenant colonel and first aide de camp to King George II, who was the last British king to fight on a battlefield.

When the Highland Regiment (then numbered the 43rd Foot) had mutinied the same year while assembling near London for overseas service, the monarch had no doubt questioned his Scottish aide closely as to the likely causes. Lord John firmly believed that the good conduct of a Highland regiment depended principally upon the proper choice of officers and probably made his views freely known. Lord John, in a letter to his brother the Duke of Athol, confided that he believed that the simple Highlanders of the regiment had been "spirited up for some reason or the other" and that Lord Sempill, a Lowlander who had skimped on the men's plaids and clothing, could no longer "have any satisfaction in commanding them."

"I have, by good advice," concluded a hopeful Lord John, "made application to the Duke of Newcastle and Mr. Pelham to succeed his Lop [Lordship]; as I am an elder Lieutenant-Colonel than Sir Robert Munro, and your Interest in the Highlands far superior to his. I must therefore beg the favour of you to write to Gen[l] Clayton to Recommend me for that Reg[t], whose opinion will have great weight." But Lord Sempill would not move on for another two years, eventually transferring to the command of a more prestigious cavalry regiment. Thus in April 1745 Lord John was finally gazetted colonel of the Black Watch, an appointment he would cherish for the next forty-two years. Lord John became a major general in 1755, a lieutenant general in 1758 and a full general in 1770.

Lord John was married at Sheffield, 13 September 1758, to Miss Dalton of Banner Cross Hall, a Yorkshire lady of property. They had one daughter, Mary, who married Captain (later Lieutenant General) William Foxlowe, who took the name of Murray in 1782. Lord John died in Paris on 26 May 1787 at the age of seventy-seven. The *Scots Magazine* for July 1787 recorded his passing: "May 26. At Paris, Lord John Murray, the eldest General in his Majesty's service." Major General Hector Munro of Novar, KB, replaced Lord John as colonel of the Royal Highlanders.

CBs; SBs; BALs; *Black Watch at Ticonderoga*, 73-75; TNA, WO 34/55: f. 58; "Lord John Murray," *A Military History of Perthshire, 1660-1902*, Marchioness of Tullabardine, ed. (Perth, 1908), 407-10.

Captain William Murray (1737–77), *British army officer.*

Born on 30 November 1737, William Murray was the second son of John Murray of Lintrose and his wife, Amelia Murray, daughter of Sir William Murray, 3rd Baronet of Ochtertyre. Lintrose was about 12 miles (19 km) northwest of Perth; half the estate of Lintrose was in Perthshire, the other portion with the mansion house was in Angus. In December 1755, at the age of eighteen, William Murray was commissioned an ensign in the 34th Regiment and subsequently promoted in that regiment to lieutenant in September 1757.

Later in his career, he described his early life in the army in a Memorial seeking preferment and promotion to lieutenant colonel which his regimental colonel, Lord John Murray, forwarded to the Secretary of War on 19 March 1776. It opened: "That your Memorialist was appointed an Ensign in the 34th Regiment of Foot in the Year 1755. That he joined his Regiment at Gibraltar soon after. In the year 1757 he was appointed a Lieutenant in the 34th Regiment of Foot, & in the Year 1758 went upon an Expedition to the East of France under the Command of His Grace the Duke of Marlborough. When he returned from that Expedition he was appointed Captain to a Company in the second Battalion of the 42d, or Royal Highland Regiment of Foot...."

The captaincy in the 2nd/42nd was dependent on his ability to raise men and his Memorial takes up the tale: "Your Memorialist went immediately to North Britain & raised fifty Men, being his proportion as Captain, & in the Month of October embarked at Grenock [*sic*] & landed in the face of the Enemy at Gudalope [*sic*] in the latter end of the Year 1758...." He participated in Major General Peregrine Hopson's 1759 expedition to capture Martinique and Guadeloupe, his Black Watch company one of two blown off course (the other was John Grant's company commanded by David Haldane) and believed lost at sea. He thus participated in the attack on Fort Louis, Guadeloupe, with the fleet's Marine battalion as well as the capture of Montreal, 1760, and the 1762 Caribbean campaigns at Martinique and Havana.

His Memorial stated: "the Year 1759 he went to North America & was in the Field until Novemr – In the Year 1760 he was under the Command of Jeffery Amherst at the Reduction of all Canada. In the years 1761 & 1762 Your Memorialist was at the reduction of Martansee [Martinique] & the Havanna, at the last of which place, he was taken ill of a Malignant Fever which Confined him to his Bed above Eight Months...." Murray and some of the recovered Highlanders of the 42nd were then sent from Long Island to quell Pontiac's Rebellion and to reinforce Fort Pitt. Murray and his Highlanders fought a fierce battle with Indians at the Battle of Bushy Run, Pennsylvania, 3 August 1763. In Murray's words: "Your Memorialist served a very Fatiguing Campaign under the Command of Colonel Bouquet, against the Savages & in 1764 Served a Second Campaign against the Savages & penetrated into their Country which obliged them to beg for Peace – During that campaign had a brevet from General Gage to act as Major – Your Memorialist returned with the Army to Fort Pitt where he remained Commanding Officer until the Year 1767 when he was relieved & returned to Britain....

Murray was made the commandant of Fort Pitt in Western Pennsylvania 1764-66 with five companies of the 42nd Foot to police the Proclamation Line of 1763 which prohibited illegal settlement west of the Allegheny Mountains. Murray returned with the regiment to Ireland in 1767, and as its senior captain was promoted to major in September 1771 in place of Major THOMAS STIRLING, who moved up to the lieutenant colonelcy of the 42nd Foot.

In January 1776, as the regiment prepared for service in America, Lord John Murray recommended William Murray as his choice to command a proposed 2nd Battalion of the 42nd stating: "Major William Murray to be Lieut. Colonel, who went a Captain to America, and since his Return purchased the majority, and above Twenty years in the Service...." Unfortunately for Major Murray, the 2nd Battalion was not authorised until later in the war and a different officer received the position.

Soon after the regiment arrived in North America however, General Orders issued on 6 August 1776 directed that the "42nd Regiment to be formed into two battalions under the command of Lt. Col. Stirling." Accordingly, the line companies of the regiment were split into two smaller battalions of about 400 men each. Major Murray was appointed to command the 1st Battalion and commanded it for the duration of the New York/New Jersey campaign of 1776-77.

In a July 1777 letter to his regimental colonel, Lord John Murray, William apologetically turned down the latter's offer to lobby on his behalf for a promotion to brevet lieutenant colonel "in the Army," bluntly explaining the politics of preferment on his side of the Atlantic: "Getting me Brevet Rank as Lieut. Col. would not be in my favor at Present, as I am the oldest Major in America, and therefore has reason from my Service, to be promoted to the first Lieutenant Colonelcy that falls vacant," he observed, "whereas were I a Brevet Lieut. Col. I might be told I had got the Rank, and a Younger Major Might be made Lieut. Col. to a Regt and it would be looked upon as no injury done me." Despite Murray's concern, the War Office announced on 6 September 1777 his promotion to lieutenant colonel "in the Army."

Murray sailed with the regiment to the Chesapeake for the Philadelphia campaign of 1777, and the day after the battle of Germantown, 5 October 1777, he was made lieutenant colonel of the 27th Foot (Enniskillens) in place of Lieutenant Colonel JOHN MAXWELL, who moved over to command the 15th Foot. A happy Murray wrote to his brother claiming: "By the friendship of my good friend Lord Cornwallis I am now appointed Lt. Colo. to the 27th Regt."

Soon after his promotion, William was informing his brother, the Duke of Athol, that he had "been very bad of a fever but am now perfectly recovered...." Sadly, just a week after writing this, William succumbed to another bout of fever and died, much mourned by his men, on 2 November 1777. He was buried in Christ Churchyard in Philadelphia, next to Ann Dashwood Grant, the wife of his closet friend and comrade in the regiment, Brevet Lieutenant Colonel William Grant of Rothiemurchas.

CBs; SBs; BALs; "List of the Officers of the 42nd or Royal Highland Regiment according to seniority dated December 29th, 1762," BL Add. MSS 21,634: f.178c; Stewart, *Sketches*, I-II; TNA, *Journal of the Commissioners for Trade and Plantations*, Vol. XII, January 1764 - December 1767, 818; TNA, Home Office Papers, 1773-5; *Bouquet Papers.*

Captain Lieutenant John Peebles (1739–1824), *British army officer, customs officer.*
John Peebles was born 11 September 1739 in Irvine, Ayrshire, to John Peebles Sr. and his wife, Mary Reoch. He was appointed surgeon's mate to the 2nd Battalion, Virginia Regiment, in 1758 and was then appointed by Colonel Archibald Montgomery of the 77th Foot (Montgomery's Highlanders) to the same position in his own regiment the following year. In September 1762 Peebles sailed from Louisbourg with the 77th Foot as part of an expedition

to recapture St. John's, Newfoundland, from the French. The French surrendered the post 20 September 1762 and Surgeon's Mate Peebles was later recognized for his gallant behaviour during the expedition.

On 14 June 1763 Peebles was approved to serve as a volunteer in Montgomery's Highlanders and he was severely wounded at Battle of Bushy Run, Pennsylvania, in August 1763 during Pontiac's Rebellion. Colonel Henry Bouquet reported to Major General JEFFERY AMHERST from Fort Pitt on 11 August 1763 that he could not "omit to mention the only Volunteer with us, Mr. Palles [Peebles] dangerously wounded...." Peebles' performance in the battle prompted General Amherst to write to Colonel Henry Bouquet on 25 August 1763 stating that the "Behavior of Mr. Peebles, on former Occasions, particularly at Newfoundland, and his being wounded now makes me Break thro' the Orders I Have Received from His Majesty respecting the Reduced Officers, that I may provide for him. As I Flatter myself the King will be graciously Pleased to approve thereof: And I Enclose you a Commission Appointing Mr. Peebles to be Ensign in the 42nd Regiment, which you will please to Deliver to him: Acquainting both Captain Lt. Balneavis and Ensign Peebles that they have no Fees to pay for those Commissions...."

Ensign Peebles had recovered sufficiently from his wounds by fall 1764 to command at Fort Ligonier from December 1764 to the summer of 1765 and returned with his regiment to Ireland in 1767. He was promoted to lieutenant in March 1770 and served detached with part of the regiment on the Isle of Man. At the outbreak of the American War for Independence, Peebles was a senior grenadier lieutenant in that elite company commanded by Brevet Major William Grant.

Upon the 42nd Foot's arrival in New York, grenadiers of the army were brigaded into composite battalions and Peebles was appointed adjutant of the 4th Grenadier Battalion on 16 August 1776. The battalion was, however, disbanded in October 1776 due to the level of sickness of the 71st Regiment's two grenadier companies. Lieutenant Peebles returned to his own grenadier company, which served for the remainder of the New York campaign of 1776 and the Rhode Island campaign of 1776-77 as part of the 3rd Grenadier Battalion.

Following its return from Rhode Island, the 3rd Grenadiers were broken up, its companies rejoining their respective regiments. Peebles and the 42nd Grenadiers were re-assigned to the 2nd Grenadier Battalion under Lieutenant Colonel Henry Monckton on 26 March 1777. Because Captain Charles Graham, who had replaced Murray as company commander, fell

Grenadier officer. Captain Lieutenant John Peebles (1739-1824) started his regular military career as a surgeon's mate in the 77th Foot (Montgomery Highlanders) in the French and Indian War, finishing as a captain of grenadiers in the Black Watch during the American Revolution. Peebles kept a set of detailed notebooks of his experiences during the Revolutionary War, which are now held in the National Archives of Scotland and have been handsomely reprinted and edited as a book entitled *John Peebles' American War* by Ira D. Gruber. Portrait miniature, artist unknown, c.1778. (National Museums of Scotland M.1952.213. Editors' photo)

ill and was left in New York for the beginning of the Philadelphia campaign of 1777, Peebles, as senior lieutenant, would have commanded the 42nd Grenadiers for the Battle of Brandywine, the capture of Philadelphia and the Battle of Germantown.

About four weeks after the Battle of Germantown, Peebles was promoted to Captain Lieutenant in Lord JOHN MURRAY's Company, 31 October 1777, and the following year Swiss artist Pierre Eugene du Simitiere painted a miniature of Captain Lieutenant Peebles in Philadelphia which now resides in the National Museum of Scotland. Peebles was promoted to captain on 18 August 1778 in place of Captain ALEXANDER DONALDSON, who was promoted to major of the 76th Foot (MacDonald's Highlanders). Peebles remained in America and took command of the 42nd Grenadier Company on 27 August 1778 when Captain Charles Graham was promoted to major. The 42nd Grenadier Company was transferred to the 1st Grenadier Battalion on 10 August 1778 and was part of the consolidated Grenadier Battalion when the two remaining battalions were merged 3 November 1778. Peebles commanded the Grenadier Company for the Siege of Charleston, South Carolina, in 1780.

In January 1781, Peebles, worn out from the service, attempted to retire from the army and entered into negotiations with Lieutenant Alexander Macgregor to purchase his captaincy but the discussions fell through as his commanding officer was unwilling to let him go. Peebles remained in command of the Grenadier Company, thus taking part in the relief attempt for Cornwallis's besieged army at Yorktown in October 1781. Peebles finally succeeded in retiring in February 1782 when Lieutenant Colonel THOMAS STIRLING was replaced as commanding officer by John's old friend, Charles Graham, and he returned to his hometown, Irvine, Ayrshire, where he married his longtime sweetheart, Anna Hamilton, daughter of Charles Hamilton of Craighlaw. Peebles became a surveyor for the port of Irvine in the customs service.

His military service would not end with his soldiering in North America. On 5 March 1797 the War Office announced that a new unit, to be known as the Irvine Volunteers, would be formed and Peebles was listed as captain of one of its companies. In December 1798 Peebles was promoted to major and took command of the Volunteers. His wife, Anna, died at Irvine 19 December 1811 at age seventy, and thirteen years later *Blackwood's Magazine* recorded Peebles' death, writing: "[Jan. 1824] At Irvine, John Peebles, Esq. late Captain 42nd Regiment, in the 85th year of his age." Peebles is buried in the Irvine Old Parish Churchyard, his tomb tablet inscribed:

HERE RESTS THE MORTAL PART
John Peebles
Late Captn of Grenadiers 42nd Regt:
SUBSEQUENTLY MAJOR COMMANDANT
OF THE IRVINE VOLUNTEERS
Born 11th: Septr: 1739. Died 7th Decr: 1824
(AGED EIGHTY FOUR YEARS)
FOR UPWARDS OF FORTY YEARS
HE SERVED HIS KING
AND COUNTRY WITH FIDELITY
AND WAS SEVERELY
WOUNDED AT THE *Battle of Bushy Run*
IN THE WARFARE
With the American Indians in 1763
HE CLOSED A LONG AND ACTIVE LIFE IN HIS
NATIVE PLACE, IN THE EXERCISE OF FAITH
HOPE
AND CHARITY, IN THE SERVICE OF HIS GOD
THIS SMALL TRIBUTE TO HER FATHER'S MEMORY
IS AFFECTIONATELY OFFERED BY
HIS ONLY CHILD

Captain Peebles kept a set of detailed notebooks of his experiences during the American War for Independence which are now held in the National Archives of Scotland and have been handsomely reprinted and edited as a book entitled *John Peebles' American War* by Ira D. Gruber.

CBs; SBs; BALs; "List of the Officers of the 42nd or Royal Highland Regiment according to seniority dated December 29th, 1762," BL Add. MSS 21,634: f.178c; Stewart, *Sketches*, I-II; TNA, Journal of the Commissioners for Trade and Plantations, Vol. XII, January 1764 - December 1767, 818; TNA, Home Office Papers, 1773-5; *Bouquet Papers*; William John Potts, "Du Simitiere, Artist, Antiquary, and Naturalist, Projector of the First American Museum, with Some Extracts from his Notebook," *The Pennsylvania Magazine of History and Biography*, vol XII (Philadelphia, 1889), 341- 375; *Blackwood's Edinburgh Magazine*, vol XV, January – June, 1824 (Edinburgh, 1824), 132; *John Peebles' American War*, Ira D. Gruber, ed. (Mechanicsburg, Pennsylvania, 1998), 554.

"Uncle David." David Ross of Tarlogie, later Lord Ankerville (1727-1805), Lord of Session, was the step-uncle of John Grant, and he and his brother, Charles Ross, MP, were two of the "friends" instrumental in securing young John Grant's coveted commission with Britain's senior Highland regiment. Caricature etching by John Kay, 1799. (NPG D16892. Editors' photo)

David Ross, later Lord Ankerville (1727–1805), *Lord of Session, barrister, landowner, John Grant's maternal step uncle.*

Born at Inverchasley near Tain, Scotland, in 1727, the son of David Ross, 1st of Inverchasley and Tarlogie, and his first wife, Isabella Munro. He received a liberal education and studied Scottish law, being admitted to the bar in 1751. By 1756 he obtained the office of steward-depute of Kirkcudbright in Galloway, Scotland, and, in 1763, was appointed one of the principal clerks of Session. In 1776, with the death of Lord Alemore (Andrew Pringle), one of the Lords of Session, he was promoted to the vacancy on the bench with the title of Lord Ankerville. In the mid-18th century, Ankerville was the richest portion of the Inverchasley Estates and Lord Ankerville would successfully combine the career of an agricultural innovator with that of senator of the College of Justice. He married Mary Cochrane in 1755, who bore him two sons and three daughters, two of the latter dying young.

His oldest sister, Anne, married John Haldane of Aberuthven, by whom she had an only son, David, John Grant's step cousin, and the latter's first company commander in the newly-raised 2nd/42nd. David's second sister, Margaret, married Charles Urquhart of Braelangwell, whose estate was the refuge of John Grant's family after Culloden and the harrowing of the glens. David's stepsister, Mary, by his father's second marriage to Mary Ross, married John Grant of Ballintomb, John's father.

While in Edinburgh, David's principle residence was in St. Andrew Square. Every year he travelled north to his seat in Tarlogie, near Tain in Ross-shire. During these long treks, David's "hosts" along the Highland road were always careful to have a "select portion of their best claret set apart for their guest." The old judge's love of claret "did not abate with his increase of years."

Lord Ankerville and his brother Charles, a Member of Parliament, were no doubt some of the "friends" whose influence was instrumental in securing John Grant a lieutenancy in the 42nd Foot. Ankerville died at his seat in Tarlogie, aged seventy-eight, on 16 August 1805.

JGM; "Davis Ross, 1st of Inverchasley and Tarlogie," *The Scottish Antiquary: or, Northern Notes & Queries*, vol V (Edinburgh: 1886), 63-4; John Kay, *A Series of Original Portraits and Caricature Etchings: With Biographical Sketches & Illustrative Anecdotes*, vol 1, 248-9; Alexander Mackenzie, *History of the Munros of Fowlis: with genealogies of the principal families of the name to which are added those of Lexington and New England* (1898), 196-7.

Ensign Patrick Sinclair (1736–1820), *British army officer, colonial administrator.*

Patrick Sinclair was born in 1736 at Lybster, Scotland, the son of Alexander Sinclair and Aemilia Sinclair. He would appear to have had some naval training and sailing experience prior to joining the new-raising 2nd/42nd as an ensign in July 1758. A brother officer but junior to John Grant, he fought at Martinique and Guadeloupe as part of Major General Peregrine Hopson's 1759 expedition and, while at Fort Ontario, Oswego, was promoted lieutenant "in room of Lt. Murray" July 1760. During the army's descent down the Saint Lawrence to capture Montreal in 1760, Sinclair was appointed captain of the captured French brig *L'Outaouaise,* which was renamed *Williamson* by Major General Jeffery Amherst to honour the bravery of the Royal Artillery row galleys that captured it. He remained detached "on command" with his ship while the 42nd went on to capture and subsequently garrison Montreal in 1760-61.

He exchanged into the 15th Foot, 24 October 1761, and remained on the Great Lakes until 1767 commanding various vessels. He was the first Briton to sail a ship on Lake Huron and Lake Michigan and was ordered by Colonel John Bradstreet to construct a stockade fort on the Huron River (Port Huron, Michigan), which he was permitted to name Fort Sinclair. He returned in 1767 with the 15th Foot to England and was promoted to captain in April 1772. He went out on half-pay the following year and returned to his family estate at Lybster in Inverness-shire, whence he lobbied for a job on the Great Lakes in any capacity.

His efforts bore fruit, for he was appointed lieutenant governor and superintendent of Michilimackinac, 7 April 1775, though it took him four years to reach his new post because of the American War of Independence. Once there, Sinclair constructed a new fort, re-located the town and gave large quantities of gifts to the western Indians to keep them loyal. He subsequently incurred huge cost overruns and was officially investigated but cleared of any wrongdoing. During his time there, he purchased a captaincy in the 2nd/84th Foot (Royal Highland Emigrants) and went out on half-pay in 1784, returning to England.

On his arrival, his creditors had him thrown into Newgate Prison for debt. After obtaining sufficient funds for his release, he promptly sued Governor Frederick Haldimand for 50,000 pounds to pay off the costs associated with Fort Michilimackinac and won his case. It was a pyrrhic victory, however, as he was subsequently impoverished by the hefty legal bills required to clear his name and credit. Sinclair retired to Lybster, a half-pay officer, and despite subsequent promotions to lieutenant colonel (1793), colonel (1797) and major general (1803), he declared bankruptcy in 1804 and died destitute 30 June 1820, a lieutenant general (1810) and still drawing a salary as the lieutenant governor of Michilimackinac.

CBs; SBs; BALs; Stewart, *Sketches*, I-II; "Patrick Sinclair," *DCB*, vol V (1801-1820); H.B. Eaton, "Lieutenant-General Patrick Sinclair: An Account of His Military Career," *JSAHR*, vol 56 (Autumn, Winter 1978), 128-42, 215-32; vol 57 (Spring 1979), 45-55.

Colonel David Stewart, later Stewart of Garth (1772–1829), *British army officer, author, colonial administrator.*

David Stewart was born 1772 at Kynachan, Scotland, the second son of Robert Stewart of Garth, Perthshire, a direct descendant of James Stewart (grandson of Robert II), who built the castle of Garth at the end of the 14th century. He initially obtained an ensign's commission in the 77th (Atholl Highlanders) on 21 April 1783, but that regiment was disbanded a week later and the eleven-year-old youth went on half-pay, his seniority in the army secure. After a few years, in which he continued his studies, he returned to active service as an ensign with the 42nd Foot (Royal Highlanders), his commission dated 10 August 1787. Promoted lieutenant on 8 August 1792, he soldiered with his regiment in Flanders in 1794, then went with it to the West Indies in October 1795, and the following year he was made the captain lieutenant (24 June 1796) commanding the colonel's company. He participated in the captures of St. Lucia and St. Vincent and the unsuccessful expedition against Puerto Rico in 1797.

Stewart returned from the West Indies with his regiment to garrison Gibraltar and was part of the force mounted to retake Minorca from the French in November 1798. Unfortunately his troop transport was captured and he was detained five months a prisoner of war in Spain before an exchange could take place. His regiment then went to Egypt with General Ralph Abercromby's expedition and Stewart was severely wounded at the battle of Alexandria, 21 March 1801.

After his recovery and three years later, he obtained a majority in the 78th Highlanders on 17 April 1804 by raising recruits for the 2nd Battalion, an easy task for the well-liked officer. His men were so much attached to him that when he was training them at Shorncliffe the following year, an observant Sir John Moore interposed to prevent him from being sent to India to join the 1st Battalion. Instead, Stewart remained with the 2nd/78th and went to the Mediterranean in September 1805 and shared in the descent on Calabria, Italy. At Maida, on 4 July 1806, Stewart was again severely wounded, this time leading the composite battalion of the various regiments' light companies.

Pride of race. David Stewart of Garth's only modern biographer is the first to admit that the good colonel was not a very precise or impartial historian, given that his protagonist was a direct descendant of the fierce and terrible Wolf of Badenoch, bastard son of King Robert II, and imbued with all his ancestor's pride of race. "He is a great authority," claims James Robertson, and correctly identifies Stewart's *Sketches* as "the source book for countless works on the history and the customs of the Highlands," but confesses in the same sentence that Stewart's "history could now be thought a little weak." Engraved by George Baird Shaw after the portrait by Sir John Watson Gordon. (Illustration from Chambers, *Lives of Illustrious and Distinguished Scotsmen*. Editors' photo)

Once he had recovered, he was appointed lieutenant colonel of the West India Rangers, 21 April 1808, and took part in the 1810 capture of Guadeloupe. He received a medal with one clasp for this victory as well as one for Maida. He was promoted colonel "in the Army" on 4 June 1814, and the following year he went out on half-pay and was created a Commander of the Bath.

It was at this time he was to secure his place in the history of the Highlands: he became the first chronicler of the histories of the early Highland regiments and a staunch advocate of Highland dress. His two-volume book *Sketches of the Character, Manners, and Present State of the Highlanders of Scotland...*, first published in 1822, has underpinned every subsequent account of the Highlands to this day. In some cases long tracts of his original text were subsumed, word-for-word, into later histories of his regiment and others raised for the service of the British Crown. But Stewart's only modern-day biographer is the first to admit that the good colonel was not a very precise or impartial historian, given that his protagonist was a direct descendant of the fierce and terrible Wolf of Badenoch, bastard son of King Robert II, and imbued with all his ancestor's pride of race.

"He is a great authority," claims James Robertson, and correctly identifies Stewart's *Sketches* as "the source book for countless works on the history and the customs of the Highlands," but confesses in the same sentence that Stewart's history "could now be thought a little weak." Well-known historian John Prebble, author of *Culloden* and *Mutiny*, is less charitable, willing to aver that Stewart's *Sketches* are still "rich in knowledge and anecdote" but, as history, reek of "the sweet smell of romantic anesthesia that softened any guilty pain his class may have felt at the manner in which a way of life had passed."

The research for his *Sketches* was conducted between 1816 and 1821, and it was sometime during this period that he contacted Major John Grant (late of the Royal Invalids) for his memories and stories of service during the French and Indian War. Thus, John Grant's first appearance to the British public was as a footnote in volume one of Stewart's bestseller. It reads: "Capt. [John] Peebles, wounded at Bushy Run, and residing in Irvine, and Major John Grant, late of the Invalids, are the only officers alive in the year 1822, who served in the regiment during the Seven Years' War."

Soon after publishing *Sketches* in March of 1822, Stewart succeeded to the estate of Garth by the death of his elder brother. When George IV visited Edinburgh in August later that year, Stewart of Garth helped Sir Walter Scott with the royal reception arrangements, headed by the Celtic Club in the welcoming procession, personally adjusted His Highness' royal plaid for the Levée, and pronounced the king "a verra pretty man."

Stewart was promoted major general on 27 May 1825 and in 1829 was sent to St. Lucia as its new governor. He was dead of fever by 18 December 1829, but the dispatch carrying news of his death did not reach London until 11 February 1830. In its obituary the *Gentleman's Magazine* summed up his career, stating: "In every relation of life, Gen. Stewart was highly esteemed; – a brave and gallant soldier, a patriotic and warm lover of his country, he was known to a very wide circle in society; and whether as the officer, the citizen, the Scotsman, or the man, he was covered with golden opinions by all ranks and classes."

CBs; SBs; BALs; Gentleman's Magazine, February 1830, 276; Stewart, *Sketches*, I, 588; James Irvine Robertson, *The First Highlander: Major General David Stewart of Garth CB, 1768-1829* (East Linton, 1998).

Lieutenant Colonel Thomas Stirling (1731–1808), *British army officer.*

Thomas Stirling was born 8 October 1731 in St. Petersburg, Russia, second son to Sir Henry Stirling, 3rd Baronet of Ardoch (Perthshire) and his wife, Anne Gordon (daughter of Admiral Thomas Gordon, a native of Aberdeen, Admiral of the Russian Baltic Squadron and Governor of Kronstadt, Russia). Commissioned originally as an ensign in the Dutch service, 30 September 1747, he was placed on half-pay in 1753. He was restored to service, as ensign in the 1st Battalion of Colonel Marjoribanks' regiment, 31 October 1756. In 1757, when three additional companies were raised as reinforcement companies to Lord John Murray's 42nd Highland Regiment of Foot, Stirling was recommended by the Duke of Athol as one of the prospective company commanders. Stirling duly raised the requisite number of men for the 42nd and was gazetted a captain, 24 July 1757.

Stirling sailed for North America in November of the same year but was not present at the 1758 attack on Ticonderoga, his company being stationed at Fort Edward. He served with the 42nd in Major General Jeffery Amherst's 1759 expedition against Ticonderoga and Crown Point and the 1760 campaign against Montreal via Oswego. He took part in the capture of Martinique in 1762 and was wounded, 24 January 1762, but was sufficiently recovered to serve in the capture of Havana later that year. Like many others during the siege, Stirling fell seriously ill with fever and returned to Scotland on sick leave to recover, not returning to America until around 1765.

In August 1765 Captain Stirling gained considerable notoriety when he was ordered to take a company-sized detachment, drawn from all the companies of the regiment, down the Ohio River from Fort Pitt (present-day Pittsburgh) to the Illinois country. The trip took from 24 August 1765 to 9 October 1765, and on arrival Stirling accepted the French surrender and transfer of Fort De Chartres (near Prairie du Rocher, Illinois) and surrounding territory to British arms. After being relieved by a detachment of the 34th Foot under the command of Major Robert Farmar, Stirling and his detachment went down the Mississippi River by boat to New Orleans and Pensacola before catching a ship back to New York, arriving there in June 1766 after a trip of over 3,000 miles (4,828 km). The following summer, Stirling and what remained of the 42nd Foot left for garrison duty in Ireland and Scotland and in 1770 he was gazetted major to the regiment. The following year he was promoted to lieutenant colonel on the retirement of Lieutenant Colonel Gordon Graham.

In 1776 and the outbreak of the American Revolution, his regiment was told off for North American service and Stirling raised the strength of his regiment from 350 men to 1,200 in five months, returned with it in the following spring to America, where he commanded it continuously for three years during the war. While acting as a brigade commander, Stirling was badly wounded in 1779 at Springfield, New Jersey, and was invalided home. He was made colonel by brevet, 19 February 1779, while continuing to serve as lieutenant colonel in the Royal Highlanders. He was also made aide de camp to King George III.

Stirling was made colonel of the 71st Highland Regiment of Foot, 13 February 1782, and was made major general, 20 November 1782.

Mississippi Highlander. General Sir Thomas Stirling, 5th Baronet (1733-1808), had a long, active military career in the British Army and fought in all the North American campaigns of the Black Watch. As a young captain, he was the first British officer to command a military expedition sent down the Ohio and subsequently down the Mississippi River to New Orleans. He returned to North America a second time during the American Revolutionary War, this time as the commanding officer of the 42nd Foot. He proved to be the major stumbling block in John Grant re-securing a captain's berth in his old regiment of the previous war. Oil on canvas after Benjamin West. (BWCM. Editors' photo)

He went on half-pay when the 71st was disbanded, 4 June 1784, but returned to active status when appointed colonel of the 41st Regiment of Foot, 13 January 1790, and created a baronet. After General James Murray's death in 1794, he purchased the estate of Strowan. He was made lieutenant general, 1796. On 26 July 1799, on the death of his brother, Stirling succeeded to the baronetcy of Ardoch and two years later, in 1801, achieved the rank of full general. He died in 1808.

CBs; SBs; BALs; *DNB*, XVIII, 1270-1271; *Black Watch at Ticonderoga,* 80-81; TNA, WO 34/55: f. 58; "General Sir Thomas Stirling of Ardoch and Strowan," *A Military History of Perthshire, 1660-1902*, Marchioness of Tullabardine, ed. (Perth, 1908), 407-10.

Captain William Sutherland (1741–89),
British army officer.
William Sutherland was born 6 August 1741, first son of Reverend Hugh Sutherland of Rogart and his wife, Janet MacLean. He was older brother to Lieutenant Colonel Alexander Sutherland of Culmaily of the Sutherland militia (1743-1822). William entered the army as an ensign in the new-raising Sutherland Regiment of Fencible Men, 10 September 1759, and the following year transferred to the new-raising 88th Foot on the regular army establishment as a 2nd lieutenant (5 January 1760). William was promoted lieutenant on 17 October 1761 in the 1st Battalion of the 105th Foot, commonly known as the Queen's Own Royal Regiment of Highlanders, and went on Irish half-pay when that regiment disbanded on 31 March 1763.

He returned to active service three years later as a lieutenant with the 68th Foot stationed in the West Indies, 9 April 1766, but he exchanged two months later into the 38th Foot, 18 June 1766, then stationed in Ireland. When his regiment was sent to North America, the long-serving Lieutenant Sutherland was in his regiment's elite grenadier company and was described as "a long-legged fellow." Marching with the British column at the North Bridge in Concord on 19 April 1775, his company was engaged by 400 Massachusetts militia and minutemen. Sutherland attempted to rally the troops and hold the bridge when the colonial militia opened fire but was quickly wounded in the engagement and forced to retire. Sutherland would later co-author a detailed account of the events on that fateful day in a pamphlet entitled "Late News of the Excursions and Ravages of the King's Troops on the nineteenth of April 1775 as set forth in the Narrative of Lt. William Sutherland of His Majesty's 38th Regiment of Foot and of Richard Pope of the 47th Regiment."

Shortly afterwards, Sutherland was given a captaincy in a provincial unit, the Royal Fencible Americans (25 July 1775), by General Thomas Gage and the following summer was commissioned a substantive captain in the 55th Foot (14 April 1776). On 30 May 1778 William was appointed aide de camp to Sir Henry Clinton, the commander-in-chief, while the army was at Philadelphia. A few weeks later he reputedly saved General Clinton's life at the battle of Monmouth in New Jersey, 28 June 1778.

The following month a notice appeared in the 9 July 1778 edition of the Royal Gazette in New York inviting "all gentlemen, natives of North Britain" to enlist in a new provincial corps to be called the "Caledonian Volunteers" and "to be commanded by their countryman, Captain William Sutherland, ADC to the Commander in Chief." He was made captain commandant, 31 July 1778, of the Caledonian Volunteers but was only able to raise one company, which was then incorporated into the newly-formed British Legion under the command of Lord Cathcart.

A grateful Clinton, obviously still wishing to reward his young aide de camp with a plum command, appointed him major commandant of the newly-raising Garrison Battalion on 26 September 1778. William sailed with two companies of this battalion of invalids and recovering men from New York on 25 October bound for Bermuda, where their main duty would be to suppress rebellious inhabitants and their thriving contraband trade with the rebels in the mainland colonies.

At first all went well, the governor writing to General Clinton on 24 November 1778 that "Major Sutherland and his troops arrived in time to prevent insult by privateers and rebellious inhabitants." But unhappily some men of his battalion ran amuck and perpetrated several indignities on the Bermudans, with their commanding officer himself, allegedly, committing some major abuses of his own. Subsequently, Articles of Complaint were lodged by the governor against Sutherland citing his various abuses of power, and his former mentor and benefactor, Sir Henry Clinton, was forced to recall him to New York.

While in New York, cooling his heels, Major Sutherland was placed in temporary command of the British fort at Paulus Hook, a sandy promontory on the New Jersey side of the Hudson River opposite New York. On 19 August 1779 Major Henry "Lighthorse Harry" Lee of Virginia led a surprise night assault against the British fort, General Clinton later observing that he feared the rebels "found the garrison so scandalously absorbed in confidence of their own security that they [Lee's men] made themselves masters of a blockhouse and 2 redoubts with scarcely any difficulty." His hands were again tied when it came to his former protégé. Clinton subsequently ordered "Major Sutherland to be tried on a charge of general misconduct as commandant" and told him to prepare for a court martial for his "misconduct as commandant of Paulus Hook on the morning of 19 August."

By 4 September 1779 William had been tried and honourably acquitted. However, there was no question of his returning as commandant to the Garrison Battalion in Bermuda as the governor had written to Sir Henry Clinton early in 1781 stating that "Sutherland's conduct has injured the Garrison." Clinton accordingly re-assigned his former aide de camp on 5 May 1782 to Colonel John Simcoe's Queen's Rangers as a captain of cavalry. However, Sutherland was struck off strength of his new unit shortly afterwards when it was found that he had retained his commission in the 55th Foot.

Up until that point in the war, British officers were able to retain their regular commissions in the British Army when they held commissions in provincial units but the King had ruled at the end of 1779 that regulars could no longer hold commissions in both regular and provincial units, and that officers so situated had to choose one and resign the other.

Thus, Sutherland returned to the 55th Foot and remained with that regiment until the end of the war. He exchanged to the 45th Foot as a captain on 26 April 1786 and died of disease three years later on the island of Grenada. A widower, he left four children "all minors ... the natural and lawful children and only next of kin of the deceased." They were Mary Anne Sutherland, Sophia Blaney Sutherland, Hugh Alexander Sutherland and Henry Clinton Sutherland.

CBs; SBs; BALs; Malcolm Sutherland, *A Fighting Clan: Sutherland Officers, 1250-1850* (London, 1996), 202-4; David Hackett Fischer, *Paul Revere's Ride* (New York: Oxford University Press, 1994); Walter T. Dornfest, *Military Loyalists of the American Revolution: Officers and Regiments, 1775-1783* (Jefferson, NC, 2011).

APPENDIX A

JOHN GRANT'S COMMISSION

"To Our Trusty and Welbeloved [*sic*] John Grant...." So reads John Grant's "renewed" lieutenant's commission "... in Our Forty Second, or Royal Highland, Regiment of Foot, commanded by Our Trusty and Welbeloved [*sic*] John Murray Esq., commonly called Lord John." All officer commissions came from the king, and when George II died on 25 October 1760, they had to be renewed under the authority of the new king, George III. John's renewed commission is dated 27 October 1760 and signed by the Secretary of State (North), the Earl of Holdernesse. It was likely presented to John during the winter of 1760-61 while he was "quartered 20 miles from Montreal in the Parish of Saint Genevieve...." John's original lieutenant's commission was dated 22 July 1758. (MCA)

George the Third, by the Grace of God, King of Great Britain, France and Ireland; Defender of the Faith, &c.ª To Our Trusty and Welbeloved John Grant Gent: Greeting: We do, by these Presents, Constitute and Appoint you to be Lieutenant to that Company whereof Esq.r is Captain, in Our Forty Second, or Royal Highland, Regiment of Foot, commanded by Our Trusty and Welbeloved John Murray Esq.r; commonly called Lord John Murray, Lieutenant General of Our Forces — You are therefore carefully and diligently to discharge the Duty of Lieutenant by Exercising and Well-disciplining both the inferior Officers and Soldiers of that Company, and We do, hereby, Command them to Obey you as their Lieutenant and you are to observe and follow such Orders and Directions, from Time to Time, as you shall receive from your Colonel, Captain or any other your Superior Officer, according to the Rules and Discipline of War, in pursuance of the Trust hereby reposed in you. Given at Our Court at Savile House the Twenty Seventh Day of October 1760 in the First Year of Our Reign.

Entered in the Office of Thomas Tyrwhitt Esq.r Comry Genl. of Musters.

Entered with the Secretary at War

By His Majesty's Command
Holdernesse

John Grant Gent: Lieutenant, in the Forty Second or Royal Highland Regiment of Foot.

DJQ J332/1

John Grant Gent:
Lieutenant
In the Forty second or Royal
Highland Regiment of
Foot

APPENDIX B

JOHN GRANT'S FAMILY TREE

Part of the so-called "loose sheets," the pages of John Grant's memoirs not part of the original binding, this family tree shows seven generations of the Grant family, ending with our hero, John, and his wife, Isobel. The tree includes two small sketches: the family motto, *Te Favente virebo* ("Under thy favour, I shall flourish"); and a crest depicting three antique crowns, presumably the family crest taken by the Dalrachney Grants. There is a poorly drawn figure above the motto, likely an attempt to draw "the trunk of an oak-tree sprouting out some leaves, with the sun shining thereon," the crest of the Laird of Grant, Sir Ludovick. In his memoirs, John would recall the elderly Laird singling him out by name at a fair at Castle Grant in 1757, the year before he went into the army. "Your family were always our *Lam á chrest*, John," he said, the term literally meaning "the hands closest to a belted shirt" – a feudal analogy reserved for family counsellors closest to the chief (the modern-day sense for this type of relationship would be "right-hand man"). This close relationship between the Dalrachney Grants and their chief would explain why John included Sir Ludovick's crest (oak-tree) on the same page as his own (three crowns). The dates above each generation are the marriage dates. (Editors' photo)

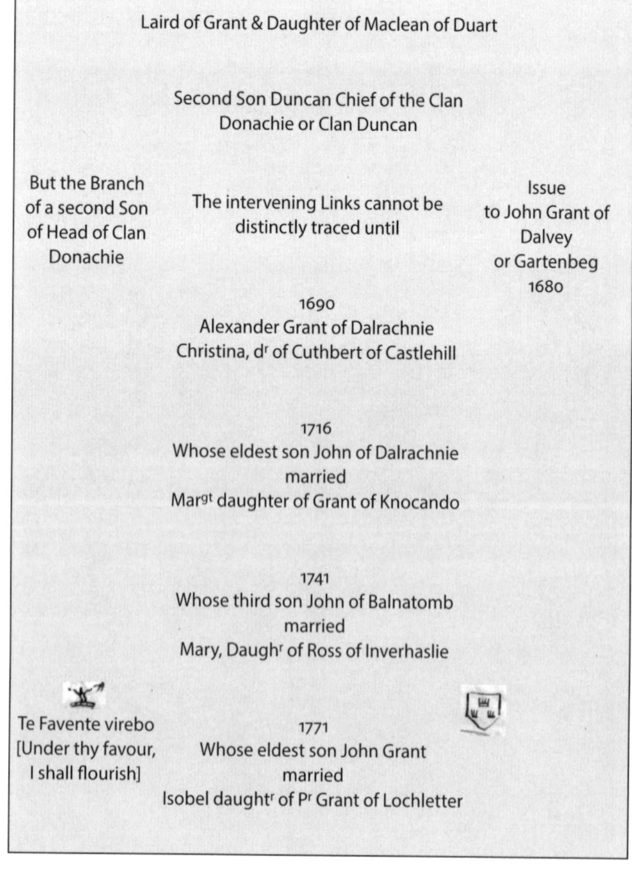
Laird of Grant & Daughter of Maclean of Duart

Second Son Duncan Chief of the Clan
Donachie or Clan Duncan

But the Branch
of a second Son
of Head of Clan
Donachie

The intervening Links cannot be
distinctly traced until

Issue
to John Grant of
Dalvey
or Gartenbeg
1680

1690
Alexander Grant of Dalrachnie
Christina, dr of Cuthbert of Castlehill

1716
Whose eldest son John of Dalrachnie
married
Margt daughter of Grant of Knocando

1741
Whose third son John of Balnatomb
married
Mary, Daughr of Ross of Inverhaslie

Te Favente virebo
[Under thy favour,
I shall flourish]

1771
Whose eldest son John Grant
married
Isobel daughtr of Pr Grant of Lochletter

Laird of Grant. & Daughter of Maclean of Duart

Second Son Duncan Chief of the Clan Donachie or Clan Duncan

But the Brave of a second son of Head of Clan Dunachie

The intervening Links cannot be distinctly traced untill

ancest[illegible] to Jer[illegible] Gran[illegible] Dala[illegible] or Galatl[illegible] 1680

1690

Alexander Grant of Dalrachnie
Christina Dr of Cuthbert of Castlehill

1710

Whose eldest Son John of Dalrachnie
married
Marg^t daughter of Grant of Knocando

1740

Whose third Son John of Balnatomb
married
Mary Daug^tr of Ross of Inverhaslie

Te Favente Virebo.

1770.

Whose eldest Son John Grant
married
Isobel daug^tr of Dr Grant of Lochletter

APPENDIX C

TIMELINE

Date	John Grant's World	World Events
1741	2 December: John born at Ballintomb Farm, Strathspey.	10 April: Austrian army is defeated by Frederick II of Prussia at Mollwitz. British joint expedition against Cartagena in Spanish America fails spectacularly (War of Jenkin's Ear). Staggering casualties among British and American provincial troops. Royal Military Academy established at Woolwich. Two future sons-in-law and the grandson of John Grant will attend. Sir Ludovick Grant elected MP for Elgin and Forres, a seat he holds until 1761, when his son, Sir James, replaces him.
1742	Grant family move to Balmacaan in Glenurquhart where John's father takes up duties as factor to the Laird of Grant. John's uncle, Alexander Grant, 6th Dalrachney, becomes collector of cess (tax) for the Regality of Grant.	13 April: Handel's *Messiah* first performed in Dublin, Ireland. 17 May: Frederick the Great defeats the Austrians at the battle of Chotusitz in Bohemia. Benjamin Franklin invents his Franklin stove.
1743	Balmacaan, Glenurquhart.	27 June: George II and British/Hanoverian forces defeat French at the battle of Dettingen, the last time a British monarch personally leads his troops in battle.
1744	Balmacaan, Glenurquhart.	France formally declares war on Britain (War of the Austrian Succession).
1745	Balmacaan, Glenurquhart.	11 May: Allied army defeated by French at Fontenoy. 19 August: Prince Charles Edward Stuart raises his Royal Standard at Glenfinnan, Scotland, marking the commencement of the most famous and final Jacobite Rising. 21 September: Battle of Prestonpans. Jacobite army defeats British army led by Sir John Cope. 28 November: French and Indian allies raid Saratoga in upstate New York, killing thirty and capturing over 100 prisoners, mostly Dutch settlers.
1746	February: Bonnie Prince Charlie sleeps overnight at Inverlaidnan, home of John's uncle, Alexander Grant, 6th Dalrachney. July: The harrowing of Glenurquhart and "the coming of troopers" at Balmacaan. The Grant family moves to Braelangwell, Ross-shire. July: John's future wife's grandfather, the infamous Alexander Grant of Shewglie, dies imprisoned in Tilbury Fort near London. August: John survives a bout of smallpox.	17 January: Jacobite army defeat British forces at Falkirk Muir. 16 April: Battle of Culloden. Jacobite army defeated and dispersed by Duke of Cumberland's army. 1 August: Act of Proscription bans Highland dress, weapons, and bagpipe music. August-October: Cumberland's forces encamp at Fort Augustus and begin the harrowing of the glens. September: Bonnie Prince Charlie escapes to France from Scotland after five months of pursuit by government forces.

Date	John Grant's World	World Events
1747	John lives at Inverlaidnan in Strathspey with Uncle Alex and attends school in nearby Duthil. 1 October: John's cousin, Lieutenant John Grant (64th Foot), younger son of Dalrachney, killed at the siege of Bergen-op-Zoom in Flanders.	16 January: Sir James Grant, 6th Laird of Grant, dies. Succeeded by his oldest surviving son, Sir Ludovick Grant of Grant. 9 April: Simon Fraser, Lord Lovat, beheaded on Tower Hill for high treason. Last person in Britain to be beheaded.
1748	Inverlaidnan, Strathspey.	14 March: General George Wade dies in London, England. 24 April: War of Austrian Succession ends with Treaty of Aix-le-Chapelle. Construction of Fort George commences at Ardesier, northeast of Inverness, built to pacify the Scottish Highlands in the aftermath of the Jacobite rebellion of 1745.
1751	John boards at Inverness Grammar School. Town garrisoned by James Wolfe's 20th Foot. 2 March: John's future wife, Isobel Grant, born in Glenurquhart.	John Smith & Sons bookshop in Glasgow established, claiming to be the oldest surviving bookseller in the English-speaking world.
1752	25 December: John's father dies suddenly; his mother and sisters move to Inverness.	18 March: The Parliament of Great Britain passes an act to bestow estates forfeited by Jacobites to the Crown and to use the revenue to develop the Scottish Highlands. June: Benjamin Franklin's kite experiment takes place in Philadelphia.
1753	John's future son-in-law, John Johnson Sr., is born at the Tower of London.	7 June: The British Museum is established in London.
1754	John's mother, Mary, dies of apoplexy. John sent by Uncle Alexander to boarding school in Fortrose.	28 May: Battle of Jumonville Glen, Western Pennsylvania. 3 July: George Washington's force defeated by French at Fort Necessity. Expulsion of the Acadians from Nova Scotia and New Brunswick.
1755	Fortrose, Black Isle.	16 June: Capture of Fort Beausejour in Acadia by British. 9 July: Massacre and destruction of Braddock's British-American expedition sent to take Fort Dusquesne. 8 September: Battle of Lake George, French defeated by Sir William Johnson and provincial army.
1756	June: John returns to Strathspey. September: John travels to Aberdeen to attend King's College.	May: Britain declares war on France. Official beginning of the Seven Years' War. June: 1st division of the 42nd Foot (Black Watch) arrive at New York; the regiment will serve in North America for next eleven years. June: British prisoners die in the Black Hole of Calcutta. August: Montcalm and his army besiege and capture three forts at Oswego on Lake Ontario. August: Frederick the Great of Prussia invades Saxony, officially starting the Seven Years' War in Europe.
1757	June: John returns to Inverlaidnan. July: The Laird of Grant, Sir Ludovick, singles him out by name at a clan fair held at Castle Grant. September: John is sent for private tutoring in Tain by his uncle, David Ross, Lord Ankerville.	23 June: Robert Clive's victory at Plassey secures Bengal in India for the British. August: Lord Loudoun's expedition to Louisbourg cancelled. 42nd Foot return to New York from Halifax. 8 August: Siege of Fort William Henry on Lake George by French-Canadian army under Montcalm and a host of Indian allies. A "massacre" occurs the day after the surrender, courtesy of the latter.

Date	John Grant's World	World Events
1758	22 July: John obtains a lieutenant's commission in the newly-raised 2nd Battalion, 42nd Foot. November: John embarks at Greenock for the West Indies.	8 July: 42nd Foot (less the newly-formed 2nd Battalion) participate in the battle of Ticonderoga in North America. Suffer 65 per cent casualties. 22 July: George II grants "Royal" status upon his senior Highland Regiment, the 42nd Foot. 26 July: Successful siege and capture of Louisbourg on Cape Breton Island by Major General Jeffery Amherst. 28 August: Lieutenant Colonel John Bradstreet successfully raids Fort Frontenac (Cataraqui). 14 September: Major James Grant's failed raid against Fort Duquesne at the Forks of the Ohio.
1759	January: John serves in Guadeloupe July: Sails to New York. September-October: Works on Fort Ontario at Oswego. October-November: On the "Battoe Service" between Oswego and Fort Stanwix. October-December: Winter quarters in Albany. Back home in Strathspey, his cousin Gregor Grant dies, the only remaining son and heir of his Uncle Alexander Grant of Dalrachney.	25 January: Robert Burns born. 19 April: Guadeloupe capitulates. 26 July: French surrender Fort Niagara to British after a short siege and their relief force is defeated at the battle of Belle Famille. August: 1st Battalion, 42nd Foot participate in General Amherst's capture of Forts Ticonderoga and Crown Point. 13 September: Battle on the Plains of Abraham. Wolfe and Montcalm killed. 18 September: Quebec capitulates and is garrisoned by British for the winter. 20 November. British naval victory over French at Quiberon Bay.
1760	January-April: Winter quarters in Albany. August-September: John's battalion sets off from Oswego to capture Montreal. September-December: Garrisons Sainte-Geneviève parish on Island of Montreal.	April: French and Canadian forces besiege Quebec under General Lévis. 28 April: The battle of Sillery (Sainte Foy). British army under James Murray defeated and retreats inside Quebec to await relief. Siege lifted following month by Royal Navy. May: 77th Foot (Montgomery's Highlanders) and 1st Foot ("Royals") dispatched to South Carolinas to fight Cherokees. August-September: Amherst's army descends Saint Lawrence River. Montreal capitulates 8 September, effectively completing Britain's conquest of New France, but Seven Years' War continues until 1763. 25 October: George II dies. 26 October: George III crowned, beginning a 60-year reign, one of the longest in British history.
1761	January-April: Winter quarters on Montreal Island. May: Departs for Staten Island, New York via Lake Champlain and Crown Point. June: Arrives at Crown Point and spends six weeks working on the fortifications. July: Travels to Staten Island and prepares for Caribbean campaign. December: Embarks for Barbados with General Robert Monckton's expedition sent to capture Martinique.	October: William Pitt the Elder resigns his ministry after a dismal General Election. December: Spain declares war on Britain. December: General Sir Eyre Coote takes Pondicherry, India from the French.

Date	John Grant's World	World Events
1762	February: John's regiment participates in the capture of Martinique. March: John transfers to the 42nd/44th Foot's composite light infantry company. June: Participates in the landings and siege of Havana. August: Contracts fever, sent back with remnants of his regiment to recover on Long Island.	May: Earl of Bute replaces Duke of Newcastle as prime minister. Land tenure reform in Scotland leads to commencement of the Highland Clearances and sparks massive emigration for next several decades. 13 August: Havana capitulates. Full possession of the city occurs the following day.
1763	John convalesces from sickness on Long Island and considers his future.	10 February: Treaty of Paris ends Seven Years' War. Confirms most of Britain's overseas gains, notably Canada and India. March: Western Indians under Pontiac attack forts in western Pennsylvania, putting the two largest, Forts Detroit and Pitt, under siege. 5-6 August: Composite battalion of 42nd/77th Foot under Colonel Henry Bouquet wins battle of Bushy Run. Fort Pitt relieved 9 August. October: Fort Detroit siege lifted.
1764	2 April: John exchanges onto half-pay with Lieutenant George Rigge, 86th Foot. Returns to Scotland.	July: Colonel Bouquet's punitive expedition against the Ohio Valley Indian tribes commences and is successfully concluded at Muskingum in November with Indians agreeing to restore all hostages and to cease hostilities.
1765	John's uncle, Alexander Grant, now styled of Inverlaidnan, dies, the last male survivor of the Dalrachney Grants.	22 March: To help defray the cost of keeping troops in America, the British Parliament enacts the Stamp Act which taxes printed materials. This act is followed shortly by the Quartering Act, requiring the Thirteen Colonies to provide housing, food and other provisions to British troops on demand. "Sons of Liberty" organize. The seeds of revolution are sown. October: Black Watch contingent under Captain Thomas Stirling take possession of Fort de Chartres in the Illinois country. Grantown-on Spey founded as a planned settlement on a low plateau at Freuchie beside the River Spey by "Good Sir James" Grant of Grant, son of Sir Ludovick.
1766	Glenurquhart.	1 January: James Stuart the "Old Pretender" dies. 18 March: Parliament repeals the Stamp Act and issues the Declaratory Act asserting that the British government had free and total legislative power over the Colonies.
1767	June: 42nd Foot relieved by 17th Foot and sent back to Ireland. Remnants land at Cork, the following month.	Joseph Priestley discovers a method of producing carbonated water and publishes *The History and Present State of Electricity.*
1768	Glenurquhart.	9 January: Philip Astley stages the first modern circus, with acrobats on galloping horses, in London. 10 May: John Wilkes is imprisoned for writing an article for *The North Briton* criticizing King George III of Great Britain. 26 August: James Cook departs from Plymouth on his first voyage of discovery.
1769	Glenurquhart.	James Watt patents steam engine condenser. 1 May: Arthur Wellesley (future Duke of Wellington) born in Dublin, Ireland. 15 August: Napoleon Bonaparte born in Corsica.

Date	John Grant's World	World Events
1770	Glenurquhart.	5 March: Boston Massacre. 29 April: Captain James Cook lands at Botany Bay, Australia. 17 December: Ludwig von Beethoven baptized in Bonn, Germany.
1771	John marries Isobel Grant in Urquhart.	12 July: Captain James Cook completes his first voyage around the world. 15 August: Novelist and poet Sir Walter Scott born. Thomas Pennant publishes *A Tour in Scotland MDCCLXIX.*
1772	28 April: Only daughter, Penuel Grant, born in Glenurquhart.	1 June: David Stewart (later of Garth) born in Perthshire, Scotland, the future author of *Sketches of the Character, Manners, and Present State of the Highlanders of Scotland...* July: James Cook starts his second circumnavigation of the world.
1773	Large numbers of neighbours and families from Glenurquhart, Glenmoriston and Strathglass emigrate to North America to take up lands on the Mohawk River Valley as tenants of Sir William Johnson.	18 March: Clan chieftain, Sir Ludovick Grant, 6th Laird of Grant, dies, and with him, the last vestiges of the old clan system. His son "Good Sir James" becomes 7th Laird. 21 April: Fort Crown Point on Lake Champlain catches fire and burns for several days. It is never rebuilt. 10 May: Parliament passes the Tea Act and East India Company given the monopoly to supply tea to the Thirteen Colonies. August-November: Samuel Johnson tours Western Highlands with friend, James Boswell. Remarks on the "epidemick" of emigration. 16 December: Boston Tea Party.
1774	July: John, his small family and followers go down the Great Glen to Fort William, where they take ship to Loch Doun, Mull. There, they charter the *Moore of Greenock*, arriving New York September-October and take winter lodgings.	March: Montfort Browne appointed governor of the Bahamas. 5 September: First Continental Congress held in Philadelphia. Twelve of Thirteen colonies attend. Joseph Priestley discovers oxygen.
1775	May: John travels up Hudson to Skeneboro to prepare for reception of his family and settlers on his Vermont land grant. Arrested by rebels and imprisoned at Crown Point. June: Escapes to Montreal and interviewed by Sir Guy Carleton. July: Returns to New York to pick up family and returns to the UK to look for employment or commission. August: Makes the rounds in London looking for commission as captain on full pay, or in lieu of that, permission to raise an independent company in the Highlands.	19 April: Battles of Lexington and Concord start the American Revolution. 10 May: Ethan Allen and Green Mountain Boys seize Fort Ticonderoga. A week later they take Crown Point. July: James Cook returns to England after his second circumnavigation of the world. 23 August: George III issues the Proclamation of Rebellion. Declares that the Thirteen colonies are in open rebellion against Great Britain and will be subdued by force. 14 November: Quebec placed under siege by rebels. 31 December: American night assault on Quebec by forces under Richard Montgomery and Benedict Arnold fails.
1776	10 April: Black Watch sails for service in America (without John Grant who is still on half-pay and trying to secure a captain's command in the regulars).	10 January: Thomas Paine publishes *Common Sense.* 3 March: American ships raid New Providence in the Bahamas looking for gunpowder. 9 March: Adam Smith publishes *The Wealth of Nations.* 6 May: Siege of Quebec lifted. Americans retreat to Fort Ticonderoga. 4 July: American Declaration of Independence signed in Philadelphia. Battles of Long Island, Brooklyn, Harlem Heights, Valcour Island, White Plains, Fort Washington, Fort Lee and Trenton fought.

Date	John Grant's World	World Events
1777	April: John ordered to report to commander in chief in New York. Crosses Atlantic with wife and child and settles them on Long Island.	Battles of Princeton, Hubbardton, Saratoga, Bennington, Oriskany, Bennington, Paoli, Germantown, Monmouth, Stony Point and Paulus Hook fought. September: British occupy Philadelphia. December: Continental Army winters at Valley Forge.
1778	25 September: John commissioned senior captain in Provincial Garrison Battalion and deploys with two companies to garrison New Providence, Bahamas. Family returns to Scotland. December: John and his two companies arrive in Nassau to find no preparations have been made for their arrival or quarters provided.	First Relief Act passed by Parliament which enables Roman Catholics in Britain to purchase property, such as land. 23 February: Friedrich Wilhelm von Steuben arrives at Valley Forge to begin training the Continental Army. 11 May: Death of William Pitt the Elder. 28 June: Washington's Continental Army battles British forces under Sir Henry Clinton to a draw near Monmouth, New Jersey.
1779	John clashes with the governor of Bahamas, Montfort Browne, on several issues concerning the garrison, the security of the islands and the governor's complete disregard for the Articles of War. July: After being threatened physically several times by henchmen of the governor, John is forced to write to Lord Germain with backing of other colonial officials that Browne is unfit to govern and associating with "disaffected and infamous Characters."	14 February: Captain James Cook is murdered by natives of Hawaii during his third visit to the islands. June: Spain declares war on Britain. The Great Siege of Gibraltar (fourteenth and last military siege) starts on 24 June. 14 August: John Maxwell appointed the new governor of the Bahamas by George III, and Browne ordered back to England for an Inquiry. 19 August: Harry "Light-horse" Lee attacks Paulus Hook by night. Garrison Battalion commanding officer court martialed for negligence, then acquitted and transferred. October: Major Robert Donkin, 44th Foot, appointed lieutenant colonel commandant of the Garrison Battalion; Captain William Anstruther, late 26th Foot, appointed new major of the Garrison Battalion, over John's head.
1780	January: John accidentally learns that he has been passed over for command of the Garrison Battalion by Sir Henry Clinton following false complaints made by Governor Browne. 8 May: John Maxwell arrives in New Providence to take up governorship of the Bahamas. John Grant learns full extent of why he has been passed over and is ordered to report to Sir Henry Clinton in New York to explain his side of the Browne affair. September: Requests reimbursement for funds expended in the feeding and clothing of his troops while stationed in the Bahamas during a visit to headquarters in New York. October: Granted leave to return home because of sick wife and pressing financial obligations.	16 January: British Admiral Sir George Rodney defeats a Spanish fleet at Cape Saint Vincent. 12 May: Charleston, South Carolina is taken by British forces. June: Gordon Riots erupt in London, public anger against Catholics one of the key causes of unrest. July: Hyder Ali begins his campaign against British holdings in India.
1781	On leave.	William Herschel announces discovery of Uranus, expanding the known boundaries of the solar system for the first time in modern history. 19 October: Cornwallis surrenders to Americans at Yorktown virtually ending Britain's efforts to realistically subdue America.

Date	John Grant's World	World Events
1782	February: John ordered back to the Bahamas. March: Applies to General Amherst for permission to stay in Britain and recruit a company in the Highlands, or be allowed to rejoin regulars as a lieutenant. Request denied. April: Returns to New York where he picks up new drafts and proceeds to the Bahamas. 8 May: Made prisoner on capitulation of the Islands to the Spanish. 4 October: Lands at Harwich by Spanish transports. He and his men garrison Landguard Fort.	9-12 April: British defeat French fleet in the West Indies at the four-day battle of the Saintes. 22 April: Captain General Juan Manuel Cagigal y Monserrat, at the head of a joint Spanish and America armada, leaves Havana bound for the Bahamas. 5 May: Cagigal's force arrives at New Providence. Bahamas capitulate 8 May. 1 July: Proscription Act repealed, thus restoring the wearing of the belted plaid and the carrying of weapons in Scotland.
1783	10 October: John out of the army on captain's half pay as the Royal Garrison Battalion (now on regular establishment) disbanded.	February: Franco-Spanish siege of Gibraltar fails. 3 September: Treaty of Versailles formally ends American War of Independence; Britain cedes all lands west to Mississippi and recognizes the United States as an independent nation. October: First piloted flight of a hot air balloon (created by the Montgolfier brothers in France). 19 December: William Pitt the Younger begins his ministry.
1784	Half-pay.	India Act of 1784 reorganizes the East India Company.
1785	Half-pay.	1 January: First issue of the *Daily Universal Register* (later known as *The Times)* is published in London. 6 July: The dollar is unanimously chosen by Congress as the new unit of currency for the United States. Coal gas is used for illumination for the first time. Napoleon Bonaparte becomes a lieutenant in the French Royalist artillery.
1786	13 September: John returns to army full time from half-pay and given command of the North British Invalid Company in Berwick-on-Tweed.	1 August: German astronomer Caroline Herschel, sister of William Herschel, discovers a comet (the first to be discovered by a woman). 17 August: Frederick the Great of Prussia dies. John Molson founds his first brewery in Montreal, Canada.
1787	Berwick-on-Tweed.	George III shows first signs of instability. 17 September: The United States Constitution is created by the Constitutional Convention in Philadelphia (ratified 21 June 1788).
1788	Berwick-on-Tweed.	20 January: First Fleet carrying British convicts arrives in Botany Bay, Australia. 31 January: Charles Edward Stuart, "Bonnie Prince Charlie," dies in exile.
1789	Berwick-on-Tweed.	30 April: George Washington inaugurated as first president of the United States in New York. 14 July: Storming of the Bastille symbolizes the outbreak of the French Revolution.
1790	Berwick-on-Tweed.	8 January: President George Washington delivers his first State of the Union address to the assembled Congress in New York City. 17 April: Benjamin Franklin dies. Forth and Clyde Canal opens.

Date	John Grant's World	World Events
1791	13 July: John transfers to command of the Guernsey Invalid Company on isle of Alderney, closest of the Channel Islands to France.	James Boswell's *Life of Johnson* published. Thomas Paine publishes volume 1 of *Rights of Man.*
1792	Alderney.	Thomas Paine publishes volume 2 of *Rights of Man.* 21 May: Eruption of the Unzen Volcano in Japan kills 15,000 people when the collapse of an underground lava dome triggers a mega-tsunami in Japan's worst-ever volcanic disaster. 21 September: Monarchy abolished in France. Inverness Grammar School closes. Replaced by Inverness Royal Academy.
1793	July: John returns to England with family to take up command of one of the Portsmouth Invalid companies. Relocates family to Portsmouth. Penuel marries an officer of the Royal Engineers, Captain Lieutenant John Johnson.	1 February: Revolutionary France declares war on Britain. Louis XVI executed; Siege of Toulon. Catholic Relief Act passed by Irish Parliament allows some Irish Catholics to vote and makes them eligible for civil service appointments.
1794	John's grandson, John Johnson Jr., born to Penuel Grant and John Johnson Sr. in Portsea, Hampshire. John's son-in-law, Captain Lieutenant Johnson of the Royal Engineers, serves in the Low Countries with the Duke of York. 12 November: John and his family, including Penuel and grandson, relocate to Kingston upon Hull, where he takes up command of one of the two Invalid companies stationed there.	April: Pitt the Younger clamps down on political radicalism: suspends *habeas corpus.* 1 June: The Glorious First of June sees Admiral Richard Howe defeat French fleet. Thomas Paine publishes *The Age of Reason.*
1795	May: Son-in-law Captain Lieutenant Johnson returns from the Continent. June: Penuel and grandson relocate to Gosport where Johnson is posted and looking for a house. November: Captain Lieutenant Johnson dies suddenly in Gosport, leaving Penuel Grant pregnant. She moves back with her parents in Kingston upon Hull, where John is captain of an invalid company stationed there.	16 January: Holland occupied by the French. 7 April: France adopts the metric system. 19 May: Death in Auchinleck, Scotland, of James Boswell, biographer of Dr. Johnston. 21 September: Protestant forces defeat Catholic troops in Loughgall, Ireland, at the battle of the Diamond, leading to the foundation of the Orange Order.
1796	May: John's granddaughter, Isabella Grant Johnson, is born, never having seen her father.	21 July: Robert Burns dies in Dumfries. East India Company forces are reorganized in India again. French attempt to invade Ireland fails.
1797	10 July: Daughter Penuel remarries, wedding Lieutenant Harcourt Forde Holcombe, RA, in Drypool, Hull.	14 February: British naval victory at Cape Saint Vincent. 3 August: John's old commander in chief, Lord Amherst dies. 11 October: British naval victory at Camperdown over Dutch fleet.
1798	Kingston upon Hull.	May-September: United Irishmen inspired by American and French revolutions stage an uprising against British rule in Ireland lasting from May to September. All hopes extinguished when Royal Navy intercept French troops attempting to land in Donegal. 1 July: Napoleon occupies Egypt. 1-3 August: Admiral Horatio Nelson wins a decisive naval victory over the French at the Nile.

Date	John Grant's World	World Events
1799	Kingston upon Hull.	Income tax is introduced. April-May: Tipu Sultan defeated and killed by the British at siege of Seringapatam in India. 14 December: George Washington dies at Mount Vernon. Napoleon Bonaparte orders ten days mourning in France.
1800	Kingston upon Hull.	1 August: Act of Union brings about parliamentary union of England and Ireland. William Herschel discovers infrared radiation.
1801	Kingston upon Hull.	8 March: British land at Aboukir and liberate Egypt. 2 April: British fleet under Nelson defeat a Danish fleet at Copenhagen.
1802	December: John retires onto full pay and returns to Scotland.	27 March: Short-lived Peace of Amiens signed. Fourteen months later, all the signatories are back at war.
1803	Drynie, Black Isle (near Munlochy).	18 May: Britain declares war on France following the breakdown of the Treaty of Amiens. 23 September: The future Duke of Wellington defeats a larger Maratha army near Assaye in western India.
1804	Drynie, Black Isle.	21 February: The first steam locomotive makes its successful run in South Wales. 14 May: Napoleon declares himself Emperor of France.
1805	Drynie, Black Isle.	21 October: While Nelson's decisive victory off Cape Trafalgar secures Britain from a French invasion, the admiral dies of wounds received on his quarterdeck. All Britain mourns. 2 December: Napoleon defeats a larger Russian and Austrian army at Austerlitz.
1806	Drynie, Black Isle.	23 January: Death of William Pitt the Younger. July: British raid Calabria, Italy; battle of Maida
1807	Drynie, Black Isle.	25 March: Parliament passes the Slave Trade Act which outlaws the slave trade, but not slavery itself. Abolition of the slave trade throughout the British Empire will not occur until 1833. 22 June: HMS *Leopard* fires on USS *Chesapeake* when latter refuses to be searched for Royal Navy deserters. Major diplomatic incident. November: France invades Portugal, England's oldest ally. The war on the Iberian Peninsula would last until Napoleon was defeated in 1814.
1808	31 October: Grandson, John Johnson, admitted to Woolwich as a gentleman cadet in the Royal Artillery.	France turns on Spain, previously its ally. July: Wellington starts his Peninsular Campaign. 21 August: Wellington beats French army at battle of Vimeiro, effectively ending the first French invasion of Portugal.
1809	Drynie, Black Isle.	January: British defeated at Corunna, Spain. 12 February: Abraham Lincoln is born in a one-room log cabin at Sinking Spring Farm near Hodgenville, Kentucky. 27-28 July: British defeat French at Talavera, Spain.
1810	Drynie, Black Isle.	Second invasion of Portugal by French. Stymied by Duke of Wellington's forces retiring behind the defensive lines of Torres near Lisbon. George III's mental illness recurs.

Date	John Grant's World	World Events
1811	Drynie, Black Isle.	5 February: Regency declared: future George IV becomes Prince Regent. May: Battles of Fuentes de Oñoro and Albuera fought.
1812	Drynie, Black Isle.	7-20 January: British capture fortress city of Ciudad Rodrigo. March-April: Wellington openly weeps at the carnage in the breach after the storming and capture of Badajoz on 7 April. 18 June: War of 1812 with the United States commences. 24 June: Napoleon leads Grande Armée into Mother Russia. 22 July: Duke of Wellington defeats French at Salamanca. 7 September: Napoleon tactically defeats Russian army at Borodino but achieves only strategic stalemate with the capture of Moscow one week later. October: Retreat from Moscow and destruction of the Grande Armée. 15 August: First commercial steamboat service from Glasgow to Greenock in operation.
1813	Drynie, Black Isle.	27 April: American forces capture York (Toronto), but the explosion of a powder magazine kills many of them, including Brigadier Zebulon Pike. Americans burn York. 21 June: Wellington wins battle of Vittoria, effectively ending French occupation of Spain.
1814	Drynie, Black Isle.	11 April: Napoleon abdicates. Exiled to Elba. 7 July: First publication of Walter Scott's *Waverley* novels. 25 July: British and American forces fight to a tactical stalemate at the battle of Lundy's Lane, fought within earshot of Niagara Falls, one of the bloodiest battles of the war, and one of the deadliest battles ever fought in Canada. December: Treaty of Ghent signed formally ending the War of 1812 with the United States, but fighting continues at the battle of New Orleans in the New Year.
1815	Drynie, Black Isle. John now blind in one eye.	18 February: War of 1812 ends. 26 February: Napoleon escapes from Elba. Returns to France. 18 June: Wellington defeats Napoleon at the battle of Waterloo.
1816	John contacted by Colonel David Stewart, who is collecting information and anecdotes of the Black Watch in the Seven Years' War and American War of Independence.	20 February: Gioachino Rossini's opera buffa *The Barber of Seville* premières at the Teatro Argentina in Rome. 22 February: Adam Ferguson, former Black Watch chaplain, Scottish philosopher and father of modern sociology dies.
1817	Granddaughter Isabella Johnson, marries Dr. James Errol Gray at Inverness.	A typhus epidemic occurs in Edinburgh and Glasgow. *The Scotsman* newspaper first published.
1818	Blervie, Forres.	6 January: Treaty of Mandeswar brings an end to the Third Anglo-Maratha War in India, extending the control of the British East India Company over territory containing some 180 million Indians. 11 March: Mary Shelley's *Frankenstein* is published anonymously in London.

Date	John Grant's World	World Events
1819	Blervie, Forres.	16 August: The Peterloo Massacre in Manchester. British cavalry charge large crowds numbering 60,000 gathered to demand parliamentary reform. 26 December: Duke of Wellington made Master General of Ordnance.
1820	Dr. Gray, husband to granddaughter Isabella Johnson, dies suddenly at the age of 30, leaving his widow with a young son.	29 January: George III dies. George IV crowned King of England.
1821	Blervie, Forres.	March: War of Greek Independence starts eleven years of conflict to end the Ottoman Empire's occupation of Greece. 24 June: Battle of Carabobo: Simón Bolívar wins Venezuela's independence from Spain. 27 September: The Army of the Three Guarantees enters Mexico City, and the following day proclaims Mexico's independence from Spain.
1822	Grandson John Johnson marries Emily Anderson.	First publication of Stewart of Garth's *Sketches of the Character, Manners, and Present State of the Highlanders of Scotland...* August: Visit of King George IV to Scotland organized by Sir Walter Scott. Caledonian Canal between Inverness and Fort William opened.
1823	Blervie, Forres.	Work begins on the British Museum in London, designed by Robert Smirke, and the Altes Museum in Berlin, designed by Karl Friedrich Schinkel.
1824	Blervie, Forres.	15-21 November: Great Fire of Edinburgh, starting in Old Assembly Close, kills eleven residents and two firemen, destroying twenty-four tenements leaving 400 families homeless.
1825	Blervie, Forres.	2 September: The world's first modern railway, the Stockton and Darlington Railway, opens in England. 26 October: The Erie Canal opens, providing passage from Albany, New York to Buffalo and Lake Erie.
1826	Granddaughter Isabella (*née* Johnson) Gray remarries, wedding John Anderson Robertson at Urquhart, Scotland.	First publication of *Last of the Mohicans* by James Fenimore Cooper. 4 July: Former United States presidents Thomas Jefferson and John Adams both die on the 50th Anniversary of the signing of the United States Declaration of Independence.
1827	1 February: Grandson John Johnson retires on half-pay from Royal Artillery to start medical training. John's son-in-law, Colonel Harcourt Forde Holcombe, RA retires on half pay. He and wife, Penuel (*née* Grant, Johnson), settle in Aberdeen.	7 January: Sandford Fleming, future Canadian engineer and surveyor, born in Kirkcaldy. Georg Ohm pioneers his theories of electricity, marking the beginning of circuit theory and modern applications of electric current. George Ballantine sets up a grocery store in Edinburgh, the predecessor of Ballantine's whisky blenders. 26 March: Ludwig von Beethoven dies in Vienna.
1828	24 January: John, "the last of his line," dies. His descendants believe his remains were interred in the graveyard of the original Forres Parish Kirk. His grandson, John Johnson Jr., is his sole beneficiary.	22 January: Duke of Wellington resigns as field marshal and commander of the Army to become Prime Minister of Great Britain.

BIBLIOGRAPHY

Primary sources

1. Manuscripts

Ballindalloch Castle, Banffshire, Scotland.
Macpherson-Grant Papers.

Archives of Ontario.
MSS 497: Gilkison Family Papers, 1786-1910.

British Library, London.
Sir Fredrick Haldimand Papers: 21673, 21728-29.
Bouquet Collection: 21640.
Add. MSS 21,634.

Huntingdon Library, San Marino, California.
AB: Abercromby Papers.
LO: Loudoun Papers.

John Carter Brown Library, Brown University, Providence, Rhode Island
"Journal of the Proceedings of the 35th Regiment of Foot," b6123117

Kent History and Library Centre (formerly Centre for Kentish Studies), Maidstone, Kent.
U1350: Amherst Family Papers.

Library of Congress, Washington, D.C.
Peter Force Collection.
James Grant Papers.

Library and Archives Canada.
Bouquet Papers.
MG 11: Colonial Office Papers.
MG 13: War Office Papers.
MG 18-M: Northcliffe Collection.
MG 23: Frederick Mackenzie Papers.

Moray Council Archives and Local Heritage Centre, Elgin, Moray, Scotland.
"Family and Military Papers of Captain John Grant and Captain John Johnson of Forres, 1777-1888" (Reference DJQ).

National Portrait Gallery, London

New York Archives, Department of State.
Military Patents, 1764-1797, Series A0447.

Public Record Office of Northern Ireland.
Perceval-Maxwell Papers.

Register House Series Microfilms.
RH 4/77: Journal of Lieutenant John Grant, 42nd Foot, 1758-62.

Stewart Museum, Montreal.
William Forbes Papers.

The National Archives, Kew, Surrey, England.
PRO 30/55: Headquarters Papers of the British Army in America.
Home Office Papers.
42: George III.
Probate Records.
11/1739.
SP 44: Secretaries of State: Correspondence, commissions and warrants.
Colonial Office Papers.
CO 5: America and West Indies, 1606-1807.
War Office Papers.
1: In-Letters.
4: Out-Letters, Secretary at War.
12: Muster Books and Pay Lists.
17: Returns.
25: General Registers.
34: Amherst Papers.
72/2: Judge Advocate General, Rules, etc., Articles of War.
116: Out-Pension Records, Royal Hospital, Chelsea.

The National Archives of Scotland, Edinburgh.
Gifts and Deposits.
GD 24: Abercairny Muniments.

William L. Clements Library, Ann Arbor, Michigan.
Jeffery Amherst Papers.
Sir Henry Clinton Papers.
Thomas Gage Papers.
Germain Papers.
Frederick MacKenzie Papers.

2. Printed original sources

Andrews, R.J. ed. *The Journals of Jeffery Amherst 1757-1763*, 2 vols (East Lansing, 2015).

Askwith, W.H. ed. *List of Officers of the Royal Regiment of Artillery from the Year 1716 to the Year 1899* (London, 1900).

Boswell, James. *Journal of a Tour to the Hebrides*, Frederick A. Pottie and Charles H. Bennett, eds. (New York, 1936).

———. *The Earlier Years, 1740-1769*, Frederick A. Pottie, ed. (New York, 1966).

———. *The Life of Samuel Johnson* (London, 1791).

British Army Lists.

Burt, Edward. *Letters from the North of Scotland.* vol I (Edinburgh, 1876).

Callaghan, E.B. and Fernow, B., eds. *Documents Relative to the Colonial History of the State of New York.* 15 vols (Albany, 1853-87).

Chapman, E.J. and McCulloch, I.M., eds. *A Bard of Wolfe's Army: James Thompson, Gentleman Volunteer, 1733-1830* (Montreal, 2010).

Commission Books.

Doughty, A.G., ed. *An Historical Journal of the Campaigns in North America for the Years 1757, 1758, 1759, and 1760 by Captain John Knox*, 3 vols (Toronto: The Champlain Society, 1914).

Edwards, R.F. *Roll of Officers of the Corps of Royal Engineers from 1660 to 1898* (Chatham, England, 1898).

Gardiner, Captain Richard. *An Account of the Expedition to the West Indies, against Martinico, With the Reduction of Guadelupe, And Other the Leeward Islands; Subject to the French King, 1759* (Birmingham, 1762).

Grant, Anne MacVicar. *Memoirs of an American Lady* (London, 1808).

Grant, Elizabeth. *Memoirs of a Highland Lady 1797-1827* (London, 1898).

Gruber, Ira D., ed. *John Peeble's American War: The Diary of a Scottish Grenadier, 1776-1782* (Mechanicsburg, PA, 1998).

Historical Manuscripts Commission. *Report on American Manuscripts in the Royal Institution of Great Britain*, vol 29, No. 169.

Hervey, William. *Journals of the Hon. William Hervey, in North America and Europe from 1755 to 1814; with Order Books at Montreal, 1760-1763* (Bury St. Edmunds, 1906).

James, A.P., ed. *Writings of General John Forbes Relating to his Service in North America* (Menasha, 1938).

Johnson, Samuel. *A Journey to the Western Isles of Scotland* (London, 1816).

Kane, J., and W.H. Askwith, eds. *List of Officers of the Royal Regiment of Artillery from the year 1716 to the year 1899* (London, 1900).

Kay, John. *A Series of Original Portraits and Caricature Etchings: With Biographical Sketches & Illustrative Anecdotes* (Edinburgh, 1877).

Kemble, Stephen. *The Kemble Papers.* 2 vols. Collections of the NY Historical Society ..., (New York, 1884-85).

Kimball, G.S., ed. *The Correspondence of William Pitt, when Secretary of State, with Colonial Governors and Military and Naval Commanders in America*, 2 vols (London, 1906, reprint New York, 1969).

Kirk[wood], Robert. *"Through So Many Dangers": The Memoirs and Adventures of Robert Kirk, Late of the Royal Highland Regiment*, edited by Ian McCulloch and Tim Todish (Limerick, 1775, reprint New York, 2004).

Ledward, K.H., ed. *Journals of the Board of Trade and Plantations*: vol 14, January 1776-May 1782 (H.M. Stationary Office, London, 1938).

Legge, William. *The Manuscripts of the Earl of Dartmouth,* vol 2, American Papers (London, 1895).

Mackintosh, Charles Fraser, ed. *Invernessiana: Contributions toward a History of the Town & Parish of Inverness, from 1160 to 1599* (Inverness, 1875).

———. *Letters of Two Centuries: Chiefly Connected with Inverness and the Highlands* (Inverness, 1890).

MacLeod, Rev. Walter, ed. *A List of the Persons Concerned in the Rebellion Transmitted to the Commissions of Excise ... in Obedience to a General Letter of 7th May 1746 ...* (Edinburgh, Scottish History Society, 1890).

Mante, Thomas. *The History of the Late War in North-America and the Islands of the West-Indies* (London, 1772, reprint New York, 1970).

Millar, Alexander Hastie. *A Selection of Scottish Forfeited Estates Papers* (Edinburgh, 1909).

Moore, Frank, ed. *Diary of the American Revolution*, vol 2 (New York, 1850).

Pargellis, Stanley M., ed. *Military Affairs in North America 1758-1763: Selected Documents from the Cumberland Papers in Windsor Castle* (London and New York, 1936).

Pennant, Thomas. *A Tour in Scotland MDCCLXIX* (London, 1776).

Pouchot, Pierre. *Memoirs on the Late War in North America between France and England,* M. Cardy, trans., B.L. Dunnigan, ed. (Youngstown, 1994).

St. Andrews Church Roster, Charlotte County, Nova Scotia.

Slezer, John. *Theatrum Scotiae, Containing the Prospects of their Majesties Castles and Palaces...* (London, 1693)

Steuart, John. *The Letterbook of Bailie John Steuart of Inverness, 1715-1752* (Edinburgh, 1915).

Stevens, Sylvester E. *et al*, eds. *The Papers of Colonel Henry Bouquet*, vol III (Harrisburg, 1976).
Sullivan, James, *et al*, eds. *The Papers of Sir William Johnson*, 14 vols (Albany, 1921-1965).
Todish, T.J. *The Annotated and Illustrated Journals of Major Robert Rogers* (Purple Mountain Press, 2002).
Webster, J.C. ed. *The Journal of Jeffery Amherst: Recording the Military Career of General Amherst in America from 1758 to 1763* (Toronto, 1931).
Willson, Beckles, ed. *The Life and Letters of James Wolfe* (London, 1909).

Newspapers and periodicals
Aberdeen Journal: 1774.
Annual Register: A Record of World Events: 1758-1764.
Blackwood's Edinburgh Magazine: 1824; 1828.
Edinburgh Advertiser: 1773.
Edinburgh Evening Courant: 1773.
Gentleman's Magazine: 1757-1764; 1800; 1822; 1828; 1830.
London Gazette: 1747.
London Magazine: 1757.
New-York Gazette: 1760-61.
Pennsylvania Gazette: 1758-1764.
Royal American Gazette: 1778.
Scots Magazine: 1739; 1747; 1786.
Sydney Herald: 1839-40.
Weekly Magazine or Edinburgh Amusement: 1774.

Secondary sources

1. Books
Adams, Ian and Somerville, Meredyth. *Cargoes of Despair and Hope: Scottish Emigration to North America 1603-1803* (Edinburgh, 1993).
Alden, J.R. *General Gage in America* (Baton Rouge, 1948).
Anderson, Fred. *Crucible of War: The Seven Years' War and the Fate of Empire in British North America, 1754-1766* (New York, 2000).
Anderson, P.J. *Major Alpin's Ancestors and Descendants* (Aberdeen, 1904).
———. *The Grammar School and Royal Academy of Inverness...* (Inverness, 1907).
Axelrod, Alan. *The Real History of the American Revolution: A New Look at the Past* (New York, 2007).
Bellico, Russell. *Chronicles of Lake George: Journeys in War and Peace* (Fleischmanns, NY, 1995).
Bradley, A.G. *Sir Guy Carleton* (Toronto, 1907).
Brander, Michael. *The Scottish Highlanders and their Regiments* (Haddington, 1996).
Brumwell, Stephen. *Redcoats: The British Soldier and the War in the Americas, 1755-1763* (Cambridge, 2002).
Buckley, R.N. *The British Army in the West Indies: Society and the Military in the Revolutionary Age* (Gainesville, FL, 1998).
Bumsted, J.M. *The People's Clearance: Highland Emigration to British North America, 1770-1815* (Edinburgh, 1982).
Burt, Edward. *Burt's Letters from the North of Scotland*, vol 1 (Edinburgh, 1876).
Butler, Jon. *Becoming America: The Revolution before 1776* (Cambridge, 2000).
Butler, Lewis. *The Annals of the King's Royal Rifle Corps, "The Royal Americans,"* vol I (London, 1913).

Campbell, Alexander V. *The Royal American Regiment: An Atlantic Microcosm, 1755-1772* (Univ. of Oklahoma Press, 2010).
Campey, Lucille H. *After the Hector: The Scottish Pioneers of Nova Scotia and Cape Breton 1773-1852* (Toronto, 2007).
Carp, Benjamin L. *Rebels Rising: Cities and the American Revolution* (Oxford, 2007).
Chambers, Robert. *Lives of Illustrious and Distinguished Scotsmen, from the Earliest Period to the Present Time, Arranged in Alphabetical Order, and Forming a Complete Scottish Biographical Dictionary,* vol 4 (Glasgow, 1841).
Clyde, Robert. *From Rebel to Hero: The Image of the Highlander, 1755-1830* (East Linton, 1995).
Cokayne, George E. *Complete Baronetage* (Gloucester, 1983).
Colley, Linda. *Britons: Forging the Nation, 1707-1837* (New Haven, 1992).
Craton, Michael and Saunders, Gail. *Islanders in the Stream: A History of the Bahamian People,* 2 vols (Athens, GA, 1992).
Cubbison, Douglas R. *All Canada in the Hands of the British: General Jeffery Amherst and the 1760 Campaign to Conquer New France* (Univ. of Oklahoma Press, 2014).
Cuneo, John R. *Robert Rogers of the Rangers* (New York, 1959, reprint, 1988).
Duane, William. *A Military Dictionary…* (Philadelphia, 1810).
Dunbar, John Telfer. *History of Highland Dress, a Definitive Study of the History of Scottish Costume and Tartan, both Civil and Military, including Weapons* (Edinburgh, 1962).
Dictionary of Canadian Biography, Toronto.
Dictionary of National Biography, London, England.
Devine, T.M. *The Scottish Nation, 1700-2000* (London, 1999).
Donkin, Major Robert. *Military Collections and Remarks* (New York, 1777).
Dornfest, Walter T. *Military Loyalists of the American Revolution: Officers and Regiments, 1775-1783* (Jefferson, NC, 2011).
Doughty, A.G., ed. *The Siege of Quebec and the Battle of the Plains of Abraham*, 6 vols (Quebec, 1901).
Dowd, G.E. *War Under Heaven: Pontiac, the Indian Nations, and the British Empire* (Baltimore, 2002).
Dunnigan, Brian L. *Siege - 1759: The Campaign Against Niagara* (Youngstown, NY, 1986).
Ferling, John E. *A Leap in the Dark: The Struggle to Create the American Republic* (Oxford University Press, 2003).
Field, Cyril. *Britain's Sea Soldiers: A History of the Royal Marines and Their Predecessors and of Their Services in Action, Ashore and Afloat, and upon Sundry Other Occasions of Moment* (Liverpool, 1924).
Fischer, Hackett. *Paul Revere's Ride* (Oxford University Press, 1994).
Flexner, James Thomas. *Lord of the Mohawks: A Biography of Sir William Johnson* (Boston, 1979).
Forbes, Archibald. *The Black Watch: The Record of an Historic Regiment* (London, 1896).
Ford, Worthington Chauncey. *British Officers Serving in America 1754-1774, Compiled from the Army Lists* (Boston, 1894, reprint Oldwick, New Jersey, 1999).
Forsyth, Rev. W. *In the Shadow of the Cairngorm: Chronicles of the United Parishes of Abernethy and Kincardine* (Inverness, 1900).
Fortescue, J.W. *A History of the British Army*, vol II (London, 1899-1930).
Fraser, Sarah. *The Last Highlander: Scotland's Most Notorious Clan-Chief, Rebel and Double-Agent* (London, 2012).
Fraser, William. *The Chiefs of Grant*, 2 vols (Edinburgh, 1883).
———. *The Chiefs of Colquhoun and Their Country*, vol I (Edinburgh, 1869).
Frégault, Guy. *La Guerre de la Conquête* (Montreal,1975).
Fremont-Barnes, Gregory. *The Jacobite Rebellion 1745-46* (Oxford, 2011).
Fuller, J.F.C. *British Light Infantry in the Eighteenth Century* (London, 1925).

Gilbert, J.A. *The Change, or The Passage from Death unto Life: A Memoir of Lieut.-Col. Holcombe* (Binns and Goodwon, 1847).
Gipson, L.H. *The British Empire before the American Revolution*, vol 7: The Great War for the Empire: The Victorious Years, 1758-1760 (New York, 1967).
Graham, Ian Charles Cargill. *Colonists from Scotland: Emigration to North America, 1707-1783* (Ithaca, NY, 1956).
Grant, Alistair. *General James Grant of Ballindalloch* 1720-1806 (London, 1930).
Grant, Francis J. *The Grants of Corrimony* (Berwick, 1885, privately printed).
Graves, Donald E. *Fighting for Canada: Seven Battles* (Toronto, 2000).
Haldane, J.A.L. *The Haldanes of Gleneagles* (Edinburgh, 1929).
Halsey, Francis Whiting. *The Old New York Frontier: Its Wars with Indians and Tories, Its Missionary Schools, Pioneers and Land Titles, 1614-1800* (New York, 1901).
Hibbert, Christopher. *Redcoats and Rebels: The American Revolution through British Eyes* (New York, 2002).
Houlding, John A. *Fit for Service: The Training of the British Army, 1715-1795* (Oxford, 1981).
Jennings, Francis. *Empire of Fortune: Crowns, Colonies & Tribes in the Seven Years War in America* (New York, 1988).
Jones, R.J. *A History of the 15th (East Yorkshire) Regiment ...* (Beverly, Yorkshire, 1958).
Journal of the Society for Army Historical Research (Hendon, England).
Keltie, Sir John Scott. *A History of the Scottish Regiments, Scottish Highlands and the Highland Clans and Regiments*, 8 vols (Edinburgh, 1889).
Laffin, John. *Scotland the Brave: The Story of the Scottish Soldier* (London, 1963).
Lees, J. Cameron. *A History of the County of Inverness (Mainland)* (Edinburgh, 1897).
Leslie, Major John Henry (RA). *The History of Landguard Fort in Suffolk* (London, 1898).
Lewis, James A. *Neptune's Militia: the frigate South Carolina during the American Revolution* (Kent State University Press, 1999).
Linklater, Eric and Andros. *The Black Watch: The History of the Royal Highland Regiment* (London, 1977).
Long, J.C. *Lord Jeffery Amherst: A Soldier of the King* (New York, 1933).
Lossing, Benson J. *The Pictorial Fieldbook of the Revolution*, 2 vols (New York, 1859 and 1860).
Mahon, Major General R.H. *Life of General the Hon. James Murray* (London, 1921).
Macdonald, M.A. *By the Banks of the Ness* (Edinburgh, 1982).
MacKay, Donald. *Scotland Farewell: The People of the Hector* (Toronto, 1980).
Mackay, William. *Urquhart and Glenmoriston: Olden Times in a Highland Parish* (Inverness, 1893).
Mackenzie, Alexander. *History of the Munros of Fowlis: with genealogies of the principal families of the name to which are added those of Lexington and New England* (Inverness, 1898).
MacLean, J.P. *An Historical Account of the Settlements of Scotch Highlanders in America* (Glasgow, 1900).
MacLeod, D. Peter. *The Canadian Iroquois and the Seven Years' War* (Toronto, 1996).
MacLeod, Norman, and Dewar, Daniel. *Dictionary of the Gaelic Language* (Edinburgh, 1909).
McConnell, Michael N. *Army & Empire: British Soldiers on the American Frontier 1758-1775* (Lincoln, NE, 2004).
McCulloch, I.M. *Sons of the Mountains: The Highland Regiments in the French & Indian War, 1756-1767*. 2 vols (Purple Mountain Press, 2006).
———. *Highlander in the French-Indian War: 1756-67* (Osprey, 2008).
McCulloch, Ian and Todish, Tim. *British Light Infantryman, North America 1757-63* (Oxford, 2004).
McKillop, A. *More Fruitful than the Soil: Army, Empire and the Scottish Highlands, 1715-1815* (East Lothian, 2000).
Miller, James. *Inverness* (Edinburgh, 2004).

Morton, Doris. *Philip Skene of Skenesborough* (New York, 1959).
Nelson, Paul. *General James Grant: Scottish Soldier and Royal Governor of East Florida* (Gainesville, 1993).
Newton, Michael. "*We're Indians Sure Enough*": *The Legacy of the Scottish Highlanders in the United States* (Auburn, NH, 2001).
Norman, C.B. *Battle Honours of the British Army* (London, 1911).
Oates, Jonathan. *Sweet William or The Butcher: the Duke of Cumberland and the '45* (Pen and Sword, South Yorkshire, 2008).
Pargellis, Stanley M. *Lord Loudoun in North America* (New Haven, 1933).
———. *Military Affairs in North America, 1748-1765: Selected Documents from the Cumberland Papers in Windsor Castle* (Hamden, 1969).
Parkman, Francis. *Montcalm and Wolfe*, 2 vols (London, 1899).
Paul, Sir James Balfour, ed. *The Scots Peerage...* (Edinburgh, 1904-14).
Pelham, Camden. *The Chronicles of Crime; or the New Newgate Calendar...*, vol 1 (London, 1887).
Platts, Una. *19th-Century New Zealand Artists: A Guide and Handbook* (New Zealand, 1980).
Pollard, Tony. *Culloden: The History and Archaeology of the Last Clan Battle* (Barnsley, 2009).
Prebble, John. *The Highland Clearances* (Harmondsworth, 1963).
———. *Glencoe: The Story of the Massacre* (New York, 1966).
———. *Culloden* (London, 1961).
———. *Mutiny: Highland Regiments in Revolt 1743-1804* (Harmondsworth, 1975).
Reid, Stuart. *Culloden Moor, 1746: the death of the Jacobite cause* (Oxford, 2002).
Reynolds, P.R. *Guy Carleton: a biography* (New York, 1980).
Rocque, Mary Ann. *A Set of Plans and Forts in America Reduced from Actual Surveys* (London, 1763).
Robertson, James Irvine. *The First Highlander: Major-General David Stewart of Garth, C.B.* (East Linton, 1988).
Sadler, John. *Culloden: Last Charge of the Highland Clans 1746* (Stroud, 2008).
Schofield, Victoria. *The Highland Furies: The Black Watch 1739-1899*, vol 1 (London, 2012).
Shy, John. *Towards Lexington: The Role of the British Army in the Coming of the American Revolution* (Princeton, 1965).
Skaggs, David C. and Nelson, Larry L. *The Sixty Years' War for the Great Lakes, 1754-1814* (East Lansing, 2001).
Smelser, Marshall T. *The Campaign for the Sugar Islands, 1759: A Study of Amphibious Warfare* (Chapel Hill, 1955).
Spring, Matthew H. *With Zeal and With Bayonets Only: The British Army on Campaign in North America, 1775-83* (Norman, 2008).
Stacey, C.P. *Quebec, 1759: The Siege and the Battle*, D.E. Graves, ed. (Toronto, reprint 2002).
Stanley, George F. G. *Canada's Soldiers: The Military History of an Unmilitary People* (Toronto, 1954).
———. *New France: The Last Phase, 1744-1760* (Toronto, 1968).
Steele, Ian K. *Guerillas and Grenadiers: The Struggle for Canada, 1689-1760* (Toronto, 1974).
———. *Betrayals: Fort William Henry and the 'Massacre'* (New York, 1990).
Stevenson, Roger. *Military Instructions for Officers Detached in the Field...* (Philadelphia, 1775).
Stewart, Colonel David. *Sketches of the Character, Manners and Present State of the Highlanders of Scotland with Details of the Military Service of the Highland Regiments*, 2 vols (Edinburgh, 1822, reprint 1977).
Sutherland, Malcolm. *A Fighting Clan: Sutherland Officers, 1250-1850* (London, 1996).
Tullabardine, Marchioness of. *A Military History of Perthshire, 1660-1902* (Perth, 1908).
Willcox, William. *Portrait of a General: Sir Henry Clinton in the War of Independence* (New York, 1964).

2. Articles

Axtell, James. "The White Indians of Colonial America," *William and Mary Quarterly* (Third Series), 32 (1975), 55-88.

Beerman, Eric. "The Last Battle of the American Revolution: Yorktown. No, the Bahamas," *The Americas* 45 (1988), 79-95.

Brumwell, Stephen. "Home from the Wars," *History Today* (March 2002), 41-47.

———. "'A Service Truly Critical': The British Army and Warfare with the North American Indians, 1755-1764," *War in History*, 5 (1998), 146-75.

Brunton, D. "Smallpox inoculation in eighteenth-century Scotland," *Cambridge Medical History*, vol 36, No.4. (1992 October), 403–429.

Campbell, Alexander V. "Anvil of Empire: The Royal American Regiment, 1756-1775." Ph.D. dissertation (University of Western Ontario, 2003).

Eaton, H.B. "Lieutenant-General Patrick Sinclair: An Account of His Military Career," *JSAHR*, vol 56 (Autumn, Winter 1978), 128-42, 215- 32; vol 57 (Spring 1979), 45-55.

Eccles, W.J. "The French Forces in North America During the Seven Years' War" in *Dictionary of Canadian Biography*, vol III (Toronto, 1974), 89-99.

Fisher, G.H. "Brigadier-General Henry Bouquet," *The Pennsylvania Magazine of History and Biography* vol 111, no.2. (1879), 125-130.

Fraser, Marie. "Descendants of Alexander Grant, 4th Sheuglie," *Clan Fraser Society of Canada.*

McCulloch, I.M. "'Within Ourselves': The Development of British Light Infantry in North America During the Seven Years' War," *Canadian Military History*, 7 (1998), 41-55.

Nicolai, Martin. "A Different Kind of Courage: The French Military and the Canadian Irregular Soldier during the Seven Years' War," *Canadian Historical Review*, 70, No.1. (1989), 53-75.

Pargellis, Stanley M. "Braddock's Defeat," *American Historical Review*, vol XLI (1936), 253-69.

Potts, William John. "De Simitiere, Artist, Antiquary, and Naturalist, Projector of the First American Museum, with Some Extracts from his Notebook," *The Pennsylvania Magazine of History and Biography*, vol XII (Philadelphia, 1889).

Robson, E. "British Light Infantry in the Mid-18th Century: The Effect of American Conditions," *Army Quarterly* (1952), 209-222.

Richards, Frederick B. "The Black Watch at Ticonderoga and Major Duncan Campbell of Inverawe," *Proceedings, New York State Historical Association*, vol X (1910).

"Ross of Inverchasley," *The Scottish Antiquary: or, Northern Notes & Queries*, vol V (Edinburgh, 1891), 63-66.

Russell, P.E. "Redcoats in the Wilderness: British Officers and Irregular Warfare in Europe and America, 1740-1760," *William and Mary Quarterly*, XXXV, (1978), 629-652.

Sears, Stephen. "The Lion's-eye-view: A British officer portrays colonial America," *American Heritage*, vol 29, no 4 (June/July 1978), 98-107.

Smith, D.E. Huger. "Commodore Alexander Gillon and the Frigate South Carolina," *The South Carolina Historical and Genealogical Magazine*, vol 9, no 4 (October 1908).

Stacey, C. P. "Lieutenant-General Thomas Davies: Soldier, Painter and Naturalist," in *Thomas Davies – An Exhibition Organized by the National Gallery of Canada* (Ottawa, 1972), 44-70. (This book is the official catalog for the exhibit.)

———. "Thomas Davies – Soldier and painter of 18th-century Canada," *Canadian Art*, 13.3 (1956), 275.

Wallace, R.F.H. "42nd Foot Regimental Routine and Army Administration in North America in 1759," *JSAHR*, XXXIII (1955), 2-4.

Whitworth, R. "Field Marshal Lord Amherst, a military enigma," *History Today*, vol IX (1959), 132-7.

INDEX

Notes: 'n' following a page number denotes a footnote is referred to; page numbers in **bold type** indicate an illustration or map; ranks after names reflect the persons rank at the time of their first appearance in John Grant's memoirs; estate names after surnames, while not technically correct (e.g. John Grant of Ballintomb) and usually reserved to denote the laird, have been inserted to help differentiate the many cadet branches or families that share the same surname.

Readers of *A Dangerous Service* will also enjoy...

A Bard of Wolfe's Army: James Thompson, Gentleman Volunteer, 1733-1830

Edited by Earl John Chapman & Ian Macpherson McCulloch

As a young grenadier in Fraser's Highlanders, Sergeant James Thompson served in the capture of Louisbourg in 1758, the battle of the Plains of Abraham at Quebec in 1759 and the battle of Sillery the following year. Later he experienced the American blockade of Quebec by Generals Richard Montgomery and Benedict Arnold during the Revolutionary War. He remained in Quebec the rest of his long life. His collected anecdotes form one of the most interesting personal accounts of soldiering during the Seven Years' War, and his journal offers an authentic first-hand view of life in Quebec in the years that followed. An astute observer with an eye for a humorous story, by the time he reached old age he was sought out by governors general and royalty to recount his stories of earlier times. In this book, editors Earl Chapman and Ian McCulloch not only present Thompson's anecdotes in one volume for the first time, but they also provide a wealth of explanation and historical background that helps to bring the period to life and places Thompson's experiences in context.

From the foreword by Peter MacLeod, Historian, Pre-Confederation, Canadian War Museum:

"In the course of his short but adventurous military career, Thompson met James Wolfe, who addressed him as 'Brother Soldier,' at the siege of Louisbourg, carried a wounded French soldier to an aid station after the Battle of the Plains of Abraham, and kept the sword of the commander of the American assault on Quebec City as a souvenir. Striking as they are, these are just three examples of a cascade of sparkling vignettes covering crime, scandal, valour, victory, defeat, honour, humour, a pet puppy and day-to-day life as a soldier."

Dr. Stephen Brumwell, award-winning author of* Paths of Glory: The Life and Death of General James Wolfe*:

"In the rich and colourful memoirs of James Thompson we hear the authentic voice of a Highland veteran of Wolfe's army. Enhanced here by expert editorial notes, Thompson's unique 'oral history' of the campaigns that decided the destiny of North America will undoubtedly appeal to specialists and general readers alike."

384 pages • 6.75 x 9.75 inches • 100+ illustrations • notes, index
Paperback • 978-1-896941-62-2
Hardcover limited edition signed by the editors • 978-1-896941-63-9

About the Editors

Earl John Chapman, a native of Montreal, is an avid military historian specializing in the Seven Years' War in North America and in the early years of Canada's volunteer militia force. As a member of the History and Heritage Committee of Canada's Black Watch, the country's senior Highland regiment, Earl is a regular contributor to its publication, *Canada's Red Hackle*. In 2012 he authored *Canada's Black Watch 1862-2012: Legacies of Gallantry & Service*, an important vehicle to showcase the regiment's many treasures. Earl is also the historian of the 78th Fraser Highlanders, a ceremonial regiment raised in 1965 by Montreal's David M. Stewart Museum to perpetuate the history of the old 78th Regiment of Foot which played such an important role in the founding years of Canada's history. He has published numerous articles, many appearing in international journals and magazines, and has written several books, the most recent being *A Bard of Wolfe's Army: James Thompson, Gentleman Volunteer, 1733-1830,* which he co-edited with Ian M. McCulloch in 2010. He was the 2008 recipient of the prestigious Gordon Atkinson Memorial Prize in Highland Military History, awarded annually by the Quebec Thistle Council.

Ian Macpherson McCulloch, a native of Halifax, Nova Scotia, is the former commanding officer of Canada's Black Watch (1993-96) and retired from the Canadian Forces in 2014, his last posting in uniform as the Director of the National Security Studies Centre at Toronto. As a military historian specializing in the Seven Years' War in North America, Ian has authored numerous articles and written several books in his field, including *Sons of the Mountains: A History of the Highland Regiments in North America, 1756-1767* (two volumes); *Highlander in the French-Indian War, 1756-1767* for Osprey, and his most recent book for Robin Brass Studio, *A Bard of Wolfe's Army: James Thompson, Gentleman Volunteer, 1733-1830*. He won the Gordon Atkinson Memorial Prize in Highland Military History in 2009.

www.robinbrassstudio.com